EVOLUTIONARY PERSPECTIVES ON HUMAN DEVELOPMENT

SECOND EDITION

EDITORS

ROBERT L. BURGESS
The Pennsylvania State University

KEVIN MacDONALD
California State University, Long Beach

SAGE Publications
Thousand Oaks ▪ London ▪ New Delhi

For information:

Sage Publications, Inc.
2455 Teller Road
Thousand Oaks, California 91320
E-mail: order@sagepub.com

Sage Publications Ltd.
1 Oliver's Yard
55 City Road
London EC1Y 1SP
United Kingdom

Sage Publications India Pvt. Ltd.
B-42, Panchsheel Enclave
Post Box 4109
New Delhi 110 017 India

Printed in the United States of America

Library of Congress Cataloging-in-Publication Data

Evolutionary perspectives on human development / edited by Robert L. Burgess and Kevin MacDonald.— 2nd ed.
    p. cm.
Includes bibliographical references and index.
ISBN 0-7619-2790-5 (pbk.)
    1. Developmental psychology. 2. Evolutionary psychology. I. Burgess, Robert G. II. MacDonald, Kevin B.
BF713.5.E95 2005
155.7—dc22   2004006222

04   05   06   07   08   10   9   8   7   6   5   4   3   2   1

Acquisitions Editor:	Jim Brace-Thompson
Editorial Assistant:	Karen Ehrmann
Production Editor:	Kristen Gibson
Copy Editor:	Carla Freeman
Typesetter:	C&M Digitals (P) Ltd.
Proofreader:	Kevin Gleason
Indexer:	Rachel Rice
Cover Designer:	Janet Foulger

Contents

Foreword

We have friends, and we have colleagues. Sometimes these roles are combined in a single person—and that is how I remember Linda Mealey. She has been in my thoughts a great deal lately, during preparation of my contribution to this volume, as well as other articles and presentations. Her criticism and advice were honest, accurate, and always welcome.

Linda Mealey was a true scholar in every sense of the word. As I reread her publications and our one joint paper (Mealey & Segal, 1993), I cannot help but be impressed over and over again. Her breadth of knowledge, grasp of concepts, and ability to synthesize were so impressive. Her loss leaves a huge gap in our field. Looking over her résumé, I see several papers in progress and regret that they will never come to fruition. It is, therefore, to the credit of Robert Burgess and Kevin MacDonald, the editors of this volume, that they have included her contribution, and have allowed me to review it and modify it, where appropriate. I trust that Linda would approve of any changes and additions!

As a behavioral geneticist with a special interest in twins, I gained many insights into evolutionary psychology in my discussions with Linda. I believe that she, in turn, gained interest and respect for how twin methods could be used to test evolutionary hypotheses. My favorite paper is her 1999 study, "Symmetry and Perceived Facial Attractiveness: A Monozygotic Co-Twin Comparison," published in the *Journal of Personality and Social Psychology*. I believe it continues to be one of the most creative applications of behavioral genetic methodology to a problem of evolutionary significance. Of course, Linda authored many outstanding works. Her 1995 article, "The Sociobiology of Sociopathy: An Integrated Evolutionary Model," published in *Behavioral and Brain Sciences*, is widely cited. Her 2000 textbook, *Sex Differences: Development and Evolutionary Strategies*, received glowing reviews.

Linda Mealey will not be forgotten soon, either as a friend or as a colleague. A list of her publications appearing during the last 10 years is reproduced below.

—Nancy L. Segal

Books and Book Chapters

Mealey, L. (1996). Evolutionary psychology: The search for evolved mechanisms underlying complex human behavior. In James Hurd (Ed.), *The biology of morality*. Edwin Mellen.

Mealey, L. (1997). The sociobiology of sociopathy: An integrated evolutionary model. Reprinted in Simon Baron-Cohen (Ed.), *The maladapted mind*. Erlbaum/ Taylor-Francis.

Mealey, L. (2000). *Sex differences: Development and evolutionary strategies*. Academic Press.

Mealey, L. (2000). Genetic influences on human fertility and sexuality. In J. L. Rodgers, D. C. Rowe, & W. Miller (Eds.), *Genetic influences on human fertility and sexuality*. Kluwer Academic Publishers.

Mealey, L. (2001). Kinship: The ties that bind (disciplines). In Paul Davies & Harmon Holcomb III (Eds.), *Evolution of minds: Psychological and philosophical perspectives*. Kluwer Academic Publishers.

Mealey, L. (2003). Anorexia: A "disease" of low, low fertility. In J. L. Rodgers & Hans-Peter Kohler (Eds.), *The biodemography of human reproduction and fertility*. Kluwer Academic Publishers.

Mealey, L. (2003). Combating rape: Views of an evolutionary psychologist. In N. Dess & R. Bloom (Eds.), *Evolutionary psychology and violence: A primer for policymakers and public policy advocates*. Westport, CT: Praeger.

Mealey, L. (in press). The illusory function of dreams. Reprinted in Stevan Harnad, Mark Blagrove, & Mark Solms (Eds.), *Sleeping and dreaming*. Cambridge University Press.

Mealey, L., & Kinner, S. (in press). Psychopathy, Machiavellianism and theory of mind. In M. Brune, H. Ribbert, & W. Schiefenhovel (Eds.), *The social brain: Evolution and pathology*. New York: John Wiley.

Journal Articles

Mealey, L., & Segal, N. (1993). Heritable and environmental variables affect reproduction-related behaviors, but not ultimate reproductive success. *Personality and Individual Differences, 14,* 783-794.

Mealey, L., & Theis, P. (1995). The relationship of mood and preferences among natural landscapes: An evolutionary perspective. *Ethology and Sociobiology, 16,* 247-256.

Mealey, L. (1995). The sociobiology of sociopathy: An integrated evolutionary model. *Behavioral and Brain Sciences, 18,* 523-599.

Mealey, L., Daood, C., & Krage, M. (1996). Enhanced memory for faces associated with potential threat. *Ethology and Sociobiology, 17,* 119-128.

Mealey, L. (1997). Bulking up: The roles of gender and sexual orientation on attempts to manipulate physical attractiveness. *Journal of Sex Research, 34,* 223-228.

Klopp, B., & Mealey, L. (1998). Experimental manipulation of mood does not induce change in preferences for natural landscapes. *Human Nature, 9,* 391-399.

Mealey, L., Bridgstock, R., & Townsend, G. (1999). Symmetry and perceived facial attractiveness: A monozygotic co-twin comparison. *Journal of Personality and Social Psychology, 76,* 157-165.

Mealey, L. (1999). The multiplicity of rape: From life history strategies to prevention strategies. *Jurimetrics, 39,* 217-226.

Mealey, L. (1999). To sleep, perchance to dream: Sleep in birds. *Interpretive Birding Bulletin (Australasian Edition), 3,* 1-5. Reprinted in the *Interpretive Birding Bulletin (North American Edition), 1,* 1-5.

Mealey, L., & Townsend, G. C. (1999). The role of fluctuating asymmetry on judgments of physical attractiveness: A monozygotic co-twin comparison. *Perspectives in Human Biology, 4,* 219-224.

Mealey, L. (2000). Anorexia: A "losing" strategy? *Human Nature, 11,* 105-116.

McAndrew, F. T., Akande, A., Bridgstock, R., Mealey, L., Gordon, S. C., Scheib, J. E., Akande-Adetoun, A. E., Odewale, F., Morakinyo, A., Nyahete, P., & Mubvakure, G. (2000). A multicultural study of stereotyping. *Journal of Social Psychology, 140,* 487-502.

Mealey, L. (2000). What? Me worry? The state of human ethology in the year 2000 (ISHE Presidential Address). *The Human Ethology Bulletin, 15*(4), 2-8.

Connolly, J., Mealey, L., & Slaughter, V. (2000). Development of preference for body shapes. *Perspectives in Human Biology, 5,* 19-25.

Bryant, J., Mealey, L., Herzog, E., & Rychwalski, W. (2001). Paradoxical effect of surveyor's conservative versus provocative clothing on rape myth acceptance of male and female participants. *Journal of Psychology and Human Sexuality, 13,* 55-66.

Connolly, J., Slaughter, V., & Mealey, L. (submitted). Children's preferences for waist-to-hip ratios: A developmental strategy.

Preface

In 1988, Springer-Verlag published a book edited by Kevin MacDonald, titled *Sociobiological Perspectives on Human Development*. That book was among the first to explore how the revolution in evolutionary biology inaugurated by E. O. Wilson's monumental *Sociobiology: The New Synthesis* could be linked to the more proximate focus of developmental psychology. This book represents an updated and expanded version of that work. The title of the new version reflects the general shift away from the usage of the term *sociobiology*. This shift was necessitated not only by the opprobrium that had become attached to the term by the critics of evolutionary approaches in the social sciences but also because the field had expanded beyond the area of social behavior to include evolutionary influences on all areas of human cognition and behavior.

Robert Burgess, who was a contributor to the first edition, is a coeditor for the new edition. Several of the other authors in the original edition are represented in this volume: Dennis Krebs on moral development; Nancy Segal on cooperation, competition, and altruism among twins; Glenn Weisfeld (with Donyell K. Coleman) on adolescence; William Charlesworth on socialization of children in cohesive, strategizing groups, Robert Burgess (with Alicia A. Drais-Parrillo) on child abuse; and Kevin MacDonald on personality development and (with Scott Hershberger) on developmental theory. Several authors who have made important contributions to the field since the publication of the first edition are also represented here: Mark Flinn on the behavioral ecology of child development; David Geary on cognitive development; D. Kimbrough Oller and Ulrike Griebel on language development; Sarah Hrdy on the evolution and culture of motherhood; and Peter LaFreniere on emotional development.

Another new contributor is Linda Mealey, whose essay on developmental psychopathology appears after her untimely death in 2002 (Nancy Segal's tribute precedes this preface). Linda was an important scholar and a wonderful person. She is greatly missed, not only by her close personal friends and colleagues but also by those of us who appreciated her stimulating ideas and her friendly manner at conferences over the years. Her attitude was that scholarship and personal integrity are more important than the fads and cliques that are so much a part of academic life. We are proud to dedicate this volume to her memory.

1

Evolutionary Theory and Human Development

Robert L. Burgess

Because of the complexity of human behavior and its development, it is essential that our research be theoretically driven and that care be taken to integrate biological as well as environmental factors in our explanations. Indeed, for several decades, increasing attention has been devoted to exploring the joint function of nature and nurture for understanding human behavior and its development. Most of the effort on the nature side of the equation has been focused on the proximate emphases of quantitative genetics and, increasingly, molecular genetics. Much less attention has been given to the implications of evolutionary theory, which underlies both. It is for this reason that the central theme of this book is the importance of evolutionary biology for understanding the nature and directions of human development.

A reader might well ask: "Why the theory of evolution?" The reason is that it is the most general theory we have in the life sciences. It unifies the disciplines of microbiology, medicine, psychology, anthropology, and sociology. Theories are important because science is concerned not only with establishing relationships between phenomena (empirical research) but also explaining why these relationships obtain. Theories, in other words, are explanations of empirically established relationships. The general theories of relativity and quantum mechanics have allowed physicists to understand (explain) the nature of our universe writ large, as well as the nature of atomic structure. These theoretical developments have transformed chemistry from being a phenomenology into an analytic science, and they have made remarkable inroads into molecular biology.

Empirically based general theories add simplicity and parsimony to the understanding of how our complex world works. Simplicity and simplistic, however, are not equivalent. Even though general theories usually consist of a few general and simple principles, the derivation or deduction of complex phenomena from these general principles is seldom a simple matter. For example, the principle "Warmer water tends to rise" can be explained by a few principles of Newtonian mechanics. But the process of doing so is far from simple and requires incorporation of principles of thermodynamics and some sophisticated mathematics.

Once we have identified general theoretical principles, we then are able to make predictions about other phenomena. If we know why warmer water rises, we can make a much wider range of predictions under a variety of given conditions. We can predict, for example, that the surface water along a coastline in the summer will be warmer when the wind is onshore than when it is offshore. Or we can predict that the air near the ceiling in a room is likely to be warmer than the air nearer the floor, and explain *why*. Predictions like these can and should, of course, be tested empirically.

To suggest, as the authors of this book have, that evolutionary theory is important because it is the most general theory in the life sciences is not to deny the significance of the disciplines of anthropology, psychology, or sociology nor the middle-range theories that have emerged and been tested therein, such as attachment theory, learning theory, exchange theory, and rational choice theory, to name a few. The behavioral and social sciences have made many empirical discoveries, but the central intellectual problems of these fields are not *analytic,* that is, discovering new and fundamental general theories. My view, and at least implicitly the view of the other contributors to this book, is that our most important general theoretical principles have already been discovered and they are the principles of the theory of evolution by natural selection.

The problems facing the behavioral and social sciences are essentially *synthetic*: showing how genes and environments in accordance with evolutionary principles combine to produce our common human nature and the diversity of ways in which this nature is manifested. This is precisely what the various contributors to this book have attempted, from the evolution and function of human intelligence (Chs. 2, 3, and 4) and language (Ch. 5), to the evolution, function, and development of social emotions (Ch. 7) and personality traits (Ch. 8). Similar efforts are directed to explaining the development of moral judgments (Ch. 9) and psychopathology (Ch. 14), the range and function of parental investment (Chs. 6 and 11), the structure and function of adolescence (Ch. 12), the ways in which vital resources are acquired in different cultural contexts (Ch. 13), and the importance of the coefficient of relatedness for understanding altruism, cooperation, and competition (Ch. 10). In each chapter, new insights into old topics emerged from the authors' use of the telephoto lens of evolutionary theory in combination with the wide-angle lens of anthropology and sociology and the macro lens of psychology and behavior genetics.

Another reason for examining the developmental implications of evolutionary theory is that empirical support for the theory has been increasing at such an increasing rate that it can no longer be ignored by the behavioral and social sciences. This has been the case ever since the breaking of the genetic code. Genes produce proteins, and proteins, which are the building blocks of bodies, consist of a linear sequence of amino acids that combine and fold in unique ways to produce particular proteins. Given the fact that there are 20 amino acids, by comparing specific proteins from different species and the number of associated amino acid changes, we have now what is essentially a molecular time clock that allows us to estimate the elapsed time since species split off from a common ancestor (Wells, 2002).

Differences do exist about how evolutionary theory can best be used to explain human behavior and its development in different contexts (Smith, 2000). Evolutionary psychologists have emphasized the role of evolved psychological mechanisms (e.g., Barkow, Cosmides, & Tooby, 1992; Symons, 1992). Behavioral ecologists, instead, have emphasized how ecological factors influence adaptive behavior (e.g., Irons, 1979). These differences notwithstanding, evolutionary scientists have been primarily interested in explaining pan-human traits, that is, those behaviors that all humans share. Such traits include biparental care, long-term pair bonding, language, our lengthy childhood, deception, cooperation, trust, jealousy, violence, and so on. We take these traits for granted, and we should, because we all share a common human nature. To be sure, there are differences. There are different languages, different dialects of the same language, and different customs, for example, afternoon siestas, genital mutilation, residential seclusion, and different rules of inheritance and residence. But there are limits to these differences, and no societies or cultures have succeeded in banishing other common human behaviors, such as fear, lust, sloth, adultery, or theft.

What needs to be understood is that the only viable scientific theory we have to explain this common, species-specific nature is the theory of evolution. There is no competitor. Beginning with Darwin, biologists have explained the complexity in nature, of flora as well as fauna, as various designs to solve adaptive problems, that is, problems of survival and reproduction. For Darwin, and for evolutionary scientists today, complex designs are the products of gradual step-by-step changes in the traits of living things.

These steps were small, and they occurred over millions of years, involving millions of individuals.

For this process of natural selection to be true, however, there had to be a way for these changes to be passed on from one generation to the next. Darwin was not quite sure how this worked, but work it must. Today, of course, we know. We have identified the conditions necessary for evolution by natural selection to take place. First, there must be a continual source of genetic variation. This source is *random mutation,* which refers to DNA copying errors that occur during cell division. The current estimate is that there are approximately 30 mutations per genome per generation (Wells, 2002, p. 18). Second, there must be *nonrandom selection* of those genetic variations that solve adaptive problems better than earlier versions. Third, there is a mechanism that permits these variations (adaptations) to be passed on to future generations, namely, the amazing, self-copying DNA molecule. Genetic diversity, then, is essential for evolution by natural selection to occur. Random mutation is therefore the most basic force in evolution because without it, polymorphisms (genetic diversity) would not exist. Once mutation occurs, nonrandom selection can take place. Finally, there is a fourth important force in evolution, *genetic drift.* Given geographic mobility, individuals who split off from parent populations may, because of different selection pressures, eventually become genetically dissimilar in certain ways from the population from which they originated.

Despite the fact that these conditions are well established, there are those who refuse to accept the importance and relevance of evolutionary theory, especially for understanding human behavior. One reason for this reluctance, from the perspective of some, is that it is *just a theory.* Those who take this position do not seem to understand what a "theory" is in science. It is not simply a guess or hypothesis, but, instead, it is a set of logically interrelated and empirically supported propositions or principles.

Other sources of resistance include the idea that because of language and culture, we have managed to escape from the constraints of our biological nature. The reasoning here is that we humans are unique. Yes, we are unique, but we are not unique in being unique (van den Berghe, 1990). A third source is the product of the logical fallacy of exclusive determinism. It takes the form that if learning and culture are important, and they are, then genes and biology must not be. But, of course, genetically influenced traits are not expressed in a vacuum. They are always expressed in, and are influenced by, the environmental context.

A fourth source of resistance is the concern about genetic determinism. For some critics, genetic determinism is determinism in the full philosophical sense of absolute, irreversible inevitability. All scientists are determinists in the sense that we assume there are causes or bases for all of our actions. But for some reason, genetic determinism is considered to be more troubling than environmental determinism. Fifth, too many people simply have not received sufficient training in biology, and therefore they do not understand how genes and evolution actually work. They apparently do not appreciate the fact that environmental factors, both internal (e.g., the effects of other genes or nutritional status) and external (e.g., social status) can modify the effects of genes and the effects of other environmental events (van den Berghe, 1990).

Finally, there is the fear of reductionism. However, reductionism need not mean replacing one field of knowledge with another, but rather, linking them. The bad reputation of reductionism stems in part from a concern for disciplinary loyalty. There need be no concern here. In biology, explanation is generally felt to occur on four complementary levels of analysis, and these different levels reflect the often different concerns and theories of the various behavioral and social sciences. These four levels include the evolutionary history of a trait, the adaptive function of a trait, the development of the trait in an individual's life span, and the specific and proximate mechanisms that cause a trait to be expressed at a particular time and place (Tinbergen, 1963). It should be recognized that a common thread runs through each of these analytical levels and that the first two levels (evolutionary history and adaptiveness) are more general than the last two (development and proximate antecedents). A moment's reflection will reveal why this is the case: A genetic process must be involved in each of the four levels. The development of a behavior must involve genetic action in some way, and the potential or capacity to exhibit a behavior must have been adaptive at some point in time. All four levels of analysis appear in the chapters of this book.

Regarding these levels of analysis, it must be understood that to claim that a trait is a product of natural selection does not imply that it can occur without experience, without development, or without a particular environmental stimulus. It is also important to remember that human traits, as evolved designs, can be and often are manifested in different ways in different circumstances. That is why biologists distinguish between genotypes and phenotypes. So, concern about genetic determinism is a straw man. Human behavior and its development reflect the importance of open versus closed genetic systems or obligate versus facultative traits (Mayr, 1982). That is why context is so important. Behavior, in other words, is often contingent.

Evolved Traits

There are, as noted earlier, different ways in which the general theory of evolution could be used to explain human behavior and its development. For this reason, a central issue raised in several chapters of this book concerns the nature and importance of evolved psychological mechanisms (Chs. 1, 2, 3, 4, 6, 7, 8, and 11). Drawing upon cognitive science, some evolutionary scientists who identify themselves as evolutionary psychologists (e.g., Buss, 1995; Cosmides & Tooby, 1987; Symons, 1992) have maintained that human behavior is influenced by evolved domain-specific psychological mechanisms, rather than by domain-general learning mechanisms that generalize across multiple behavioral domains. Domain-specific mechanisms are said to have evolved because they solved adaptive problems throughout human history; and because these problems were many, we possess many specific psychological mechanisms. These mechanisms include the ability to recognize faces, read emotions, infer mood, fear snakes, be generous to one's children, prefer certain traits in potential mates, acquire grammar, infer semantic meaning, calculate social obligations, and so on (Ridley, 1993).

Evolutionary psychologists representing this view are often quite dismissive of traditional learning theorists, sociobiologists, and human behavioral ecologists. The views represented in this book are much less doctrinaire. For example, I agree that mechanisms that make up the human mind can be usefully analyzed as evolved adaptations and that many of these mechanisms are domain-specific. I disagree, however, that the brain can be composed only of domain-specific mechanisms or that domain-general mechanisms are unimportant for understanding human behavior. In several of the following chapters, it is argued that the very uncertainty and diversity of the environments that our ancestors faced led to the selection of psychological mechanisms of sufficient generality to permit adaptation to changing and unpredictable environments, perhaps especially because of the challenges produced by competitive conspecifics. This is not to deny the importance of domain-specific mechanisms nor that some behaviors, such as language and others historically correlated with survival, reproductive success, and inclusive fitness, are more easily learned than others, such as abstract mathematics.

My point here is that the human brain consists of a variety of evolved domain-general mechanisms, such as respondent and operant conditioning, direct tuition, and social learning, as well as domain-specific mechanisms. As Ridley (2003) put it, "Thinking is a general activity that integrates vision, language, empathy, and other modules: mechanisms that operate as modules presuppose mechanisms that don't" (p. 66; see also Fodor, 2001). While we have much to learn about how domain-general and domain-specific mechanisms are linked, certain things are known: (a) Our behavior often is contingent, and (b) we often behave as if we assess the relative costs and benefits of actions associated with outcomes that historically have been correlated with reproductive success or inclusive fitness. Cost-benefit analysis has a distinguished lineage in evolutionary biology (Hamilton, 1964; Trivers, 1974; Williams, 1966).

Development and Individual Differences

Traditionally, evolutionary biologists began their research by identifying a trait, examining how it is expressed in the typical environments of a species, and then attempting to determine the adaptive significance of the trait. Only later might the issue of the trait's ontogeny or development be addressed. This approach, as Alexander (1979) noted, "thus parallels the way in which natural selection actually works. It does not matter, in selection, how a trait comes to be expressed—only that it is expressed in the optimal way and at the optimal time and place" (p. 202).

Individual development is, of course, the main topic of this book. Nor have evolutionary scientists ignored development. The concept of the phenotype, as a product of genotypes, is to acknowledge the flexible ways in which individuals respond to varying environmental circumstances. The ability to adapt to different environments and to learn different things is surely a product of natural selection. This, in turn, suggests that learning is a product of the action of genes—it is, in other words, an evolved ability. This does not mean, however, that learning and phenotypes are necessarily independent of evolutionary history. As Cohen (1999) put it, "Nature limits and channels nurture" (p. 68). Nevertheless, to the extent that genes are switched on and off in response to environmental input, it is also true that nature is expressed through nurture (Ridley, 2003).

Behavioral and social scientists have always been interested in human differences as well as similarities. Cultural and evolutionary anthropologists, for example, have been interested in both. The field of developmental psychology, especially, has been interested in individual differences. Up to this point, I have emphasized similarity—our shared human nature—and the importance of evolutionary theory to explain that nature. We will now turn our attention to individual differences. Yet we need not put away our evolutionary telephoto lens, because there exists an interesting apparent paradox; namely, the same differences are found all over the world and in all cultures. Everywhere, we find similar individual differences in personality, temperament, intelligence, psychopathology, antisocial behavior, and so on.

In a somewhat different context, Ridley (2003) put it this way: "Similarity is the shadow of difference. . . . Difference is the shadow of similarity" (p. 7).

That said, how exactly do we reconcile the idea that all humans, fundamentally, are the same while also acknowledging that we are all individuals and unique in some ways? How can there be a universal, species-specific human nature when every human being is unique? The answer to this apparent paradox begins with our genetic code, which makes us uniquely human *and* uniquely different from every other person on this planet. Those very mechanisms that are responsible for our common human nature also play a role in human diversity. Remember, genetic variation originating in mutation is where it all begins. The blood groups found in human populations originated as mutations, as have all other polymorphisms. Natural selection is the second mechanism. It occurs, of course, when a particular trait confers a reproductive advantage on those individuals who possess it. For example, individuals (usually of northern European descent) who have historically lived in environments where there is little sun, and the low ultraviolet radiation associated with chronic vitamin D deficiency, possess the genes for lactose tolerance. The lactose of fresh milk functions as a vitamin D supplement, facilitating the absorption of calcium from the small intestine.

The third mechanism is sexual reproduction. Sex mixes the genes of a man and a woman after one half of the mixture has been discarded, which occurs during the presexual mixing of genes from the maternal and paternal genomes when sperm and eggs are formed. This process of sexual recombination results in no child being an exact replica of either parent. It also means that with the exception of identical twins, no two siblings will be genetically alike. A fourth mechanism responsible for genetically based differences between individuals is frequency-dependent selection, which is a sort of balancing mechanism such that some phenotypes are reproductively successful to the extent that they are relatively rare in the population (Maynard-Smith, 1982).

But there are limits to genetic diversity. Natural selection uses up somewhere between 70% and 85% of genetic variance. There are also other limitations. It is beginning to appear as if human DNA has been inherited generation after generation in large, unchanged blocks from ancestral populations, with less mixing and shuffling of DNA from maternal and paternal chromosomes than once thought. To use a deck-of-cards analogy, it would be as if the dealer dealt from a deck from which all players received the same set of cards glued together, along with those cards that differed from one player to another. Another limiting factor may reside in evolutionary convergence. Convergence is said to occur when two or more species have independently evolved the same trait. Examples of convergence can be found at the most basic level of molecular biology. Despite the incredible number of forms that proteins could conceivably take, the actual forms observed are quite limited. For example, the proteins that are functional in respiration (i.e., the oxygen-carrying molecule, hemoglobin) are similar from bacteria to humans (Morris, 2003), although the more closely related species are, the fewer the number of amino acid changes in the molecule (Wells, 2002). These processes, natural selection, the swapping of genetic material in relatively large blocks, and evolutionary convergence, combine to produce the effects that all of the genes that make up the human genome remain in the gene pool, that individual differences are virtually the same all over the world, and that the majority (c. 85%) of these differences are found within populations rather than between ethnic groups or races. On a macrolevel, it has been calculated that there are more than 100 million possible combinations of cultural forms, yet only a tiny fraction are actually found (Cronk, 1999; see also van den Berghe, 1979).

Even though there are limits to genetic diversity, it does exist. One estimate is that 15% to 30% of human genes vary between any two individuals. Behavior genetics is the research speciality that has been most interested in exploring the role of genetic diversity as a source of individual differences. Behavior geneticists who study human behavior have had to rely on the "natural experiments" of twinning and adoption. For Caucasian populations, approximately 1 in every 120 or so births consists of fraternal, or dizygotic, twins, and 1 in 250 consists of identical, or monozygotic, twins, which originate from a single fertilized egg. By comparing fraternal and identical twins for some trait, and by comparing both types of twins when they have been adopted into different families, it is possible to estimate the heritability of a trait. Because of the large proportion of the human genome that is invariant, heritability, which is a population average, refers only to that 15% to 30% of the genes that vary between individuals. Thus, when behavior geneticists use the coefficient of relatedness and calculate that fraternal twins, like other non-twin siblings, share approximately 50% of their genes or that grandparents and grandchildren share 25% of their genes, they are referring only to variant genes. Here is another apparent paradox, namely, that our least "heritable" traits are the most genetically determined: For example, with few exceptions, we are all born with 10 fingers and two kidneys and can learn language. While each of the various research designs and analytic methods used by behavior geneticists has limitations, collectively, they indicate hereditary influences for virtually all psychological traits. This is true for intelligence, academic achievement, personality, psychopathology, antisocial behavior, and so on.

Genes, of course, are not the whole story. Individuals differ not only in their genetic makeup but also in the environmental influences to which they have been exposed. The phenotype is a product of the mix of these two influences. Research with twins and adoptees allows us to estimate the relative importance of genes and environments as determinants of individual differences in psychological traits. Behavior genetics research has also alerted us to the importance of distinguishing between two classes of environmental influences. Some influences are consistent within a family. These are termed *shared environments* and include any experiences that are relatively uniform for all children within a family but different for children in another family. Examples would include parental personality traits, parental social attitudes, parenting style (to the degree that it is constant across siblings), religious beliefs, social class, and so on. But, of course, not all influences within families are shared. Parents may prefer one child over another. Major family events, such as divorce or parental loss, may occur for children at different ages. They may have different teachers. They usually have different friends. They, of course, have different birth orders. One sibling may have required extensive hospitalization. And before all of this, they would have had different prenatal experiences. Experiences such as these are analyzed as *nonshared environments*.

When examining individual differences within cultures rather than the effects of different cultures, nonshared environmental experiences have generally been found to have a greater influence on psychological traits than do shared environmental influences (e.g., Plomin & Daniels, 1987). This finding has often been misunderstood and has led to the conclusion that families do not matter (Bouchard, Lykken, McGue, Segal, & Tellegen, 1990). Limited influence, however, does not mean there is no influence. Given the importance of learning, it is to be expected that it can occur in a variety of contexts. Throughout human history, children have been exposed to a variety of family forms. Moreover, as children age, they are exposed to an increasing number of role models and socialization influences other than their parents: teachers, neighbors, friends, the parents of friends, and, of course, older siblings. Parental influence can channel how genetically influenced traits are manifested, and they can encourage children to optimize their talents. Parents also have an impact on these extrafamilial experiences both directly and indirectly. By purchasing a home in a particular neighborhood, parents have some influence on who their children's peers are likely to be, on the block and at school.

Unfortunately, in all too many families today, the tasks and responsibilities of parents have been made more difficult than perhaps ever before in human history. Given high geographic mobility, families are often cut off from the kin support emphasized by Hrdy in Chapter 6. Effective parental and adult monitoring become more difficult, especially with both parents in the workforce. Add to all of this the lengthening of adolescence, the mobility that the automobile provides, increasing affluence with too few contingencies and responsibilities placed on our youth, and the incendiary nature of the drug culture, it is perhaps surprising that parents have as much influence as they do. Some children are clearly at risk for getting into trouble, and those with certain genetic tendencies are more at risk than others. There are several lessons to be drawn here. First, the concept of nonshared environments serves to remind us that the same environmental event can impact on different people differently, even within the same family. That is the principal reason why operant conditioning and behavior modification research emphasized single-subject research designs. A second lesson is that families do matter, although their influence may be more limited than sometimes assumed. There is a substantial research literature documenting that misguided or inept parenting promotes inappropriate or antisocial behavior, that good parenting encourages admirable, prosocial behavior (although there are no guarantees), and that well-designed interventions have significant ameliorative effects (e.g., Patterson & Dishion, 1988). As Cohen (1999, p. 228) noted, our genes make us uniquely human, and the family, when functioning well, makes us optimally human.

A third lesson is that the relative strength of genetic and environmental effects is trait- and population-specific. For example, while differences in personality and intelligence may be more a product of differences in genes than in rearing environments, families do influence the degree to which these traits are optimized. It is also the case, however, that intelligence and personality differ in the relative influences of genes and shared and nonshared environments. Differences in intelligence, more than personality, are influenced by shared environment, although heritability is greater in high socioeconomic status (SES) families, and shared environment is more important in low-SES families (Neiss & Rowe, 2000; Turkheimer, Haley, Waldron, D'Onofrio, & Gottesman, 2002). The causal mechanisms responsible for greater shared environmental influence for intelligence in low-SES families are unknown at present, although two possibilities are likely. The first is that there may simply be more variability in early stimulation, nutrition, and exposure to environmental toxins in low-SES than in high-SES families. In other words, SES may be a marker for the quality of the environments in which children are born and reared that affect intellectual competence. An alternative explanation is that children reared in low-SES families may differ from other children genetically as well as environmentally. As Plomin and Bergeman (1991) demonstrated, markers of environmental quality also reflect genetic variability.

A fourth lesson is that it is necessary that we think of nonshared environments broadly. For example, environmental influences begin in utero.

How well nourished a baby is prenatally may have long-term developmental consequences (Barker, Winter, Osmond, Margetts, & Simmonds, 1989). The prenatal environment is not shared with siblings, except for twins. Even for twins, there may be important differences due to how long they shared the same placenta (Cohen, 1999, pp. 179-182). There are also nongenetic yet biological (epigenetic) processes that occur prenatally and contribute to subsequent individual differences. As genes are switched on and off (often in response to environmental input), they manufacture proteins. These proteins interacting with other proteins link together to create parts of cells. These cells reacting to other proteins form tissues; the tissues form organs linked by neural networks; these organs interact to produce organisms; and, as the latter interact with the environment, multiple nonlinear effects can occur anywhere along this line and contribute to individual differences later in life (Burgess & Molenaar, 1993; Molenaar, Boomsma, & Dolan, 1993). These nonlinear effects could contribute, for example, to individual differences in sensitivity to certain smells and tastes, susceptibility to allergies, perfect pitch, the eventual malfunction of vital organs, or a tendency toward shyness or boldness. Thus, in addition to genetic and environmental sources of developmental variability, there is an indication of a third important source: nonlinear epigenetic influences.

The fifth lesson is that aside from nonshared prenatal and epigenetic effects, there are nonshared gene-environment relationships. Behavior geneticists typically look at gene-environment relationships as genetic effects, but it is also reasonable to examine them as environmental effects, and if we do, they are clearly nonshared effects. While it has proven difficult to document gene-environment interactions in human behavior genetic research, the concept has been found to be important in animal experimental work and useful to developmental theorists. Gene-environment interactions refer to situations where the effects of an environmental circumstance vary with a genotype, and conversely. Although compelling examples are difficult to find in the empirical literature, there are some. For example, Kendler, Kessler, Walters, MacLeon, and Neale (1995) found that sensitivity to the depression-inducing effects of stressful life events was greater for those at greater genetic risk. Parental discord, parental psychopathology, or inept parenting (e.g., a tendency toward noncontingent reinforcement or poor monitoring) could affect one child in a family differently than a sibling, and gene-environment interactions would be one reason why. Gene-environment correlations occur when individuals with genotypes that have a particular effect tend to interact with environments that have similar effects. Gene-environment correlations draw our attention to the fact that we are active agents in our own development. By virtue of possessing certain genetically influenced traits, we may evoke, select, or modify the environments to which we are exposed (Scarr &

McCartney, 1983). Evocation would occur when genetically influenced traits elicit predictable reactions from others. A child might be identified as gifted in some domain and be given special opportunities to express and practice that gift. Selection occurs when we expose ourselves to certain environments. A child with genetically influenced athletic skill might gravitate toward sports and thereby differentially associate with peers who have similar interests. There is nothing too surprising here. Most people, given the chance, will spend more time doing that which they do best. To accomplish this, sometimes it may even be necessary to manipulate or orchestrate our environments so that selection can occur (Cohen, 1999, Ch. 4).

Selection and manipulation combine to produce what is often called "niche picking," which should be examined as a domain-general mechanism that functions in a wide variety of circumstances, including different cultural and historical contexts, to gain access to resources that historically have been correlated with reproductive success. Viewed this way, niche picking is an example of "genetic action at a distance" (Dawkins, 1982). Niche picking has been systematically explored by Sulloway (1996), who used Darwin's Principle of Divergence to make predictions about differences among siblings in their personalities and life strategies. While assuming the role of genetic diversity in personality, his chief focus was on systematic nonshared environmental influences. He views families as ecosystems where children, possessing evolved motivational systems, attempt to maximize parental investment by carving out and occupying different niches within their families. Among the factors influencing niche choice that he tested were birth order, parent-child conflict, and family size.

How all of this works out in an individual case can, of course, be quite complicated and multiply determined. For example, how a person expresses the personality traits of openness to experience and risk taking (both of which have significant heritability) will depend on the developmental context. These traits could be manifested in prosocial ways by becoming an astronaut, a downhill racer, or a venture capitalist. Alternatively, those same traits, as a result of quite different environmental and developmental circumstances, could be expressed through antisocial behavior by becoming a thief, a con man, or a drug dealer. Sulloway (1996), in a remarkable intellectual achievement, not only used general trends to test his family dynamics model but also made predictions about specific individuals. Nor did he stop there. He attempted to understand exceptions to his predictions by gathering more detailed biographical information about the individual exceptions and then testing his new hypotheses with his entire sample. In doing so, it became possible to specify the conditions under which his basic model does and does not apply. When all was said and done, he was able to conclude, as predicted, that siblings employ strategies aimed at maximizing parental investment. For this reason, laterborn children were more likely to be unconventional and radical than firstborn children. But as seen from his tests of exceptions to the rule, radical behavior can also be influenced by other factors operating inside families (e.g., parent-child conflict or parental loss) and outside the family (e.g., national styles, personal influences, or interpersonal rivalry).

Just as there have been critics of evolutionary theory, so too have there been persistent critics of behavior genetics. In Chapter 2 of this volume, MacDonald and Hershberger discuss the prominent critique offered by Gottlieb (1992, 1995). According to Gottlieb, the field of behavior genetics is of little relevance to the study of individual development because of its failure to identify specific bidirectional mechanisms linking genetic, neural, behavioral, and environmental activity. In one limited sense, Gottlieb's critique is correct. It is not possible to generalize from the population level analysis of interindividual differences to the developmental structure of specific individuals. Nevertheless, given the multitude of factors that can influence development, interindividual factors identified in population-based investigations are essential and can inform inferences at an individual level of analysis. Because of the complexity of human behavior and its development, we need to use multiple research methods: person-centered research, variable-centered research, replication studies, experiments, and cross-sectional as well as longitudinal designs (e.g., Molenaar & Boomsma, 1987; Vreeke, 2000). The focus, as always, should be on the identification of the conditions under which the relationships between phenomena do and do not obtain, and do so in a theoretically informed way. Just as no one research methodology is sufficient to study human behavior, neither is just one level of analysis. Focusing on intraindividual analyses of development adds detail but it exacts a cost in scope and generality. Finally, as discussed in Chapter 2, Gottlieb's developmental systems approach is inconsistent with evolutionary principles and research because of the failure of his perspective to recognize constraints on the range of interactions among his four levels of bidirectional influences that result from selection pressures on adaptation (see also Burgess & Molenaar, 1995). To fully understand any biological phenomenon, we need to be sensitive to all four of Tinbergen's complementary levels of analysis discussed earlier.

Conclusions

In this chapter, I have sketched in broad strokes the importance of general theory in science and the significance of evolutionary theory for understanding the nature of human nature and individual development. It is impossible to discuss this topic without encountering controversy. The very reality of evolution is challenged by some. Even if it is real, its relevance to understanding human behavior and development is questioned by others (e.g., Lerner & von Eye, 1992). Evolutionary scientists themselves sometimes overemphasize their differences rather than the bedrock of shared views that is the foundation of their work. Thus, some claim, the human mind could not possibly be composed of all-purpose domain-general psychological mechanisms. That, we are told, was the folly of behaviorism. Instead, only a modular brain made up of many evolution-based, special-purpose, domain-specific mechanisms makes sense. For others, such as the contributors to this book, both types of psychological mechanisms are important. For still others, the field of behavior genetics rests on flawed research designs and questionable political motives. What are we to make of this? One reaction is simply to despair and reject it all. A more realistic view is to recognize these disagreements as signals of the vitality of a science finally coming to grips with the often surprising ways in which nature and nurture combine to produce who we are as humans and as unique individuals.

The fruits of this endeavor are scattered throughout this book. For example, in Chapter 2, MacDonald and Hershberger examine motivational systems as important framing mechanisms necessary to solve adaptive problems for which the solutions are contextually varied and "underspecified." In this way, linkages are formed between domain-general and domain-specific mechanisms. Similarly, Flinn in Chapter 3 remarks that learning is not random, nor could it have evolved if it led to behaviors that were random with respect to adaptation. This does not mean that all behavior is adaptive. Some behavior may be historically and culturally specific. Yet even here, culturally unique behavior (e.g., scarification, or the practice of purdah) may lead to outcomes that are correlated with reproductive success in particular cultures (e.g., social status and paternity certainty). In each of these chapters, as well as in Chapter 4 by Geary, the importance of general intelligence (g) is emphasized as a domain-general mechanism facilitating survival and reproductive success in circumstances that vary across generations and lifetimes.

Oller and Griebel, in Chapter 5, discuss the evolution of language as part of a suite of adaptations that were selected because they increased the ability of dependent offspring to communicate their needs to caretakers. This was undoubtedly important throughout human evolution, not only because of child dependency and its unique length but also because of the uncertainty and contingent nature of parental investment (Hrdy, Ch. 6; Burgess & Drais-Parrillo, Ch. 11). For the same reasons, child sensitivity to parental cues (Hrdy, Ch. 6; LaFreniere, Ch. 7) would have been selected for, as would neoteny and hormonal priming, as mechanisms to encourage attachment and parental investment. Once in place, of course, language skills would become more sophisticated to deal with the complexity of social life as population expansion and density increased.

Other examples of the fruitfulness of an evolutionary perspective on development is evident in Krebs's (Ch. 9) examination of moral judgments and moral behavior as adaptations to deal with the conflicts of interests endemic to living in social groups. Complying with rules of morality is most notable in kin relations and probably evolved therein. The connection between altruistic behavior and kin relations is seen in the ancient Arab proverb: "I against my brother, my brother and I against our cousin, my brother, my cousins and I against the world." Beyond kin-based altruism, moral behavior is often sustained through reciprocal altruism or exchange among non-kin and by coercion in more complex societies (van den Berghe, 1979). In this manner, Kohlberg's Stages 4 through 6 of moral development come to resemble Stage 1. In Chapter 8, MacDonald examines personality, not just as a set of individual differences, but as an evolved emotional and motivational system. Among the benefits for doing so, sex differences in personality traits and changes over the life span become more understandable. In Chapter 10, Segal discusses the advantages of combining the dual perspectives of evolutionary biology and behavior genetics for understanding differential parental investment and sibling relationships. Chapter 11 illustrates how Tinbergen's four levels of analysis can be combined to provide a comprehensive explanation of child maltreatment. In Chapter 12, Weisfeld and Coleman gain added purchase on the nature of human adolescence by examining the importance of dominance striving, and the formation of romantic relationships and competition for mates during this stage of the life span. Acquiring resources is essential for any evolutionarily successful species. By comparing the Amish and Gypsies, Charlesworth, in Chapter 13, illustrates how universal adaptations can be manifested differently in different ecological and cultural circumstances. In Chapter 14, Mealy shows that by taking an evolutionary approach, it is possible to distinguish between true pathologies, modern pathologies, ethical pathologies, and evolutionary compromises.

These represent just a few examples of the insights provided by an evolutionary perspective. Each of the contributions to this book, separately and in concert, illustrates how far we have come in recognizing that despite all the individual differences we see around us, there is a common human nature, and the rules of survivorship and inclusive fitness ultimately govern the final outcome. This is seen once we recognize the similarity of individual differences around the world. Our fundamental human nature never departs very far from a golden mean.

References

Alexander, R. D. (1979). Natural selection and social exchange. In R. L. Burgess & T. L. Huston (Eds.), *Social exchange in developing relationships* (pp. 197-221). New York: Academic Press.

Barker, O. J., Winter, P. D., Osmond, C., Margetts, B., & Simmonds, S. J. (1989). Weight in infancy and death from ischaemic heart disease. *Lancer, 8663,* 577-580.

Barkow, J. H., Cosmides, L., & Tooby, J. (1992). *The adapted mind: Evolutionary psychology and the generation of culture.* Oxford, UK: Oxford University Press.

Bouchard, T. J. Jr., Lykken, D. T., McGue, M., Segal, N. L., & Tellegen, A. (1990). Sources of human psychological differences: The Minnesota study of twins reared apart. *Science, 250,* 223-228.

Burgess, R. L., & Molenaar, P. C. M. (1993). Commentary. *Human Development, 36,* 45-54.

Burgess, R. L., & Molenaar, P. C. M. (1995). Commentary. *Human Development, 38,* 159-164.

Buss, D. M. (1995). Evolutionary psychology: A new paradigm for psychological science. *Psychological Inquiry, 6*(1), 1-30.

Cohen, D. B. (1999). *Stranger in the nest: Do parents really shape their child's personality, intelligence, or character?* New York: John Wiley.

Cosmides, L., & Tooby, J. (1987). From evolution to behavior: Evolutionary psychology as the missing link. In J. Dupne (Ed.), *The latest on the best: Essays on evolution and optimality* (pp. 277-306). Cambridge: MIT Press.

Cronk, L. (1999). *That complex whole: Culture and the evolution of human behavior.* Boulder, CO. Westview.

Dawkins, R. (1982). *The extended phenotype.* Oxford, UK: Oxford University Press.

Fodor, J. (2001). *The mind doesn't work that way.* Cambridge: MIT Press.

Gottlieb, G. (1992). *Individual development and evolution: The genesis of novel behavior.* New York: Oxford University Press.

Gottlieb, G. (1995). Some conceptual deficiencies in "developmental" behavior genetics. *Human Development, 38,* 131-141.

Hamilton, W. D. (1964). The genetical evolution of social behavior. *Journal of Theoretical Biology, 7,* 1-52.

Irons, W. G. (1979). Natural selection, adaptation, and human social behavior. In N. Chagnon & W. Irons (Eds.), *Evolutionary biology and human social behavior* (pp. 4-39). North Scituate, MA: Duxbury Press.

Kendler, K. S., Kessler, A. C., Walters, E. E., MacLeon, C., & Neale, M. C. (1995). Stressful life events, genetic liability, and onset of an episode of major depression in women. *American Journal of Psychiatry, 152*, 833-842.

Lerner, R. M., & von Eye, A. (1992). Sociobiology and human development: Arguments and evidence. *Human development, 35*, 12-33.

Maynard-Smith, J. (1982). *Evolution and the theory of games.* Cambridge, UK: Cambridge University Press.

Mayr, E. (1982). *The growth of biological thought: Diversity, evolution and inheritance.* Cambridge, MA: Harvard University Press.

Molenaar, P. C. M., & Boomsma, D. I. (1987). The genetic analysis of repeated measures. II. The Karhunen-Loeve expansion. *Behavior Genetics, 17*, 229-242.

Molenaar, P. C. M., Boomsma, D. I., & Dolan, C. V. (1993). A third source of developmental differences. *Behavior Genetics, 25*, 519-524.

Morris, S. C. (2003). *Life's solution: Inevitable humans in a lonely universe.* Cambridge, UK: Cambridge University Press.

Neiss, M., & Rowe, D. C. (2000). Parental education and child's verbal IQ in adoptive and biological families in the National Longitudinal Study of Adolescent Health. *Behavior Genetics, 30*, 487-495.

Patterson, G. R., & Dishion, T. J. (1988). Multilevel family process models: Traits, interactions, and relationships. In R. A. Hinde & J. Stevenson-Hinde (Eds.), *Relationships within families: Mutual influences* (pp. 283-310). Oxford, UK: Clarendon.

Plomin, R. & Bergeman, C. S. (1991). The nature of nurture: genetic influences on environmental measures. *Behavioral and Brain Sciences, 14*, 373-427.

Plomin, R., & Daniels, D. (1987). Why are children in the same family so different from each other? *Behavioral and Brain Sciences, 10*, 1-16.

Ridley, M. (2003). *Nature via nurture: Genes, experience, and what makes us human.* New York: HarperCollins.

Ridley, M. (1993). *The red queen: Sex and the evolution of human nature.* New York: Macmillan Publishing Company.

Scarr, S., & McCartney, K. (1983). How people make their own environments: A theory of genotype environment effects. *Child Development, 54*, 424-435.

Smith, E. A. (2000). Three styles in the evolutionary analysis of human behavior. In L. Cronk, N. Chagnon, & W. Irons (Eds.), *Adaptation and human behavior: An anthropological perspective* (pp. 27-46). New York: Aldine de Gruyter.

Sulloway, F. J. (1996). *Born to rebel: Birth order, family dynamics, and creative lives.* New York: Pantheon.

Symons, D. (1992). *On the use and misuse of Darwinism in the study of human behavior.* In J. H. Barkow, L. Cosmides, & J. Tooby (Eds.), *The adapted mind: Evolutionary psychology and the generation of culture* (pp. 137-159). Oxford, UK: Oxford University Press.

Tinbergen, N. (1963). On the aims and methods of ethology. *Zeitschnifr für Tienpsychologie, 20*, 410-433.

Trivers, R. L. (1974). Parent-offspring conflict. *American Zoologist, 14*, 249-264.

Turkheimer, E., Haley, A., Waldron, M., D'Onofrio, B., & Gottesman, T. (2002). Socioeconomic status modifies heritability of IQ in young children. *Psychological Science, 14,* 623-628.

van den Berghe, P. L. (1979). *Human family systems: An evolutionary view.* Amsterdam, The Netherlands: Elsevier.

van den Berghe, P. L. (1990). Why most sociologists don't (and won't) think evolutionarily. *Sociological Forum, 5*(2), 173-185.

Vreeke, G. J. (2000). Nature and nurture and the future of the analysis of variance. *Human Development, 43,* 32-45.

Wells, S. (2002). *The journey of man: A genetic odyssey.* Princeton, NJ: Princeton University Press.

Williams, G. (1966). *Adaptation and natural selection.* Princeton, NJ: Princeton University Press.

2

Theoretical Issues in the Study of Evolution and Development

Kevin MacDonald and Scott L. Hershberger

When the first author wrote the introductory chapter of *Sociobiological Perspectives on Human Development* (MacDonald, 1988a), the basic approach was to attempt to integrate evolutionary thinking with prominent strands of theory already influential in developmental psychology—particularly social learning theory, cognitive developmental theory, behavior genetics, and ethology. The intent was not to provide an alternative to these theoretical contributions, but to show how the revolution in evolutionary thinking inaugurated by William Hamilton, Robert Trivers, and G. C. Williams and culminating in E. O. Wilson's (1975) *Sociobiology* could add richness and insight into many areas of developmental psychology.

Whatever the merits of this approach, it soon became eclipsed by a much more radical approach, that of evolutionary psychology (Tooby & Cosmides, 1992). Evolutionary psychology offered radical critiques of all of the theories that traditionally held sway in developmental psychology. The attempt was not to integrate and amend, but to overthrow and discard. The following describes the program of evolutionary psychology and evaluates its critiques of influential theories of development. The chapter concludes with an updated version of the integrative approach adopted in the 1988 article. An important point is that the big story of childhood is the development of the extraordinary human brain and our uniquely human domain-general cognitive abilities, which have resulted in the extraordinary cultural developments of the last several thousand years.

Evolutionary Psychology and Development

Evolutionary psychologists propose the human mind consists predominantly of highly specialized mechanisms designed to solve specific problems. The specific problems that the human mind is designed to solve are those that repeatedly confronted our ancestors over evolutionary time. When organisms are repeatedly confronted by challenges or opportunities, the optimum response is to develop specialized methods of dealing with them.

The ancestral environment in which humans evolved is termed the *environment of evolutionary adaptedness* (EEA). This environment consists of a set of problems that must be solved if the animal is to avoid extinction. For example, over evolutionary time, humans and their primate ancestors had to be able find mates and raise children, and they had to form alliances with others. They had to be able to find food, and they had to avoid dangerous predators and poisonous plants and animals. There were a great many other problems that humans had to solve, but the point is that all of these problems presented themselves repeatedly over evolutionary time. According to evolutionary psychology, these problems were solved by evolving a set of psychological mechanisms designed to deal with these specific problems. These mechanisms are *adaptations,* mechanisms designed by natural selection to solve particular problems. For example, on the basis of a large body of theory and data, evolutionary psychologists argue that humans evolved mechanisms that allow them to choose mates in an adaptive manner: Women are attracted to men willing to invest in their children, and men are attracted to youthful, physically attractive women because these traits are signs of fertility (e.g., Buss, 1999).

A fundamental premise of evolutionary psychology is that evolutionary adaptations equip animals to meet recurrent challenges of the physical, biological, and social environment. When the environment presents long-standing problems and recurrent cues relevant to solving them, the best solution is to evolve domain-specific mechanisms, or *modules,* specialized to handle specific inputs and generate particular solutions. Modules are designed to solve problems in specific domains by mapping characteristic inputs onto characteristic outputs (Fodor, 1983, 2000). Their operation is mandatory (i.e., they are automatically triggered in the presence of appropriate environmental stimulation), fast, and unconscious. For example, when we look around the room, our brains are automatically carrying out millions of operations that allow us to see the objects in the room. The calculations are done very rapidly, and we are unaware of them. They carry out their operations by consulting a proprietary database: Each module processes information with mechanisms peculiar to its own area of "expertise," so that, for example, verbal and spatial information are processed with different mechanisms. Modules are also information encapsulated: Although information relevant to solving a particular problem may be accessible to other parts of the cognitive system, it is not necessarily available to a module (Fodor, 1983).

The modular view is likely a correct account of how the mind responds to recurrent, highly stable patterns of evolutionarily significant information (Geary & Huffman, 2002). For example, the three-dimensional structure of the physical world contains a large number of constantly recurring contours (invariances) that have resulted in genetic systems that are sensitive to spatial information related to finding prey and to migration (Gallistel, 1990, 1999).

There are no provisions for responding to variation within categories in the highly constrained modules proposed by Tooby and Cosmides (1992). Geary and Huffman (2002; see also Geary, Ch. 4, this volume) have described "soft modules" as sensitive to accommodating variation within a circumscribed range on analogy with the exoskeleton of invertebrates: The hard exoskeleton responds to invariances related, say, to physical space, language, or the human face, while the soft "innards" respond to variable patterns within a prespecified range. For example, human speech occurs within a genetically specified range, but the system is also open to variant patterns, for example, discriminating the speech patterns of different people.

Developmentally, these soft modules result in biases in children's attentional, affective, and information-processing capacities (Gelman & Williams, 1998), as well as biases in self-initiated behavioral engagement with the environment, such as play and exploration (Geary & Huffman, 2002). For example, the proposed face perception module is designed to make babies pay special attention to faces; this results in exposure to information needed to adapt the module to variation in the faces actually seen, such as parents and other family members.

Soft modules go some way toward accommodating traditional developmental theory with approaches derived from evolutionary psychology based on highly constrained modules. Soft modules raise the issue that modules often cannot prespecify the entire range of environmental variation to which they are attuned. Another critical issue is that animals often must find novel solutions to old problems of survival and reproduction. Evolutionary psychologists posit an EEA composed of recurrent cues signaling adaptive dangers and opportunities (Tooby & Cosmides, 1992). However, this leaves unexplained how humans and many animals are routinely able to solve novel problems and learn novel contingencies. It leaves unexplained how humans have been able to create the extraordinary human culture characteristic of the last 50,000 years of human evolution and cope with life in a constantly changing world far removed from our evolutionary past.

Adaptations sensitive to environmental regularities are of critical importance for all animals. However, there is no reason to restrict adaptations to mechanisms responsive to environmental regularities (Chiappe & MacDonald, 2005). The human EEA contained far more than a set of recurrent cues to dangers and opportunities. Rather, humans were forced to adapt to rapidly shifting ecological conditions by developing adaptations geared to novelty and unpredictability. For example, during the Pleistocene, there were unpredictable and nonrepetitive climatic shifts. There were shifts between cold steppe and warm, forested conditions interspersed with periods of climatic stability (Potts, 1998). These shifts occurred within a century or even decades—far too short a period to evolve adaptations sensitive to environmental regularities.

Moreover, even without a lot of climatic variation, environments are never completely stable and predictable for any animal. Animals and humans often have to make decisions about how to attain their goals in situations where past learning, whether by specialized or unspecialized simple learning mechanisms, is ineffective in attaining evolved goals. For example, rats are able to invent new ways to obtain food rewards by combining information from different sources (Anderson, 2000). Tomasello (1999) noted that most mammals and virtually all primates are able to use insight in learning. For example, ravens are able to solve novel problems by formulating goals, building mental scenarios, and evaluating possible sequences of actions without having to endure their consequences (Heinrich, 2000). The goals are evolutionarily ancient, but the methods used to obtain them do not rely on recurrent environmental cues.

The main criticism rendered by evolutionary psychologists against traditional psychology is that domain-general learning mechanisms are unlikely to have evolved. According to Cosmides and Tooby (2002), domain-general mechanisms are inherently weak because "jacks of all trades are masters of none. They achieve generality only at the price of broad ineptitude" (p. 170). From their perspective, a basic problem is that there are no particular problems that social learning mechanisms are designed to solve. For example, social learning mechanisms, as described in standard accounts (e.g., Bandura, 1977), have no preset goals and no way to determine when goals are achieved. A child confronted by an aggressive model must have a reason for imitating the model and must have ways of evaluating when the goal is achieved.

This is an example of the *frame problem* discussed by cognitive scientists (e.g., Dennett, 1987; Fodor, 1983; Gelman & Williams, 1998). The frame problem is the problem of determining which problems are relevant and what actions are relevant for solving them. A blank-slate organism is unable to determine which of the infinite number of problems it must solve to survive and reproduce. Without framing mechanisms guiding it toward the solution of adaptive problems, a problem solver would "go on forever making up solutions that have nothing to do with a non-assigned problem" (Gelman & Williams, 1998, p. 596). Due to the frame problem, it is difficult to see how domain-general processes could evolve. Modular systems, on the other hand, provide a built-in sense of relevance—a built-in sense of what the problem is and how to solve it. They easily solve the frame problem because environmental input is automatically framed by the relevant modules.

The above is a compelling argument for the existence of at least some modular, domain-specific mechanisms. Nevertheless, an important aspect of evolution has been to solve the frame problem in a manner compatible with the evolution of domain-general mechanisms (Chiappe & MacDonald, 2005; MacDonald, 1991). The basic idea is that humans and other animals have evolved motivational systems that help to solve the frame problem by equipping them with systems that provide signals when their goals are being met. For example, the hunger mechanism provides a signal telling the child to look for food and begin feeding. How the child goes about getting food is unspecified, but the motivational system effectively frames the problem: It tells the child what the problem is (the feeling of hunger), and it tells the child when the problem has been solved (satiation).

From this perspective, a watershed event in evolutionary history was the evolution of psychological signals—positive or negative feelings—that inform the animal when its goals of survival and reproduction are being met or unmet. Imagine a primitive organism equipped only with "if *p,* then *q*" devices, where *p* represents recurrent environmental events and *q* represents an evolved response to the event: If a certain environmental situation *p* occurs (e.g., presence of food), then respond with behavior *q* (eating). Such an organism would completely satisfy the requirements for a psychological adaptation as posed by evolutionary psychologists: The mind is constructed with mechanisms designed to respond adaptively to recurrent environmental events. The mechanism is entirely modular, designed to deal exclusively with a particular kind of input and produce a particular kind of output. Its disadvantage would be that there would be no way to take advantage of non-recurrent information in order to find food, for example, the information that a certain stimulus is a cue for food (classical conditioning), the chance discovery that a certain behavior is a good way to obtain food (operant conditioning), or observing another animal successfully obtaining food (social learning).

Examples of "if p, then q" systems are the fixed signaling systems of nonhuman primates and other animals discussed by Oller and Griebel (Ch. 5, this volume). Such signals occur in particular contexts (e.g., threat, danger, alarm, greeting) and are coupled to the specific circumstances surrounding their use and the functions they serve. Their meaning is therefore fixed. The breakthrough in human language, however, was the evolution of *contextual freedom*, in which each sound can be produced voluntarily and can be coupled, via learning, to an endless variety of social functions. These functions can change quickly over time, making them ideal for dealing with uncertain, novel situations. As in the case of social learning (see below), there is undoubtedly a great deal of specialized neural machinery underlying human language ability. However, like social learning, it functions as a domain-general system, with no evolutionarily fixed inputs or outputs. Even infants 3 to 6 months of age show "complex many-to-many mapping between signal and function, and the signals themselves are produced with great variability and often with no social function at all" (Oller & Griebel, Ch. 5, this volume).

The evolution of motivating systems goes a long way toward solving the frame problem. (It is also, quite probably, the evolutionary origin of consciousness, because by definition, the animal must be aware of these motivational cues.) A hungry child may indeed be confronted with an infinite number of behavioral choices, but such a child easily narrows down this infinite array by choosing behaviors likely to satisfy his or her hunger. The motive of hunger and the fact that certain behaviors reliably result in satiating hunger give structure to the child's behavior and enable him or her to choose adaptively among the infinite number of possible behaviors. The child's behavior is not random, because it is motivated by the desire to assuage the feeling of hunger.

Motivational mechanisms can be thought of as a set of adaptive problems to be solved but whose solution is massively underspecified. Learning mechanisms are examples of the evolution of *hyperplastic* mechanisms, mechanisms such as the immune system, which are unspecialized because they are not responsive to recurrent environmental events and because there is no selection for a particular phenotypic result (West-Eberhard, 2003, p. 178). Such systems enable the evolution of any cognitive mechanism, no matter how opportunistic, flexible, or domain-general, that is able to solve the problem (Chiappe & MacDonald, 2005; MacDonald, 1991). The child could solve his or her hunger problem by successfully getting the attention of the caregiver. The problem could be solved if the child stumbled onto a novel contingency (how to open the refrigerator door); or it could be solved

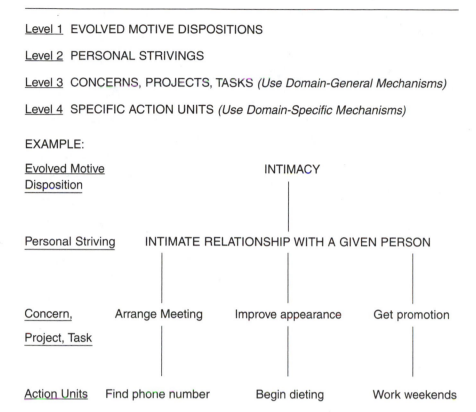

Level 1 EVOLVED MOTIVE DISPOSITIONS

Level 2 PERSONAL STRIVINGS

Level 3 CONCERNS, PROJECTS, TASKS *(Use Domain-General Mechanisms)*

Level 4 SPECIFIC ACTION UNITS *(Use Domain-Specific Mechanisms)*

EXAMPLE:

Evolved Motive   INTIMACY
Disposition

Personal Striving   INTIMATE RELATIONSHIP WITH A GIVEN PERSON

Concern,   Arrange Meeting   Improve appearance   Get promotion

Project, Task

Action Units   Find phone number   Begin dieting   Work weekends

Figure 2.1   Hierarchical Model of Motivation Showing Relationships Between
Domain-Specific and Domain-General Mechanisms
SOURCE: Adapted from Emmons (1989).

by imitating others eating a novel food; or the child could develop a sophisticated plan based on imagining possible outcomes and relying on mechanisms of general intelligence, the *g factor* of intelligence research. None of
these ways of solving the problem need result in solutions that were successful in our evolutionary past. This is illustrated in Figure 2.1.

Motivation represents a major point of contact between evolutionary
approaches and approaches based on learning theory. Learning theories
generally suppose that some motivational systems are biological in origin,
but traditionally they have tended toward *biological minimalism.* They
posit only a bare minimum of evolved motivational systems. For example,
traditional drive theory proposed that rats and people have drives to
consume food, satisfy thirst, have sex, and escape pain. For an evolutionist, this is a good start, but leaves out a great many other things that

organisms desire innately. Personality theory provides a basis for supposing there are several evolved motivational systems, including ones for seeking out social status, sexual gratification, felt security (safety), love, and a sense of accomplishment (MacDonald, 1995b, 1998, and Ch. 8, this volume). Glenn Weisfeld (1997) has provided an expanded list of affects that provide positive or negative signals of adaptive significance: tactile pleasure and pain, thirst, tasting and smelling, disgust or nausea, fatigue, drowsiness, sexual feelings, loneliness and affection receiving, interest and boredom, beauty appreciation, music appreciation and noise annoyance, humor appreciation, pride and shame, anger, and fear. One can quarrel with the details of such a list, but there is little doubt that there is a wide range of positive feelings that humans are innately designed to experience and a wide range of negative feelings that humans are innately designed to avoid.

The pursuit of evolved motives allows for flexible strategizing and the evolution of domain-general cognitive mechanisms—learning mechanisms and the mechanisms of general intelligence useful for attaining evolved desires. This fits well with research showing that problem solving is opportunistic: People satisfy their goals, including evolved goals such as satisfying hunger, by using any and all available mechanisms. For example, children typically experiment with a variety of strategies and then select the ones that are effective. Children are *bricoleurs,* tinkerers who constantly experiment with a wide range of processes to find solutions to problems as they occur. Children "bring to bear varied processes and strategies, gradually coming through experience to select those that are most effective. . . . Young bricoleurs . . . make do with whatever cognitive tools are at hand" (Deloache, Miller, & Pierroutsakos, 1998, p. 803).

Indeed, a common evolutionary mechanism for dealing with unpredictability is the initial overproduction of variants followed by selective retention by those that work (West-Eberhard, 2003, p. 41). Overproduction of dendrites followed by synaptic pruning occurs in many brain regions (e.g., stereoscopic depth perception) and is associated with a highly reliable source of environmental information that guides the elimination process (Greenough & Black, 1992). This *experience-expectant information* allows the fine-tuning of adaptive systems during a sensitive period, which is defined as the period when excess connections exist. This also fits well with Thelen's (1995) findings on motor development: Babies initially produce a wide range of unfocused movements, followed by selective retention of movements that are effective in attaining goals. Such mechanisms are adaptive because the outcome of the selection process is not genetically transmitted; flexibility is not diminished between generations.

The following sections discuss social learning theory, cognitive developmental theory, behavior genetics, and ethology. Each section includes the critique made by evolutionary psychologists, an evaluation of the critique, and a discussion of the theory from the integrative perspective developed here. A major theme is that general intelligence and the big brain that it entails are the central facts of human development—that the contours of human development are shaped by the requirements of producing a large-brained organism with the most powerful domain-general mechanisms known to nature.

Social Learning Theory

Social learning theory remains an important theoretical approach in developmental psychology (see also Flinn, Ch. 3, this volume). The critique proposed by evolutionary psychology emphasizes that social learning cannot be truly domain-general because it requires

> a rich battery of domain-specific inferential mechanisms, a faculty of social cognition, a large set of frames about humans and the world drawn from the common stock of human metaculture, and other specialized psychological adaptations designed to solve the problems involved in this task. (Tooby & Cosmides, 1992, p. 119)

The critique of social learning theory therefore emphasizes the need for domain-specific mechanisms as a precondition for social learning. Social learning no doubt requires a great deal of evolved machinery; otherwise, it would be far more common among animals. Indeed, Tomasello (1999) emphasized the uniqueness and incredible power of human social learning as deriving from an adaptation for the ability to engage in joint attention at around 9 months of age. This allows humans to see others as having goals and selecting among possible alternatives, thereby allowing them to take advantage of the way others have achieved their goals.

However, even if one accepts the premise that certain domain-specific mechanisms are prerequisites for social learning, this is insufficient to establish social learning as domain-specific. To be interesting, the argument must entail that the content of what is learned is evolutionarily circumscribed, and there is no evidence that this is the case. Evolved biases are indeed important in social learning, as emphasized in the original version of this chapter (MacDonald, 1988a; see also below). However, this does not imply that social learning evolved to solve a particular, highly discrete problem recurrent in the EEA. There is no evidence at all that the information available to social learning mechanisms or transmitted by social learning mechanisms is restricted to a specific set of messages important for adaptation in the EEA. We can use social learning to learn how to fix TV sets as easily as for learning how to hunt for wild boars. Social learning systems in humans are domain-general in the critical sense that they allow us to benefit from the experience of others, even when their behavior was not recurrently adaptive in the EEA but is effective in achieving evolved goals in the current environment.

For humans, the types of behaviors that can be successfully transmitted by social learning are not limited to behaviors useful to meeting recurrent challenges of the EEA. They are limited only by general cognitive and motor limitations: limitations on the informational complexity of modeled behavior, limitations on attentional processes and memory, and limitations on human motor abilities (Bandura, 1969, 1977; Shettleworth, 1994). Even among rats, Kohn and Dennis (1972) found that animals that were able to observe other rats solve a discrimination problem (and thus avoid shock) were quicker to learn this discrimination than rats that were prevented from the opportunity to observe. The patterns that were discriminated were entirely arbitrary and in no sense elements of the EEA. The response pattern involved motor activity to escape the shock by going through the appropriate door. The mechanism therefore was not domain-specific: It was not triggered by a highly delimited stimulus recurring in the EEA, and it did not result in a highly discrete response designed specifically to deal adaptively with this problem.

In general, we expect that domain-general learning will be most important in highly variable environments (Boyd & Richerson, 1985, 1988). The reason for this is that when environments change rapidly, it is not possible for an animal to track the changes genetically. Domain-specific, modular mechanisms evolve by tracking environmental cues that recur over and over again across generations, as in the example of three-dimensional space mentioned above. Animals must accommodate to a three-dimensional world repeatedly, over many generations, and the input useful for tracking this world is the same as it was in the EEA. On the other hand, if the usefulness of a particular behavior is only transient or local, there would be no possibility (or need) for the evolution of a genetic system devoted to producing this behavior.

We also expect that domain-general learning devices will evolve if there are low costs to learning. On the other hand, natural selection has sometimes molded learning mechanisms away from domain-generality if the costs of domain-general learning are too high (Garcia & Koelling, 1966; Öhman &

Mineka, 2001; Rescorla, 1988). A good example is taste aversion learning in a wide range of species, including quail, bats, catfish, cows, coyotes, and slugs (Kalat, 1985). If a rat consumes food and later feels nauseous, it associates the illness with the food rather than with other more recent stimuli such as lights and sounds, and it will make this association over much longer periods of delay than is typical for other examples of learning. The association of food with poison is greatly influenced by whether the food is unfamiliar to the animal. This indicates that taste aversion learning in rats is an adaptation to nonrecurrent and unpredictable features of the environment.

In this case, novel food items are a potential resource for the animal and must not be ignored even though they are more likely to be dangerous. Novel food items were a recurrent but unpredictable feature of the rat's EEA, with the result that the animal has evolved adaptations that minimize the cost of sampling this novelty. Because domain-general learning in this case is so costly, evolution has designed a constrained, biased learning mechanism. Rats preferentially eat novel food that they have smelled on the breath of another rat (Galef, 1987), thereby minimizing the danger of trial-and-error learning. This shows the utility of specialized social learning mechanisms that evolved to adapt to recurrent problems involving specific sources of novelty.

There are many recurrent but contingent aspects of an animal's microenvironment that must be learned. This learning is best performed by specialized learning mechanisms that allow for rapid and efficient learning of specific types of information. For example, there are specialized mechanisms that allow children to learn language (Oller & Griebel, Ch. 5, this volume). The language acquisition device makes learning any human language an effortless task, whereas the task is impossible for animals not so equipped. There certainly are mechanisms that make possible learning certain types of recurrently important information. However, it does not follow that the language acquisition device or other "learning instincts" (Tooby & Cosmides, 1992) should be viewed as a general paradigm for all human learning or even that language learning itself does not exhibit aspects of domain-generality (Oller & Griebel, Ch. 5, this volume). Language acquisition is more the exception than the rule in human learning. Unlike social learning and associative learning, there is a critical period for language acquisition, during which it is most efficient (Pinker, 1994; Spelke & Newport, 1998). Moreover, the capacity to acquire language can be selectively impaired. Children with *specific language impairment* have normal intelligence, but their ability to acquire language is disrupted (Pinker, 1994). However, not all forms of learning can be selectively impaired, suggesting that at least some learning mechanisms apply to a wide range of domains.

Domain-generality is apparent in Pavlovian conditioning and instrumental conditioning in animals and humans (Chiappe & MacDonald, 2004). Both systems allow animals and humans to make opportunistic associations between local, transient events not recurrent in their EEA. As mentioned above, there are well-documented cases where there are evolved biases away from domain-generality, as in taste aversion learning in rats (e.g., Garcia & Koelling, 1966; Rescorla, 1980). In general, however, animals rely on "rules of thumb" based on very broad, general features of the environment. For example, in Pavlovian conditioning, the main general predictors are contiguity (including temporal order and temporal contiguity) and contingency (reliable succession). These predictors reflect the fact that causes are reliable predictors of their effects, that causes precede their effects, and that in general, causes tend to occur in close temporal proximity to their effects (Revulsky, 1985; Staddon, 1988). Causes that are temporally far removed from their effects are difficult to detect, and the temporal contiguity of cause and effect is a general feature of the world. The fact that there are exceptions, as in taste aversion learning, where noncontiguous causes have a special status because of the evolutionary history of the animal, does not detract from the general importance of temporal contiguity. From the animal's perspective, in the absence of such a prepared association, the best default condition is to suppose that causes precede the unconditioned stimulus (UCS) and are temporally contiguous. While temporal contiguity is neither a necessary nor a sufficient condition for associating events, in general, it is a main source of information on causality (Shanks, 1994).

Tooby and Cosmides (1992) claimed that support for domain-generality in learning relies on data from "experimenter-invented, laboratory limited, arbitrary tasks" (p. 95). They criticized traditional learning experiments for not focusing exclusively on ecologically valid, natural tasks—tasks that deal with problems that were recurrent in the animal's EEA. Such a stance obviously begs the question of whether there are nonrecurrent problems that can be solved by learning. While it is certainly true that investigations of such tasks are likely to reveal specialized learning mechanisms in some cases, an equally remarkable aspect of learning is that pigeons *can* learn to peck keys to satisfy their evolved goals of staving off hunger and eating tasty foods even in experimenter-contrived situations. Although pecking for food is undoubtedly a species-typical behavior for pigeons, pigeons, like rats learning to push levers, are also able to learn a variety of arbitrary, experimenter-contrived behaviors that are not components of the animal's species-typical foraging behavior. In other words, they are able to solve a fundamental problem of adaptation (getting food) in a novel and even arbitrary environment that presents few, if any, of the recurrent associations between the animal's behavior and obtaining food experienced in the animal's EEA. Similarly, humans are able to learn lists of nonsense syllables—another example highlighted by Tooby and Cosmides (1992), despite the fact that learning such lists was not a recurrent problem in the EEA. People can learn such lists because their learning mechanisms can be harnessed to new goals, such as getting course credit as a subject in a psychology study.

In general, neither operant nor classical conditioning evolved to exclusively link specific events or behaviors recurrent in the EEA. The mechanisms underlying these abilities imply a great deal of evolved machinery, and there are important cases where evolution has shaped learning in ways that depart from domain-generality. In general, there is no characteristic input to these systems, because the input to associational mechanisms of rats and humans verges on whatever is detectable by the sense organs, and operant behaviors span virtually the entire range of physically possible motor behaviors. Because of their domain-generality, these mechanisms allow humans to solve problems with features not recurrent in the EEA.

There are important evolved mechanisms guiding human social learning in adaptive ways. Parent-child affection channels children's social learning within the family (MacDonald, 1992, 1997a). The human affectional system is designed to cement long-term relationships of intimacy and trust by making them intrinsically rewarding (MacDonald, 1992). A continuing relationship of warmth and affection between parents and children is expected to result in the acceptance of adult values by the child, identifying with the parent, and a generally higher level of compliance: "the time-honored concept of warmth and identification" (Maccoby & Martin, 1983, p. 72). The finding that warmth of the model facilitates imitation and identification has long been noted by social learning theorists (e.g., Bandura, 1969).

Domain-general learning mechanisms interact with other personality systems. For example, the fear system illustrates the complex interplay between domain-specificity and domain-generality (see LaFreniere, Ch. 7, this volume). The fear system is selective in its inputs: Certain stimuli recurrently associated with danger in the EEA are particularly easy to acquire and difficult to extinguish (e.g., Öhman & Mineka, 2001; Seligman, 1971). However, other stimuli can gain control of the fear system. The adaptiveness of domain-general aspects of the fear system can be seen from data showing that when the unconditioned stimulus is highly aversive or when a conditioned stimulus without any evolutionary significance is known to be very dangerous, the differences between evolutionarily primed fears and nonevolutionarily primed fears disappear (Chiappe & MacDonald, 2005; Öhman & Mineka, 2001, p. 513). As a result, intense trauma may result in phobias even toward normally benign objects with no evolutionary prepotency (Campbell,

Sanderson, & Laverty, 1964; Lautch, 1971). This modification of the fear system by what one might term "system-specific stimulation" is quite likely a general phenomenon in personality (Segal & MacDonald, 1998; see MacDonald, Ch. 8, this volume).

Piagetian Psychology and Information Processing

Research in cognitive development reveals an important role for the types of modular architecture posited by evolutionary psychologists as central to human cognition (e.g., Bjorklund & Pellegrini, 2002; Gelman & Williams, 1998). The 1988 chapter highlighted aspects of Piagetian theory that are consonant with an evolutionary perspective:

1. Intrinsic motivation: the child as a curious and interested explorer of the world rather than a passive recipient of environmental influences. The pleasure infants feel when they solve problems and understand the world a bit better is another example of the affective motivational mechanisms discussed above as critical to the evolution of domain-general cognitive mechanisms.

2. There are universal features of human social development and universal, age-graded differences among children. These universal features are products of human genetic invariance, the common human genetic heritage, interacting with universal features of the environment. The universal features of the pan-human EEA include the world of three-dimensional objects and very general features of the social world common to all human groups.

The 1988 chapter reflected the criticisms of stage theories that were already current at that time (Flavell, 1985; Gelman & Baillargeon, 1983), but the domain-general nature of Piagetian stages was not proposed as an important problem. This is because domain-generality itself was not seen as necessarily incompatible with an evolutionary perspective, as indeed it is not. In recent years, neo-Piagetian stage models have been elaborated incorporating modular, domain-specific mechanisms along with nonmodular, domain-general mechanisms. Case (1998) described domain-general central conceptual structures (CCS) that serve to integrate and organize information from modular systems of number, space, and theory of mind: "Although the content that they serve to organize is modular, the structures themselves reflect a set of principles and constraints that are systemwide in their

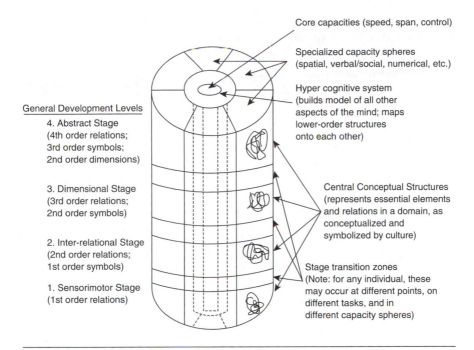

Core capacities (speed, span, control)

Specialized capacity spheres
(spatial, verbal/social, numerical, etc.)

Hyper cognitive system
(builds model of all other
aspects of the mind; maps
lower-order structures
onto each other)

General Development Levels
4. Abstract Stage
(4th order relations;
3rd order symbols;
2nd order dimensions)

3. Dimensional Stage
(3rd order relations;
2nd order symbols)

Central Conceptual Structures
(represents essential elements
and relations in a domain, as
conceptualized and
symbolized by culture)

2. Inter-relational Stage
(2nd order relations;
1st order symbols)

1. Sensorimotor Stage
(1st order relations)

Stage transition zones
(Note: for any individual, these
may occur at different points, on
different tasks, and in
different capacity spheres)

Figure 2.2   Integrated Model of the Developing Mind

SOURCE: From Demetriou, Efklides, and Platsidou (1993). Copyright: Society for Research in Child Development. Reprinted with permission.

NOTE: The Core Capacities are domain-general abilities; the Specialized Capacity Spheres are modular abilities.

nature, and that change with age in a predictable fashion" (p. 770). Among the factors thought to be important for stage advances in CCS is working memory, a domain-general ability that is also implicated in the model of Demetriou, Christou, Spanoudis, and Platsidou (2002). Their model includes domain-general abilities revealed by research in the tradition of IQ testing (speed of processing, working memory, and attentional control), lower-level, domain-specific ability modules (quantitative/relational, spatial/imaginal, verbal/propositional, qualitative/analytic, and causal/experimental), and stage transitions, that is, transition zones in which there are major developmental changes in these domain-specific and domain-general abilities (see Figure 2.2).

These models illustrate the continued power of models integrating both domain-general and domain-specific mechanisms. Both domain-general and domain-specific systems are supported, and both are compatible with the importance of stagelike transitions. It is noteworthy that these models integrate the modular, domain-specific mechanisms of the information-processing tradition with mechanisms of working memory, speed of processing, and inhibitory ability discovered to underlie general intelligence in the psychometric tradition. Indeed, in a study combining standard IQ tasks (the WISC) with neo-Piagetian tasks, Case, Demetriou, Platsidou, and Kazi (2001) found support for the five domain-specific abilities noted above (quantitative/ relational, spatial/imaginal, verbal/propositional, qualitative/analytic, and causal/experimental) as well as for a general intelligence factor representing the correlations among all of these subfactors (see Figure 2.3). The specific abilities have their own evolutionary histories, unique set of underlying operations, and unique logic—hallmarks of evolved modules.

At the same time, the general intelligence factor, *g*, was more robust when age effects were included, suggesting that changes in *g* are the main factor responsible for developmental shifts in mental ability:

> Although there may be additional sources of variability in children's reasoning on Piagetian tasks, the sources of variability isolated by psychometric theorists are powerful because they differentially affect the rate at which children construct new conceptual understandings in many of the different fundamental areas identified by Kant: areas such as space, number, causation, and social cognition. (Case et al., 2001, p. 326)

Supporting the importance of age changes in domain-general processes, Kail (1996) has shown that developmental increase in speed of processing is a critical mechanism of children's cognitive development, linked to increases in working memory and increases in performances on IQ instruments such as the Raven's Progressive Matrices. In a later section, I will argue that the most important story of human development—the reason why human development takes so long and why children require so much adult investment in time and energy—is the maturation of the brain's information-processing capabilities and specifically, the structures underlying general intelligence.

There is excellent evidence that general intelligence is an adaptation underlying the ability of humans to create novel solutions to ancient problems of survival and reproduction (Chiappe & MacDonald, 2005; Geary, Ch. 4, this volume). From an evolutionary perspective, a critical function of general intelligence is the attainment of evolutionary goals in unfamiliar and novel conditions characterized by a minimal amount of prior knowledge. Tests of Cattell's (1963) fluid intelligence, such as Raven's Progressive Matrices and Cattell's Culture Fair Test, are strongly associated with the ability to solve novel problems (Horn & Hofer, 1992). They

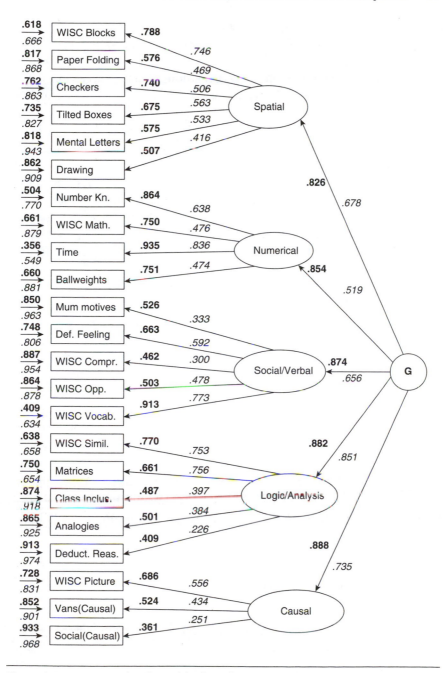

Figure 2.3   Hierarchical Model of Intelligence, With Modular Abilities
Arrayed Under the General Intelligence Factor

reflect the capacity "to adapt one's thinking to a new cognitive problem" (Carpenter, Just, & Shell, 1990, p. 404). Fluid intelligence lies at the heart of the concept of *g*. As several researchers have pointed out, tests of fluid intelligence produce the highest *g* correlations (Carpenter et al., 1990; Carroll, 1993; Duncan, Burgess, & Emslie, 1995; Duncan, Emslie, Williams, Johnson, & Freer, 1996).

Research on intelligence has consistently found that more-intelligent people are better at attaining goals in unfamiliar and novel conditions characterized by a minimal amount of prior knowledge. People with high intelligence have a variety of real-world advantages (Gottfredson, 1998; Herrnstein & Murray, 1994). They tend to make more money and achieve higher social status than people on the low end of the IQ distribution. The *g* factor is the best single predictor of job performance. Correlations between *g* and job performance range between 0.2 and 0.8, with greater predictive validity achieved for jobs of greater complexity. Thus, people with higher intelligence are more adept at attaining their evolutionary goals in situations of novelty, complexity, and unpredictability—precisely the functions of *g* as a psychological adaptation designed by natural selection (Chiappe & MacDonald, 2005; Geary, Ch. 4, this volume).

General intelligence is therefore at the heart of an evolutionary analysis. Although modules designed to process specific types of information are unquestionably important to an evolutionary analysis, evolutionary psychology has overemphasized modularity and ignored the vast data indicating a prominent role for domain-general mechanisms in human and animal cognition. Domain-general mechanisms are not weak "jacks of all trades but masters of none," as evolutionary psychologists would have it. They are powerful but fallible mechanisms that are the basis for solving a fundamental problem faced by all but the simplest organisms: the problem of navigating constantly changing environments that present new challenges that have not been recurrent problems in the EEA. Most important, the domain-general mechanisms at the heart of human cognition are responsible for the decontextualization and abstraction processes critical to the scientific and technological advances that virtually define civilization (Chiappe & MacDonald, 2005).

The Developmental Systems
Perspective and Behavior Genetics

The 1988 introductory chapter contained no mention of developmental systems theory (DST) associated most prominently with Gilbert Gottlieb (e.g., Gottlieb 1992; Gottlieb, Wahlsten, & Lickliter, 1998; see also Lickliter & Honeycutt, 2003) because it did not seem compatible with the findings of behavior genetic research or with a modern evolutionary perspective. Because of its focus on universal adaptations, evolutionary psychology has also shown no interest in behavior genetics or, indeed, individual differences in general—conceptualizing individual differences as "noise" without adaptive significance (Tooby & Cosmides, 1992).

However, there are good theoretical reasons to suppose that natural selection has shaped the enormous interest people have in individual differences in personality and other types of individual differences (e.g., intelligence) (Lusk, MacDonald, & Newman, 1998; MacDonald, 1995b, 1998, and Ch. 8, this volume). People choose mates, friends, allies, and leaders based partly on their personalities. Reflecting the importance of personality as a resource in human transactions, people often go to great lengths to convince others of their personal qualities (e.g., their honesty and intellectual competence), processes that often involve deception and self-deception. Behavior genetics, as the science of understanding the genetic and environmental influences on human diversity, is thus central to an evolutionary approach to development. Also, because different human groups evolved in somewhat different EEAs, understanding between-group genetic variation will shed light on the origins of human differences, for example, the tendency for children from the Mongoloid gene pool to be lower on affect intensity, aggression, and disruptiveness and to be more cooperative than Caucasian children (Brazelton, Robey, & Collier, 1969; Freedman & Freedman, 1969; Orlick, Zhou, & Partington, 1990).

DST is a prominent opponent of behavior genetic analysis. It deserves scrutiny because of its widespread influence within developmental psychology (as indicated, e.g., by its prominence in Richard Lerner's 1998 edited volume in the authoritative *Handbook of Child Psychology* series) and because it forms the theoretical basis of Bjorklund and Pellegrini's (2002) recent attempt to reconcile evolutionary psychology and human development.

As represented in Figure 2.4, DST proposes that there are reciprocal influences at all levels of development, from genes to the environment. Development occurs in a set of hierarchically organized systems of increasing size, differentiation, and complexity, in which each component affects, and is affected by, all the other components, not only at its own level but at lower and higher levels as well. Genes do indeed influence physiology, behavior, and the environment, but the reverse also occurs: The external environment influences behavior, which influences physiology and eventually turns particular genes on and off. The result is "a totally interrelated, fully coactional system in which the activity of the genes themselves can be affected

BIDIRECTIONAL INFLUENCES

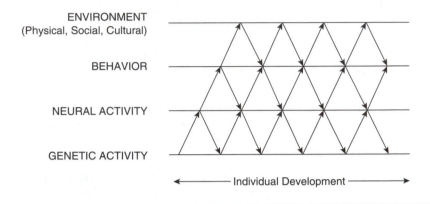

ENVIRONMENT
(Physical, Social, Cultural)

BEHAVIOR

NEURAL ACTIVITY

GENETIC ACTIVITY

◄─────── Individual Development ───────►

Figure 2.4   Gottlieb's Model of Bidirectional Influences

SOURCE: The probablistic epigenetic conceptual framework, showing a hierachy of four mutually coacting levels of analysis in which there are "top-down" as well as "bottom-up" bidirectional influences. From *Individual Development and Evolution; The Geneds of Novel Behavior by Gilbert Gottlieb. Copyright* 1991 by Oxford University Press. Inc. Reprinted by permission.

through the cytoplasm of the cell by events originating at any other level in the system, including the external environment" (Gottlieb, 1992, p. 145).

Gottlieb regards his theory as incompatible with the reaction range idea and with behavioral genetic research in general. The common response of behavioral geneticists to Gottlieb's theory is a mixture of outrage combined with charges of fundamental misunderstandings and suggestions of political motivation (e.g., Turkheimer, Goldsmith, & Gottesman, 1995). All sides agree that there are complex interactions among genes and environments and that environments affect genetic activity—that, for example, genes are turned on and off during development by exposure to environmental stimulation.

It is important to have a concept of an evolutionarily expected environment (EEE) and the closely related concept of the EEA. These concepts, originating with Bowlby (1969), highlight the idea that species are designed to solve the problems encountered in the environments in which they evolved and animals are designed to expect the range of environments typically encountered during their evolution. Gottlieb's argument rests on "what if" theorizing that stresses the unpredictable and unusual effects of major deviations from the expected environment (Scarr, 1995). Evolutionary approaches ranging from evolutionary psychology (Tooby & Cosmides, 1992) to the developmental systems approach of Bjorklund and Pellegrini

(2002) to the integrative approach discussed here suppose that it is meaningful and important to speak of a universal, species-typical environment: the environmental invariance that, as noted in the above discussion of cognitive developmental theory, combines with normal human genetic commonality to result in reliably developing human phenotypes. Gottlieb's theory is profoundly antievolutionary because it ignores the actual evolution of developing systems—the typically encountered environmental problems that these systems were designed to solve. Recurrent environmental events are a critical force in evolution:

> It is only those conditions that recur, statistically accumulating across many generations, that lead to the construction of complex adaptations. . . . For this reason, a major part of adaptationist analysis involves sifting for these environmental or organismic regularities or invariances. (Tooby & Cosmides, 1992, p. 69)

While this statement goes too far in emphasizing the importance of environmental invariance for designing adaptations (Chiappe & MacDonald, 2005), there is no question that a fundamental aspect of evolution is the design of adaptive systems in response to environmental regularities. By ignoring environmental invariance, Gottlieb effectively undercuts the entire concept of an adaptation.

This same objection applies as well to Lickliter and Honeycutt's (2003) critique of evolutionary psychology from the standpoint of DST. If development were truly as contingent and unspecified genetically as these authors have claimed, there would be no way to explain the overwhelming regularity of developmental outcomes: the fact that development within the normal range of human environments reliably results in normally formed, psychologically functioning children.

Bjorklund and Pellegrini's (2002) acceptance of the standard evolutionary concept of an EEE goes some way toward providing a minimally acceptable evolutionary theory of development. However, they accept Gottlieb's ideas that genetic and environmental sources of individual differences cannot be literally partitioned via the standard techniques of behavioral genetics, and they have claimed that Gottlieb is correct in arguing that behavioral genetic research provides an overly simple characterization of the environment (p. 79). At the same time, they proposed, "We believe that the expression of many genes that influence individual differences is robust to the perturbations of a wide range of 'ordinary' environments, accounting for the impressive predictions of behavior genetics" (p. 85). But such a claim is exactly what is embedded in the concept of additive genetic variance that has been shown to be the most important genetic contribution to individual differences: Additive genes have their effect in a wide range of environments typically encountered by the organism. There is no reason whatever to avoid studying such genes or to reject the idea of partitioning the components of variance, as is done in standard behavior genetics research.

Gottlieb's (1995) "norm of reaction" concept implies that "it is not possible to predict outcomes from one rearing circumstance to the next" (p. 133). Gottlieb also argues that the reaction range idea sets "strict and predictable upper and lower limits for a genotype" (p. 134). At the heart of Gottlieb's theory is the idea that complex, idiosyncratic interactions with environments are the rule rather than the exception (also apparent in Lickliter & Honeycutt, 2003), with the result that development is unpredictable—apparently implying that parents really couldn't have any good reason to suppose that talking to their children and taking them to museums would be a better way to treat them than locking them in a closet.

Gottlieb's theory implies that the concept of additive genetic variance is vacuous, and although Gottlieb embraces average effects of environments, his position of omnipresent interactions implies that there are no expectable average effects of rearing in different environments. All of these propositions are incorrect. In fact, Gottlieb does not provide a single study from the human psychological literature showing that there are high levels of genotype-environment interactions within normal ranges of environmental variation. The single animal example discussed in Gottlieb involves both artificial selection for maze learning and extreme rearing conditions, and thus says nothing about the importance of genotype-environment interaction in natural populations within the range of the EEE. Even using extreme environments under controlled conditions, animal studies have typically not shown an important contribution of genotype-environment interaction (Rutter & Silberg, 2002).

As conceptualized by Gottlieb and others, genotype-environment interaction (GXE) occurs when the effects of the environment depend on genetic differences among individuals. This definition of GXE is comparable to the definition of an interaction in the analysis of variance: The effect of one independent variable (genotypic differences) on a dependent variable (phenotypic differences) varies as a function of a second independent variable (environmental differences). GXE can be represented schematically as a 2×2 factorial arrangement in which one variable is the genotype and the other is the environment (see Figure 2.5). For any dependent variable, the design can be used to investigate the effect of genotype independent of the environment (i.e., the genetic main effect or *heritability* of the dependent variable),

	G_1	G_2
E_1	G_1E_1	G_2E_1
E_2	G_1E_2	G_2E_2

Figure 2.5   Genotype-Environment Interaction in the Form of 2×2 Analysis of Variance (ANOVA)

the effect of the environment independent of genotype (i.e., the environmental main effect or *environmentality* of the dependent variability), and GXE. One example of GXE could be that a child having a high genetic value for introversion may be moderately interactive with a small group of friends but very inhibited within a large group of unfamiliar children, whereas a child having a low genetic value for introversion (i.e., extraversion) may be uninhibited in both situations.

We believe that GXE is of dubious importance for explaining individual differences in human behavior. Our belief is based on two considerations: (1) the vast empirical evidence *against* the significance of GXE and (2) the inconsistency of GXE and evolutionary theory. To more clearly communicate why GXE is a trivial source of variance, we first describe the model underlying most quantitative investigations of phenotypic variation. In the simplest form of the model, a phenotype (P) is a linear function of genetic (G) and environmental (E) causes. However, because the purpose is to explain the variance of a phenotype, G is expressed as a deviation score from the genotypic mean, and E is expressed as a deviation score from the environmental mean, while allowing for the possibility of genotype-environment interaction (GXE) and random error (e):

$$Pi = Gi + Ei + (GXE)i + ei$$

where the *i* refers to the *ith* individual's deviation from the mean.

G can be partitioned further into three separate elements, each expressed as a deviation score—the additive genetic deviation (A), the dominance deviation (D), and the epistatic deviation (I):

$$Gi = Ai + Di + Ii$$

and

$$Pi = Ai + Di + Ii + Ei + (AXE)i + (DXE)i + (IXE)i + ei$$

The additive genetic value (A) is the sum of the effects of the genes across all the loci influencing the trait. In an analysis of variance sense, the additive gene effect is the main effect of the genes on the phenotype. Dominance deviation (D) occurs when the two alleles *within* a locus are not of equivalent influence. At a locus, a gene may be recessive and not be manifested in the phenotype unless paired with another recessive gene at the same locus. Dominant genes will often, but not always, neutralize the effects of recessive genes, depending on whether the dominant gene exerts complete, over-, or partial dominance. Dominance effects cause the genotype to deviate from its expected value based on the additive genetic effect. Epistatic interaction deviation (I) refers to the interaction of alleles *between* loci. Epistatic interaction deviation represents the remaining influence of genetic variation on phenotypic variation after additive genetic and dominance effects have been removed, and is typically small. Collectively, dominance deviation and epistatic interaction deviation are known as nonadditive genetic effects, the "nonadditive" a lexical gift from the analysis of variance signifying their interactional nature.

Because each of the genetic and environmental influences has been expressed as a deviation score, the model is revised to express the contribution of each of the sources to the variance in the phenotype. First, taking the genetic effects over all N individuals in the population, we find by the rules for the variance of an unweighted composite:

$$VG = VA + VD + VI + 2Cov(A, D) + 2Cov(D, I)$$
$$+ 2Cov(I, A) + VAXD + VDXI + VIXA$$

This model for the total genetic variance may be greatly simplified. Additive, dominance, and epistatic effects may be assumed to be uncorrelated (Kempthorne, 1957, provided a rather complex explanation for this assumption). The three interaction terms may also be removed from the equation. Although interactions among the three genetic effects do occur, their identification, especially with human data, is difficult, if not impossible, with the methods currently available. In addition, their contribution to the total phenotypic variance can be expected to be quite small, relative to the other variance components. Typically, epistatic interaction variance is left confounded with dominance variance, for the detection of the unique contribution of each in humans is extraordinarily difficult. Therefore, the model for the total genetic variance is:

$$VG = VA + VD$$

If the environmental deviation score is incorporated into the variance partitioning, the total variance in a phenotype over all N members of the population is:

$$VP = VA + VD + VE + 2Cov(A, E)$$
$$+ 2Cov(D, E) + VAXE + VDXE + Ve$$

According to the model, the total variance in a phenotype is a function of the variance in both additive and nonadditive genetic effects, variance in the environment, and the variance due to the correlation and interaction between the various genetic and environmental effects. As in any correlation, where certain values of one variable tend to occur in concert with certain values of another variable, a significant genotype-environment correlation represents the nonrandom distribution of the values of one variable (genotype) across the values of another variable (environment). Consequently, different phenotypes are selectively exposed to environmental experiences based upon their differing genetic propensities. As one example, genotype-environment correlation may be of importance when young adults differing in intelligence select different career paths. If the more-intelligent young adults select more intellectually demanding occupations, then a positive association is found between genotype and environment. But genotype-environment correlation can be negative as well, a situation that could occur, for instance, when young adults of lower intelligence are coerced by their parents to pursue the same intellectually demanding occupations as the more-intelligent young adults. The foregoing examples imply a linear correlation between genotypes-environments; genotype-environment correlations can also be nonlinear. Cattell's (1982) idea of "coercion to the biosocial mean" is an example of a nonlinear genotype-environment correlation, in which the correlation tends to be negative for individuals at high and low levels of a trait, and positive in-between the two levels. Supposedly, society attempts to moderate the "extreme" behavior of individuals by coercing them to behave more moderately; for example, too much or too little aggression is usually discouraged or even punished. Of course, there must be a significant genetic component to the trait.

It should be noted that traits differ in the extent to which additive genetic and nonadditive genetic effects are both influential in individual differences. In the case where the two genetic sources of variance have not been differentiated or only additive genetic variance is of concern, the total genetic variance can be represented as before, VG. In the situation where a trait is influenced by both additive and nonadditive genetic variance, we ask whether it is possible for the two components of variance to differentially correlate with the environment; the situation where Cov(A, E) is significant but Cov(D, E) is not. For example, where directional selection occurs, only Cov(A, E) is likely to be significant; where stabilizing selection occurs, only Cov(D, E) is likely to be significant. Generally, if directional or stabilizing selection is not of particular concern, genotype-environment can be neutrally written as "Cov(G, E)."

Therefore, the total variance in a phenotype is expressed as:

$$VP = VG + VE + 2Cov(G, E) + VGXE + Ve$$

In the model, GXE is considered simply as another source of variance contributing to individual differences on a trait, exerting influence above and beyond the influence of genetic and environmental main effects.

One difficulty with accepting GXE as an important influence on human behavior is the virtual absence of evidence of its significance; on the contrary, evidence is readily available that GXE is generally not significant. For example, three books report the exhaustive attempts that have been made to detect GXE in data from the Colorado Adoption Project (DeFries, Plomin, & Fulker, 1994; Plomin & DeFries, 1985; Plomin, DeFries, & Fulker, 1988), a longitudinal adoption study examining the development of a number of cognitive ability and personality variables from infancy through young adulthood, in a sample that includes adopted children and their adoptive and biological families. Of the hundreds evaluated, the number of significant GXE does not exceed the nominal Type I error rate of 5%.

A number of methods have been proposed to detect GXE. We illustrate the application of two methods to work on environment-related variables from the Swedish Adoption/Twin Study of Aging (Hershberger, Lichtenstein, & Knox, 1994), a longitudinal study of adult reared-together and reared-apart monozygotic and dizygotic twins. In both methods, data from only reared-apart monozygotic twins (MZA) are used.

The first method, proposed by Jinks and Fulker (1970), involves correlating the means of MZA pairs with the corresponding absolute intra-pair differences. Applying this test to MZAs detects genetic effects on sensitivity to the environment that are correlated with genetic effects on average trait value. The variables examined for GXE were the 10 scales from the Work Environment Scale (WES) (Moos, 1981): Work involvement, peer cohesion, supervisor support, work autonomy, task orientation, pressure, role clarity, control, innovation, and physical comfort. None of the correlations was significant, thus implying that GXE was not present in these data.

In the second method of detecting GXE, hierarchical regression is used to remove joint effects of genotype and environment and then to assess their interaction in predicting a twin's report of the work environment (Plomin, DeFries, & Loehlin, 1977). In addition to the 10 scales of the WES, three "objective" environmental variables are included in the analysis: (1) occupation type (whose four categories range from "unskilled" to "professional"), (2) level of education required for the occupation, and (3) the amount of physical labor involved in the occupation. The method assumes that the response of one of the twins within each MZA pair serves as an estimate of the co-twin's genotype. In the first step of the hierarchical regression, one twin's response to a scale from the WES is regressed onto the co-twin's response in order to assess the significance of genetic effects. In the second step, one of the three objective work environment variables is included in the model in order to assess the significance of environmental effects. In the third and last step, the product between the WES and the work environment is added to the model in order to assess the significance of GXE. Because there are 10 scales from the WES and 3 work environment variables, 30 hierarchical regression analyses were conducted. Of these 30, only 3 were significant—approximately what would be expected using a nominal Type I error rate of 5%. Thus, in these data, no evidence was found for GXE.

Also suggestive of GXE's dispensability is the finding that even if GXE is significant, failing to specify it as a parameter in the quantitative genetic model does not significantly affect the values of the model's other parameters (e.g., the heritability does not change) (Molenaar & Boomsma, 1987). In contrast, if Cov(G, E) is significant but not specified, the other parameters become biased: If Cov(G, E) is positive, the estimated heritability is too high; if Cov(G, E) is negative, the estimated heritability is too low (Hershberger, 1991).

A statistical red herring is occasionally introduced to avert attention away from the theoretical and statistical shortcomings of GXE. GXE apologists emphasize the exceptional power requirements for detecting significant interactions (e.g., Wahlsten, 1990). So be it. It is the responsibility of those who want to detect interactions to design more powerful studies. Detecting significant Cov(G, E) also requires exceptional power (e.g., Eaves, Last,

Martin, & Junks, 1977), but as indicated below, this does not seem to have seriously affected our ability to find Cov(G, E) when we look for it. A statistical anomaly of GXE that *is* troubling is the possibility of finding significant GXE effects in the absence of significant genetic and environmental main effects. In contrast, for Cov(G, E) to be significant, *both* genetic and environmental main effects must be significant. In natural environments, it is extremely unusual to find an animal or human phenotype that does not have significant genetic and environmental main effects of some type (Falconer, 1981). In fact, significant GXE without significant genetic and environmental effects is a spurious result of exposing organisms to unnatural environments, environments they would never encounter without the assistance of researchers.

From an evolutionary perspective, the ubiquitous GXEs envisioned by Gottlieb are not expected. Additive genes have their effects on a wide range of normal genetic backgrounds and across a wide range of normal environments. The evolutionary logic of such genes is that when a trait such as intelligence is under directional selection, there would be selection for genes that provide a general positive effect on the trait that is more or less independent of genetic background and a wide range of normal environmental rearing conditions. For example, the genes for intelligence are predominantly additive (e.g., Plomin, 2003). Given that intelligence (or increased lung capacity or increased oxygen efficiency) is a valuable trait for the organism, genes that contributed to intelligence in one commonly encountered environment but lowered intelligence in another commonly encountered environment would be at a disadvantage. The presence of complex, unpredictable, and idiosyncratic interactions envisioned in DST would make it very difficult for natural selection to construct complex adaptations. Complex adaptations require multiple, smoothly meshing genes that produce qualitatively similar phenotypes throughout the entire range of environments encountered in the EEA. This does not imply that there are no interactions at all or that individual differences would be absolutely preserved over a wide range of normal environments (Turkheimer et al., 1995). It does mean that such interactions are not expected to disrupt the design plan of complex adaptations.

Another reason why a major influence of GXE is inconsistent with evolutionary theory is suggested by the ubiquitous significance of Cov(G, E). This is because Cov(G, E) and GXE are fundamentally incompatible processes if one accepts that the results of natural selection are organisms adapted to their environments. Recall that significant Cov(G, E) implies that genotypes are systematically matched to environments. This is exactly what would be expected under natural selection. On the other hand, for GXE to be significant, a range of genotypes must be found within each environment. This is highly unlikely, if not impossible, under natural selection. Natural selection severely reduces the variety of genotypes found within any environment; greater reductions result in higher Cov(G, E). Natural selection never gives GXE much of a chance.

Evidence for the importance of Cov(G, E) for many human phenotypes is not difficult to find; for example, in contrast to GXE, Cov(G, E) has been found for many of the cognitive ability and personality variables measured in the Colorado Adoption Project. As is the case for GXE, a number of methods have been proposed for detecting Cov(G, E). We will describe one such method and its application to data from the Colorado Adoption Project. This method is designed to detect "reactive" Cov(G, E), in which individuals evoke experiences that derive from the reactions of others to the individual's genetically influenced behavior. To compute Cov(G, E), measures of genotypes and environments are required. In the Colorado Adoption Project, the genotype of adopted children can be indexed by scores from their biological parents, and the environment of adopted children can be estimated using any measure of the adoptive home environment or characteristics of the adoptive parents (Plomin et al., 1977). If adoptive parents react to their adopted children on the basis of genetic differences among the children, correlations between the scores of the biological parents and environmental measure should be significant. In the absence of selective placement, this method will detect Cov(G, E) when there is a heritable relationship between the phenotype of biological parents and their adopted-away children and when there is a relationship between the environmental measure and the phenotype of adopted children. The correlation computed under this method is consistent with the definition of Cov(G, E): Genetic differences among children are correlated with differences among their environments.

From the Colorado Adoption Project data, a set comprising 15 birth mother characteristics was correlated with a set comprised of 10 scales from the Family Environment Scale (Moos & Moos, 1981) when adopted children were 1, 3, 5, 7, 9, 10, and 11 years of age. This canonical Cov(G, E) was significant at each age, increasing from its lowest value of .32 at 1 year of age to its highest value of .59 at 11 years of age.

Those theorists who insist on the importance of GXE for human behavior are motivated by an *idée fixe*: If only we could place individuals within their optimal environments, individual differences would disappear. Disappearing with them would be a multitude of undesirable phenotypes: At last, the uneducable would become educable; the poor, wealthy; and the emotionally disturbed, well. GXE is not the first time interactions have been used to satisfy the utopian fantasies of social scientists. Aptitude X treatment effects were once hypothesized to be of the greatest importance in education (Cronbach & Snow, 1977). According to the proponents of this interaction, finding optimal methods of instruction for each student leads to the eradication of individual differences in learning. However, several decades of nonreplicable findings have convinced most researchers otherwise. After birth, the idea of aptitude X treatment effects died from a failure to thrive in a research setting. We predict that GXE will meet a similar fate. We live in a world primarily of main effects, with a few true interactions complicating the picture. And given enough time, these interactions will themselves evolve into main effects. These are the logical consequences of natural selection.

One is struck in reading the debate between Gottlieb and his critics that both sides have paid homage to the idea that DST is an accurate picture of the real nature of developing systems. For example, Turkheimer et al. (1995) noted that "ultimately the relationship between genotype and phenotype cannot possibly be linear" (p. 148). Scarr (1995) stated that "we do not fully understand the complex, nonlinear web of mechanisms involved in producing these outcomes" (p. 155). Behavior genetic methods are therefore seen as useful simplifications of a complex reality that can be captured only by probabilistic, nonlinear models.

We suggest the reverse: Models stressing additive genes and additive environmental effects reflect the fundamental reality discussed above. The genes that are most easily incorporated into many complex adaptations are selected (a) because they result in reliably developing phenotypes across a wide range of environments, (b) because additive genes are most easily incorporated into complex adaptations due to the fact that such genes have predictable effects on the phenotype independent of genetic background, and (c) because naturally occurring environments are often structured to result in additive increments to the phenotype for genetically normal people.

In the case of personality systems, there is reason to expect that nonadditive genetic variation will be more common (MacDonald, 1998; Segal & MacDonald, 1998; see also MacDonald, Ch. 8, this volume). This is because personality systems function to deal with conflicting demands of the environment and because personality systems are likely to be shaped by stabilizing selection rather than directional selection. Personality systems are profoundly interactive at the physiological level, with mutual inhibitory linkages among systems (Fox, 1994; see MacDonald, Ch. 8, this volume): Events that trigger behavioral withdrawal and fear also trigger inhibition of other personality systems underlying behavioral approach and positive emotions. As a result, genes that strengthen an animal's fear system may work by more effectively inhibiting behavioral approach mechanisms and therefore have different effects depending on the strength of the organism's approach systems. The result is that unlike the case for intelligence, there are relatively high levels of nonadditive genetic variation associated with personality systems (Segal & MacDonald, 1998).

In the case of personality systems, it is likely that stabilizing selection (i.e., selection against extremes) rather than directional selection occurred. Individuals who are extremely high or extremely low on particular traits would appear to be at a disadvantage, but there is a broad range of genetic variation in the middle of the distribution underlying a range of viable strategies. Indeed, extremes on personality distributions are associated with psychopathology. Extreme sensation seeking, for example, would tend to result in dangerous risk taking and impulsivity, while individuals who are extremely low on these appetitive traits would lack motivation to pursue goals related to the accumulation of sexual and personal resources. Extremes in either direction would appear to be maladaptive. On the other hand, the wide diversity of intermediate individuals resulting both from genetic variation and developmental plasticity would be able to occupy different social roles and have differing balances between caution and impulsivity.

Gottlieb has made much of findings of average effects on IQ in adoption studies (e.g., Capron & Duyme, 1989; Scarr & Weinberg, 1983). Both Gottlieb (1995) and Bjorklund and Pellegrini (2002) ignored the results of follow-up studies that indicate a much-attenuated average effect as adopted children approach adulthood (Weinberg, Scarr, & Waldman, 1992; see also Bouchard, 1993). Positive effects of adoption are likely when children are adopted out of abusive environments (e.g., Dennis, 1973); but such results imply that in general and averaged over all genotypes sampled in the population, the difference in environments has a consistent, unidirectional effect on the adopted children. This additive environmental effect is a common finding in animal studies and makes excellent evolutionary sense: For example, it is well-known in ecology that environments vary from marginal to excellent. These gradients in quality (relative lack of nutrients, poor climate, high risk of predation) imply that there would be average effects on a wide range of characteristics depending on environmental quality. In IQ research, the Flynn effect of increasing IQ scores over historical time has been attributed to better nutrition (Lynn, 1996). Better nutrition and other improvements in the modern world have resulted in large increases in height and earlier ages of menarche. The general positive effect of enriched versus deprived environments is central to the reaction range concept defended by Turkheimer et al. (1995) and, despite his misgivings, is apparent in Gottlieb's (1995, p. 135) own presentation. This implies that the effects of the environment are far from capricious or unpredictable, as implied in Gottlieb's description of his model. If they were, parents could not reasonably suppose that feeding a child a diet with an adequate amount of protein would be better than no protein at all. These findings also show that genotype-environment interactions are not the main story in development.

We conclude that there is no theoretical problem with the standard behavioral genetic practice of partitioning additive and nonadditive genetic variance and shared and unshared environmental variance. Additive genetic and environmental effects make excellent evolutionary sense for systems such as intelligence that are beneficial for organisms in the entire gamut of environments normally encountered by the species. However, the peculiar nature of personality systems as responsive to a variety of often incompatible environmental demands and the complex interaction among personality systems at the physiological level means that nonadditive genetic variance (but not GXE interaction) plays an important role.

A major difference between evolutionary approaches and behavior genetics is that the former attempts to "carve nature at its joints": That is, it attempts to discover the actual systems that have been under natural selection and serve adaptive functions. Behavior geneticists, on the other hand, have not limited themselves to finding the contributions of genetic and environmental sources of variation in naturally evolved systems, but have applied their methods to any trait that shows variation. For example, behavior genetics research shows that the propensity for divorce is heritable (McGue & Lykken, 1992; Turkheimer, Lovett, Robinette, & Gottesman, 1992). Evolutionary psychology can undoubtedly shed some light on divorce. For example, infidelity is the leading cause of divorce (Betzig, 1989), a result expected because spousal infidelity imposes costs on both partners. However, the genetic variation for divorce is not only likely to be "radically polygenic" (Turkheimer et al., 1995, p. 152), it is likely to be radically poly-systemic, spread among a wide range of evolved systems: People with a wide range of differences in personality that make them difficult to live with (e.g., high on neuroticism/emotional reactivity), prone to philandering (high on behavioral approach), have low sex drives (low on behavioral approach), unrewarding as mates (low on nurturance/love), and poor providers (low on conscientiousness and intelligence) would all be more likely to get divorced. People also get divorced because their mates gain weight, lose hair, or are infertile. As a result, the genetic variation for divorce is spread among a wide range of evolved systems, so that behavior genetics analysis of this trait is of little interest to an evolutionist. To make matters worse, the likelihood of divorce also depends on the legal climate: Divorce was essentially unheard of until about 50 years ago in Western cultures, and provisions for finding fault and dividing assets also affect divorce rates. However, heritability studies of divorce have a certain practical interest; for example, it is relevant to clinical practice to know the heritability of traits in normally occurring environments (Scarr, 1995), although, of course, even a high heritability would not prevent an inventive clinician from designing interventions that could change the probability of divorce or the sequelae of divorce, even if such environments were never encountered in the EEA.

The behavior genetics analysis of evolved systems is of considerable interest. The most important of the evolved systems are those related to general intelligence and the major personality systems (Chiappe & MacDonald, 2005; see MacDonald, Ch. 8, this volume). Although evolutionary psychologists have suggested that genetic variation in evolved systems is mere noise (Tooby & Cosmides, 1990), there is good reason to suppose that genetic variation in evolved systems is adaptive—that genetic variation promotes occupying different niches and that people possess adaptations that allow them to assess phenotypic variation of themselves and others in order to advance their interests (MacDonald, 1998). The general theory for understanding the methods by which individuals interact with the phenotypic and genotypic resource environment represented by human diversity may be termed *intraspecific diversity theory,* that is, the theory of the assessment and manipulation of within-species diversity as a resource environment. The reality is that people are acutely interested in the phenotypic variation in themselves and others. Different qualities are important in different relationships—for example, honesty, intelligence, and conscientiousness in many job situations, and affection in close romantic relationships. If genetic variation were mere noise, we would not be so deeply interested in this variation.

Within an evolutionary systems perspective, environmental influences are conceptualized as involving specific types of stimulation directed at particular evolved systems. Thus, environmental influences affecting the Conscientiousness system would be expected to be events related to possible threats to personal safety or long-term goals, while environmental influences related to Nurturance/Love would be expected to involve warmth and affection that typically occur in close family relationships.

Developmental Plasticity

The first author's 1988 introductory chapter accepted the traditional notion of developmental plasticity rooted in the reaction range idea (Gottesman & Shields, 1982) as compatible with an evolutionary perspective (see also Bjorklund & Pellegrini, 2002). Evolutionary psychologists have problematized the traditional notion of developmental plasticity. Tooby and Cosmides

(1992) claimed that "plasticity" can be retained only if it guides behavior into "an infinitesimally small adaptive space" (p. 101). Such plasticity is really only apparent, the result of large numbers of conditional "if-then" mechanisms responsive to recurrent contingencies in our evolutionary past.

An example that fits this analysis is the life history model of Belsky, Steinberg, and Draper (1991), in which resource scarcity results in a pattern of exploitative interpersonal relationships and precocious sexuality, whereas resource security results in trusting personal relationships and delayed sexual maturation. Another type of developmental plasticity that can be accommodated by this sort of model is the "fine-tuning" of the nervous system by synaptic pruning in the presence of a highly reliable source of environmental information that can guide the elimination process (see above). Fine-tuning is also central to Geary and Huffman's (2002) proposal on soft modules as underlying play and exploration. Fairbanks (2000) reviewed evidence indicating that play functions to prune synapses in the cerebellum and elsewhere in the brain.

Despite surface appearances, there isn't any logical difference between the traditional idea of developmental plasticity based on a reaction range notion and the proposal of Tooby and Cosmides (1992). If one construes a normal reaction range for a trait as the EEE, then any point in the range can be considered as responsive to recurrent environmental cues. From this perspective, the reaction range from deprived to enriched environments for a particular trait represents a continuum of if-then relationships defining the plasticity for the trait. Of course, this way of thinking about plasticity renders Tooby and Cosmides's claim for an infinitesimally small adaptive space true by definition. It also seems odd to think of reaction ranges as composed of large numbers of adaptations, each aimed at some particular infinitesimally small range, as opposed to, say, one adaptation that responds predictably to a range of environments—a fairly wide range in the case of the effects of nutritional variation on stature. Such a notion of plasticity is compatible with the quantitative models of behavior genetics.

The theory of plasticity proposed by Tooby and Cosmides does not address examples where plasticity is blind, that is, examples where environmental events that are not part of an organism's EEA are able to influence the phenotype. But there are myriad examples showing that people and other organisms are able to respond adaptively to environmental novelty and uncertainty. As discussed above, learning and general intelligence function exactly this way, and learning has effects on the brain. For example, Greenough and Black (1992) provided evidence for effects on the brain of unpredictable environmental influences, as when learning results in changes in synaptic organization. Similarly, human-reared chimpanzees show superior symbol-learning ability and social learning compared with nonhuman-reared chimpanzees (Tomasello, 1999). Since being reared by humans is not part of the chimpanzee's EEA, this example suggests that plasticity carries with it the possibility that natural capabilities may be enhanced in environments that were not characteristic of the animal's EEA.

Tooby and Cosmides's theory implies that events outside those recurrent in the EEA would tend to produce pathology, and there certainly are examples of such events. Extreme abuse and lack of stimulation or social contact come to mind. However, in addition to mechanisms of learning and general intelligence, there are a variety of other mechanisms for dealing with uncertainty. Although recurrent and expected environments are of fundamental importance to an evolutionary account, organisms have evolved mechanisms of plasticity that allow accommodation to at least some genetic mutations and to at least some extreme environments that were not recurrent in the EEA (West-Eberhard, 1989, 2003). The changes following a mutation that shortened the front legs of a goat are a classic example. This mutation resulted in a large number of compensatory changes in the animal's skeletal and muscular systems resulting from the fact that the animal now walked on its rear legs. This ability to compensate for unexpected developmental disruptions is a powerful example of plasticity.

The importance of domain-general psychological mechanisms for human adaptation implies a high level of human plasticity, indeed. For example, as a result of their high level of cognitive abilities—prototypically human general intelligence—humans are able to create cultural mechanisms ranging from social controls and ideologies that regulate sexual behavior to medical technology able to cure genetic diseases (Laland, Odling-Smee, & Feldman, 2000; Li, 2003; MacDonald, 1988b, 1995a). The claim that human adaptations respond to an infinitesimally small adaptive space implies that humans would not be able to change their sexual behavior even after contraception and the availability of safe abortion dramatically lowered the cost of sex, especially for women. However, there is a great deal of evidence that sexual behavior has changed dramatically since the advent of safe and reliable contraception and abortion (e.g., Furstenberg, 1991).

Plasticity is also implicated in traits produced by environmental induction as a result of extreme or unusual environmental influences, as in genetic assimilation and similar phenomena (West-Eberhard, 2003, pp. 151-154). For example, in the *Baldwin effect,* there is a phenotypic response to variable or extreme environments made possible by plasticity. Genetic mechanisms then accommodate to the new phenotypic change via natural selection on "variation in the regulation, form or side effects of the novel trait" (West-Eberhard, 2003, p. 140). In other words, genetic changes accommodate to the new phenotype, for example, by making it work more smoothly; but the original alteration of the phenotype occurs as the result of plasticity. As a result, the new trait becomes heritable. A possible example is dwarfism in elephants, caused originally by inadequate nutrition on islands affecting the phenotype via developmental plasticity. The inadequate nutrition causes stunting, followed by selection on previously existing genetic variation. The trait then becomes genetically consolidated, with the result that better nutritional conditions do not result in the return of the large phenotype.

Indeed, according to West-Eberhard (2003), developmental plasticity is central to the entire evolutionary process. Evolution begins with a recurrent developmental change brought about either by a mutation or (more commonly) by developmental plasticity interacting with environmental events. Selection then consolidates the trait by modifying genes influencing the regulation of the trait. An example of this would be when learning particular contingencies is shaped by natural selection: If there is genetic variation for the ability to learn a particular contingency, natural selection may act to strengthen the ability to learn this contingency. Examples where natural selection has shaped learning are central to evolutionary accounts of learning, as in taste aversion learning among rats (see above), but the central role of plasticity in initiating the changes wrought by natural selection is typically left out of the accounts produced by evolutionary psychologists.

Human Growth as an Example of Plasticity

Variation in nutrition is attractive for studying plasticity because nutritional variation is a recurrent environmental feature and thus likely to result in adaptations designed to cope with it. The effects of malnourishment are also well studied and easily controlled for genetic factors, quite unlike the situation with many other psychological systems. In general, it is reasonable to suppose that environmental influences are system-specific, for example, that the fear system is influenced by traumatic events and the affectional system by warmth and affection (Segal & MacDonald, 1998).

Researchers in the area of the plasticity of human growth have found irreversible changes in stature and other anthropomorphic measures in response to variation in caloric intake and other components of nutrition during development (Bogin, 2001; Mascie-Taylor & Bogin, 1995; Roberts, 1995; Schell, 1995; Stoch, Smythe, Moodie, & Bradshaw, 1981). For example, malnourishment before birth has a series of long-term medical consequences, such as increased likelihood of type 2 diabetes, even when the children achieve normal weight and height as a result of high caloric intake during childhood (Forsén et al., 2000).

However, the brain retains "preferential access to nutrients even in conditions of semi-starvation" (Stevens, 1998, p. 257), an indication of the importance of the brain for later functioning. Research on environmental insults to the brain during development supports the generalization that periods of rapid change are most open to environmental influence (Morgan & Gibson, 1991), the classic sensitive-period notion deriving from ethology. A great many influences that are deleterious to the developing brain have little or no effect on the adult brain, and in general, the effects of early experience become increasingly irreversible with age (Shonkoff & Phillips, 2000). Animal studies indicate that severely malnourished brains never recover fully, even when subjected to intensive nutritional rehabilitation in the post-weaning period. Catch-up growth does occur in children, but best results are achieved if rehabilitation is begun during the period when cell division is still occurring and continuing through the period of myelination and dendritic arborization (Morgan & Gibson, 1991). Indeed, Morgan and Gibson described the second trimester as a "'critical period' for the formation of cortical neurons" (p. 98). For the critically important variable of intelligence, nutritional rehabilitation of severely malnourished children treated before 2 years of age resulted in the children attaining American norms for intelligence, but children rehabilitated after this age remained below the norms (Lien, Meyer, & Winick, 1977; Winick, Meyer, & Harris, 1975).

As indicated above, the model of West-Eberhard for the evolution of dwarfism in elephants suggests that cultures subjected to a diet deficient in protein and calories over many generations would develop a hereditary tendency toward small stature, low energy output, and low intelligence. Bogin (2001) has interpreted his work comparing Mayans in the United States and in Guatemala as indicating that the relatively enriched environment of the United States resulted in the Mayan children approaching U.S. norms in one generation, results suggesting that natural selection had not effected a genetic tendency toward the low-energy phenotype. However, although there were large gains in both height and weight during childhood compared with Guatemalan norms, at age 15, the children were much closer to U.S. norms for weight than for height. At age 15, height remained intermediate between U.S. norms and Guatemalan norms, suggesting that developmental plasticity is more important for weight than height and, at the least, that more than one generation would be required to attain U.S. norms in height.

West-Eberhard (2003) has argued for the transmission of environmental influences between generations. For example, in migratory locusts, effects of maternal crowding on adult phenotypes accumulate over four generations before leading to a migratory phenotype. Such cumulative, between-generation effects may be important for humans in the area of nutrition. For example, Asian immigrants to Scotland increased in height every generation since their arrival (Shams & Williams, 1997). In general, degree of plasticity "correlates with degree of environmental variation in the parameter to which plasticity responds" (West-Eberhard, 2003, p. 179), and there is little doubt that variation in nutritional regime has been common for humans over evolutionary time. The suggestion is that humans are adapted to respond quickly to improvements in nutrition but that several generations may be required to maximize traits such as height within a particular nutritional regime. Of course, this generalization is compatible with average racial/ethnic differences in the maximum attainable within any given nutritional regime.

Bogin's (2001) finding that the height of Mayan children in the United States increasingly resembles the height of Guatemalan Mayans with age may well reflect the general tendency for heritability for a wide range of traits to increase with age. For example, the heritability of the critical trait of general intelligence ranges from 0.2 in infancy to 0.4 in childhood to 0.6 in adulthood (McClearn et al., 1997; McGue, Bouchard, Iacono, & Lykken, 1993). This implies that environmental influences on individual differences in intelligence become less important as people age. It is a remarkable fact that unrelated children living in the same household become less and less like each other as they approach adulthood, and by the time they reach adulthood, their correlation for IQ is zero (Rowe, 1994; Scarr & Weinberg, 1983).

Human Life History Characteristics: The Most Important Single Fact About Human Development Is the Development of the Adult Brain

A major point of the preceding is the central importance of domain-general psychological mechanisms of general intelligence for thinking about human adaptation. Developmental increases in speed of processing and of mechanisms underlying increases in general intelligence are the central story, perhaps *the* central story of children's cognitive development. Moreover, there is excellent evidence that general intelligence is an adaptation underlying the ability of humans to create novel solutions to ancient problems of survival and reproduction. There is little doubt that general intelligence underlies the human ability to create the extraordinary culture characteristic of the last 50,000 years of human evolution.

This suggests that the development of the human brain is also the central fact of human life history theory, the theory of how organisms allocate energy toward growth, maintenance, reproduction, and rearing offspring (Allman, 1999). According to Charnov's (2001) theory, what needs explaining in life history is the length of the prereproductive period. Among mammals, there is a relatively constant relationship between life span and age of first reproduction. While animals benefit from a longer prereproductive period by increasing in size and obtaining other resources that will benefit future reproductive ability (e.g., a more efficient brain), a lengthy prereproductive period is enormously costly because it increases the cost of parenting and increases the changes of mortality prior to reproduction.

One theory that has attempted to explain the prolonged human prereproductive period is that children benefit by being able to learn information and hone abilities that are critical for successful adult functioning (e.g. Bjorklund & Pellegrini, 2002; Flinn, Ch. 3, this volume; Geary, Ch. 4, this volume; Kaplan, Hill, Lancaster, & Hurtado, 2000; MacDonald, 1997a). Learning accounts are called into question by several considerations (see Bogin, 2001, p. 103; Deaner, Barton, & van Schaik, 2003). If learning was so important to human development as to result in the enormous costs of a prolonged preadulthood, it is surprising that children's cognitive and learning abilities are so limited and inefficient compared with adults', at least until late adolescence. Indeed, Kail (1991) found that the average performance of 8- to 10-year-old children for response times on a wide range of intellectual tasks is typically 5 to 6 standard deviation units below the mean for young adults; even 12- and 13-year-olds perform more than a full standard deviation below the young adult mean. Moreover, Blurton Jones and Marlowe (2002) found no evidence that children require prolonged periods to learn the skills of hunting and gathering. Bogin (2001, p. 103) also noted that the learning hypothesis can't account for the alternating fast and slow growth pattern characteristic of humans, and it can't explain the length of the prereproductive period in humans.

The relatively trivial benefits accruing from "the adaptive uses of immaturity" (Bjorklund & Pellegrini, 2002, p. 203) also seem insufficient to account for such an enormously costly childhood. Indeed, the principal example of adaptive immaturity, children's tendency to overestimate their cognitive ability, would be obviated if children's cognitive ability were more sophisticated to begin with. Finally, the finding of increased genetic influence with age on a wide variety of measures of individual differences (see above) suggests that many early environmental influences wash out prior to adulthood.

An alternative set of hypotheses—all mutually compatible—center on the idea that the prolonged prereproductive period of human development is needed to produce the extraordinarily powerful human brain because of physiological constraints on brain development (see Deaner et al., 2003). Childhood is so lengthy because Mother Nature simply cannot construct the human brain in a shorter period. Such an extended childhood is extremely costly, but it can evolve because it has huge delayed benefits. In particular, the advanced cognitive abilities of the adult brain reduce adult mortality due to predation or food shortages and eventually, with *Homo erectus,* produce cultural shifts that have resulted in the complete ecological dominance of humans throughout the world. Such a brain would also be useful in navigating the social world of competing humans (see Flinn, Ch. 3; Geary, Ch. 4; Oller & Griebel, Ch. 5, this volume).

Any hypothesis for explaining the prolonged developmental period of children must take account of the fact that brain development is the driving force of human development and by far the most important contributor to human life history characteristics. Newborns use 87% of their resting metabolic rate for brain growth and functioning, a figure that declines to 44% by age 5 and 25% in adulthood (Bogin, 2000). These percentages are more than twice the levels for chimpanzees. Because of their relatively large brains, humans must have access to a diet that is rich in energy (Leonard & Robertson, 1994). As noted above, the brain is relatively buffered from nutritional deprivation compared with other systems (Stevens, 1998). According to Gibson (1991; see also Deaner et al., 2003), the dependence of this enormously costly organ on adequate resources favors extended developmental periods, because only by extending development can adequate nutrition be obtained. A rapidly developing large brain would be more susceptible to temporary nutritional deficits, while the slowly developing myelination of the human brain affords a prolonged period during which nutritional rehabilitation is possible (Morgan & Gibson, 1991). This fits well with evidence indicating that the normal response of humans to lowered levels of nutrition or other stressors is to delay development, while better nutrition results in earlier puberty (MacDonald, 1997b, 1999).

Another possible physiological limit has been described by McKinney (2000), attributing the unique features of human brain development to a *predisplacement* process in which a larger proportion of embryonic neuron stem cells produces a larger, slow-growing brain. This process involves terminal extension or overdevelopment—additions to the primate brain, rather than neotenous processes in which adult forms retain juvenile characteristics (e.g., Langer, 2000; McKinney, 2000). Because of inherent limits on mitotic cell division processes for nerve cells, terminal extension results in a very long developmental period required for full brain development. Postnatal brain development is quite slow, but body growth is also slow until the adolescent growth spurt, resulting in an energetically efficient body sustaining a slow-growing brain. Dendritic growth and myelination (critical to efficient nerve transmission) continue well into the adolescent period.

In general, compared with other primates, peak rates of neurogenesis, dendritogenesis (and pruning), synaptogenesis, and myelination occur later in modern humans, and each process is itself extended (Gibson, 1991). Significantly, myelination is completed last in the neocortex and prefrontal cortex, the seat of working memory and general intelligence. The human prefrontal cortex is more than twice the size of an anthropoid ape corrected for body size—an indication of the importance of the domain-general processes underlying intelligence in human evolution (see above; see also Geary, Ch. 4, this volume). Among primates, size of the neocortex is significantly associated with life span, data consistent with the hypothesis that decreased adult mortality mediated by human intelligence is a driving force of human evolution (Deaner et al., 2003).

Hawkes, O'Connell, and Blurton Jones (2002) have argued against the brain development hypothesis by pointing to the separation by 1 million years between the evolution of human life history characteristics (attributed to *Homo erectus*) and the major increases in brain size (attributed to *Homo sapiens*). While it is true that *H. sapiens* represents a major increase in brain size compared with *H. erectus,* the brain size of *H. erectus* was also a major advance from previous hominids. *H. erectus* brains range from 850 to 900 cm^3. A brain size of this magnitude is above Martin's (1983) threshold for requiring a shift to a humanlike pattern of brain and body growth: a great deal of postnatal brain development combined with slow growth of the body (Bogin, 2001). This results from limits on the size of the pelvic birth canal.

Corresponding to the increased brain size, *H. erectus* also represented a major advance in the use of technology (tools, fire, shelter) and social organization (Klein, 1989), presumably a reflection of major increases in general intelligence. We have seen that general intelligence is linked with adapting to new habitats. *H. erectus* was the first hominid species to disperse out of Africa into the temperate climates of Eurasia; within Africa, it colonized dry areas that had been unoccupied (Klein, 1989). There is thus little reason to reject the brain development hypothesis for explaining human life history characteristics based on what we know of *H. erectus*.

Hawkes et al.'s (2002) alternative hypothesis is that the basic trade-off is between the benefits of increased adult size (produced by a longer developmental period) and the risks of not reproducing as adulthood is delayed. As adult mortality declines, animals benefit from having a prolonged juvenile phase because it allows the animal to attain a greater body size. The difficulty with this hypothesis is the adolescent growth spurt. For the four primate species with sufficient data (humans, macaques, mangabeys, and chimpanzees), a growth spurt follows the termination of brain growth (Deaner et al., 2003). This is consistent with the hypothesis of inherent limits in brain growth, because the end of brain growth should permit body growth to be optimized, while requiring less energy during the period when the brain is immature. However, if increased physical size were the focus of natural selection for humans, there would be no adolescent growth spurt. Instead, there would be a consistent pattern of growth until the optimum size was achieved, and it would be much earlier than in fact occurs in children. This is because, all things being equal, our ancestors would have benefited from attaining adult size as soon as possible. The fact that somatic growth is very slow during the period when children are still undergoing enormous increases in cognitive functioning, followed by a period of rapid growth to attain adult physical size, is much more compatible with brain development being the fundamental driving force of human development. Indeed, gorillas, with a much larger body size than humans, have a much shorter developmental period between weaning and maturity (see Hawkes et al., 2003, p. 217), indicating that attaining a large size in a much shorter period poses no insurmountable evolutionary problems. Reinforcing this argument is the fact that at all stages of the human life cycle after birth, humans have brains that are much larger than expected on the basis of body size (Bogin, 2000, p. 108). This conclusion fits well with Ward, Flinn, and Begun (2004), who have shown that changes in body size alone cannot explain changes in brain size, although they may well have worked synergistically to increase human ecological dominance; there must have been selection for intelligence itself.

The big picture, then, is that cognitive development is the critical force in human evolution. The vast gap in cognitive development between humans and other species can be seen from the fact that nonhuman primates do not progress to the level of a 3-year-old child (Langer, 2000); all human brain development beyond this point is via the process of terminal extension (e.g., Langer, 2000; McKinney, 2000). With the achievement of concrete operations in middle childhood and the onset of abstract reasoning ability around the time of puberty, children achieve the basics of adult level cognition as well as sexual competence (but not reproductive competence). Prior to adolescence, children are relatively inexpensive because of their small body size, because they contribute some economic benefit to the family (e.g., girls' babysitting), and because alloparents are available from other family members and relatives (Bogin, 1997; Hrdy, Ch. 6, this volume). Children then undergo a growth spurt, thereby achieving the more energetically costly adult body size required for adult activities, such as fighting in men, childbirth (via increased pelvic size) in women, and obtaining material resources. Because of their adult level cognitive abilities, adolescents are able to rapidly absorb the culture around them and prepare to fit into the world of adults. Cognitive development continues after adolescence, however, ending at around age 30, after which there are declines in fluid intelligence (Gibson, 1991; Langer, 2000).

Within this overall picture, there is an important role for plasticity: The most important general influence on long-term development is that lowered resource availability during development has the effect of prolonging development and decreasing adult stature and brain development (Gibson, 1991), although, as we have noted, brain development is relatively well buffered from such environmental influences. Indeed, captive chimpanzees attain menarche at earlier ages than wild chimpanzees, presumably as a result of better nutrition (Goodall, 1986). Modernization has resulted in better nutrition and health care, with the result that the average age of menarche has been declining for at least 150 years in Western societies. Life history theory converges on the proposition that for humans, cues to environmental adversity (poor nutrition, downward social mobility) would result in a delay of physical maturation and postponement of marriage and childbearing (MacDonald, 1997b, 1999).

Conclusion

The main "take-home" message is that attention to evolutionary theory results in an integration and enrichment of other theoretical perspectives in developmental psychology without eradicating them. Rather than an exclusive emphasis on domain-specific modules, there is a robust role for domain-general processes of intelligence and learning. There is a great deal of evidence for additive and nonadditive genetic variation in evolved systems and for correlations between genes and environments, but little evidence for interactions between evolved systems and environmental variation. There is also an important role for human plasticity in many developing systems. And perhaps most important, child development is seen as mainly the story of the development of the extraordinary human brain and our uniquely human domain-general cognitive abilities, which have resulted in the phenomenal cultural developments of the last several thousand years.

References

Allman, J. M. (1999). *Evolving brains.* New York: Scientific American Library.

Anderson, B. (2000). The *g* factor in non-human animals. In G. R. Bock, J. A. Goode, & K. Webb (Eds.), *The nature of intelligence* (pp. 79-95). New York: John Wiley.

Bandura, A. (1969). Social learning theory of identificatory processes. In D. A. Goslin (Ed.), *Handbook of socialization theory and research*. New York: Rand McNally.

Bandura, A. (1977). *Social learning theory*. Englewood Cliffs, NJ: Prentice Hall.

Belsky, J., Steinberg, L., & Draper, P. (1991). Childhood experience, interpersonal development, and reproductive strategy: An evolutionary theory of socialization. *Child Development, 62*, 647-670.

Betzig, L. L. (1989). Causes of conjugal dissolution: A cross-cultural study. *Current Anthropology, 30*, 654-676.

Bjorklund, D., & Pellegrini, A. (2002). *The origins of human nature*. Washington, DC: American Psychological Association.

Blurton Jones, N., & Marlowe, F. W. (2002). Selection for delayed maturity: Does it take 20 years to learn to hunt and gather? *Human Nature, 13*, 199-238.

Bogin, B. (1997). Evolutionary hypotheses for human childhood. *Yearbook of Physical Anthropology, 40*, 63-89.

Bogin, B. (2000). Basic principles of human growth and development. In S. Stinson, B. Bogin, R. Huss-Ashmore, & D. O'Rourke (Eds.), *Human biology: An evolutionary and biocultural perspective* (pp. 377-424). New York: Wiley-Liss.

Bogin, B. (2001). *The growth of humanity*. New York: Wiley-Liss.

Bouchard, T. J. (1993). The genetic architecture of human intelligence. In P. A. Vernon (Ed.), *Biological approaches to the study of human intelligence* (pp. 33-93). Norwood, NJ: Ablex.

Bowlby, J. (1969). *Attachment and loss: Vol. I. Attachment*. New York: Basic Books.

Boyd, R., & Richerson, P. (1985). *Culture and the evolutionary process*. Chicago: University of Chicago Press.

Boyd, R., & Richerson, P. (1988). An evolutionary model of social learning: The effects of spatial and temporal variation. In T. Zentall & B. Galef (Eds.), *Social learning: Psychological and biological perspectives* (pp. 29-48). Hillsdale, NJ: Erlbaum.

Brazelton, T. B., Robey, J. S., & Collier, G. A. (1969). Infant development in the Zinacanteco Indians of Southern Mexico. *Pediatrics, 44*, 274-290.

Buss, D. M. (1999). *Evolutionary psychology*. Boston: Allyn & Bacon.

Campbell, D., Sanderson, R., & Laverty, S. G. (1964). Characteristics of a conditioned response in human subjects during extinction trials following a simple traumatic conditioning trial. *Journal of Abnormal and Social Psychology, 68*, 627-639.

Capron, C., & Duyme, M. (1989). Assessment of effects of socio-economic status on IQ in a full cross-fostering study. *Nature, 340*, 552-554.

Carpenter, P., Just, M., & Shell, P. (1990). What one intelligence test measures: A theoretical account of the processing in the Raven Progressive Matrices Test. *Psychological Review, 97*, 404-431.

Carroll, J. B. (1993). *Human cognitive abilities*. New York: Cambridge University Press.

Case, R. (1998). The development of conceptual structure. In W. Damon (Series Ed.) & D. Kuhn & R. S. Siegler (Vol. Eds.), *Handbook of child psychology: Vol. 2. Cognition, perception, and language* (5th ed., pp. 745-800). New York: John Wiley.

Case, R., Demetriou, A., Platsidou, M., & Kazi, S. (2001). Integrating concepts and tests of intelligence from the differential and developmental traditions. *Intelligence, 29,* 307-336.

Cattell, R. B. (1963). Theory of fluid and crystallized intelligence: A critical experiment. *Journal of Educational Psychology, 54,* 1-22.

Cattell, R. B. (1982). *The inheritance of personality and ability: Research methods and findings.* New York: Academic Press.

Charnov, E. L. (2001). Evolution of mammal life histories. *Evolutionary Ecology Research, 3,* 521-535.

Chiappe, D., & MacDonald, K. (2005). The evolution of domain-general mechanisms in intelligence and learning. *Journal of General Psychology,* in press.

Cosmides, L., & Tooby, J. (2002). Unraveling the enigma of human intelligence: Evolutionary psychology and the multimodular mind. In R. J. Sternberg & J. C. Kaufman (Eds.), *The evolution of intelligence* (pp. 145-198). Mahwah, NJ: Erlbaum.

Cronbach, L. J., & Snow, R. E. (1977). *Aptitudes and instructional methods: A handbook for research on interactions.* New York: Irvington.

Deaner, R. O., Barton, R. A., & van Schaik, P. (2003). Primate brains and life histories: Renewing the connection. In P. M. Kappeler & M. E. Pereira (Eds.), *Primate life histories and socioecology* (pp. 233-265). Chicago: University of Chicago Press.

DeFries, J. C., Plomin, R., & Fulker, D. W. (Eds.). (1994). *Nature and nurture during middle childhood.* Cambridge, MA: Blackwell.

Deloache, J. S., Miller, K. F., & Pierroutsakos, S. L. (1998). Reasoning and problem solving. In W. Damon (Series Ed.) & D. Kuhn & R. S. Siegler (Vol. Eds.), *Handbook of child psychology: Vol. 2. Cognition, perception, and language* (5th ed., pp. 801-850). New York: John Wiley.

Demetriou, A., Christou, C., Spanoudis, G., & Platsidou, M. (2002). The development of mental processing: Efficiency, working memory and thinking. *Monographs of the Society for Research in Child Development, 67*(1, Serial No. 268), 1-154.

Demetriou, A., Elklides, A., & Platsidou, M. (1993). The architecture and dynamics of the developing mind. *Monographs of the Society for Research in Child Development, 58*(5/6, Serial No. 234).

Dennett, D. (1987). Cognitive wheels: The frame problem of AI. In Z. Pylyshyn (Ed.), *The robot's dilemma* (pp. 41-64). Norwood, NJ: Ablex.

Dennis, W. (1973). *Children of the crèche.* New York: Appleton.

Duncan, J., Burgess, P., & Emslie, H. (1995). Fluid intelligence after frontal lobe lesions. *Neuropsychologia, 33,* 261-268.

Duncan, J., Emslie, H., Williams, P., Johnson, R., & Freer, C. (1996). Intelligence and the frontal lobe: The organization of goal-directed behavior. *Cognitive Psychology, 30,* 257-303.

Eaves, L. J., Last, K. A., Martin, N. G., & Jinks, J. L. (1977). A progressive approach to non-additivity and genotype-environment covariance in the analysis of human differences. *British Journal of Mathematical and Statistical Psychology, 30,* 1-32.

Emmons, R. A. (1989). The personal striving approach to personality. In L. A. Pervin (Ed.), *Goal concepts in personality and social psychology* (pp. 87-126). Hillsdale, NJ: Erlbaum.

Fairbanks, L. A. (2000). Developmental timing of primate play. In S. T. Parker, J. Langer, & M. L. McKinney (Eds.), *Biology, brains, and behavior: The evolution of human development.* Santa Fe, NM: School of American Research Press.

Falconer, D. S. (1981). *Introduction to quantitative genetics* (2nd ed.). London: Longman.

Flavell, J. H. (1985). *Cognitive development.* Englewood Cliffs, NJ: Prentice Hall.

Fodor, J. A. (1983). *The modularity of mind.* Cambridge: MIT Press.

Fodor, J. A. (2000). *The mind doesn't work that way.* Cambridge: MIT Press.

Forsén, T., Eriksson, J., Tuomilehto, J., Reunanen, A., Osmond, C., & Barker, D. (2000). The fetal and childhood growth of persons who develop type 2 diabetes. *Annals of Internal Medicine, 133,* 176-182.

Fox, N. A. (1994). Dynamic cerebral processes underlying emotion regulation. In N. Fox (Ed.), The development of emotion regulation: Biological and behavioral considerations. *Monographs for the Society for Research in Child Development, 59(2/3,* Serial No. 240), 152-166.

Freedman, D. J., & Freedman, N. C. (1969). Behavioral differences between Chinese-American and European-American newborns. *Nature, 224,* 1227.

Furstenberg, F. (1991). As the pendulum swings: Teenage childbearing and social concern. *Family Relations, 40,* 127-138.

Galef, B. G. Jr. (1987). Social influences on the identification of toxic foods by Norway rats. *Animal Learning and Behavior, 15,* 327-332.

Gallistel, C. R. (1990). *The organization of learning.* Cambridge: MIT Press.

Gallistel, C. R. (1999). The replacement of general purpose learning models with adaptively specialized learning modules. In M. S. Gazzanigz (Ed.), *The new cognitive neurosciences* (2nd ed.). Cambridge: MIT Press.

Garcia, J., & Koelling, R. (1966). Relation of cue to consequence in avoidance learning. *Psychonomic Science, 4,* 123-124.

Geary, D. C., & Huffman, K. J. (2002). Brain and cognitive evolution: Forms of modularity and functions of mind. *Psychological Bulletin, 128,* 667-698.

Gelman, R., & Baillargeon, R. (1983). A review of some Piagetian concepts. In J. H. Flavell & E. Markman (Eds.), *Handbook of child psychology: Vol. 3. Cognitive development.* New York: John Wiley.

Gelman, R., & Williams, E. M. (1998). Enabling constraints for cognitive development and learning: Domain-specificity and epigenesis. In W. Damon (Series

Ed.) & D. Kuhn & R. S. Siegler (Vol. Eds.), *Handbook of child psychology: Vol. 2. Cognition, perception, and language* (5th ed., pp. 575-630). New York: John Wiley.

Gibson, K. R. (1991). Myelination and behavioral development. In K. R. Gibson & A. C. Petersen (Eds.), *Brain maturation and cognitive development: Comparative and cross-cultural perspectives* (pp. 29-63). New York: Aldine de Gruyter.

Goodall, J. (1986). *The chimpanzees of Gombe: Patterns of behavior.* Cambridge, MA: Harvard University Press.

Gottesman, I. I., & Shields, J. (1982). *Schizophrenia: The epigenetic puzzle.* New York: Cambridge University Press.

Gottfredson, L. S. (1998). The general intelligence factor. *Scientific American Presents, 9*(4), 24-29.

Gottlieb, G. (1991). *Individual development and evolution: The genetics of novel behavior.* Oxford, UK: Oxford University Press.

Gottlieb, G. (1992). *Individual development and evolution.* New York: Oxford University Press.

Gottlieb, G. (1995). Some conceptual deficiencies in "developmental" behavior genetics. *Human Development, 38,* 131-141.

Gottlieb, G., Wahlsten, D., & Lickliter, R. (1998). The significance of biology for human development: A developmental psychobiological systems view. In R. Lerner (Ed.), *Handbook of child psychology: Vol. 1. Theoretical models of human development* (pp. 233-273). New York: John Wiley.

Greenough, W. T., & Black, J. E. (1992). Induction of brain structure by experience: Substrates for cognitive development. In M. R. Gunnar & C. A. Nelson (Eds.), *Minnesota Symposia on Child Psychology: Vol. 24. Developmental behavioral neuroscience* (pp. 155-200). Hillsdale, NJ: Erlbaum.

Hawkes, K., O'Connell, J. F., & Blurton Jones, N. (2002). The evolution of human life histories: Primate trade-offs, grandmothering socioecology, and the fossil record. In P. M. Kappeler & M. E. Pereira (Eds.), *Primate life histories and socioecology* (pp. 204-227). Chicago: University of Chicago Press.

Heinrich, B. (2000). Testing insight in ravens. In C. Heyes & L. Huber (Eds.), *The evolution of cognition* (pp. 289-305). Cambridge: MIT Press.

Herrnstein, R. J., & Murray, C. (1994). *The bell curve: Intelligence and class structure in American life.* New York: Free Press.

Hershberger, S. L. (1991, June). *The underestimation of genotype-environment covariance by structural equation modeling methods.* Paper presented at the meeting of the Behavior Genetics Association, St. Louis, MO.

Hershberger, S. L., Lichtenstein, P., & Knox, S. S. (1994). Genetic and environmental influences on perceptions of organizational climate. *Journal of Applied Psychology, 79,* 24-33.

Horn, J. L., & Hofer, S. M. (1992). Major abilities and development in the adult period. In R. J. Sternberg & C. A. Berg (Eds.), *Intellectual development.* New York: Cambridge University Press.

Jinks, J. L., & Fulker, D. W. (1970). Comparison of the biometrical genetical, MAVA, and classical approaches to the analysis of human behavior. *Psychological Bulletin, 73,* 311-349.

Kail, R. (1991). Developmental change in speed of processing during childhood and adolescence. *Psychological Bulletin, 109,* 490-501.

Kail, R. (1996). Nature and consequences of developmental change in speed of processing. *Swiss Journal of Psychology, 55,* 133-138.

Kalat, J. W. (1985). Taste-aversion learning in ecological perspective. In T. Johnston & A. Pietrewicz (Eds.), *Issues in the ecological study of learning* (pp. 119-141). Hillsdale, NJ: Erlbaum.

Kaplan, H., Hill, K., Lancaster, J., & Hurtado, A. M. (2000). A theory of human life history evolution: Diet, intelligence, and longevity. *Evolutionary Anthropology, 9,* 156-185.

Kempthorne, O. (1957). *Introduction to genetic statistics.* Ames, IA: Iowa State Press.

Klein, R. G. (1989). *The human career: Human biological and cultural origins.* Chicago: University of Chicago Press.

Kohn, B., & Dennis, M. (1972). Observation and discrimination learning in the rat: Specific and non-specific effects. *Journal of Comparative and Physiological Psychology, 78,* 292-296.

Laland, K. N., Odling-Smee, J., & Feldman, M. W. (2000). Niche construction, biological evolution and cultural change. *Behavioral and Brain Sciences, 23,* 131-175.

Langer, J. (2000). The heterochronic evolution of primate cognitive development. In S. T. Parker, J. Langer, & M. L. McKinney (Eds.), *Biology, brains, and behavior: The evolution of human development.* Santa Fe, NM: School of American Research Press.

Lautch, H. (1971). Dental phobia. *British Journal of Psychiatry, 119,* 151-158.

Leonard, W. R., & Robertson, M. L. 1994. Evolutionary perspectives on human nutrition: The influence of brain and body size on diet and metabolism. *American Journal of Human Biology, 6,* 77-88.

Lerner, R. (Ed.). (1998). *Handbook of child psychology: Vol. 1. Theoretical models of human development.* New York: John Wiley.

Li, S. (2003). Biocultural orchestration of developmental plasticity across levels: The interplay of biology and culture in shaping the mind and behavior across the life span. *Psychological Bulletin, 129,* 171-194.

Lickliter, R., & Honeycutt, H. (2003). Developmental dynamics: Toward a biologically plausible evolutionary psychology. *Psychological Bulletin, 129,* 819-835.

Lien, N. M., Meyer, K. K., & Winick, M. (1977). Early malnutrition and "late" adoption: A study of their effects on the development of Korean orphans adopted into American families. *American Journal of Clinical Nutrition, 30,* 1734-1739.

Lusk, J., MacDonald, K., & Newman, J. R. (1998). Resource appraisals among self, friend and leader: Implications for an evolutionary perspective on individual differences and a resource/reciprocity perspective on friendship. *Personality and Individual Differences, 24,* 685-700.

Lynn, R. (1996). *Dysgenics: Genetic deterioration in modern populations.* Westport, CT: Praeger.

Maccoby, E., & Martin, J. (1983). Socialization in the context of the family. In P. H. Mussen (Series Ed.) & E. M. Hetherington (Vol. Ed.), *Handbook of child psychology: Vol. 4. Socialization, personality, and social development* (pp. 1-102). New York: John Wiley.

MacDonald, K. B. (1988a). The interfaces between developmental psychology and evolutionary biology. In K. B. MacDonald (Ed.), *Sociobiological perspectives on human development.* New York: Springer-Verlag.

MacDonald, K. B. (1988b). *Social and personality development: An evolutionary synthesis.* New York: Plenum.

MacDonald, K. B. (1991). A perspective on Darwinian psychology: The importance of domain-general mechanisms, plasticity, and individual differences. *Ethology and Sociobiology, 12,* 449-480.

MacDonald, K. B. (1992). Warmth as a developmental construct: An evolutionary analysis. *Child Development, 63,* 753-773.

MacDonald, K. B. (1995a). The establishment and maintenance of socially imposed monogamy in Western Europe. *Politics and the Life Sciences, 14,* 3-23.

MacDonald, K. B. (1995b). Evolution, the five factor model, and levels of personality. *Journal of Personality, 63,* 525-567.

MacDonald, K. B. (1997a). The coherence of individual development: An evolutionary perspective on children's internalization of parental values. In J. Grusec & L. Kuczynski (Eds.), *Parenting and children's internalization of values: A handbook of contemporary theory* (pp. 362-397). New York: John Wiley.

MacDonald, K. B. (1997b). Life history theory and human reproductive behavior: Environmental/contextual influences and heritable variation. *Human Nature, 8,* 327-359.

MacDonald, K. B. (1998). Evolution, culture, and the five-factor model. *Journal of Cross-Cultural Psychology, 29,* 119-149.

MacDonald, K. B. (1999). An evolutionary perspective on human fertility. *Population and Environment, 21*(2), 223-246.

Martin, R. D. (1983). Human brain evolution in an ecological context. *Fifty-second James Arthur Lecture.* New York: American Museum of Natural History.

Mascie-Taylor, C. G. N., & Bogin, B. (1995). *Human variability and plasticity.* Cambridge, UK: Cambridge University Press.

McClearn, G., Johansson, B., Berg, S., Pedersen, N. L., Ahern, F., Petrill, S. A., et al. (1997). Substantial genetic influence on cognitive abilities in twins 80 or more years old. *Science, 276,* 1560-1563.

McGue, M., Bouchard, T. J., Iacono, W. G. Jr., & Lykken, D. T. (1993). Behavioral genetics of cognitive ability: A lifespan perspective. In R. Plomin & G. E. McClearn (Eds.), *Nature, nurture, and psychology* (pp. 59-76). Washington, DC: American Psychological Association.

McGue, M., & Lykken, D. T. (1992). Genetic influence on risk of divorce. *Psychological Science, 3,* 368-373.

McKinney, M. L. (2000). Evolving behavioral complexity by extending development. In S. T. Parker, J. Langer, & M. L. McKinney (Eds.), *Biology, brains, and behavior: The evolution of human development.* Santa Fe, NM: School of American Research Press.

Molenaar, P. C., & Boomsma, D. I. (1987). Application of nonlinear factor analysis to genotype-environment interaction. *Behavior Genetics, 17,* 71-80.

Moos, R. H. (1981). *Work environment scale manual.* Palo Alto, CA: Consulting Psychologists Press.

Moos, R. H., & Moos, B. H. (1981). *Family environment scale manual.* Palo Alto, CA: Consulting Psychologists Press.

Morgan, B., & Gibson, K. R. (1991). Nutrition and environmental interactions in brain development. In K. R. Gibson & A. C. Petersen (Eds.), *Brain maturation and cognitive development: Comparative and cross-cultural perspectives* (pp. 91-106). New York: Aldine de Gruyter.

Öhman, A., & Mineka, S. (2001). Fears, phobias, and preparedness: Toward an evolved module of fear and fear learning. *Psychological Review, 108,* 483-522.

Orlick, T., Zhou, Q., & Partington, J. (1990). Co-operation and conflict within Chinese and Canadian kindergarten settings. *Canadian Journal of Behavioural Sciences, 22,* 20-25.

Pinker, S. (1994). *The language instinct.* New York: William Morrow.

Plomin, R. (2003). Genes, genomics, and *g. Molecular Psychiatry, 8,* 1-5.

Plomin, R., & DeFries, J. C. (1985). *Origins of individual differences in infancy: The Colorado Adoption Project.* Orlando, FL: Academic Press.

Plomin, R., DeFries, J. C., & Fulker, D. W. (1988). *Nature and nurture during infancy and early childhood.* New York: Cambridge University Press.

Plomin, R., DeFries, J. C., & Loehlin, J. C. (1977). Genotype-environment interaction and correlation in the analysis of human behavior. *Psychological Bulletin, 84,* 309-322.

Potts, R. (1998). Variability selection in hominid evolution. *Evolutionary Anthropology, 7,* 81-96.

Rescorla, R. A. (1980). *Pavlovian second-order conditioning: Studies in associative learning.* Hillsdale, NJ: Erlbaum.

Rescorla, R. A. (1988). Pavlovian conditioning: It's not what you think it is. *American Psychologist, 43,* 151-160.

Revulsky, S. (1985). The general process approach to animal learning. In T. D. Johnston & A. T. Pietrewicz (Eds.), *Issues in the ecological study of learning* (pp. 401-432). Hillsdale, NJ: Erlbaum.

Roberts, D. F. (1995). The pervasiveness of plasticity. In C. G. Mascie-Taylor & B. Bogin (Eds.), *Human variability and plasticity* (pp. 1-17). Cambridge, UK: Cambridge University Press.

Rowe, D. C. (1994). *The limits of family influence: Genes, experience, and behavior.* New York: Guilford Press.

Rutter, M., & Silberg, J. (2002). Gene-environment interplay in relation to emotional and behavioral disturbance. In S. T. Fiske (Ed.), *Annual Review of Psychology, 53*, 463-490.

Scarr, S. (1995). Commentary. *Human Development, 38*, 154-158.

Scarr, S., & Weinberg, R. (1983). The Minnesota adoption studies: Genetic differences and malleability. *Child Development 54*, 260-267.

Schell, L. M. (1995). Human plasticity, history, and future research. In C. G. Mascie-Taylor & B. Bogin (Eds.), *Human variability and plasticity* (pp. 213-237). Cambridge, UK: Cambridge University Press.

Segal, N., & MacDonald, K. B. (1998). Behavior genetics and evolutionary psychology: A unified perspective on personality research. *Human Biology, 70*, 159-184.

Seligman, M. E. P. (1971). Phobias and preparedness. *Behavior Therapy, 2*, 307-320.

Shams, M., & Williams, R. (1997). Generational changes in height and body mass differences between British Asians and the general population in Glasgow. *Journal of Biosocial Science, 29*, 101-109.

Shanks, D. R. (1994). Human associative learning. In N. J. Mackintosh (Ed.), *Animal learning and cognition* (pp. 335-374). San Diego: Academic Press.

Shettleworth, S. (1994). Biological approaches to the study of learning. In N. J. Mackintosh (Ed.), *Animal learning and cognition* (pp. 185-219). San Diego: Academic Press.

Shonkoff, J. P., & Phillips, D. A. (2000). *From neurons to neighborhoods: The science of early childhood development*. Washington, DC: National Academy Press.

Spelke, E., & Newport, E. (1998). Nativism, empiricism and the development of knowledge. In R. M. Lerner (Vol. Ed.), *Handbook of child psychology: Vol. 1. Theoretical models of human development* (pp. 275-340). New York: John Wiley.

Staddon, J. E. R. (1988). Learning as inference. In R. C. Bolles & M. D. Beecher (Eds.), *Learning and evolution* (pp. 59-78). Hillsdale, NJ: Erlbaum.

Stevens, R. (1998). Nutrition and cognitive development. In S. Ulijasek et al. (Eds.), *Cambridge encyclopedia of growth and development*. Cambridge, UK: Cambridge University Press.

Stoch, M. B., Smythe, P. M., Moodie, A. D., & Bradshaw, D. (1981). Psychosocial outcome and CT findings after gross undernourishment during infancy: A 20-year developmental study. *Developmental Medicine and Child Neurology, 24*, 419-436.

Thelen, E. (1995). Motor development: A new synthesis. *American Psychologist, 50*, 79-95.

Tomasello, M. (1999). *The culture origins of human cognition*. Cambridge, MA: Harvard University Press.

Tooby, J., & Cosmides, L. (1990). On the universality of human nature and the uniqueness of the individual: The role of genetics and adaptation. *Journal of Personality, 58*, 17-67.

Tooby, J., & Cosmides, L. (1992). The psychological foundations of culture. In J. Barkow, L. Cosmides, & J. Tooby (Eds.), *The adapted mind: Evolutionary psychology and the generation of culture* (pp. 19-136). New York: Cambridge University Press.

Turkheimer, E., Goldsmith, H. H., & Gottesman, I. I. (1995). Commentary: Some conceptual deficiencies in "developmental" behavior genetics. *Human Development, 38,* 142-153.

Turkheimer, E., Lovett, G., Robinette, C. D., & Gottesman, I. (1992). The heritability of divorce: New data and theoretical implications. *Behavior Genetics, 22,* 757 (Abstract).

Wahlsten, D. (1990). Insensitivity of the analysis of variance to heredity-environment interaction. *Behavioral and Brain Sciences, 13,* 109-161.

Ward, C. V., Flinn, M. V., & Begun, D. (2004). Body size and intelligence in Hominoid evolution. In A. E. Russon & D. R. Begun (Eds.), *The evolution of thought: Evolutionary origins of great ape intelligence.* Cambridge, UK: Cambridge University Press.

Weinberg, R. A., Scarr, S., & Waldman, I. D. (1992). The Minnesota transracial adoption study: A follow-up of IQ test performance at adolescence. *Intelligence, 16,* 117-135.

Weisfeld, G. (1997). Research on emotions and future developments in human ethology. In A. Schmitt, K. Atzwanger, K. Grammer, & K. Schäfer (Eds.), *New aspects of human ethology* (pp. 25-46). New York: Plenum.

West-Eberhard, M. J. (1989). Phenotypic plasticity and the origins of diversity. *Annual Review of Ecology and Systematics, 20,* 249-278.

West-Eberhard, M. J. (2003). *Developmental plasticity and evolution.* New York: Oxford University Press.

Wilson, E. O. (1975). *Sociobiology: The new synthesis.* Cambridge, MA: Harvard University Press.

Winick, B., Meyer, K. K., & Harris, R. (1975). Malnutrition and environmental enrichment by early adoption. *Science, 190,* 1173-1175.

3

Culture and Developmental Plasticity

Evolution of the Social Brain

Mark V. Flinn

The relation between culture and biology emerged as one of anthropology's first intellectual responsibilities. It remains one of our most frustrating enigmas. The dichotomy of "nature and nurture" has been a persistent obstacle to consilience between the biological and social sciences. Anthropology has traditionally recognized that culture is inextricably linked to the evolution of mind and that the converse is equally important. In this chapter, I review a scenario in which the mind evolved as a "social tool" in an increasingly cultural environment. I posit that the human psyche was designed primarily to contend with social relationships, whereas the physical environment was relatively less important. Most natural selection in regard to brain evolution was a consequence of interactions with conspecifics, not with food and climate. The primary mental chess game was with other intelligent hominid competitors and cooperators, not with fruits, tools, prey, or snow. An extended juvenile period was favored by natural selection because of the need for more time to develop mental competencies used in forming coalitions and other aspects of social competition. "Culture," shorthand for the information acquired and used by minds in social ways, was a key component of the emerging hominid social environment. Humans are unique in the extraordinary levels of novelty that are generated by the cognitive processing of abstract mental representations. To a degree that far surpasses that of any other species, human mental processes must contend with a constantly changing information environment of their own creation. This perspective may reconcile important aspects of the current biology-culture gap because it suggests an evolved human psychology that is creative, dynamic, and responsive to cultural context, rather than being rigidly constrained by domain-specific modules.

Social Sensitivity, Hormones, and Health: Why Can Words Make Us Sick?

Wayonne's dirt bomb struck the bright yellow dress hanging on the clothesline, making an impressive star-shaped smudge. His older cousin Jenny turned angrily from sweeping the house yard to chase him with her broom. Granny Deedee's yell halted their squabble. Jenny's face morphed from stifled argument to guilt, head bowed. She later told me she felt upset because granny did not understand; her frustration was compounded by the rule that she must accept granny's authority without disagreement. Jenny's cortisol (a stress hormone) level, measured from her saliva that I collected several times a day, rose from 1.4 to 4.2 µg/dl. The next day, her secretory immunoglobulin-A levels dropped from 6.04 to 3.6 mg/dl. Four days later, she had common cold symptoms: runny nose, headache, and low-grade fever (see Figure 3.1).

This anecdote contributes to a common pattern. Children in this rural Dominican community are more than twice as likely to become ill during the week following a stressful event (Flinn & England, 2003). People everywhere appear sensitive to their social environments, often with negative consequences for their health (Cohen, Doyle, Turner, Alper, & Skoner, 2003; Maier, Watkins, & Fleschner, 1994; Marmot & Wilkinson, 1999). Mortality rates were appalling during the early 20th century for children in orphanages and hospitals lacking the evolutionarily normal intimacy of the family: "In the last report of the State Board of Charities of New York, it is stated that 57.2 per cent of infants died in infant asylums through the state" (Chapin, 1928, p. 214). It is not just the occurrence of traumatic events that affects health, but the lack of social support, including parental warmth and other factors that influence emotional states. Why should this be so? Why do social interactions, and a child's perceptions of them, affect physiology and

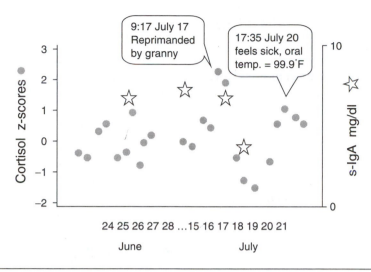

Figure 3.1   Cortisol and s-IgA Levels of a 12-Year-Old Girl Living in Bwa Mawego

morbidity? And, more generally, why is the social environment of such paramount importance in a child's world (e.g., Hirschfeld, 2002)?

In this rural Dominican village that I have lived in and studied over the past 16 years, most of a child's mental efforts seem focused on negotiating social relationships with parents, siblings, grandparents, cousins and other kin, peers, teachers, bus drivers, neighbors, shop owners, and so forth. Foraging for mangos and guavas, hunting birds with catapults, or even fishing in the sea from rock cliffs are relatively simple cognitive enterprises, complicated by conflicts with property owners and decisions about which companions to garner and share calories with. The mind seems more involved with the social chess game than with the utilitarian concerns of the ecological.

I pose these questions as an introduction to the broader issue of the biology-culture gap that pervades anthropology, psychology, and other social and behavioral sciences. The relation between biology and culture is the nexus of anthropology and child development. It is arguably one of our most important scientific and philosophical problems; it underpins mind, thought, and action. It is the keystone of anthropology's holistic approach. And yet it is a perennial source of rancor and disagreement. For many, anthropology "has become polarized into two tribes—one oriented toward biology, the other toward culture—who seem unable or unwilling to understand one another" (Holden, 1993, p. 1641). This "biology-culture gap" has a history and a potential solution.

A Brief History of Culture

In 1900, the President of the Royal Society (London) suggested that everything of great importance had already been discovered by science. Perhaps he overlooked anthropology and its problem of culture—at least we were in good company, alongside black holes and the like. Certainly Taung, "Argonauts," Gombe, DNA, and the many other jewels of the past 100 years challenge his speculation.

In hindsight, the 20th century began with formidable empirical, theoretical, and ideological obstacles to understanding the biological significance of culture. The hominid fossil record was sparse and crudely interpreted. Ethnography was slapdash. Archeology was still engaged in treasure hunts. Primatology was limited to circus and zoo anecdotes. Genetics and psychology were just getting started. Linguistics lacked integration with neurobiology. Evolutionary theory had not yet benefited from the insights of the new synthesis and subsequent refinements. Religious and spiritual beliefs of "human uniqueness" were pervasive. Ethnocentrism clouded analysis of cultural diversity. Racism, sexism, and socioeconomic inequalities called for a politically active as well as a scientific anthropology. Even the term *culture* was contentious.

I hope that it is not complacent to observe that anthropology has made significant inroads against these obstacles. We have learned a great deal about human biology and culture; however, we still have not been able to put the two together satisfactorily. We need a comprehensive explanation for the evolution of the extraordinary aptitudes of humans for abstract mental representation and social learning.

Traditional culture theory, however, did not seek answers to the riddles of culture in the evolution of the brain. The "symbol" was posited as a novelty that uncoupled the human mind from biology (Boas, 1911). The physical mechanisms and functional reasons for the origin(s) of culture were considered speculative details lost to prehistory; the important thing was that symbolic representation had sparked a new informational universe with its own set of open rules (Washburn, 1978). The diversity of culture would not be explicable by reference to neurons and synapses. The preconditions were not supposed to constrain or direct culture.

The recent works of behavioral ecologists, evolutionary psychologists, primatologists, and others inspired by the new developments in evolutionary biology, however, suggest otherwise. The biology-culture gap was widened for some by the sociobiology confrontation, but new bridges were built. Although it is difficult to generalize about theoretical positions in anthropology, I think it is fair to summarize that while most anthropologists were comfortable with the idea that the human brain was a product of natural selection, many were uncomfortable relating this truism to direct connections to informational content, that is, to cultural specifics. The conceptual dichotomy of "nature and nurture" persisted.

Current Ideas

There seems a growing dissatisfaction with the old concepts of culture. A self-reflective anthropology has begun turning over some interesting academic stones. "Culture" was many cherished things: our discipline's authoritative domain, our explanation of our species' uniqueness, and the source of our political influence. It seems surprising that something we had so much difficulty agreeing upon what it was nevertheless could be so important. Let me reiterate the casual definition that I dangled at the beginning of this paper: Culture is shorthand for the information acquired and used by minds in social ways. This definition is undoubtedly problematic. It does not justify territoriality of theory. It does not support a view of our species as qualitatively unique. It does not scientifically privilege the information acquired and processed by humans.

Considering the alternatives, "culture as information" is too simple: It neglects the evident emergent properties of psychological development and social and historical process. And yet "culture as that complex whole" is vague and imprecise (but see Cronk, 1999). Even the middle ground is shaky. The goals of our definition of culture have changed. The superorganic concept of culture has crumbled under the scrutiny of individual variability (Barth, 2002). The species-centric perspective has been challenged by primatology (McGrew, 2003; Stanford, 2001; de Waal, 2001; Whiten et al., 1999; Wrangham, McGrew, de Waal, & Heltne, 1994) and ethology (Mann & Sargeant, 2003; de Waal & Tyack, 2003). Perhaps most important, a much more powerful understanding of ontogeny is beginning to emerge from developmental biology (West-Eberhard, 2003) that places culture into a different relation with biology: one that requires an evolutionary theory of phenotype that meshes mind with social and historical process.

A Potential Solution

The culture side of the gap has traditionally identified a number of important and unique characteristics distinguishing human culture. These include:

1. Culture content is *transmitted by learning processes* (i.e., cognitive information transfer) and not by the transfer of genetic materials. Hence, culture appears to be a separate inheritance system, uncoupled from genetics.

2. Culture (or its effects) is partly *extrasomatic*. Cultural traits (e.g., stone points, political monuments) exist outside the soma (physical body) of the culture-bearing organism.

3. Human culture, by most definitions, involves *mental phenomena*, including conscious thought.

4. Human culture involves the *use of arbitrary symbols* to form mental representations and to communicate information.

5. Culture appears to have *emergent properties at the group level,* such as shared values and beliefs resulting in political and religious institutions.

6. Culture involves *historical processes*. History constrains the options (cultural traits) available for individual choice and modification, and culture can change rapidly, apparently outracing genetic evolution.

7. Complex culture is *uniquely human.*

These characteristics of human culture make it a most challenging and difficult aspect of life to understand in scientific terms. However, they do not necessarily cause culture to become a "nonevolutionary" or "separate evolutionary" phenomenon, independent of biological adaptation. Two of the above characteristics stand out as especially important for resolution of the biology-culture gap: (1) the biological basis of social learning and (2) the evolution of human cognitive abilities and associated cultural aptitudes. We need to understand what the mind was designed to do by the selective pressures of hominid evolutionary history. What tasks were accomplished by Woody Allen's second favorite organ that resulted in the survival and reproduction of our ancestors?

The Mechanisms: Biology and Social Learning

It is difficult to conceive of a process responsible for systematic, incremental development of the human brain over several million years that did not involve differential replication of genes (i.e., natural selection), and yet, this is what a "blank-slate" model of the central nervous system requires. If cultural learning is uncoupled from natural selection, then once culture developed, the brain (more specifically, those parts of the brain involved with cultural information) would no longer evolve. Increasingly refined aptitudes for social learning via symbolic communication would not have evolved if the information obtained did not result in adaptive behavior.

Organic or Darwinian evolution is usually defined as a change in gene or allele frequencies over time. Cultural evolution is usually defined as a change in cultural trait frequencies (or mental information) over time. Because cultural transmission (e.g., imitating a song or adopting a technique for making stone tools) occurs without concomitant genetic transmission, it has been argued that cultural evolution is independent of genes. This leads to the conclusion that cultural evolution is independent of organic evolution. If biology = genetics, and culture = learning, then if learning ? genetics, culture ? biology.

The logic underlying the above conclusion is an important aspect of the biology-culture gap. It distinguishes learning from other flexible responses (e.g., physiological changes) to environmental influences in the production of the phenotype. This is a critical assumption underlying the view that culture is an autonomous inheritance system. "Cultural" evolution is distinguished from "biological" evolution on the basis that cultural evolution involves a distinct mode of information transmission (learning on one hand, genetics on the other). The analogy between cultural evolution and organic evolution, however, may be inappropriate if cultural information is mediated via organically evolved mental faculties, including social learning processes (Flinn, 1997).

Phenotypes are generally accepted to be the products of genes + environment. The directions and degrees to which organisms modify their phenotypes in response to environmental conditions result from a past history of natural selection on abilities to modify phenotypes in response to environmental changes (Alexander, 1979; Stearns, 1992; West-Eberhard, 2003). Arctic hares have seasonal changes in fur color, humans develop calluses on their hands and feet, fig wasps alter the sex-ratios of their broods, sweat bees learn by association and similarity whom to let into the nest, chimps observe and imitate termiting with sticks, and so forth.

The point here is that phenotypic modification, whether achieved via learning or physiological change, is not random. The environment is a causal factor during the development of the phenotype in the context of an evolutionary history of selection for modifications in response to environmental changes (West-Eberhard, 2003; Williams, 1966). Environments do not have random effects on phenotypes. Among Arctic hares, winter conditions result in white coats, summer in brown coats. Other species of rabbit lack this capability; they do not have genetic materials that allow for this adaptive response. Similarly, chimpanzees lack aptitudes for most aspects of human culture, presumably because chimps do not have genetic materials necessary for development of the requisite central nervous system—especially an expanded prefrontal cortex—and associated psychological mechanisms. Regardless of environment, chimpanzees cannot acquire and transmit knowledge of black holes, despite their remarkable cognitive abilities (Tomasello, Kruger, & Ratner, 1993). Clearly, there are evolved differences between chimps and humans in regard to mental processes that underlie human culture (e.g., de Waal & Tyack, 2003; Wrangham, Jones, Laden, Pilbeam, & Conklin-Brittain, 1999). These differences involve the underlying neural architecture.

Humans have brains that are roughly 2 to 3 times larger than that of our clever phylogenetic cousins, the chimpanzees (*Pan troglodytes* and *Pan paniscus*), the gorilla (*Gorilla gorilla*), and the orangutan (*Pongo pygmaeus*), and our distant ancestors, the australopithecines (e.g., *Australopithecus afarensis*). Our enormous neural structures are not cheap: they consume 20% of our metabolic resources and are energetically and developmentally expensive to build as well. Hence, the evolution of the human brain requires an extraordinary functional payoff (Dunbar, 1996). But the differences are not in size and calories alone. In addition to the much more complex patterns of cerebral convolutions, there are many unusual and unique aspects of the human brain. For example, humans have relatively dense connections between parts of the brain that are involved with emotion and higher cognitive skills. The anterior cingulate cortex (ACC) receives strong projections from the amygdala, providing higher-order cognitive regulation of fear and anxiety. Like our close hominoid relatives, albeit in much greater numbers, humans possess a unique type of neuron, the spindle cell, found in layer 5B of Brodmann's area 24 (Nimchinsky et al., 1999). These spindle cells potentially link distinct components of the brain, providing a mechanism for monitoring performance and rewarding success via the rich dopaminergic cells of the ACC (Allman, Hakeem, Erwin, Nimchinsky, & Hof, 2001). These and other structures provide the neurobiological bases for the remarkable human abilities of self-awareness, theory of mind, empathy, and consciousness (Adolphs, 2003; Seigal & Varley, 2002).

What are the functions of all this magnificent neural hardware? The simple answer is increased abilities to process information, providing enhanced response to environmental contingencies. The brain provides a means for phenotypic flexibility via adjustable behaviors. Genes evolved to produce phenotypes, including capabilities for learning, because phenotypes provide a means of responding to changing environments:

> The whole reason for phenotypes having evolved is that they provide flexibility in meeting environmental contingencies that are only predictable on short-term bases. Learned behavior is the ultimate of all such flexibilities. Not just humans

and higher mammals but animals in general develop their behavior, or "learn" to do what is appropriate in their particular life circumstances. Even the remarkably distinctive castes of the social insects are in nearly all cases determined *not* by genetic differences, but by variations in experiences with food or chemicals while they are growing up. The ranges of variation, and the adaptive "peaks" along the axes of such variations (in the case of the social insects, the actual worker and soldier castes), are finite and predictable (e.g., Oster & Wilson, 1978). I believe that we will eventually discover that exactly the same is true for the range and relative likelihoods of composites of learned behavior (or "learning phenotypes") in humans. (Alexander, 1979, p. 14)

Learning capabilities (and neuropsychological mechanisms that use information acquired by learning) would not have evolved if they produced behaviors that were random with respect to biological adaptation. Organisms have evolved to learn in ways that enhance fitness; they have *evolved* to learn nothing else. This is not to deny that learning can result in maladaptive behavioral modifications; imperfection is the bedfellow of unpredictable environments and novelties that favor learning capabilities in the first place. Hence, perhaps, our evolved abilities to analyze and learn from mistakes and successes of others (Flinn & Alexander, 1982). The degree of skepticism with which we view teachings of others, particularly nonrelatives or others whose interests do not coincide with our own, suggests that deception and manipulation are additional concerns.

Learning is a type of phenotypic modification, one way that environmental conditions are used to adjust responses of the organism:

> The alternative to cultural behavior is not "genetically transmitted" behavior: the environment always participates in ontogenesis, even when it is invariable. Plasticity is the rule rather than the exception for all aspects of phenotypes, and imitation and other learning are not restricted to human culture. (Flinn & Alexander, 1982, p. 384)

Cultural differences are due not to genetic differences, but to a *history* of learned responses to different environmental conditions. To take a simple example, just as the white coat is advantageous for the Arctic hare in winter, knowledge of seal hunting is advantageous for the Eskimo. In both cases, there is an evolved ability to respond in a flexible way to varying environmental conditions. In both cases, the phenotype is adjusting itself in a way that is consistent with adaptation. In the case of seal hunting, psychological mechanisms using social transmission of information are involved.

Learning capabilities involve specific propensities and constraints (e.g., Gould & Marler, 1987; Heyes & Galef, 1996). Cognitive capacities, including complex features such as personality development, are influenced by genetic factors (e.g., Plomin, 1990; Scarr, 1992). The important questions here are whether learning propensities and constraints are adaptations produced by natural selection and whether they influence transmission of cultural information.

Learning allows modification of behavior based on experience. Behavioral modifications are no less "biological" than physiological modifications; both involve chemical-neurological mechanisms, and both are products of evolution. There are several general "methods" or pathways by which adaptive learning can occur (e.g., Shettleworth, 1998). The simplest method is behavior modification based on the "trial and error" of individual experience within specific domains (e.g., rats develop aversions to foods that result in nausea; Garcia, 1974).

More complex learning methods use information transfer from one individual to another via "imitation" (for more specific use of the term, see Heyes, 1994; Galef, 1996; Tomasello, 1999; Tomasello & Call 1995). The ability to (a) observe behavior (of parents, etc.), (b) produce a mental image, and (c) reproduce the behavior (imitate or copy) can have tremendous advantages over trial and error (e.g., Heyes & Galef, 1996). Social learning allows one to benefit from the experiences of others and to provide coresident offspring with a "head start." Aversions to poisonous mushrooms can be developed by following the example set by others rather than by direct experience. Problems with imitative learning arise if inappropriate (maladaptive) behaviors are acquired. For example, it would not suit nest parasitic species such as European cuckoos to learn their mating songs from their hosts. Imitative learning requires learning "templates" or "innately tuned sensory systems" that may be time and/or situation restricted (e.g., kin recognition; Alexander, 1990a).

Imitative learning need not be "blind." Evaluation of the relative success and failure of one's peers may allow for more sophisticated behavioral modification. For example, in some species of birds, selective imitation of songs of males that are successful in attracting females can be more advantageous than random imitation of a singing male (Baker & Cunningham, 1985). Learning via selective imitation can lead to cumulative directional change if successful innovations are passed along to the next generation (e.g., Maestripieri, 1996). Intergenerational social learning with cumulative modifications can result in "progressive" historical development of information.[1] Because the current information pool is based on experiences of past generations, this type of learning involves historical constraints. Most definitions of "culture" involve learned information of this sort and the behavior it produces (McGrew, 2003).

A further modification of learning involves selective imitation of behavior based on an individual's specific microenvironment and life history stage. Abilities to "custom-fit" acquisition of information to an individual's specific life history circumstances are advantageous if there are significant differences in individual strategies. What is best for one individual to learn at a certain time in life may be inappropriate for another. Ideally, one would learn the right thing at the right time from the right role model (e.g., MacDonald, 1988). Specialized learning of this sort requires the ability to analyze the individual's position in current social-environmental conditions (perhaps involving self-awareness and consciousness; see Adolphs, 2003; Alexander, 1989; Dennett, 1995; Povinelli, 1993, 1994; Tomasello, 1999). Such analysis probably requires extensive information storage (memory) in order to have a basis for comparison and perhaps for delayed usage (e.g., young chimps observing an alpha male may store images of his behavior for imitation later in their lives).

Humans (and perhaps other hominoids, especially chimpanzees) have developed complex forms of learning that involve behavior modification based on mental representation and scenario building. We use mental "games" to predict possible outcomes of alternatives. Should I get Aunt Leila the red sweater or the blue? Which color would she prefer? What will my other relatives think? Such decisions are based on a "theory of mind" including foresight and comprehension of thought processes (and likely behavioral strategies) of others (Adolphs, 2003; Seigal & Varley, 2002; Tomasello, 1999). Decision making based on mental scenarios allows for experience without the cost. In addition to the task-specific modular capacities (e.g., ability to recognize facial expressions), such enhanced psychological mechanisms require expanded neural capacity for increased general competencies of working memory, attentional control, and executive functions (allowing for more extensive analysis, framing, categorization, etc.; see Engle, 2002).

Humans use a combination of learning methods in day-to-day living. We obtain information from direct observation and symbolic communication. We "think over" acquired information (consciously or unconsciously) and evaluate whether it is useful (e.g., Chibnik, 1981). We modify our behavior accordingly. Unfortunately, quantitative models of cultural transmission do not yet include complex learning and information manipulation that exemplify human culture and behavior. Humans appear "smart"; we do not randomly imitate cultural traits, even from apparently successful role models. Nor are cultural traits employed randomly; individuals strategically use different behaviors to suit particular contexts.

The complexity of social learning processes is a key issue for resolving the biology-culture gap. Theories based on evolved psychological mechanisms emphasize adaptive decision making, whereas traditional theories focus on nonpsychological aspects of information transmission, such as structure of diffusion (vertical via parents, horizontal via peers, etc.). The issue involves whether learning "rules of thumb" are simple or sophisticated, and the importance of "other forces" besides evolutionary design of cognitive processes that affect culture content.

The ubiquity of apparently nonadaptive or maladaptive behaviors such as tattoos, arbitrary food taboos, religious beliefs, celibacy, ethnic markers, dress style, and so on, may be interpreted as evidence that forces besides evolved psychological mechanisms influence culture choice. Cultural traits that are maladaptive nonetheless become common by virtue of "cultural" processes such as society level functions, conformity, or blind imitation, because human psychological mechanisms are not sophisticated enough to discriminate among cultural options. There are, however, alternative explanations for the existence of nonadaptive and maladaptive behaviors, including historical lag, deception and manipulation by competitors (Krebs & Dawkins, 1984), experimentation, selective conformity, and chance (see Alexander, 1979; Dawkins, 1982, pp. 33-54, for discussion of "constraints on perfection"). Perhaps the most difficult aspect of evaluating the utility of cultural traits is determining social and historical context. Conformity, imitation of success, and other aspects of human sociality may generate complex dynamics that do not fit with simplistic utilitarian models of culture.

Evolved psychological mechanisms theory emphasizes that learning capabilities are evolved aspects of the phenotype, and, as such, have been designed by natural selection. The information bits in human minds are generated by processing of observations of the behaviors of others, and are not independent replicators (for debate, see Flinn, 1997; Laland & Brown, 2002; Sperber, 1996). Detailed descriptions of psychological mechanisms (and their ontogenetic development) are important research objectives. Social learning may involve numerous distinct processes, such as social facilitation, local enhancement, mimicking, emulation, and imitation (Heyes, 1994; Tomasello, 1999), perhaps further specialized in different functional domains (Hirschfeld & Gelman, 1994), including language (Pinker, 1997). As summarized by Leda Cosmides and John Tooby (1989),

> The study of culture is the study of how different kinds of information from each individual's environment, especially from his or her social environment, can be expected to affect that individual's behavior. The behavior elicited by this information reverberates throughout the individual's social group, as information that other individuals may act on in turn. The ongoing cycle that results is the generation of culture. By directly regulating individual learning and

behavior, those psychological mechanisms that select and process information from the individual's social environment govern the resulting cultural dynamics. (pp. 51-52)

Information, or culture, thus involves not only social interaction but also an endless history of social interaction, filtered and analyzed at each step by psychological mechanisms that are themselves developed during ontogeny in response to the particular subset of information to which each individual is exposed. This approach parallels studies of human motivation in cultural anthropology (e.g., D'Andrade & Strauss, 1992).

No one has argued that culture content can be explained by reference to evolved psychological mechanisms alone. How could we predict and explain the directions and pace of cultural changes, given that all humans have roughly the same psychological mechanisms? Environmental differences appear insufficient to account for cultural differences without including some type of interaction with historical context. A complete model of culture must include the effects of (a) social integration and shared information, "reverberation throughout the individual's social group"; (b) history, "the ongoing cycle"; (c) individual psychological and informational development (ontogeny); (d) the noncultural environment (e.g., flora and fauna, geography, and demography); (e) chance or accidental events; and (f) evolved psychological mechanisms that underlie mental representation and communication. The devil is in the details; for evolutionary psychologists such as Cosmides and Tooby, the emphasis is on the "psychological mechanisms that select and process information" because they "directly regulat[e] individual learning and behavior." Direct regulation, however, may not be the optimal strategy if the game is constantly being reinvented and is contingent upon specific social and historical context. The empirical focus on "universals" is similarly problematic in some domains: The human social environment generates conditions under which individuals may benefit from innovation and behavioral diversity.

The theoretical logic and evidence for the evolved mind are compelling. Hence the firm stance on the biology side of the gap. The view from the other side is a bit different. Many cultural anthropologists look at the situation and do not see the relevance of biology, regardless of the evolutionary basis for the mind. The nearly infinite diversity of cultural detail does not appear to be reducible to a set of biological universals. Culture does not adhere to a strict utilitarian scheme. If the evolved psychological mechanisms are so influential, why the cacophony of information? Why the riot of individual expression and yet the restraint of collective meaning? From the culture side of the gap, one can only conclude that whatever our minds might have evolved to do, it is not a collection of simple biological routines

(Mithen, 1996). Getting calories and breathing air are great, but what would life be without friends, art, sports, religion, music, sex, quarks, status, and the stars and the moon?

Hence the quandary of the biology-culture gap. One side is convinced that the mind is a product of organic evolution, designed by natural selection for specific functions and yet capable of considerable "cognitive fluidity." The other side sees little relevance of that obvious fact for understanding the diversity of culture; we spin our webs of meaning far from the apparent constraints of our DNA heritage. Both positions are backed by logical theories and mountains of empirical evidence.

The Missing Link: Why Did Human Intelligence Evolve?

Anthropology has considered many hypotheses concerning the selective advantages of human intelligence. Most explanations involve ecological problem solving, such as tool use (e.g., Byrne, 1997; Darwin, 1871; Gibson & Ingold, 1993; Washburn, 1959; Wynn, 1988, 2002), hunting (e.g., Dart, 1925; Stanford, 2001), scavenging, foraging (e.g., Isaac, 1978; Kaplan, Hill, Lancaster, & Hurtado, 2000), projectile weapons (e.g., Bingham, 1999), extended life history (e.g., van Schaik & Deaner, 2003), food processing (e.g., Wrangham et al., 1999), and savanna, aquatic (e.g., Morgan, 1995), or unstable (Potts, 1996) environments. None has achieved complete or general acceptance, even when combined in synthetic models and causally linked to social dynamics.

Common problems for these models include difficulties with explaining why humans uniquely evolved such extraordinary cognitive abilities, considering that many other species hunt, occupy savanna habitats, have long lifetimes, and so forth. Given the very high metabolic costs of evolving, building, and maintaining a human brain (20% of total caloric intake), the ecological gains required are difficult to imagine (Dunbar, 1996). Additional problems arise from the lack of clear domain-specific adaptations for the above scenarios. The exceptional human cognitive abilities of consciousness, emotions, self-awareness, and theory of mind do not make sense as adaptations for tracking prey or collecting fruit, nor as spurious outcomes of neurogenesis or other developmental processes (cf. Finlay, Darlington, & Nicastro, 2001). All of these models, moreover, have difficulties accounting for the diversification of culture into nonutilitarian areas.

One possibility is that a single genetic event resulted in a dramatic origin of cultural abilities (e.g., Calvin & Bickerton, 2000; Klein & Edgar, 2002;

cf. Enard et al., 2002). It is uncertain what benefit such a saltational mutation might have for the initial individual in which it occurred, for there would not be anyone else to talk or "culture" with. Complex adaptations and cultural abilities surely qualify as such, products of long, directional selection with successful intermediary stages (Dawkins, 1986; Mayr, 1982). The fossil record suggests a gradual, albeit rapid, pattern of increase in cranial capacity (e.g., Lee & Wolpoff, 2003; Lewin, 1998; Ruff, Trinkaus, & Holliday, 1997) among hominids. Although apparently abrupt artifact changes are suggestive of significant transitions, the hypothesis that the "creative explosion" was caused by a neurological "hopeful monster" remains tenuous. Artifacts found by future archeologists at the contemporary sites of New York City and the upper Orinoco might suggest significant differences in mental abilities between the populations, but such an inference would be wrong.

A different approach to the problem of the evolution of human intelligence involves consideration of the brain as a "social tool" (Adolphs, 2003; Alexander, 1971, 1989; Brothers, 1990; Byrne & Whiten, 1988; Dunbar, 1996; Humphrey, 1976, 1983; Jolly, 1999). This hypothesis suggests that the human psyche is designed primarily to contend with social relationships, whereas the physical (nonsocial) environment is relatively less important. Most natural selection in regard to brain evolution was a consequence of interactions with conspecifics, not with food and climate. The primary mental chess game was with other intelligent hominid competitors and cooperators, not with fruits, tools, prey, or snow (although enhanced intelligence surely was useful in dealing with such hostile forces as well).[2] Human social relationships are complex. Predicting future moves of a social competitor-cooperator, and appropriate countermoves, amplified by multiple relationships, shifting coalitions, and deception, makes social success a difficult undertaking (Alexander, 1987, 1990b; Axelrod & Hamilton, 1981; Henrich et al., 2001; de Waal, 1982).

Indeed, the potential variety of human social puzzles is apparently infinite; no two social situations are precisely identical, nor are any two individuals ever in exactly the same social environment. Moreover, social relationships can change rapidly, requiring quick modification of strategy. This unpredictable, dynamic social hodgepodge would seem to favor flexible, "open," "domain-general," or "executive" psychological mechanisms highly dependent upon social learning and capable of integrating information processed by more restricted, "domain-specific" mechanisms (e.g., Hirschfeld & Gelman, 1994; Shettleworth, 1998). These complex cognitive processes would be more capable of contending with (and producing) novelties created by cultural change and culture- and individual-specific differences. Unfortunately, such chameleonic psychological mechanisms would be nightmares to document empirically, evidenced perhaps by our meager understanding of the "black box."

The "social tool" hypothesis initially encountered the same common problems as the physical environment hypotheses. The uniqueness issue was especially difficult. Comparative analyses indicated that group size and proxy measures for intelligence (e.g., cranial capacity, neocortex ratios) were associated in a wide range of taxa, including primates (e.g., Kudo & Dunbar, 2001; Pawlowski, Lowen, & Dunbar, 1999). What was missing, however, was the reason(s) why hominids formed larger and/or more socially complex groups, hence creating an environment in which greater intelligence would have been favored by natural selection. That critical part of the puzzle was provided by the biologist Richard Alexander (1989, 1990b) in two seminal essays.

Alexander's scenario posits that hominids increasingly became an "ecologically dominant" species. Humans uniquely evolved sophisticated brains because humans were the only species to become their own "principal hostile force of nature" (Alexander, 1989, p. 469) via inter- and intragroup competition and cooperation. Increasing intellectual and linguistic capacities were favored because such skills allowed individuals to better anticipate and influence social interactions with other increasingly intelligent humans. This "runaway" directional selection produced greater and greater cerebral capabilities because success was based on relative (rather than absolute) levels of intelligence. Unlike static ecological challenges, the hominid social environment became an autocatalytic process, ratcheting up the importance of increased intelligence.

Evaluating scenarios of human evolution is necessarily speculative to varying degrees (e.g., Marks, 2002; McHenry & Coffing, 2000). Alexander's model, however, posits a wide range of interrelated phenomena, thereby generating a large number of ways to falsify it. Full discussion of his model is beyond the scope of this review (see Flinn, Geary, & Ward, in press; Geary & Flinn, 2001), but a synopsis of the key components may suffice:

- Humans have an unusual pattern of speciation. The extinction of all intermediate stages (e.g., gracile australopithecines and *Homo erectus)* and nondescendant branch species (e.g., robust australopithecines) and the absence of a pattern of adaptive radiation suggest that within-taxa competition was highly significant.
- Humans have an unusual life history pattern, with extended childhood and postreproductive stages (Bogin, 1997; Leigh, 2001; Mace, 2000). Childhood may be necessary for complex development and experience to acquire social skills (Hirschfeld, 2002; Joffe, 1997); a postreproductive stage may be useful

for caretaking of dependent offspring, grandchildren, and other relatives (Hawkes, 2003; Hawkes, O'Connell, Jones, Alvarez, & Charnov, 1998).

- Humans have a unique mating system, with extensive male parental care and long-term pair-bonding in a context of multimale/multifemale communities.
- Humans have a unique sexuality, with concealed ovulation, menopause, and other characteristics that may facilitate aspects of the unique human mating/parenting system (above).
- Humans have reduced sexual dimorphism of body size and other traits (e.g., canines). Comparative analyses of hominid fossils and primates suggest that coalitions and fighting techniques other than biting were important during human evolution.
- The neocortex is larger than that of other primates in areas that support social competencies that are unique to humans (Rilling & Insel, 1999), such as theory of mind (Adolphs, 2003; Baron-Cohen, 1999) and language (Pinker, 1994).
- Humans have unusual aptitudes for use of projectile weapons (throwing *and* dodging, suggesting that competition with conspecifics was important, because prey such as antelope do not pick up spears or stones and throw them back at hunters).
- Humans have unique aptitudes for communication, including language and specific linguistic abilities.
- Humans have unique aptitudes for developing large, complex social groups based on kinship and reciprocity.
- Humans converge with species that have competition among socially complex coalitions, for example, chimpanzees (e.g., Harcourt, 1988; Mitani & Watts, 2000; Watts & Mitani, 2001; Wrangham, 1999) and dolphins (e.g., Mann & Sargeant, 2003; Smolker, 2000).

The factor that ties all of the above components—one might consider them "evolutionary clues"—especially the rapid changes associated with the emergence of *H. sapiens,* is social competition and cooperation in the context of ecological dominance:

> The ecological dominance of evolving humans diminished the effects of extrinsic forces of natural selection such that within-species competition became the principal "hostile force of nature" guiding the long-term evolution of behavioral capacities, traits, and tendencies, perhaps more than any other species. (Alexander, 1989, p. 458)

As ecological dominance was achieved bit by bit, the traits that began to strongly covary with individual differences in survival and reproductive outcomes were those that allowed hominids to socially "outmaneuver" other hominids. These traits would include sophisticated social competencies, such as language, self-awareness, consciousness, and theory of mind; an accompanying increase in brain size; and other adaptations that facilitated kin-based social coalitions. An extended period of childhood with intensive parenting would contribute to the acquisition of social skills.

Abstract mental representation is useful, perhaps even necessary, for the complex analysis of social relationships and networks that most humans conduct with such ease. The diversity of human culture, the extraordinary range of information that we use in comparison with other species, results from the social dynamics of our complex coalitions. Alexander's model posits that we evolved our abilities for art, dance, theatre, friendship, technology, and so forth primarily as methods for contending with the social world of other humans. The advantages such abilities offered for dealing with the ecological demands of drought, food shortages, snow, and the like, are posited to be secondary.

Concluding Remarks: Reconciliation

The success of a theory of culture is not determined by its ability to smooth the ruffled feathers of disgruntled colleagues arguing across the biology-culture gap. Nonetheless, I think it is salient that Alexander's version of the social tool model for the evolution of human intelligence may explain the apparent incongruities that have plagued us for so many years.

Humans are unique in the extraordinary levels of novelty that are generated by the processing of abstract mental representations. Human culture is cumulative; human cognition produces new ideas built upon the old. To a degree that far surpasses that of any other species, human mental processes must contend with a constantly changing information-environment of their own creation. Cultural information may be especially dynamic because it is a fundamental aspect of human social coalitions. Apparently arbitrary changes in cultural traits, such as clothing styles, music, art, food, and dialects, may reflect information "arms races" among and within coalitions. The remarkable developmental plasticity and cross-domain integration of some cognitive mechanisms may be products of selection for special sensitivity to variable social context (e.g., Adolphs, 2003; Boyer, 1998; Carruthers, 2002). Human "culture" is not just a pool or source of information; it is an arena and theater of social manipulation and competition via cooperation. Culture is contested because it is a contest.

The effects of coalition conformity and imitation of success may drive culture in directions difficult to predict solely on the basis of simple functional concerns or evolved psychological mechanisms. This social dynamic would explain the apparent lack of a simple biological utilitarianism of so much of culture and the great importance of historical context and social power (e.g., Wolf, 2001). It also reconciles symbolic and interpretive approaches in cultural anthropology with the biological "evolved-mind" approaches. Deconstruction is a complicated, but necessary, enterprise, for we are all players in the social arena. The twist is that we are evolved participants.

Reconciliation of the biology-culture gap is important for anthropological contributions to child development (Bjorklund & Pellegrini, 2002) and may provide a basic underpinning for the links among the many interrelated fields that anthropologists engage in. Returning to the anecdotal example at the beginning of this essay, consider the relations among stress, health, and culture. People in difficult social environments tend to be less healthy in comparison with their more fortunate peers (e.g., Cohen et al., 2003; Dressler & Bindon, 2000; Flinn, 1999; Wilkinson, 2001). The obvious explanation of a better physical environment—improved housing, work conditions, nutrition, health care, and reduced exposure to pathogens and poisons—is insufficient (Ellis, 1994; Marmot et al., 1991). The specific mechanisms underlying the association between socioeconomic conditions and health are uncertain. Psychosocial stress and associated immunosuppression are possible intermediaries (Adler et al., 1994; Kiecolt-Glaser, Malarkey, Cacioppo, & Glaser, 1994). If the brain evolved as a social tool, then the expenditure of somatic resources via cortisol release to resolve psycho-social problems makes sense (e.g., Beylin & Shors, 2003). Relationships are of paramount importance.

Notes

1. Cultural "progress" (e.g., increasing social complexity, technology, and group size) is an incidental effect (Ingold, 1986, 2001; Wright, 1994). Apparent "intentionality" of human reason is a product of evolution, not the driving force. Competition within a cultural environment, however, may be a zero-sum, "red-queen" game in which "winners" must continually advance their tactics beyond their competitors'. Arms races are a good example.

2. This might explain the apparent lack of significant population differences in cognitive abilities: The uniquely common selective force that all humans contend with is competition with other humans, regardless of physical environment. Inter-populational gene flow further reduces potential differences among populations.

References

Adler, N. E., Boyce, T., Chesney, M. A., Cohen, S., Folkman, S., Kahn, R. L., et al. (1994). Socioeconomic status and health. *American Psychologist, 49,* 15-24.

Adolphs, R. (2003). Cognitive neuroscience of human social behavior. *Nature Reviews, Neuroscience, 4,* 165-178.

Alexander, R. D. (1971). The search for an evolutionary philosophy of man. *Proceedings of the Royal Society of Victoria, 84,* 99-120.

Alexander, R. D. (1979). *Darwinism and human affairs.* Seattle: University of Washington Press.

Alexander, R. D. (1987). *The biology of moral systems.* Hawthorne, NY: Aldine Press.

Alexander, R. D. (1989). Evolution of the human psyche. In P. Mellars & C. Stringer (Eds.), *The human revolution* (pp. 455-513). Chicago: University of Chicago Press.

Alexander, R. D. (1990a). Epigenetic rules and Darwinian algorithms: The adaptive study of learning and development. *Ethology and Sociobiology, 11,* 1-63.

Alexander, R. D. (1990b). *How did humans evolve?* (Special publication #1). Ann Arbor: University of Michigan, Museum of Zoology.

Allman, J. M., Hakeem, A., Erwin, J. M., Nimchinsky, E., & Hof, P. (2001). The anterior cingulate cortex: The evolution of an interface between emotion and cognition. *Annals of the New York Academy of Sciences, 935,* 107-117.

Axelrod, R., & Hamilton, W. D. (1981). The evolution of cooperation. *Science, 211*(4489), 1390-1396.

Baker, M. C., & Cunningham, M. A. (1985). The biology of bird song dialects. *Behavioral and Brain Sciences, 8,* 85-133.

Baron-Cohen, S. (1999). The evolution of a theory of mind. In M. C. Corballis & S. E. G. Lea (Eds.), *The descent of mind: Psychological perspectives on hominid evolution* (pp. 261-277). Oxford, UK: Oxford University Press.

Barth, F. (2002). An anthropology of knowledge. *Current Anthropology 43*(1), 1-18.

Beylin, A. V., & Shors, T. J. (2003). Glucocorticoids are necessary for enhancing the acquisition of associative memories after acute stressful experience. *Hormones and Behavior, 43,* 1124-1131.

Bingham, P. M. (1999). Human uniqueness: A general theory. *Quarterly Review of Biology, 74,* 133-169.

Bjorklund, D. F., & Pellegrini, A. D. (2002). *The origins of human nature: Evolutionary developmental psychology.* Washington, DC: APA Press.

Boas, F. (1911). *The mind of primitive man.* New York: Macmillan.

Bogin, B. (1997). Evolutionary hypotheses for human childhood. *Yearbook of Physical Anthropology, 40,* 63-90.

Boyer, P. (1998). Cognitive tracks of cultural inheritance: How evolved intuitive ontology governs cultural transmission. *American Anthropologist, 100,* 876-889.

Brothers, L. (1990). The social brain: A project for integrating primate behavior and neurophysiology in a new domain. *Concepts in Neuroscience, 1,* 27-51.

Byrne, R. W. (1997). The technical intelligence hypothesis: An additional evolutionary stimulus to intelligence? In A. Whiten & R. W. Byrne (Eds.), *Machiavellian intelligence II: Extensions and evaluations* (pp. 289-311). Cambridge, UK: Cambridge University Press.

Byrne, R., & Whiten, A. (Eds.). (1988). *Machiavellian intelligence: Social expertise and the evolution of intellect in monkeys, apes, and humans.* Oxford, UK: Oxford University Press.

Calvin, W. H., & Bickerton, D. (2000). *Lingua ex machina: Reconciling Darwin and Chomsky with the human brain.* Cambridge: MIT Press.

Carruthers, P. (2002). The evolution of consciousness. In P. Carruthers & A. Chamberlain (Eds.), *Evolution and the human mind: Modularity, language, and meta-cognition* (pp. 254-276). Cambridge, UK: Cambridge University Press.

Chapin, H. D. (1928). *Heredity and child culture.* New York: E. P. Dutton.

Chibnik, M. (1981). The evolution of cultural rules. *Journal of Anthropological Research, 37,* 256-268.

Cohen, S., Doyle, W. J., Turner, R. B., Alper, C. M., & Skoner, D. P. (2003). Emotional style and susceptibility to the common cold. *Psychosomatic Medicine 65,* 652-657.

Cosmides, L., & Tooby, J. (1989). Evolutionary psychology and the generation of culture, Part II. Case study: A computational theory of social exchange. *Ethology and Sociobiology, 10,* 51-98.

Cronk, L. (1999). *That complex whole: Culture and the evolution of human behavior.* Boulder, CO: Westview Press.

D'Andrade, R., & Strauss, C. (Eds.). (1992). *Human motives and cultural models.* Cambridge, UK: Cambridge University Press.

Dart, R. A. (1925). *Australopithecus africanus:* The man-ape of South Africa. *Nature, 115,* 195-199.

Darwin, C. (1871). *The descent of man and selection in relation to sex* (2 vols.). New York: D. Appleton.

Dawkins, R. (1982). *The extended phenotype: The gene as the unit of selection.* San Francisco: Freeman.

Dawkins, R. (1986). *The blind watchmaker.* New York: W. W. Norton.

Dennett, D. C. (1995). *Darwin's dangerous idea: Evolution and the meanings of life.* New York: Simon & Schuster.

de Waal, F. B. M. (1982). *Chimpanzee politics.* New York: Harper & Row.

de Waal, F. B. M. (2001). *The ape and the sushi master.* New York: Basic Books.

de Waal, F. B. M., & Tyack, P. L. (Eds.). (2003). *Animal social complexity.* Cambridge, MA: Harvard University Press.

Dressler, W. W., & Bindon, J. R. (2000). The health consequences of cultural consonance: Cultural dimensions of lifestyle, social support, and arterial blood pressure in an African American community. *American Anthropologist, 102,* 244-260.

Dunbar, R. I. M. (1996). *Grooming, gossip, and the evolution of language.* Cambridge, MA: Harvard University Press.

Ellis, L. (1994). Social status and health in humans: The nature of the relationship and its probable causes. In L. Ellis (Ed.), *Social stratification and socioeconomic inequality* (Vol. 2, pp. 123-144). Westport, CT: Praeger.

Enard, W., Przeworski, M., Fisher, S. E., Lai, C. S. L., Wiebe, V., Kitano, T., Monaco, A. P., & Pääbo, S. (2002). Molecular evolution of FOXP2, a gene involved in speech and language. *Nature, 418,* 869-872.

Engle, R. W. (2002). Working memory capacity as executive attention. *Current Directions in Psychological Science, 11,* 19-23.

Finlay, B. L., Darlington, R. B., & Nicastro, N. (2001). Developmental structure in brain evolution. *Behavioral & Brain Sciences, 24,* 263-308.

Flinn, M. V. (1997). Culture and the evolution of social learning. *Evolution and Human Behavior, 18,* 23-67.

Flinn, M. V. (1999). Family environment, stress, and health during childhood. In C. Panter-Brick & C. Worthman (Eds.), *Hormones, health, and behavior* (pp. 105-138). Cambridge, UK: Cambridge University Press.

Flinn, M. V., & Alexander, R. D. (1982). Culture theory: The developing synthesis from biology. *Human Ecology, 10,* 383-400.

Flinn, M. V., & England, B. G. (2003). Childhood stress: endocrine and immune responses to psychosocial events. In J. M. Wilce (Ed.), *Social & cultural lives of immune systems* (pp. 107-147). London: Routledge Press.

Flinn, M. V., Geary, D. C., & Ward, C. V. (in press). Ecological dominance, social competition, and coalitionary arms races: Why humans evolved exceptional intelligence. *Evolution and Human Behavior, 25(5).*

Galef B. G. Jr. (1996). Introduction. In C. M. Heyes & B. G. Galef Jr. (Eds.), *Social learning in animals* (pp. 3-16). New York: Academic Press.

Garcia, J. (1974). Behavioral regulation of the milieu interne in man and rat. *Science, 185,* 824-831.

Geary, D. C., & Flinn, M. V. (2001). Evolution of human parental behavior and the human family. *Parenting: Science and Practice, 1,* 5-61.

Gibson, K., & Ingold, T. (1993). *Tools, language, and cognition in human evolution.* Cambridge, UK: Cambridge University Press.

Gould, J. L., & Marler, P. (1987). Learning by instinct. *Scientific American, 256,* 74-85.

Harcourt, A. H. (1988). Alliances in contests and social intelligence. In R. W. Byrne & A. Whiten (Eds.), *Machiavellian intelligence* (pp. 142-152). Oxford, UK: Oxford University Press.

Hawkes, K. (2003). Grandmothers and the evolution of human longevity. *American Journal of Human Biology, 15,* 380-400.

Hawkes, K., O'Connell, J. F., Jones, N. G., Alvarez, H., & Charnov, E. L. (1998). Grandmothering, menopause, and the evolution of human life histories. *Proceedings of the National Academy of Sciences of the United States of America, 95(3),* 1336-1339.

Henrich, J., Boyd, R., Bowles, S., Camerer, C., Fehr, E., Gintis, H., et al. (2001). Cooperation, reciprocity and punishment in fifteen small-scale societies. *American Economic Review, 91,* 73-78.

Heyes, C. M. (1994). Social learning in animals: categories and mechanisms. *Biological Reviews of the Cambridge Philosophical Society, 69*(2), 207-231.

Heyes, C. M., & Galef, B. G. Jr. (Eds.). (1996). *Social learning in animals.* New York: Academic Press.

Hirschfeld, L. A. (2002). Why don't anthropologists like children? *American Anthropologist, 104,* 61-67.

Hirschfeld, L. A., & Gelman, S. A. (Eds.). (1994). *Mapping the mind: Domain specificity in cognition and culture.* New York: Cambridge University Press.

Holden, C. (1993). Failing to cross the biology-culture gap. *Science, 262,* 1641.

Humphrey, N. K. (1976). The social function of intellect. In P. P. G. Bateson & R. A. Hinde (Eds.), *Growing points in ethology* (pp. 303-317). New York: Cambridge University Press.

Humphrey, N. K. (1983). *Consciousness regained.* Oxford, UK: Oxford University Press.

Ingold, T. (1986). *Evolution and social life.* Cambridge, UK: Cambridge University Press.

Ingold, T. (2001). From complementarity to obviation: On dissolving the boundaries between social and biological anthropology, archaeology, and psychology. In S. Oyama, P. E. Griffiths, & R. D. Gray (Eds.), *Cycles of contingency: Developmental systems and evolution* (pp. 255-279). Cambridge: MIT Press.

Isaac, G. (1978). The food-sharing behavior of protohuman hominids. *Scientific American, 238,* 90-108.

Joffe, T. H. (1997). Social pressures have selected for an extended juvenile period in primates. *Journal of Human Evolution, 32,* 593-605.

Jolly, A. (1999). *Lucy's legacy: Sex and intelligence in human evolution.* Cambridge, MA: Harvard University Press.

Kaplan, H., Hill, K., Lancaster, J., & Hurtado, A. M. (2000). A theory of human life history evolution: Diet, intelligence and longevity. *Evolutionary Anthropology, 9,* 156-183.

Kiecolt-Glaser, J. K., Malarkey, W. B., Cacioppo, J. T., & Glaser, R. (1994). Stressful personal relationships: Immune and endocrine function. In R. Glaser & J. K. Kiecolt-Glaser (Eds.), *Handbook of human stress and immunity* (pp. 301-319). New York: Academic Press.

Klein, R. G., & Edgar, B. (2002). *The dawn of human culture.* New York: John Wiley.

Krebs, J. R., & Dawkins, R. (1984). Animal signals: Mind reading and manipulation. In J. R. Krebs & N. B. Davies (Eds.), *Behavioural ecology: An evolutionary approach* (pp. 380-402). Sunderland, MA: Sinauer.

Kudo, H., & Dunbar, R. I. M. (2001). Neocortex size and social network size in primates. *Animal Behaviour, 62,* 711-722.

Laland, K., & Brown, G. (2002). *Sense and nonsense: Evolutionary perspectives on human behaviour*. Oxford, UK: Oxford University Press.

Lee, S. H., & Wolpoff, M. H. (2003). The pattern of evolution in Pleistocene human brain size. *Paleobiology, 29,* 186-196.

Leigh, S. R. (2001). The evolution of human growth. *Evolutionary Anthropology, 10,* 223-236.

Lewin, R. (1998). *Principles of human evolution*. Malden, UK: Blackwell Science.

MacDonald, K. B. (1988). *Social and personality development: An evolutionary synthesis*. New York: Plenum Press.

Mace, R. (2000). Evolutionary ecology of human life history. *Animal Behaviour, 59,* 1-10.

Maestripieri, D. (1996). Maternal encouragement in nonhuman primates and the question of animal teaching. *Human Nature, 6,* 361-378.

Maier, S. F., Watkins, L. R., & Fleschner, M. (1994). Psychoneuroimmunology: The interface between behavior, brain, and immunity. *American Psychologist, 49,* 1004-1007.

Mann J., & Sargeant, B. (2003). Like mother, like calf: The ontogeny of foraging traditions in wild Indian Ocean bottlenose dolphins (*Tursiops* sp.). In D. Fragaszy & S. Perry (Eds.), *The biology of traditions: Models and evidence* (pp. 236-266). Cambridge, UK: Cambridge University Press.

Marks, J. (2002). *What it means to be 98% chimpanzee: Apes, people, and their genes*. Berkeley: University of California Press.

Marmot, M., Smith, G. D., Stansfield, S., Patel, C., North, F., Head, I., et al. (1991). Health inequalities among British civil servants: The Whitehall II Study. *Lancet 337,* 1387-1393.

Marmot, M., & Wilkinson, R. G. (Eds.). (1999). *Social determinants of health*. Oxford, UK: Oxford University Press.

Mayr, E. (1982). *The growth of biological thought: Diversity, evolution, and inheritance*. Cambridge, MA: Belknap Press.

McGrew, W. C. (2003). Ten dispatches from the chimpanzee culture wars. In F. B. M. de Waal & P. L. Tyack (Eds.), *Animal social complexity*. Cambridge, MA: Harvard University Press.

McHenry, H. M., & Coffing, K. (2000). Australopithecus to Homo: Transformations in body and mind. *Annual Review of Anthropology, 29,* 125-146.

Mitani, J. C., & Watts, D. P. (2000). Why do chimpanzees hunt and share meat? *Animal Behaviour, 61,* 915-924.

Mithen, S. J. (1996). *The prehistory of the mind: The cognitive origins of art, religion, and science*. London: Thames and Hudson.

Morgan, E. (1995). *The descent of the child: Human evolution from a new perspective*. New York: Oxford University Press.

Nimchinsky, E. A., Gilissen, E., Allman, J. M., Perl, D. P., Erwin, J. M., & Hof, P. R. (1999). A neuronal morphologic type unique to humans and great apes. *Proceedings of the National Academy of Sciences of the United States of America, 96*(9), 5268-5273.

Oster, G. F., & Wilson, E. O. (1978). *Caste and ecology in the social insects.* Princeton, NJ: Princeton University Press.

Pawlowski, B., Lowen, C. B., & Dunbar, R. I. M. (1999). Neocortex size, social skills and mating success in primates. *Behaviour, 135,* 357-368.

Pinker, S. (1994). *The language instinct: How the mind creates language.* New York: William Morrow.

Pinker, S. (1997). *How the mind works.* New York: W. W. Norton.

Plomin, R. (1990). The role of inheritance in behavior. *Science, 248,* 183-188.

Potts, R. B. (1996). *Humanity's descent: The consequences of ecological instability.* New York: William Morrow.

Povinelli, D. J. (1993). Reconstructing the evolution of mind. *American Psychologist, 48,* 493-509.

Povinelli, D. J. (1994). What chimpanzees (might) know about the mind. In R. W. Wrangham (Ed.), *Chimpanzee cultures* (pp. 285-300). Cambridge, MA: Harvard University Press.

Rilling, J. K., & Insel, T. R. (1999). The primate neocortex in comparative perspective using magnetic resonance imaging. *Journal of Human Evolution, 37*(2), 191-223.

Ruff, C. B., Trinkaus, E., & Holliday, T. W. (1997). Body mass and encephalization in Pleistocene *Homo. Nature, 387,* 173-176.

Scarr, S. (1992). Developmental theories for the 1990s: Development and individual differences. *Child Development 63*(1), 1-19.

Seigal, M., & Varley, R. (2002). Neural systems involved with "Theory of Mind." *Nature Reviews, Neuroscience, 3,* 463-471.

Shettleworth, S. J. (1998). *Cognition, evolution, and behavior.* New York: Oxford University Press.

Smolker, R. A. (2000). Keeping in touch at sea: Group movement in dolphins and whales. In S. Boinski & P. A. Garber (Eds.), *On the move: How and why animals travel in groups* (pp. 559-586). Chicago: University of Chicago Press.

Sperber, D. (1996). *Explaining culture: a naturalistic approach.* Oxford, UK: Blackwell.

Stanford, C. (2001). The ape's gift: Meat-eating, meat-sharing and human evolution. In F. B. M. de Waal (Ed.), *Tree of origin: What primate behavior can tell us about human social evolution* (pp. 95-119). Cambridge, MA: Harvard University Press.

Stearns, S. C. (1992). *The evolution of life histories.* Oxford, UK: Oxford University Press.

Tomasello, M. (1999). *The cultural origins of human cognition.* Cambridge, MA: Harvard University Press.

Tomasello, M., & Call, J. (1995). The social cognition of monkeys and apes. *Yearbook of Physical Anthropology, 37,* 273-305.

Tomasello, M., Kruger, A. C., & Ratner, H. H. (1993). Cultural learning. *Behavioral and Brain Sciences, 16,* 495-552.

van Schaik, C., & Deaner, R. (2003). Life history and cognitive evolution in primates. In F. B. M. de Waal & P. Tyack (Eds.), *Animal social complexity: Intelligence, culture and individualized societies* (pp. 5-25). Cambridge, MA: Harvard University Press.

Washburn, S. L. (1959). Speculations on the interrelations of the history of tools and biological evolution. *Human Biology, 31,* 21-31.

Washburn, S. L. (1978). Human behavior and the behavior of other animals. *American Psychologist, 33,* 405-418.

Watts, D. P., & Mitani, J. C. (2001). Boundary patrols and intergroup encounters in wild chimpanzees. *Behaviour, 138,* 299-327.

West-Eberhard, M. J. (2003). *Developmental plasticity and evolution.* Oxford, UK: Oxford University Press.

Whiten, A. J., Goodall, W. C., McGrew, T., Nishida, V., Reynolds, Y., Sugiyama, C. E., Tutin, G., Wrangham, R. W., & Boesch, C. (1999). Cultures in chimpanzees. *Nature, 399,* 682-685.

Wilkinson, R. G. (2001). *Mind the gap: hierarchies, health, and human evolution.* New Haven, CT: Yale University Press.

Williams, G. C. (1966). *Adaptation and natural selection.* Princeton, NJ: Princeton University Press.

Wolf, E. R. (2001). *Pathways of power: Building an anthropology of the modern world.* Berkeley/Los Angeles: University of California Press.

Wrangham, R. W. (1999). The evolution of coalitionary killing. *Yearbook of Physical Anthropology, 42,* 1-30.

Wrangham, R. W., Jones, J. H., Laden, G., Pilbeam, D., & Conklin-Brittain, N. (1999). The raw and the stolen: Cooking and the ecology of human origins. *Current Anthropology 40(5),* 567-594.

Wrangham, R. W., McGrew, W. C., de Waal, F. B. M., & Heltne, P. G. (Eds.). (1994). *Chimpanzee cultures.* Cambridge, MA: Harvard University Press.

Wright, R. (1994). *The moral animal.* New York: Pantheon.

Wynn, T. (1988). Tools and the evolution of human intelligence. In R. W. Byrne & A. Whiten (Eds.), *Machiavellian intelligence* (pp. 271-284). Oxford, UK: Oxford University Press.

Wynn, T. (2002). Archaeology and cognitive evolution. *Behavioral and Brain Sciences, 25,* 389-438.

4

Evolution and Cognitive Development

David C. Geary

The purpose of brain and mind is to allow the individual to attend to, process, and guide behavioral responses to the types of information and conditions that have covaried with survival or reproductive prospects during the species' evolutionary history (Cosmides & Tooby, 1994; Gallistel, 2000; Geary, 2004). These conditions include information patterns generated by the body shape and movement of conspecifics (Blake, 1993; Downing, Jiang, Shuman, & Kanwisher, 2001) and by species of predator and prey (Barton & Dean, 1993), as well as by environmental features (e.g., star patterns) used in navigation (Gallistel, 1990), among many other conditions. As emphasized by many evolutionary psychologists, when such information patterns are consistent from one generation to the next, then modular brain and cognitive systems that identify and process these restricted forms of information should evolve, as illustrated by the invariant end of the continuum in Figure 4.1. The systems may also include implicit (below the level of conscious awareness) decision-making heuristics (e.g., Gigerenzer & Selten, 2001). These are cognitive "rules of thumb" that represent evolved behavioral responses to evolutionarily significant conditions. In some species of bird, as an example, parental feeding of chicks can be described as a simple heuristic, "Feed the smallest, if there is plenty of food; otherwise, feed the largest." Davis and Todd (1999) demonstrated how these implicit and simple

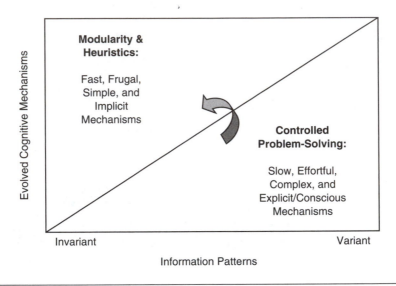

Figure 4.1   The types of cognitive mechanisms that operate on ecological or social information are predicted to vary with the extent to which that information tended to be invariant (resulting in evolved heuristics) or variant (resulting in evolved problem-solving mechanisms) during the species' evolutionary history and during a typical life span.

heuristics can explain the seemingly complex decision making involved in raising the largest number of healthy fledglings.

There can also be conditions that influence survival and reproductive prospects but that produce less predictable, or variant, information patterns across generations and within life spans. This variation might involve fluctuating climatic conditions (e.g., Potts, 1998), but is most likely to emerge from the behavioral interactions between biological organisms that have competing interests (Maynard Smith & Price, 1973). Predator-prey relationships and social competition provide examples of this type of relationship: Variability in the context of these relationships provides an advantage because it renders implicit, heuristic-based behavioral responses less effective. In any case, when the conditions that covary with survival or reproductive prospects are variable across generations or within lifetimes, then the potential for the evolution of less modularized, domain-general mechanisms emerges (Chiappe & MacDonald, 2005; Geary, 2004). As shown at the variant end of the continuum in Figure 4.1, these domain-general systems enable the explicit representation of variant information patterns in working memory and support the controlled problem solving needed to cope with these variable conditions.

My goals for this chapter are to outline both modularized and domain-general systems that vary along the continuum shown in Figure 4.1 and to discuss the interaction between these systems as related to children's cognitive development. In the first section, I describe evolved and modularized domains of the human mind and developmental mechanisms for adapting these systems to the nuances of local social and ecological conditions. In the second section, I describe domain-general brain and cognitive systems, the conditions that may have facilitated their evolution, and their relation to psychometric studies of general intelligence. In the final section, I describe how evolutionarily novel cognitive competencies, such as the ability to read, can emerge through the interaction between modularized and domain-general systems; for a more thorough treatment see Geary (2004).

Evolved Domains of Mind

The purpose of behavior is to allow the individual to gain access to and control of the types of resource that have tended to enhance survival or reproductive options during the species' evolutionary history. These resources fall into three domains: social, biological, and physical. The social domain includes the behavior of and resources controlled by conspecifics, and an example of accompanying evolutionary pressures is competing for mates. The biological domain includes other species that can be used as food and, in the case of humans, medicine. The physical domain includes the territory (e.g., nesting site) that contains biological or reproductive resources. These domains will result in information patterns (e.g., basic shape of a human face) that are important from one generation to the next and thereby create conditions that favor the evolution of the type of brain and cognitive module and behavioral heuristic represented by the invariant end of the continuum in Figure 4.1. Although this issue is vigorously debated (see Finlay, Darlington, & Nicastro, 2001; Gallistel, 2000; Pinker, 1994; Tooby & Cosmides, 1995), I am assuming that the result of these invariant information patterns is the evolution of modules and heuristics that coalesce around the domains of folk psychology, folk biology, and folk physics.

Even within these modular domains, there can be evolutionarily significant variation in information patterns. The basic shape of the human face is invariant, but, at the same time, there are differences in the shape of one face versus another. If it is important to distinguish one individual from another, then some degree of plasticity should evolve within the constraints of the modular system that processes faces (Geary & Huffman, 2002). In these situations, plasticity means there are brain and cognitive systems that are modifiable during the individual's lifetime, but within modular constraints and primarily during the developmental period. The result, in this example, is that the individual can identify other individuals by means of distinctive facial features. Thus, for many of the modular systems I describe in the following sections, the associated cognitive competencies likely emerge through an interaction between inherent constraint and patterns of developmental experience (Bjorklund & Pellegrini, 2002; Geary & Bjorklund, 2000). As I describe in the final section, plasticity within modular constraints enables these brain and cognitive systems to be adapted to create nonevolved academic abilities, such as the ability to read. These nonevolved abilities are called "biologically secondary" because their use in modern society is secondary to their primary evolved function; as an example, reading is a secondary ability that is constructed from the primary, or evolved, language system (Geary, 1995; Rozin, 1976). Figure 4.2 presents a taxonomy of evolved, biologically primary modules in folk domains.

Folk Knowledge

Folk Psychology

Folk psychology is composed of the affective, cognitive, and behavioral systems that enable people to negotiate social interactions and relationships. The function of the corresponding cognitive components is to process and manipulate (e.g., create categories) the forms of social information that have covaried with survival and reproduction during human evolution. The associated domains involve the self, relationships, and interactions with other people, and group level relationships and interactions. These dynamics are supported by the respective modular systems corresponding to self, individual, and group shown in the bottom, left-hand sections of Figure 4.2.

Self. Self-related cognitions include awareness of the self as a social being and of one's behavior in social contexts (Tulving, 2002), as well as a self schema (Markus, 1977). The self schema is a long-term memory network of information that links together knowledge and beliefs about the self, including positive (accentuated) and negative (discounted) traits (e.g.,

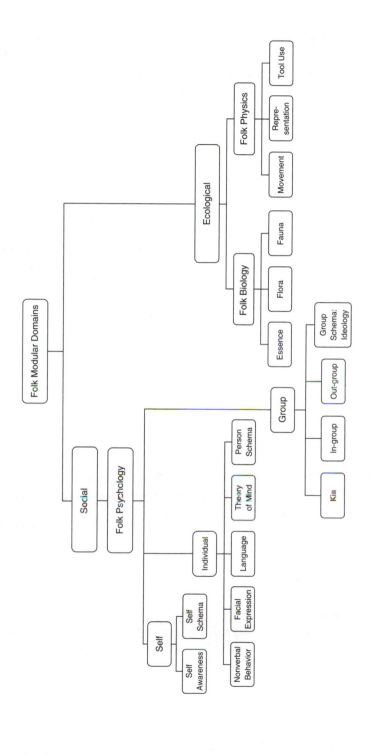

Figure 4.2 Evolved Cognitive Modules That Compose the Domains of Folk Psychology, Folk Biology, and Folk Physics

friendliness), personal memories, self-efficacy in various domains, and so forth. Whether implicitly or explicitly represented, self schemas appear to regulate goal-related behaviors, specifically, where one focuses behavioral effort and whether or not one will be persistent in the face of failure (Sheeran & Orbell, 2000). Self-related regulation results from a combination of implicit and explicit processes that influence social comparisons, self-esteem, valuation of different forms of ability and interests, and the formation of social relationships (Drigotas, 2002).

Individual. The person-related modular competencies function to enable the monitoring and control of dyadic interactions and the development and maintenance of one-on-one relationships. Caporael (1997) and Bugental (2000) have described universal forms of these interactions and relationships, including parent-child attachments and friendships, among others. There are, of course, differences across these dyads, but all of them are supported by the individual level modules shown in Figure 4.2. These modules include those that enable the reading of nonverbal behavior and facial expressions, language, and theory of mind (e.g., Baron-Cohen, 1995; Brothers & Ring, 1992; Pinker, 1994; Rosenthal, Hall, DiMatteo, Rogers, & Archer, 1979). Theory of mind refers to the ability to make inferences about the motives underlying the behavior of other people, their future intentions, and so forth.

The person schema is a long-term memory network that includes representations of another person's physical attributes (age, race, sex), memories for specific behavioral episodes, and more abstract trait information, such as the person's sociability (e.g., warm to emotionally distant) and competence (Schneider, 1973). It seems likely that the person schema will also include information related to the other person's modular systems, such as theory of mind, as well as the person's network of social relationships and kin (Geary & Flinn, 2001). The former would include memories and trait information about how the person typically makes inferences and responds to social cues, his or her social and other goals, and so forth.

Group. A universal aspect of human behavior and cognition is the parsing of the social world into groups. The most consistent of these groupings are shown in Figure 4.2 and reflect the categorical significance of kin, the formation of in-groups and out-groups, and a group schema. The latter is an ideologically based social identification, as exemplified by nationality, religious affiliation, and so forth. The categorical significance of kin is most strongly reflected in the motivational disposition of humans to organize themselves into families of one form or another in all cultures (Brown, 1991).

In traditional societies, nuclear families are typically embedded in the context of a wider network of kin (Geary & Flinn, 2001). Individuals within these kinship networks cooperate to facilitate competition with other kin groups over resource control and manipulation of reproductive relationships. As cogently argued by Alexander (1979), coalitional competition also occurs beyond the kin group, is related to social ideology, and is endemic throughout the world (Horowitz, 2001). As with kin groups, competition among ideology-based groups is over resource control. The corresponding selective pressure is the competitive advantage associated with large group size; that is, ideologies enable easy expansion of group size during group level competition (Alexander, 1989).

Folk Biology and Folk Physics

People living in traditional societies use the local ecology to support their survival and reproductive needs. The associated activities are supported by, among other things, the folk biological and folk physical modules shown in the ecological section of Figure 4.2 (Geary, 1998, 2004; Geary & Huffman, 2002). The folk biological modules support the categorizing of flora and fauna in the local ecology, especially species used as food, medicines, or in social rituals (Berlin, Breedlove, & Raven, 1973). Folk biology also includes systems that support an understanding of the essence of these species (Atran, 1998), that is, heuristic-based decisions regarding the likely behavior of these species. In particular, the essence is knowledge about growth patterns and behavior that facilitates hunting and other activities involved in securing and using these species as resources (e.g., food). Physical modules are for guiding movement in three-dimensional physical space, mentally representing this space (e.g., demarcating the in-group's territory), and using physical materials (e.g., stones, metals) to make tools (Pinker, 1997; Shepard, 1994). The associated primary abilities support a host of evolutionarily significant activities, such as hunting, foraging, and the use of tools as weapons.

Heuristics and Attributional Biases

In addition to describing "rule of thumb" patterns of behavior, heuristics also encompass inferential and attributional biases that are integral features of folk knowledge, at least for humans. For instance, social attributional biases that favor members of the in-group and derogate members of out-groups are well-known (Stephan, 1985) and facilitate coalitional competition (Horowitz, 2001). The essence associated with folk biology allows people to make inferences (e.g., during the act of hunting) about the behavior of members of familiar species, as well as about the likely behavior of less familiar but related species (Atran, 1998). Attributions about causality in the physical world have also been studied. Children and adults have, as an example, natural, naive conceptions about motion and other physical phenomena (Clement, 1992).

Cognitive Development and Modular Plasticity

Cognitive development, as contrasted with academic development (see below), is the experience-driven adaptation of biologically primary modular competencies to the nuances of the local social, biological, and physical ecologies (Geary & Bjorklund, 2000). As noted, modular systems should be plastic or open to experiential modification if sensitivity to variation within these domains is of potential survival or reproductive significance. For many folk domains (e.g., language), plasticity appears to be especially evident during the developmental period, although the benefits of plasticity are balanced by potential risk of dying before having the opportunity to reproduce. Given this potential cost, the benefits associated with a long developmental period and the corresponding increase in plasticity must be substantial.

The mechanisms involved in the experience-driven adaptation of plastic modular systems to local conditions are not well understood. At a macrolevel, and following the lead of Gelman (1990), Geary and Huffman (2002) proposed that prenatal brain organization results in an exoskeleton that comprises neural and perceptual modules that guide attention to and processing of stable forms of information (e.g., the general shape of the human face) in the folk domains shown in Figure 4.2. The result is biases in early postnatal attentional, affective, and information-processing capacities, as well as biases in self-initiated behavioral engagement of the environment (Bjorklund & Pellegrini, 2002; Scarr, 1992; Scarr & McCartney, 1983). The latter generate evolutionarily expectant experiences, that is, experiences that provide the environmental feedback needed to adjust modular architecture to variation in information patterns in these domains (Greenough, Black, & Wallace, 1987; MacDonald, 1992). These behavioral biases are expressed as common juvenile activities, such as social play and exploration of the ecology. These experience-expectant processes result in the modification of plastic features of the exoskeleton such that the individual is able to identify and respond to variation (e.g., discriminate one individual from another) within these domains and to begin to create the forms of category described above, such as in-groups/out-groups or flora/fauna.

Folk Psychology

As an illustration of plasticity in a folk domain, consider that the strong bias of human infants to attend to human faces, movement patterns, and speech reflects, in theory, the initial and inherent organizational and motivational structure of the associated folk-psychological modules (Freedman, 1974). These biases reflect the evolutionary significance of social relationships (Baumeister & Leary, 1995) and, in effect, recreate the microconditions (e.g., parent-child interactions) associated with the evolution of the corresponding modules (Caporael, 1997). Attention to and processing of this information provides exposure to the within-category variation needed to adapt the architecture of these modules to variation in parental faces, behavior, and so forth (Gelman & Williams, 1998). It allows your infant to discriminate your voice from the voice of other potential parents with only minimal exposure to your voice. Indeed, when human fetuses (gestation age of about 38 weeks) are exposed in utero to human voices, their heart rate patterns suggest they are sensitive to and learn the voice patterns of their mothers and discriminate her voice from those of other women (Kisilevsky et al., 2003).

Developmental experiences may also facilitate later category formation. Boys' group level competition (e.g., team sports) provides one example of the early formation of competition-based in-groups and out-groups and the coordination of social activities that may provide the practice for primitive group level warfare in adulthood (Geary, 1998; Geary, Byrd-Craven, Hoard, Vigil, & Numtee, 2003). These natural games may provide the practice needed for the skilled formation and maintenance of social coalitions in adulthood and result in the accumulation of memories for associated activities and social strategies. In other words, and in keeping with the comparative analyses of Pellis and colleagues (e.g., Pellis & Iwaniuk, 2000), these games may be more strongly related to learning the skills of other boys and acquiring the social competencies for coordinated group level activities, as contrasted with learning specific fighting behaviors, such as hitting. My assumption is that these activities and the accompanying effects on brain and cognition are related to the group level social selection pressures noted above and provide experience with the dynamic forming in-groups and out-groups.

Folk Biology and Folk Physics

The complexity of hunting and foraging activities varies with the ecology in which the group lives, a situation that should select for plasticity in the associated brain, cognitive, and behavioral systems. Indeed, experiences during development appear to result in the fleshing out of many of these folk systems. Children's implicit folk-biological knowledge and inherent interest in living things result, in theory, in the motivation to engage in experiences that automatically create taxonomies of local flora and fauna and in the accrual of an extensive knowledge base of these species. In traditional societies, these experiences include assisting with foraging and play hunting (e.g., Blurton Jones, Hawkes, & O'Connell, 1997). Anthropological research indicates that it often takes many years of engaging in these forms of play and early work to learn the skills (e.g., how to shoot a bow and arrow) and knowledge needed for successful hunting and foraging (Hill & Hurtado, 1996), although this is not the case with all hunting and foraging activities (Bliege Bird & Bird, 2002; Blurton Jones & Marlowe, 2002).

An example associated with folk physics is provided by the ability to mentally form maplike representations of the large-scale environment, which occurs more or less automatically as animals explore this environment (Gallistel, 1990). For humans, the initial ability to form these representations emerges by 3 years of age (DeLoache, Kolstad, & Anderson, 1991), improves gradually through adolescence, and often requires extensive exploration and exposure to the local environment to perfect (Matthews, 1992). The research of Matthews clearly shows that children automatically attend to geometric features of the large-scale environment and landmarks within this environment and are able to generate a cognitive representation of landmarks and their geometric relations at a later time. Children's skill at generating these representations increases with repeated explorations of the physical environment (see also Landau, Gleitman, Spelke, 1981; Mandler, 1992). Thus, learning about the physical world is a complex endeavor for humans and requires an extended developmental period, in comparison with the more rapid learning that occurs in species that occupy a more narrow range of physical ecologies (Gallistel, 2000). A recent study by Chen and Siegler (2000) suggests that similar processes occur for tool use. Here, it was demonstrated that 18-month-olds have an implicit understanding of how to use simple tools (e.g., a hooked stick to retrieve a desired toy) and with experience learn to use these tools in increasingly effective ways.

Summary

A long developmental period is an evolved feature of human life history and appears to function to enable the fleshing out of folk modules and knowledge. The necessity of a long developmental period results from the complexity and variability of social relationships and social competition (Alexander, 1989; Geary, 2002b; Geary & Flinn, 2001) and the wide range of biological and physical-ecological (e.g., mountainous versus desert) niches occupied by humans (Kaplan, Hill, Lancaster, & Hurtado, 2000). In each domain, there is evidence for both inherent constraints that guide attention to, and the early processing of, invariant information patterns, such as human biological motion or human voice patterns (Freedman, 1974; Kuhl, 1994) and experience-based modifications of the associated systems to accommodate variation, such as recognition of individual voices, within broader constraints (Pascalis, de Haan, & Nelson, 2002). From this perspective, cognitive development is an integral component of human life history; is centered on cognitive abilities, such as language, that define the modules shown in Figure 4.2; and functions to adapt these inherent modular systems to nuances of the local ecologies.

Evolution of General Intelligence

The above section provided an outline of how early experiences interact with inherent modular constraints to guide children's cognitive development in the domains of folk psychology, folk biology, and folk physics. However, these mechanisms do not provide a sufficient explanation for the development of nonevolved, or biologically secondary, cognitive competencies, such as reading and writing. The acquisition of these and other nonevolved cognitive competencies must involve at least one other set of mechanisms that operate on modular systems. I recently proposed that these mechanisms are captured by psychometric and cognitive research on general intelligence (Geary, 2004). The details are beyond the scope of this chapter, but an important component is shown in the right-hand section of Figure 4.1, specifically, the ability to explicitly represent information in working memory (defined below) and to systematically manipulate this information so as to engage in controlled problem solving. The brain and cognitive mechanisms that enable the explicit representation of information in working memory appear to underlie the ability to acquire biologically secondary competencies, as I elaborate in the "Academic Learning" section.

Figure 4.1 also shows that the mechanisms that enable controlled problem solving are related to conditions that covaried with survival or reproductive prospects during the species' evolutionary history but have components that are variable across generations and within lifetimes. These conditions are produced by social dynamics and some dynamics associated with ecological demands, such as hunting. In other words, aspects of the social and ecological selection pressures that resulted in the evolution of the modular systems represented in Figure 4.2 also resulted in conditions that favored the evolution of less modularized, domain-general brain   d cognitive systems. I explain the nuances of this model and supporti   evidence elsewhere (Geary, 2004). The gist is that the evolutionary funct   1 of general intelligence, the component cognitive abilities (e.g., working memory), and supporting brain regions is to cope with the unpredictability that results from fluctuating social and ecological conditions.

More precisely, these systems enable the individual to generate a self-centered mental model of the perfect world, a world in which other people behave in ways consistent with one's best interest, and biological (e.g., food) and physical (e.g., land) resources are under one's control. General intelligence, working memory, and mechanisms that represent the essential part of the ability to engage in explicit problem solving are then used to devise and simulate behavioral strategies that can be used to reduce the difference between one's current circumstances and the simulated perfect world. General intelligence is related to academic learning and learning in other evolutionarily novel contexts (e.g., work).

As noted, research on general intelligence has led to the discovery of several components of an evolved brain and cognitive system that enables the simulation of behavioral strategies to cope with social and ecological novelty (Geary, 2004). Because biologically secondary abilities are, by definition, novel from an evolutionary perspective, the cognitive systems that compose general intelligence should be engaged when these abilities are constructed from inherent modular domains. In the following sections, I provide a review of empirical research on general intelligence and then outline the evolution of the supporting cognitive and brain systems.

Psychometric Research

Research in this tradition examines individual differences in performance on various forms of paper-and-pencil abilities measures and began in earnest with Spearman's (1904) classic study. Here, groups of elementary and high school students as well as adults were administered a series of sensory and perceptual tasks (e.g., the ability to discriminate one musical pitch from another) and were rated by teachers and peers on their in-school intelligence and out-of-school common sense. Scores on standard exams in classics, French, English, and mathematics were also available for the high school students. Correlational analyses revealed that above-average performance on one task was associated with above-average performance on all other tasks, on exam scores, and for ratings of intelligence and common sense. On the basis of these findings, Spearman (1904) concluded "that all branches of intellectual activity have in common one fundamental function (or group of functions)" (p. 285). Spearman termed the fundamental function or group of functions "general intelligence," or "*g.*"

In a series of important empirical and theoretical works, Cattell and Horn (Cattell, 1963; Horn, 1968; Horn & Cattell, 1966) later argued that the single general ability proposed by Spearman should be subdivided into two equally important but distinct abilities. The first ability is called *crystallized intelligence* (gC) and is manifested as the result of experience, schooling, and acculturation and is referenced by overlearned skills and knowledge, such as vocabulary. The second ability is called *fluid intelligence* (gF), which represents a biologically based ability to acquire skills and knowledge.

Cognitive Research

Speed of Processing. With the development of computer technologies and accompanying conceptual advances, experimental psychologists can study and identify the elementary processes that underlie performance on paper-and-pencil tests, including measures of *g.* As an example of an elementary cognitive process, consider a simple task developed by Posner and his colleagues (Posner, Boies, Eichelman, & Taylor, 1969). Here, upper- and lowercase combinations of various letters, such as "AA," "Ab," "Aa," and "CE," are presented one at a time on a computer monitor. The participants indicate (by depressing a response key) whether the letters are the same or different, with the time between the presentation of the letter pair and participants' response recorded by the computer. With the use of a bit of statistics and arithmetic, the difference in speed of responding to pairs that are physically identical compared with pairs that are identical in name (e.g., "AA" versus "Aa") provides an index of the speed of accessing the name code from long-term memory. College students can access these names codes in about 80-thousandths of a second (i.e., 80 ms).

The initial foci of these studies was on identifying the elementary processes common to all people, but attention soon turned to the study of individual differences in these processes as they related to *g* (Hunt, 1978). Although many details remain to be resolved, several important patterns have emerged from this literature. First, faster speed of cognitive processing is related to higher scores on measures of *g* (e.g., Jensen, 1982; Jensen & Munro, 1979), but the strength of the relation is moderate (*rs* of about −0.3 to −0.4). Second, variability in speed of processing is also related to scores on measures of *g* (*rs* of about −0.4; Jensen, 1992). The variability measure provides an assessment of the consistency in speed of executing the same process multiple times, such as speed of retrieving the name code for "A" across multiple trials. Individuals who are consistently fast in executing these processes have the highest scores on measures of g (Deary, 2000; Jensen, 1998; Neubauer, 1997). Third, the speed with which individuals can identify very briefly (e.g., 50 ms) presented information (e.g., whether ">" is pointed left or right) is moderately correlated with g (Deary & Stough, 1996).

These studies suggest that intelligence is related to the speed and accuracy with which social or ecological information is identified and then processed by the associated brain and cognitive systems. The processing of this information is often implicit and results in fast and automatic responses to the forms of information (e.g., a facial expression) described in the folk sections above. When this happens, the information is active in short-term memory, but the individual may not be consciously aware of it. When the information is not readily processed by modular systems, the result is an automatic shift in attention to this information (Botvinick, Braver, Barch, Carter, & Cohen, 2001). When attention is focused on this information, the result is an explicit representation of the information in working memory.

Working Memory. Working memory is important for coping with conditions that cannot be handled by means of the automatic cognitive systems and heuristics that compose folk modules or by means of knowledge acquired during the life span, that is, crystallized intelligence, or gC. Basically, working memory is the information that is currently available to conscious awareness and thus available for explicit, controlled problem solving. The attentional system that controls the manipulation of information during problem solving is called the *central executive,* and the modalities in which the information is represented are typically auditory (e.g., language), visual, or spatial (Baddeley, 1986). The latter are often called *slave systems.* The mechanisms that result in an individual becoming consciously aware of information represented in a slave system appear to involve an attention-driven amplification of these short-term memory representations and synchronization of activity in the underlying brain regions with activity in the brain regions that compose the central executive (Damasio, 1989; Miller & Cohen, 2001; Posner, 1994). The latter brain regions include the dorsolateral prefrontal cortex and the anterior cingulate (Kane & Engle, 2002). At a cognitive level, individual differences in working-memory capacity are related to individual differences in the ability to focus attention and prevent irrelevant information from diverting attention from the task at hand (Engle, 2002; Kane & Engle, 2002) and individual differences in speed of processing (Fry & Hale, 1996).

Research on the relation between performance on working-memory tasks and performance on measures of g have focused on fluid intelligence, or gF (Cattell, 1963; Horn, 1968). As Cattell (1963) stated: "Fluid general ability . . . shows more in tests requiring adaptation to new situations, where crystallized skills are of no particular advantage" (p. 3). In theory then, performance on measures of gF should be strongly associated with individual differences in working memory, and this is indeed the case, whether the measure of gF is an IQ test (Carpenter, Just, & Shell, 1990; Conway, Cowan, Bunting, Therriault, & Minkoff, 2002; Engle, Tuholski, Laughlin, & Conway, 1999) or scores on psychometric tests of complex reasoning that are highly correlated with IQ scores (Kyllonen & Christal, 1990; Mackintosh & Bennett, 2003). The strength of the relation between performance on working-memory tasks and scores on measures of reasoning and gF range from moderate (rs about 0.5; Mackintosh & Bennett, 2003) to very high (rs > 0.8; Conway et al., 2002; Kyllonen & Christal, 1990). On the basis of these patterns, Horn (1968) and other scientists (Carpenter et al., 1990; Stanovich, 1999) have argued that measures of strategic problem solving and abstract reasoning define gF, and the primary cognitive system underlying problem solving, reasoning, and thus gF is working memory.

Summary. Cognitive research has revealed that (a) intelligent individuals identify and apprehend bits of social and ecological information more easily and quickly than do other people and (b) their perceptual systems process this information such that it is activated in short-term memory more quickly and with greater accuracy than it is for other people. Once active in short-term memory, the information is made available for conscious, explicit representation and manipulation in working memory, but this happens only for that subset of information that becomes the focus of attention. Once attention is focused, highly intelligent people are able to represent more information in working memory than are other people and have an enhanced ability to consciously manipulate this information. The manipulation, in turn, is guided and constrained by reasoning and inference-making mechanisms (see Stanovich, 1999). The mechanisms that enable faster and more accurate processing and an attention-driven ability to represent and manipulate information in working memory also contribute to the ease of learning biologically secondary knowledge and procedures, as I discuss in the "Academic Learning" section.

Neuroscience Research

Brain Size. Research on the relation between brain volume, as measured by neuroimaging techniques, and performance on measures of g has revealed a consistent but modest relation (r of about 0.4); the bigger the better

(Deary, 2000; Flashman, Andreasen, Flaum, & Swayze, 1998; Rushton & Ankney, 1996; Vernon, Wickett, Bazana, & Stelmack, 2000). In one of the most comprehensive of these studies, Wickett, Vernon, and Lee (2000) examined the relations between total brain volume and performance on measures of gF, gC, short-term memory, and various speed of processing measures. Larger brain volumes were associated with higher gF ($r = 0.49$), larger short-term memory capacity ($r = 0.45$), and faster speed of processing (rs about -0.4) but were unrelated to gC ($r = 0.06$). Raz et al. (1993) examined the relation between performance on measures of gF and gC and total brain volume, and volume of the dorsolateral prefrontal cortex, the somatosensory cortex, portions of the parietal cortex, and the hippocampus. Higher gF scores were associated with larger total brain volume ($r = .43$), a larger dorsolateral prefrontal cortex ($r = .51$), and more white matter (i.e., neuronal axons) in the prefrontal cortex ($r = .41$) but were unrelated to size of the other brain regions. Performance on the gC measure, in contrast, was not related to size of any of these brain regions or to total brain volume.

Regional Activation. A number of studies have examined the brain regions that become activated or deactivated while individuals solve items on measures of gF (Duncan et al., 2000; Gray, Chabris, & Braver, 2003; Prabhakaran, Smith, Desmond, Glover, & Gabrieli, 1997). These are early and pioneering studies, and thus the most appropriate interpretation of their findings is not entirely certain (Deary, 2000). Nonetheless, most of the studies reveal a pattern of activation and deactivation in a variety of brain regions, much of which is likely due to task-specific content of the reasoning measures (e.g., verbal vs. visual information). Recent studies using the imaging methods most sensitive to regional change in activation/deactivation suggest fluid intelligence may be supported in part by the same system of brain regions that supports working memory and attentional control. As noted, these regions include the dorsolateral prefrontal cortex and the anterior cingulate (Duncan et al., 2000).

Integration

Brain-imaging studies and especially those that employ the most sensitive measures of regional brain activity support the hypothesis that the same brain systems that underlie working memory and explicit controlled problem solving are engaged when people solve items on measures of gF (Duncan et al., 2000; Gray et al., 2003; Kane & Engle, 2002). High scores on measures of gF are associated with activation of the dorsolateral prefrontal cortex and several brain regions associated with attentional control, including the anterior cingulate and regions of the parietal cortex. These same regions also appear to support the ability to inhibit irrelevant information from intruding into working memory and conscious awareness (Esposito, Kirkby, van Horn, Ellmore, & Berman, 1999).

An attention-driven synchronization of the activity of dorsolateral prefrontal cortex and the brain regions that support the working-memory representations of external information or internal mental simulations would be facilitated by faster speed of processing and rich interconnections among these brain regions. The latter is associated with larger brain size and especially a greater volume of white matter (i.e., axons). Speed of processing may be important for the synchronization process: Synchronization appears to occur through neural connections that communicate back and forth between different brain regions, creating feedback cycles. Faster speed of processing would enable more accurate adjustments in synchronization per feedback cycle. With repeated synchronized activity, the result appears to be the formation of a neural network that automatically links the processing of these information patterns (Sporns, Tononi, & Edelman, 2000).

Mental Models and Fluid Intelligence

My proposal is that research on general fluid intelligence has identified many of the core features that support the use of mental simulations. These function to anticipate and generate behavioral responses to social and ecological conditions that are toward the variant end of the continuum in Figure 4.1. The core of a mental model is the generation of a "perfect world." In the perfect world, the individual is in control of the social, biological, and physical resources that have tended to covary with survival and reproductive prospects during human evolutionary history: The behavior of other people and the flow of resources align with the individual's best interests. The real world operates differently, however. The goal is to generate strategies that will reduce the difference between conditions in the real world and those simulated in the perfect world, that is, to generate ways to gain better control of important relationships and resources.

The problem-solving processes, inference making, and reasoning employed to devise the corresponding social and behavioral strategies are dependent on working memory, attentional control, and the supporting brain systems, along with a sense of self. In this view, the mechanisms that support an explicit, conscious awareness of information represented in working memory evolved as a result of the same social and ecological pressures that drove the evolution of the ability to generate and use these mental models, and gF. Self-awareness is important to the extent that one must cope with the maneuvering of other people; that is, the perfect world of most people will involve manipulating others to behave in ways that is counter to their best interests. When many people with competing interests are able to anticipate and mentally simulate these moves and countermoves, the complexity of social dynamics explodes and the predictability of the dynamics decreases accordingly (Alexander, 1989; Humphrey, 1976).

The ability to use these simulations is dependent on working memory, attentional control, and the underlying brain systems that I noted above. These brain and cognitive systems function to deal with novelty in social and ecological conditions, and thus they will not be constrained to process a particular form of information as are the modular systems shown in Figure 4.2. These domain-general systems should therefore be engaged when individuals must cope with conditions and information that cannot be automatically and implicitly processed by modular systems. In other words, 100 years of empirical research on g, and especially gF, has isolated those features of self-centered mental models that are not strongly influenced by content and that enable explicit representations of information in working memory and an attentional-dependent ability to manipulate this information in the service of strategic problem solving.

Cattell's (1963) and Horn's (1968) definition of fluid intelligence and subsequent research on the underlying cognitive and brain systems are consistent with this view: There is considerable overlap in the systems that support self-centered mental models and those that support fluid abilities (e.g., Duncan et al., 2000). One important discrepancy involves self-awareness, which is a core feature of my proposal but not an aspect of fluid intelligence (Geary, 2004). The reason for the discrepancy lies in the initial development and goal of intelligence tests, specifically to predict academic performance (Binet & Simon, 1916). Because the initial goal was to predict learning in an evolutionarily novel context (i.e., school), the content of the items that compose intelligence tests was largely asocial.

Modularity and Crystallized Intelligence

In the most comprehensive review of the psychometric literature ever conducted, Carroll (1993) concluded that most of the psychometric tests that index gC "involve language either directly or indirectly" (p. 599). Included among these are tests of vocabulary, listening comprehension, word fluency, reading, and spelling. The two latter skills are taught in school, as are some of the other competencies that index gC, such as complex arithmetic, other school-taught quantitative skills, and mechanical abilities. General cultural knowledge is also an indicator of gC, as are some measures of spatial and visual abilities. In total, these tests appear to tap many of the modular domains shown in Figure 4.2, in particular, language and spatial representation.

They do not appear to tap all of these domains, but this is potentially because not all of the modular competencies have been assessed. When other modular competencies are measured and correlated with intelligence, there is a relation. Legree (1995) found that scores on tests of knowledge of social conventions and social judgments are positively correlated with scores on measures of g. In other words, I am suggesting that the inherent knowledge represented in the modular systems defines one class of crystallized intelligence. The other class is represented by the knowledge (e.g., facts, concepts, procedures) learned during the individual's lifetime through formal or informal instruction, or just incidentally, as proposed by Cattell (1963). In the next section, I discuss how this evolutionarily novel knowledge might be constructed through the interaction of gF, plasticity in modular systems, and experience.

Academic Learning

If the evolution of fluid intelligence was driven by behavioral and social variability and unpredictability, then the mechanisms that compose fluid intelligence are designed to identify, anticipate, represent, and reason about evolutionarily novel information patterns. Novelty is a matter of degree, of course, because the variability involves social dynamics and perhaps dynamics associated with ecological conditions (e.g., hunting). Still, the mechanisms are not constrained to process highly specific forms of information (e.g., contour of a human face), as are modular systems. The implication is that the evolution of fluid intelligence, though likely driven by social competition, opened the door to the ability to develop evolutionarily novel, biologically secondary abilities during the life span (Geary, 1995; Rozin, 1976). As I describe in the sections that follow, empirical research on the relation between g and learning in evolutionarily novel contexts, such as school and work, supports this hypothesis. In the third section, I focus on brain-imaging studies of the learning process as these relate to the brain systems that support fluid intelligence and the mechanisms that appear to support the construction of secondary competencies.

School and Work

In modern society, school and work represent important but evolutionarily novel contexts. Success in these contexts is important because it influences one's ability to gain access to and control of the forms of resource (e.g., money) that are important for success in modern society. If the evolved function of general intelligence, and especially gF, is to enable the individual to cope with evolutionarily novel conditions, then performance on measures of g, such as IQ tests, should be predictive of outcomes in school and at work.

School. Walberg (1984) reviewed 3,000 studies of the relation between performance on academic achievement tests and a variety of student attributes (e.g., intelligence), home environment (e.g., television viewing), and classroom variables. By far, the best individual predictor of achievement was IQ ($r = 0.7$). Jensen (1998), Lubinski (2000), and Matarazzo (1972) also reviewed research on the relation between IQ scores and performance on academic achievement tests and reached the same conclusion. They estimated the correlation between general intelligence and academic achievement ranges between 0.6 and 0.8, indicating that between 36% and 64% of the individual differences in performance on academic achievement tests can be explained by individual differences in general intelligence. Moreover, Jensen estimated that individual differences in general intelligence explain about 36% of the individual differences in years of education completed.

Work. It is clear that individuals with higher IQ scores populate higher-status occupations in the modern work force (Gottfredson, 1997; Jensen, 1998; Nyborg & Jensen, 2001; Reynolds, Chastain, Kaufman, & McLean, 1987; Scullin, Peters, Williams, & Ceci, 2000). In an analysis of the nationally (U.S.) representative standardization sample for the Wechsler Adult Intelligence Scale-Revised (Wechsler, 1981), Reynolds et al. found that for 20- to 54-year-olds, the average IQ score of professional and technical workers was at about the 75th percentile, whereas that of unskilled workers was below the 25th percentile. Evidence for a causal relationship between g and occupational status comes from several longitudinal studies. Scullin et al. (2000) found that performance on a measure of g administered in high school was positively correlated (rs about 0.5) with occupational prestige 15 years later.

Fluid intelligence is the best single predictor of occupational performance across the broad swath of jobs (e.g., sales, scientific publications) available in modern economies (Gottfredson, 1997; Hunter & Hunter, 1984; Schmidt & Hunter, 1998). Predictive validity represents the economic value of using the test as a selection criterion, that is, increases in job-related productivity and reductions in training and retraining costs that accrue as a result of using the test to make employment decisions. For some jobs (e.g., mechanic, electrician), work samples have slightly higher predictive validities than IQ tests, but IQ is the best predictor of performance for most jobs and is the best predictor of the ability to learn on the job, including jobs in which work samples are a valid selection criterion. Across jobs, the validity coefficient for IQ tests is .51, and .56 for success in job training programs. Hunter and Hunter (1984) estimated that the widespread use of IQ tests in employment decisions would result in nearly $16 billion per year in economic benefits in the United States.

Learning and Cognition

Theory and Research. The relation between *g*, academic achievement, and job-related outcomes suggests that individuals who are high in fluid intelligence learn evolutionarily novel information more easily than do other individuals. These correlations, however, do not inform us as to how fluid intelligence actually affects the learning process. Ackerman has been at the forefront of efforts to understand this relation (Ackerman, 1988) and has proposed that the process of learning can be divided into three stages: cognitive, perceptual speed, and psychomotor (see also Anderson, 1982). The gist is that different abilities are related to individual differences in academic and job-related performance at different points in the learning process.

For school-based and job-related learning, the cognitive stage refers to the relation between fluid intelligence and initial task performance. The prediction is that novel and complex tasks will require an attention-driven, explicit representation of task goals and information patterns in working memory. During this phase, the task goals and the sequence of steps needed to perform the task are learned and memorized. With enough practice, the eventual result is the automatic, implicit processing of task features and automatic behavioral responses to these features. These phases of learning represent the shift from explicit representations and controlled problem solving to automatic, implicit, and sometimes heuristic-based processing of and responding to the task, as illustrated by the darkened arrow in the center of Figure 4.1. In this view, one difference between evolved, biologically primary modular competencies and biologically secondary competencies is the need for Ackerman's cognitive phase of learning. The inherent constraints associated with evolved competencies can be understood as putting them at Ackerman's second or third phase of learning, without the need for the first phase.

Ackerman and his colleagues have extensively tested the hypothesis that individual differences in gF and task-relevant crystallized knowledge will predict individual differences in the early phases of learning, whereas individual differences on measures of speed of perceptual and motor processes will predict individual differences after extensive task practice (Ackerman, 1988). A work-related example is provided by tasks that simulate the demands of an air traffic controller, which is clearly an evolutionarily novel demand. One task involves learning the rules that govern decision making, such as whether to keep a plane in a holding pattern or allow it to land, based on air traffic, wind, and so forth. Another task involves the especially complex demands of tracking and making decisions based on information patterns (e.g., multiple plane icons) represented on dynamic radar screens (Ackerman & Cianciolo, 2000, 2002). Performance on these tasks is indexed by the number of flights that are properly routed (e.g., landed or allowed to fly over the airport) and speed of making these decisions. Ease of initial rule learning is moderately correlated with fluid intelligence (rs of about 0.4 to 0.5) and remains so even after 6 hours of practice (r about 0.3). Performance on the radar task is moderately to highly correlated with fluid intelligence (rs from 0.4 to 0.8) and remains so throughout training. A causal relation between performance and gF was experimentally demonstrated by manipulating the number of planes the individual needed to simultaneously monitor. As the number of planes increased, the importance of fluid intelligence increased.

Mechanisms. As mentioned earlier, individual differences in fluid intelligence are determined by individual differences in attentional control, speed of processing, working-memory resources, and the ability to draw inferences from the information patterns represented in working memory (Embretson, 1995; Fry & Hale, 2000; Kane & Engle, 2002). It then follows that the initial learning of evolutionarily novel academic and job-related competencies, as illustrated by Ackerman's (1988) research, is driven by the ability to control attention, simultaneously represent multiple pieces of information in working memory, and logically piece this information together. In many cases, the drawing of inferences about information represented in working memory will be facilitated if the information is made available to conscious awareness, although pattern learning can occur without conscious awareness (Stadler & Frensch, 1997). A more fundamental issue concerns how these working-memory resources, speed of processing, attentional processes, and activities of the supporting brain systems create competencies that do not have an evolutionary history (Rozin, 1976). We are only beginning to explore these issues, and thus I can only offer speculation at this time.

As I noted earlier, the dorsolateral prefrontal regions, the anterior cingulate, and attentional regions of the parietal cortex are particularly important for explicitly representing goals and information to be manipulated in working memory (Duncan & Owen, 2000; Kane & Engle, 2002; Miller & Cohen, 2001). These ends appear to be achieved through an attention-driven amplification of neural activity in the posterior and subcortical pathways that process the information needed for goal achievement (Dehaene & Naccache, 2001; Posner, 1994). To illustrate how the process might work in an evolutionarily novel context, consider how children initially learn to read. One of the underlying component skills is phonemic decoding (Bradley & Bryant, 1983). Decoding requires an explicit awareness of and representation in working memory of a basic language sound (e.g., "ba," "da," "ka") and the association of this sound, as well as blends of sounds, with corresponding visual patterns, specifically letters (e.g., "b," "d," "k") and letter combinations. Attentional focus on the relation between the sound and the letter should, in theory, result in the amplification of the activity of the brain regions that process both forms of information and the simultaneous representation of both forms of information in working memory. The process should result in the synchronization of this brain activity with activity in the dorsolateral prefrontal cortex and, with sufficient practice, the formation of a learned association between the sound and letter.

With extended practice, the association becomes represented in long-term memory and thus becomes implicit knowledge, representing Ackerman's (1988) final stages of learning. When this is achieved, the association between the sound and letter, or letter combination and word-sound, is automatically triggered when the letter string is processed during the act of reading and thus no longer engages the prefrontal cortex, working memory, or related cognitive and brain systems, and no longer requires gF. We now have an evolutionarily novel cognitive competency (i.e., reading), the linking of a language sound with a visual pattern such that the visual pattern automatically triggers the word-sound and associated concept.

The learning of phonetic decoding is a simple task but illustrates how the processes may work for the learning of more complex skills. The primary difference across task complexity would involve the length of the first phase of learning, to use Ackerman's (1988) model. More precisely, complexity will be related to the extent to which the task is evolutionarily novel, the amount of information that must be identified and processed to deal with task demands, and the extent to which this information changes across time. As each of these features increases in complexity, there is an accompanying increase in the need for sustained attention, working memory, and the ability to reason and make inferences, that is, an increased reliance on gF.

Learning and Brain Mechanisms

In a review of brain-imaging studies of working memory, problem solving, and learning, Duncan and Owen (2000) concluded that these cognitive functions are dependent on the dorsolateral prefrontal cortex and the anterior cingulate. Other areas are also active when people are engaged in these tasks, and there are, of course, different patterns of brain activity associated with learning one type of skill or another (e.g., McCandliss, Posner, & Givón, 1997). Regardless, the brain regions identified by Duncan and Owen are consistently engaged when people are learning novel information and or coping with complex tasks that require working-memory resources and attentional control (see also Kane & Engle, 2002). Additional research is needed, but the evidence suggests the dorsolateral prefrontal cortex and anterior cingulate are engaged only during Ackerman's (1988) first phase of learning (Raichle et al., 1994), in keeping with the proposed mechanism described in the above section. Thereafter, brain activation is associated with the particular type of stimulus (e.g., visual vs. auditory) and the specifics of task demands.

Only a few studies have combined learning and brain imaging with assessments of general intelligence (e.g., Gevins & Smith, 2000; Haier, Siegel, Tang, Abel, & Buchsbaum, 1992). Haier et al. assessed the brain's use of glucose during the learning of a novel spatial problem-solving task. Individuals with high IQ scores learned the task more quickly than their less intelligent peers and showed more rapid declines in glucose metabolism across learning trials. Using electrophysiological methods, Gevins and Smith found the dorsolateral prefrontal cortex was initially engaged during the learning of a complex task that required working memory and attentional control, but engagement of this region declined as individuals learned the task. The decline was especially pronounced for intelligent individuals, who, in turn, appeared to shift the processing of task requirements to more posterior regions of the brain. The results of these studies are consistent with studies of the relation between gF and ease of learning (Ackerman, 1988); specifically, through attentional control and inhibition, intelligent individuals use only those cognitive and brain systems needed to cope with the task at hand.

At this point, it appears that one function of the dorsolateral prefrontal cortex, the anterior cingulate, and the posterior attentional system is to ensure the synchronized activity of other brain regions, such that anatomical and functional links are formed among these regions. When couched in terms of gF, it appears that the associated ability to focus attentional resources and inhibit the activation of task-irrelevant information (Kane & Engle, 2002) results in the ability to synchronize only those brain regions needed for secondary learning. The result would be lower glucose use and faster learning for individuals high in gF, because fewer unneeded brain regions are activated and thus fewer regions are anatomically linked. Functionally, the result would be a sharper representation and better understanding of the new competency, because irrelevant information and concepts would not be linked to this competency. Once formed, an evolutionarily novel, biologically secondary cognitive competency emerges.

Folk Systems

Plasticity. Fluid intelligence is involved during the initial phase of learning biologically secondary abilities, but the fully developed competencies reside in a network of cognitive and brain systems that differ from those that support gF (Gevins & Smith, 2000; Raichle et al., 1994). This network of systems represents the class of crystallized intelligence (Cattell, 1963; Horn & Cattell, 1966) or at least that class of knowledge acquired during the individual's lifetime. Such learning is possible to the extent that inherent modular systems evince some degree of plasticity and to the extent that independent modular systems can be interconnected to form unique neural networks and functional competencies (Garlick, 2002; Sporns et al., 2000).

As I explain elsewhere (Geary, 2004; Geary & Huffman, 2002), there is evidence for neural plasticity in most of the brain regions that are likely to support inherent, modular systems. The presumed evolutionary function of plasticity is to enable these systems to be fine-tuned to the nuances of the ecologies in which the individual is situated, although the fine-tuning appears to occur within inherent constraints on the forms of information the brain and cognitive systems can process (e.g., visual contours or prototypical shape of a human face). Modular plasticity also indicates that these systems can be modified to process evolutionarily novel information, if this novel information is similar to the forms of information the system evolved to process (Sperber, 1994). I give an example below. My point for now is that variability in social and ecological dynamics during human evolution not only provides an explanation for the evolution of gF but would also result in a selective advantage for plasticity within modular systems. Modular plasticity, in turn, enables the formation of crystallized knowledge during the life span.

Folk Psychology, Reading, and Writing. In the "Learning and Cognition" section, I described how the initial phase of learning how to read might occur. I now consider how reading and writing might be more broadly related to inherent, folk-psychological modules (see also Geary, 2002a). Because the function of written and therefore read material is to communicate with other people, it follows that writing and reading emerged from and currently are based on evolved social communication systems, that is, folk psychology. Writing must have emerged (culturally) from the motivational disposition to communicate with and influence the behavior of other people (e.g., morals in the Bible) and must engage the same folk-psychological systems, especially language and theory of mind. If this is correct, then writing and reading should engage many of the same brain and cognitive systems that support folk psychology. The research base on reading is larger than that on writing, and thus I focus on the former.

The research to date is not definitive, but it is consistent with the hypothesis that the acquisition of reading-related abilities (e.g., word decoding) involves the instruction-driven adaptation of primary language and language-related systems, among others (e.g., visual scanning; Rozin, 1976). Wagner, Torgesen, and Rashotte (1994) reported that individual differences in the fidelity of kindergarten children's phonological processing systems, which are basic features of the language domain, are strongly predictive of the ease with which basic reading abilities (e.g., word decoding) are acquired in first grade (Bradley & Bryant, 1983). Children who show explicit awareness of basic language sounds are more skilled than are other children at associating these sounds with the symbol system of the written language. In further support of the adaptation hypothesis, Pugh and his colleagues (1997) found that the brain and cognitive systems that are engaged during the processing of language sounds are also engaged during the act of reading.

It is also likely that reading comprehension engages theory of mind, at least for literary stories, poems, dramas and other genres that involve human relationships (Geary, 1998). This is because comprehending the gist of these stories involves making inferences about the nuances of social relationships, which, by definition, involves theory of mind. It is also of interest that some of the more popular forms of literature focus on interpersonal relationships and dynamics, typically reproductive relationships, as in the case of romance novels and the male-male competition (with unrestricted sexuality) in the case of spy novels and related genres. In these stories, a sense of self may also come into play, to the extent the individual identifies with the protagonist or antagonist in the story.

Conclusion

The function of brain and cognition is to enable the organism to attend to, process, and behaviorally respond to the forms of information and conditions that covaried with survival or reproductive prospects during the species' evolutionary history (Geary & Huffman, 2002). At a behavioral level, the organism focuses on gaining access to and control of the resources that support survival and allow one to reproduce. These resources fall into three general categories: social (e.g., mates), biological (e.g., prey species), and physical (e.g., nesting sites). The dynamics of the corresponding conditions, as in prey identification and capture, vary along a continuum ranging from information patterns that are static across generations and lifetimes to information patterns that are highly dynamic, the specifics of which can fluctuate across generations and within lifetimes. Static or invariant conditions create pressures for the evolution of modularized brain and cognitive systems (Gallistel, 2000; Tooby & Cosmides, 1995), whereas dynamic conditions create pressures for modular plasticity and the evolution of less modularized, domain-general systems (Chiappe & MacDonald, 2005; Geary, 2004). For humans, the modularized systems coalesce around the domains of folk psychology (Baron-Cohen, 1995; Brothers & Ring, 1992), folk biology (Atran, 1998), and folk physics (Pinker, 1997). There is evidence for plasticity within these modularized domains, as well as evidence for domain-general brain and cognitive systems that operate on information patterns generated by modularized brain and cognitive systems (Geary, 2004). These domain-general systems are known as general fluid intelligence (Engle, 2002; Cattell, 1963).

From this perspective, cognitive development is an inherent feature of the human life span and functions to flesh out the plastic features of modularized folk domains such that these brain and cognitive systems become sensitive to nuances in the local social, biological, and physical ecologies (Geary & Bjorklund, 2000). The experiences needed to adjust these plastic features to these ecologies are generated by children's natural social play and exploratory activities. The result of these activities, such as parent-infant social play, is the effortless and automatic adaptation of plastic systems such that the individual easily makes discriminations among different people and learns about their personality and behavioral dispositions; forms categories of local plants and animals and learns about their essence; and develops mental maps of the groups' physical territory, among many other cognitive changes. These cognitive competencies are biologically primary; that is, the human mind is inherently biased to acquire knowledge in these domains and to do so with little effort.

Academic development, in contrast, involves the experience-driven acquisition of nonevolved, or biologically secondary, cognitive competencies (Geary, 1995). The acquisition of these competencies is dependent on plasticity in modularized domains and the existence of domain-general mechanisms that can adapt these brain and cognitive systems such that they respond to evolutionarily novel information patterns. An example of the latter is formation of associations among language sounds and visual patterns to create the ability to read and write. Although not typically approached from an evolutionary perspective, research in experimental psychology has identified these domain-general systems; specifically, fluid intelligence (Kane & Engle, 2002). Fluid intelligence is composed of the attentional and working-memory systems that enable people to explicitly represent and manipulate information that has tended to be variable during human evolutionary history or is evolutionarily novel. Although it is not certain, it appears the explicit representation of information in working memory and the reasoned manipulation of this information are at the heart of the human ability to construct nonevolved cognitive competencies (Ackerman, 1988). My proposals here and elsewhere (Geary, 2004) as to how the mechanisms that may govern academic learning can be understood within a wider evolutionary perspective are speculative, but may provide a useful start.

References

Ackerman, P. L. (1988). Determinants of individual differences during skill acquisition: Cognitive abilities and information processing. *Journal of Experimental Psychology: General, 117*, 288-318.

Ackerman, P. L., & Cianciolo, A. T. (2000). Cognitive, perceptual-speed, and psychomotor determinants of individual differences in skill acquisition. *Journal of Experimental Psychology: Applied, 6*, 259-290.

Ackerman, P. L., & Cianciolo, A. T. (2002). Ability and task constraint determinants of complex task performance. *Journal of Experimental Psychology: Applied, 8*, 194-208.

Alexander, R. D. (1979). *Darwinism and human affairs*. Seattle, WA: University of Washington Press.

Alexander, R. D. (1989). Evolution of the human psyche. In P. Mellars & C. Stringer (Eds.), *The human revolution: Behavioural and biological perspectives on the origins of modern humans* (pp. 455-513). Princeton, NJ: Princeton University Press.

Anderson, J. R. (1982). Acquisition of cognitive skill. *Psychological Review, 89*, 369-406.

Atran, S. (1998). Folk biology and the anthropology of science: Cognitive universals and cultural particulars. *Behavioral and Brain Sciences, 21*, 547-609.

Baddeley, A. D. (1986). *Working memory*. Oxford, UK: Oxford University Press.

Baron-Cohen, S. (1995). *Mindblindness: An essay on autism and theory of mind*. Cambridge: MIT Press/Bradford Books.

Barton, R. A., & Dean, P. (1993). Comparative evidence indicating neural specialization for predatory behaviour in mammals. *Proceedings of the Royal Society of London B, 254*, 63-68.

Baumeister, R. F., & Leary, M. R. (1995). The need to belong: Desire for interpersonal attachment as a fundamental human motive. *Psychological Bulletin, 117,* 497-529.

Berlin, B., Breedlove, D. E., & Raven, P. H. (1973). General principles of classification and nomenclature in folk biology. *American Anthropologist, 75,* 214-242.

Binet. A., & Simon, T. (1916). *The development of intelligence in children.* Baltimore, MD: Williams & Wilkins.

Bjorklund, D. F., & Pellegrini, A. D. (2002). *The origins of human nature: Evolutionary developmental psychology.* Washington, DC: American Psychological Association.

Blake, R. (1993). Cats perceive biological motion. *Psychological Science, 4,* 54-57.

Bliege Bird, R., & Bird, D. W. (2002). Constraints on knowing or constraints on growing? Fishing and collecting among the children of Mer. *Human Nature, 13,* 239-267.

Blurton Jones, N. G., Hawkes, K., & O'Connell, J. F. (1997). Why do Hadza children forage? In N. L. Segal, G. E. Weisfeld, & C. C. Weisfeld (Eds.), *Uniting psychology and biology: Integrative perspectives on human development* (pp. 279-313). Washington, DC: American Psychological Association.

Blurton Jones, N., & Marlowe, F. W. (2002). Selection for delayed maturity: Does it take 20 years to learn to hunt and gather? *Human Nature, 13,* 199-238.

Botvinick, M. M., Braver, T. S., Barch, D. M., Carter, C. S., & Cohen, J. D. (2001). Conflict monitoring and cognitive control. *Psychological Review, 108,* 624-652.

Bradley, L., & Bryant, P. E. (1983, February 3). Categorizing sounds and learning to read—A causal connection. *Nature, 301,* 419-421.

Brothers, L., & Ring, B. (1992). A neuroethological framework for the representation of minds. *Journal of Cognitive Neuroscience, 4,* 107-118.

Brown, D. E. (1991). *Human universals.* Philadelphia, PA: Temple University Press.

Bugental, D. B. (2000). Acquisition of the algorithms of social life: A domain-based approach. *Psychological Bulletin, 126,* 187-219.

Caporael, L. R. (1997). The evolution of truly social cognition: The core configurations model. *Personality & Social Psychology Review, 1,* 276-298.

Carpenter, P. A., Just, M. A., & Shell, P. (1990). What one intelligence test measures: A theoretical account of processing in the Raven Progressive Matrices Test. *Psychological Review, 97,* 404-431.

Carroll, J. B. (1993). *Human cognitive abilities: A survey of factor-analytic studies.* New York: Cambridge University Press.

Cattell, R. B. (1963). Theory of fluid and crystallized intelligence: A critical experiment. *Journal of Educational Psychology, 54,* 1-22.

Chen, Z., & Siegler, R. S. (2000). Across the great divide: Bridging the gap between understanding toddlers' and older children's thinking. *Monographs of the Society for Research in Child Development, 65*(2, Serial No. 261).

Chiappe, D., & MacDonald, K. (2005). The evolution of domain-general mechanisms in intelligence and learning. *Journal of General Psychology,* in press.

Clement, J. (1982). Students' preconceptions in introductory mechanics. *American Journal of Physics, 50,* 66-71.

Conway, A. R. A., Cowan, N., Bunting, M. F., Therriault, D. J., & Minkoff, S. R. B. (2002). A latent variable analysis of working memory capacity, short-term memory capacity, processing speed, and general fluid intelligence. *Intelligence, 30*, 163-183.

Cosmides, L., & Tooby, J. (1994). Origins of domain specificity: The evolution of functional organization. In L. A. Hirschfeld & S. A. Gelman (Eds.), *Mapping the mind: Domain specificity in cognition and culture* (pp. 85-116). New York: Cambridge University Press.

Damasio, A. R. (1989). Time-locked multiregional retroactivation: A systems-level proposal for the neural substrates of recall and recognition. *Cognition, 33*, 25-62.

Damasio, A. (2003). *Looking for Spinoza: Joy, sorrow, and the feeling brain.* Orlando, FL: Harcourt.

Davis, J. N., & Todd, P. M. (1999). Parental investment by simple decision rules. In G. Gigerenzer, P. M. Todd, & the ABC Research Group (Eds.), *Simple heuristics that make us smart* (pp. 309-324). New York: Oxford University Press.

Deary, I. J. (2000). *Looking down on human intelligence: From psychophysics to the brain.* Oxford, UK: Oxford University Press.

Deary, I. J., & Stough, C. (1996). Intelligence and inspection time: Achievements, prospects, and problems. *American Psychologist, 51*, 599-608.

Dehaene, S., & Naccache, L. (2001). Towards a cognitive neuroscience of consciousness: Basic evidence and a workspace framework. *Cognition, 79*, 1-37.

DeLoache, J. S., Kolstad, D. V., & Anderson, K. N. (1991). Physical similarity and young children's understanding of scale models. *Child Development, 62*, 111-126.

Downing, P. E., Jiang, Y., Shuman, M., & Kanwisher, N. (2001, September 28). A cortical area selective for visual processing of the human body. *Science, 293*, 2470-2473.

Drigotas, S. M. (2002). The Michelangelo phenomenon and personal well-being. *Journal of Personality, 70*, 59-77.

Duncan, J., & Owen, A. M. (2000). Common regions of the human frontal lobe recruited by diverse cognitive demands. *Trends in Neurosciences, 23*, 475-483.

Duncan, J., Rüdiger, J. S., Kolodny, J., Bor, D., Herzog, H., Ahmed, A., Newell, F. H., & Emslie, H. (2000, July 21). A neural basis for general intelligence. *Science, 289*, 457-460.

Embretson, S. E. (1995). The role of working memory capacity and general control processes in intelligence. *Intelligence, 20*, 169-189.

Engle, R. W. (2002). Working memory capacity as executive attention. *Current Directions in Psychological Science, 11*, 19-23.

Engle, R. W., Tuholski, S. W., Laughlin, J. E., & Conway, A. R. A. (1999). Working memory, short-term memory, and general fluid intelligence: A latent-variable approach. *Journal of Experimental Psychology: General, 128*, 309-331.

Esposito, G., Kirkby, B. S., van Horn, J. D., Ellmore, T. M., & Berman, K. F. (1999). Context-dependent, neural system-specific neurophysiological concomitants of ageing: Mapping PET correlates during cognitive activation. *Brain, 122*, 963-979.

Finlay, B. L., Darlington, R. B., & Nicastro, N. (2001). Developmental structure in brain evolution. *Behavioral and Brain Sciences, 24,* 263-308.

Flashman, L. A., Andreasen, N. C., Flaum, M., & Swayze, V. W. II (1998). Intelligence and regional brain volumes in normal controls. *Intelligence, 25,* 149-160.

Freedman, D. G. (1974). *Human infancy: An evolutionary perspective.* New York: John Wiley.

Fry, A. F., & Hale, S. (1996). Processing speed, working memory, and fluid intelligence: Evidence for a developmental cascade. *Psychological Science, 7,* 237-241.

Gallistel, C. R. (1990). *The organization of learning.* Cambridge: MIT Press/ Bradford Books.

Gallistel, C. R. (2000). The replacement of general-purpose learning models with adaptively specialized learning modules. In M. S. Gazzaniga (Editor-in-chief), *The new cognitive neurosciences* (2nd ed., pp. 1179-1191). Cambridge: Bradford Books/MIT Press.

Garlick, D. (2002). Understanding the nature of the general factor of intelligence: The role of individual differences in neural plasticity as an explanatory mechanism. *Psychological Review, 109,* 116-136.

Geary, D. C. (1995). Reflections of evolution and culture in children's cognition: Implications for mathematical development and instruction. *American Psychologist, 50,* 24-37.

Geary, D. C. (1998). *Male, female: The evolution of human sex differences.* Washington, DC: American Psychological Association.

Geary, D. C. (2002a). Principles of evolutionary educational psychology. *Learning and Individual Differences, 12,* 317-345.

Geary, D. C. (2002b). Sexual selection and human life history. *Advances in Child Development and Behavior, 30,* 41-101.

Geary, D. C. (2004). *The origin of mind: Evolution of brain, cognition, and general intelligence.* Washington, DC: American Psychological Association.

Geary, D. C., & Bjorklund, D. F. (2000). Evolutionary developmental psychology. *Child Development, 71,* 57-65.

Geary, D. C., Byrd-Craven, J., Hoard, M. K., Vigil, J., & Numtee, C. (2003). Evolution and development of boys' social behavior. *Developmental Review, 23,* 444-470.

Geary, D. C., & Flinn, M. V. (2001). Evolution of human parental behavior and the human family. *Parenting: Science and Practice, 1,* 5-61.

Geary, D. C., & Huffman, K. J. (2002). Brain and cognitive evolution: Forms of modularity and functions of mind. *Psychological Bulletin, 128,* 667-698.

Gelman, R. (1990). First principles organize attention to and learning about relevant data: Number and animate-inanimate distinction as examples. *Cognitive Science, 14,* 79-106.

Gelman, R., & Williams, E. M. (1998). Enabling constraints for cognitive development and learning: Domain-specificity and epigenesis. In W. Damon (Series Ed.) & D. Kuhl & R. S. Siegler (Vol. Eds.), *Cognition, perception, and language: Vol. 2. Handbook of child psychology* (5th ed., pp. 575-630). New York: John Wiley.

Gevins, A., & Smith, M. E. (2000). Neurophysiological measures of working memory and individual differences in cognitive ability and cognitive style. *Cerebral Cortex, 10,* 829-839.

Gigerenzer, G., & Selten, R. (Eds.). (2001). *Bounded rationality: The adaptive toolbox.* Cambridge: MIT Press.

Gottfredson, L. (1997). Why g matters: The complexity of everyday life. *Intelligence, 24,* 79-132.

Gray, J. R., Chabris, C. F., & Braver, T. S. (2003). Neural mechanisms of general fluid intelligence. *Nature Neuroscience, 6,* 316-322.

Greenough, W. T., Black, J. E., & Wallace, C. S. (1987). Experience and brain development. *Child Development, 58,* 539-559.

Haier, R. J., Siegel, B., Tang, C., Abel, L., & Buchsbaum, M. S. (1992). Intelligence and changes in regional cerebral glucose metabolic rate following learning. *Intelligence, 16,* 415-426.

Hill, K., & Hurtado, A. M. (1996). *Ache life history: The ecology and demography of a foraging people.* New York: Aldine de Gruyter.

Horn, J. L. (1968). Organization of abilities and the development of intelligence. *Psychological Review, 75,* 242-259.

Horn, J. L., & Cattell, R. B. (1966). Refinement and test of the theory of fluid and crystallized general intelligence. *Journal of Educational Psychology, 57,* 253-270.

Horowitz, D. L. (2001). *The deadly ethnic riot.* Berkeley: University of California Press.

Humphrey, N. K. (1976). The social function of intellect. In P. P. G. Bateson & R. A. Hinde (Eds.), *Growing points in ethology* (pp. 303-317). New York: Cambridge University Press.

Hunt, E. (1978). Mechanics of verbal ability. *Psychological Review, 85,* 109-130.

Hunter, J. E., & Hunter, R. F. (1984). Validity and utility of alternative predictors of job performance. *Psychological Bulletin, 96,* 72-98.

Jensen, A. R. (1982). Reaction time and psychometric g. In H. J. Eysenck (Ed.), *A model for intelligence* (pp. 93-132). New York: Springer-Verlag.

Jensen, A. R. (1992). The importance of intraindividual variation in reaction time. *Intelligence, 13,* 869-881.

Jensen, A. R. (1998). *The g factor: The science of mental ability.* Westport, CT: Praeger.

Jensen, A. R., & Munro, E. (1979). Reaction time, movement time, and intelligence. *Intelligence, 3,* 121-126.

Kane, M. J., & Engle, R. W. (2002). The role of prefrontal cortex in working-memory capacity, executive attention, and general fluid intelligence: An individual-differences perspective. *Psychonomic Bulletin & Review, 9,* 637-671.

Kaplan, H., Hill, K., Lancaster, J., & Hurtado, A. M. (2000). A theory of human life history evolution: Diet, intelligence, and longevity. *Evolutionary Anthropology, 9,* 156-185.

Kisilevsky, B. S., Hains, S. M. J., Lee, K., Xie, X., Huang, H., Ye, H. H., Zhang, K., & Wang, Z. (2003). Effects of experience on fetal voice recognition. *Psychological Science, 14,* 220-224.

Kuhl, P. K. (1994). Learning and representation in speech and language. *Current Opinion in Neurobiology, 4,* 812-822.

Kyllonen, P. C., & Christal, R. E. (1990). Reasoning ability is (little more than) working-memory capacity?! *Intelligence, 14,* 389-433.

Landau, B., Gleitman, H., & Spelke, E. (1981, September 11). Spatial knowledge and geometric representations in a child blind from birth. *Science, 213,* 1275-1278.

Legree, P. J. (1995). Evidence for an oblique social intelligence factor established with a Likert-based testing procedure. *Intelligence, 21,* 247-266.

Lubinski, D. (2000). Scientific and social significance of assessing individual differences: "Sinking shafts at a few critical points." *Annual Review of Psychology, 51,* 405-444.

MacDonald, K. (1992). Warmth as a developmental construct: An evolutionary analysis. *Child Development, 63,* 753-773.

Mackintosh, N. J., & Bennett, E. S. (2003). The fractionation of working memory maps onto different components of intelligence. *Intelligence, 31,* 519-531.

Mandler, J. M. (1992). How to build a baby: II. Conceptual primitives. *Psychological Review, 99,* 587-604.

Markus, H. (1977). Self schemata and processing information about the self. *Journal of Personality and Social Psychology, 35,* 63-78.

Matarazzo, J. D. (1972). *Wechsler's measurement and appraisal of adult intelligence* (5th ed.). New York: Oxford University Press.

Matthews, M. H. (1992). *Making sense of place: Children's understanding of large-scale environments.* Savage, MD: Barnes & Noble Books.

Maynard Smith, J., & Price, G. R. (1973, November 2). The logic of animal conflict. *Nature, 246,* 15-18.

McCandliss, B. D., Posner, M. I., & Givón, T. (1997). Brain plasticity in learning visual words. *Cognitive Psychology, 33,* 88-110.

Miller, E. K., & Cohen, J. D. (2001). An integration of theory of prefrontal cortex function. *Annual Review of Neuroscience, 24,* 167-202.

Neubauer, A. C. (1997). The mental speed approach to the assessment of intelligence. In J. Kingma & W. Tomic (Eds.), *Advances in cognition and education: Reflections on the concept of intelligence* (pp. 149-173). Greenwich, CT: JAI Press.

Nyborg, H., & Jensen, A. R. (2001). Occupation and income related to psychometric g. *Intelligence, 29,* 45-55.

Pascalis, O., de Haan, M., & Nelson, C. A. (2002, May 17). Is face processing species-specific during the first year of life? *Science, 296,* 1321-1323.

Pellis, S. M., & Iwaniuk, A. N. (2000). Adult-adult play in primates: Comparative analyses of its origin, distribution and evolution. *Ethology, 106,* 1083-1104.

Pinker, S. (1994). *The language instinct.* New York: William Morrow.

Pinker, S. (1997). *How the mind works.* New York: W. W. Norton.

Posner, M. I. (1994). Attention: The mechanisms of consciousness. *Proceedings of the National Academy of Sciences USA, 91,* 7398-7403.

Posner, M. I., Boies, S. J., Eichelman, W. H., & Taylor, R. L. (1969). Retention of visual and name codes of single letters. *Journal of Experimental Psychology Monograph, 79,* 1-16.

Potts, R. (1998). Variability selection in hominid evolution. *Evolutionary Anthropology, 7,* 81-96.

Prabhakaran, V., Smith, J. A. L., Desmond, J. E., Glover, G. H., & Gabrieli, J. D. E. (1997). Neural substrates of fluid reasoning: An fMRI study of neocortical activation during performance of the Raven's progressive matrices test. *Cognitive Psychology, 33,* 43-63.

Pugh, K. R., Shaywitz, B. A., Shaywitz, S. E., Shankweiler, D. P., Katz, L., Fletcher, J. M., Skudlarski, P., Fulbright, R. K., Constable, R. T., Bronen, R. A., Lacadie, C., & Gore, J. C. (1997). Predicting reading performance from neuroimaging profiles: The cerebral basis of phonological effects in printed word identification. *Journal of Experimental Psychology: Human Perception and Performance, 23,* 299-318.

Raichle, M. E., Fiez, J. A., Videen, T. O., MacLeod, A. M. K., Pardo, J. V., & Petersen, S. E. (1994). Practice-related changes in human brain functional anatomy during non-motor learning. *Cerebral Cortex, 4,* 8-26.

Raz, N., Torres, I. J., Spencer, W. D., Millman, D., Baertschi, J. C., & Sarpel, G. (1993). Neuroanatomical correlates of age-sensitive and age-invariant cognitive abilities: An *in vivo* MRI investigation. *Intelligence, 17,* 407-422.

Reynolds, C. R., Chastain, R. L., Kaufman, A. S., & McLean, J. E. (1987). Demographic characteristics and IQ among adults: Analysis of the WAIS-R standardization sample as a function of the stratification variables. *Journal of School Psychology, 25,* 323-342.

Rosenthal, R., Hall, J. A., DiMatteo, M. R., Rogers, P. L., & Archer, D. (1979). *Sensitivity to nonverbal communication: The PONS test.* Baltimore, MD: Johns Hopkins University Press.

Rozin, P. (1976). The evolution of intelligence and access to the cognitive unconscious. In J. M. Sprague & A. N. Epstein (Eds.), *Progress in psychobiology and physiological psychology* (Vol. 6, pp. 245-280). New York: Academic Press.

Rushton, J. P., & Ankney, C. D. (1996). Brain size and cognitive ability: Correlations with age, sex, social class, and race. *Psychonomic Bulletin & Review, 3,* 21-36.

Scarr, S. (1992). Developmental theories of the 1990s: Developmental and individual differences. *Child Development, 63,* 1-19.

Scarr, S., & McCartney, K. (1983). How people make their own environments: A theory of genotype-environment effects. *Child Development, 54,* 424-435.

Schmidt, F. L., & Hunter, J. E. (1998). The validity and utility of selection methods in personnel psychology: Practical and theoretical implications of 85 years of research findings. *Psychological Bulletin, 124,* 262-274.

Schneider, D. J. (1973). Implicit personality theory: A review. *Psychological Bulletin, 79,* 294-309.

Scullin, M. H., Peters, E., Williams, W. M., & Ceci, S. J. (2000). The role of IQ and education in predicting later labor market outcomes: Implications for affirmative action. *Psychology, Policy, and Law, 6,* 63-89.

Sheeran, P., & Orbell, S. (2000). Self-schemas and the theory of planned behaviour. *European Journal of Social Psychology, 30,* 533-550.

Shepard, R. N. (1994). Perceptual-cognitive universals as reflections of the world. *Psychonomic Bulletin & Review, 1,* 2-28.

Spearman, C. (1904). General intelligence, objectively determined and measured. *American Journal of Psychology, 15,* 201-293.

Sperber, D. (1994). The modularity of thought and the epidemiology of representations. In L. A. Hirschfeld & S. A. Gelman (Eds.), *Mapping the mind: Domain specificity in cognition and culture* (pp. 39-67). New York: Cambridge University Press.

Sporns, O., Tononi, G., & Edelman, G. M. (2000). Connectivity and complexity: The relationship between neuroanatomy and brain dynamics. *Neural Networks, 13,* 909-922.

Stadler, M. A., & Frensch, P. A. (Eds.). (1997). *Handbook of implicit learning.* Thousand Oaks, CA: Sage.

Stanovich, K. E. (1999). *Who is rational? Studies of individual differences in reasoning.* Mahwah, NJ: Erlbaum.

Stephan, W. G. (1985). Intergroup relations. In G. Lindzey & E. Aronson (Eds.), *Handbook of social psychology: Vol. II. Special fields and applications* (pp. 599-658). New York: Random House.

Tooby, J., & Cosmides, L. (1995). Mapping the evolved functional organization of mind and brain. In M. S. Gazzaniga (Ed.), *The cognitive neurosciences* (pp. 1185-1197). Cambridge: Bradford Books/MIT Press.

Tulving, E. (2002). Episodic memory: From mind to brain. *Annual Review of Psychology, 53,* 1-25.

Vernon, P. A., Wickett, J. C., Bazana, P. G., & Stelmack, R. M. (2000). The neuropsychology and psychophysiology of human intelligence. In R. J. Sternberg (Ed.), *Handbook of intelligence* (pp. 245-264). Cambridge, UK: Cambridge University Press.

Wagner, R. K., Torgesen, J. K., & Rashotte, C. A. (1994). Development of reading-related phonological processing abilities: New evidence of bidirectional causality from a latent variable longitudinal study. *Developmental Psychology, 30,* 73-87.

Walberg, H. J. (1984). Improving the productivity of America's schools. *Educational Leadership, 41,* 19-27.

Wechsler, D. (1981). *Manual for the Wechsler Adult Intelligence Scale-Revised.* New York: Psychological Corporation.

Wickett, J. C., Vernon, P. A., & Lee, D. H. (2000). Relationships between factors of intelligence and brain volume. *Personality and Individual Differences, 29,* 1095-1122.

5

Contextual Freedom in Human Infant Vocalization and the Evolution of Language

D. Kimbrough Oller and Ulrike Griebel

Steps of Vocal Evolution

Behavioral adaptations often vary markedly even among related species. In such cases, the comparative enterprise offers the immediate opportunity to formulate theory regarding steps of evolution that may have led to the most elaborate forms of a particular adaptation. Oscine birds present a good example of such diversity across related species. The differing degrees of ability among species to use elaborate songs and to acquire new songs make it possible to posit not only steps of evolution but also forces of natural selection that have favored elaborate song capability in some species (Kroodsma, 1999). In the context of this sort of study, territoriality and advertisement for mating, for example, have come to be viewed as the primary forces driving the evolution of song learning capability in many species of birds (Searcy & Nowicki, 1999).

Authors' Note: The authors gratefully acknowledge support for this work from the Plough Foundation.

But nature has not always provided such clear evidence of the possible steps of evolution in behavior. Human language presents a notable problem in this regard. While the many nonhuman primate species do show observable diversity in vocal communication, virtually every scientist who has studied communication comparatively from the Enlightenment to the present has acknowledged that there is an enormous gap in type and degree of vocal communicative control manifest in human language compared with the natural communicative systems of any other primate (e.g., Condillac, 1756; Marler, 1975; Cheney & Seyfarth, 1999). In addressing how human language came to exist, the lack of species showing intermediate degrees of communicative capability, then, presents a major obstacle.

We are intrigued by the unique circumstances that must have stimulated human vocal evolution and by the steps that must have been taken as language began to emerge. Our attempt to shed light on the process has especially relied upon a new set of possibilities resulting from empirical research on human infant vocal development and related theoretical developments. In light of these efforts, a series of steps that appear universally to characterize normal infant vocal development are thought to offer clues regarding the steps that our hominid ancestors may have taken.

The approach to be presented here is based in long-standing assumptions inherent to evolutionary theory. A key is the notion of descent with modification (Darwin, 1859, 1871). Major changes of design in morphology or behavior are unlikely to occur in single leaps but are instead evolved systematically, where each step provides a modification built upon the foundations of prior evolutionary steps, each with its own fitness advantage at the time it is taken (Dawkins, 1996). The view that the whole of language capability must have evolved in a sudden burst of change corresponding to the Upper Paleolithic is seen as extremely unlikely in light of the great generality with which the principle of descent with modification is observed in evolution. Our assumption, then, is that there were many steps of descent with modification that must have been taken to provide foundations for language, perhaps over hundreds of thousands or even millions of years.

Research in infant vocalization and young child speech has not only revealed many steps of development, but has highlighted the extent to which those changes reveal successive stages of power in communication. Crucially, the very early stages of vocal development in the human show ways in which the infant communicates vocally with potential survival advantages for the individual infant, and further development reveals growth in communication with further increasing potential survival advantages. Perhaps, we have thought, the human infant provides a natural laboratory for observation, where the process of growth may be similar to the steps that were taken by our hominid ancestors.

The key matters that we wish to address in this paper concern (a) the nature of the very earliest step of differentiation in vocal communication of the hominid line from its pan-primate background and (b) the initial conditions that led to the break. By considering human infant development and comparative evidence from other vocally active species, certain key problems of explanation come into view, and possible solutions regarding the initial conditions of vocal evolution can be formulated.

Contextual Freedom as Possibly the Earliest Step in the Hominid Break

Oller (2000) has contended that the most fundamental logical requirement of the break with the primate background was the evolution of vocal "Contextual Freedom," and that all other steps of vocal evolution toward language were dependent upon that initial step. Developmental observations reviewed in the cited volume have provided empirical support for the possibilities suggested by this line of reasoning.

First then, what is Contextual Freedom, and in what sense is it a logical requirement for any sort of growth toward a linguistic system? Roughly, Contextual Freedom in vocalization is the capability to produce sounds that are free of specific stimulus conditions or requirements of function. By definition, every communicative act consists of an action that signals a function (a term intended to encompass intentions, states, and meanings). There is always a distinction to be drawn between the signal itself and the function it serves. In the absence of Contextual Freedom, signals and functions are coupled, and whenever a particular signal is delivered, it transmits the same potential function. With vocal Contextual Freedom, on the other hand, each sound (potential signal) can be produced at will and consequently is available for adaptation (by learning) to a variety of functions for the communicative needs of the individual or the group, needs that may be different day-to-day or generation to generation. Different social functions can be served by any of these sounds on different occasions or in different groups of animals.

For example, suppose an individual can produce sounds X and Y contextually freely. One indicator of Contextual Freedom is usage of a sound repetitively (for example, the individual might produce sequences of X X X X or Y Y Y Y Y Y) when the individual is alone or not engaged socially and shows no sign of emotional expression. Another indicator is substantial variability in the acoustic nature of sounds produced; the individual may seemingly wander about the articulatory/acoustic space in producing a sound class (for example, $X_1 X_2 X_3 X_4 \ldots$), again during periods when there is no indication of social engagement or emotionality. An additional sign of Contextual Freedom is systematic (that is, reliably nonrandom) alternation among classes (for example, X X X Y Y X X X X X Y Y Y Y) in uninterrupted sequences, also in circumstances of isolation and neutral emotionality. All these patterns (and especially the conjunction of all of them) provide indications that the individual can control the production of a sound, can explore the articulatory/acoustic space in its neighborhood, and can systematically contrast it with other sound types, even though no social or expressive function is being served.

Once Contextual Freedom is in place for any sound, an additional step can be taken, by which the sound can come to be used to express emotions or states. Contextual Freedom does not require a particular sound to be paired consistently with a particular emotion or state; in fact, the ability to use a particular sound in the context of *different* states of arousal or affectivity is clearly an indicator of a special kind of Contextual Freedom that can be termed "Free Expressivity" (Oller, 2000). Thus, X might be used in the context of an expression of delight or jubilation on one occasion (as indicated by postural or facial expressions), while being used to express frustration or upset on another occasion, and to express a neutral state on a third occasion. With Free Expressivity in place, Y could also be used on different occasions to express all these states. Let us note that this sort of variability of usage is precisely what we observe in human infants (Oller, 1981), and there will be more to say about it below. Such Contextual Freedom and Free Expressivity allow for a rich and variable kind of social interaction with sounds.

If a group of animals commands contextually free signals, the foundation is in place to pair the sounds specifically (and then maintain those pairings by convention) with specific new social functions. Eventually, for example, a contextually free sound such as X might become a particular greeting call used just for members of the kin group, and Y might become an appeasement signal to be used toward less closely related individuals. Eventually, through experience and convention developed within the group, sounds such as X and Y might come to be truly referential in that they could signify particular members of the group independent of such functions as greeting, praise, reprimand, or appeasement. For example, X might be used to refer to siblings both in greeting them, in labeling siblings for other individuals, in praising siblings, in reprimanding them, or in attempting to appease them. Y might be used to refer to any stranger of the same species in all the same ways. Once the sounds could be used with stable reference *and* variable function (greeting, praise, reprimand, appeasement), the sounds would have taken on key characteristics of true words. Note that to form such primitive words, the sounds would have to be paired freely with these references and functions within individuals, generation by generation, and that this ability is logically dependent upon the ability of the individuals to produce the sounds freely in the first place.

Contextual Freedom is, thus, the foundation upon which every step toward words is built. Domain specificity in the functions of a small number of preset signals (as we see in nonhuman primates; see references below) cannot give way to domain generality of an unlimited number of signals that can be attached through learning to new functions (as in speech) until there exists the potential to explore the vocal articulatory/acoustic space and to parse it into sound categories actively and freely, and thus to develop potential signals available for learning, signals that are free of fixed, specific functions predetermined by natural selection.

Fixed Signals and Contextually Free Signals

To clarify the nature of Contextual Freedom, consider the traditional ethological notion of the "fixed signal" (Lorenz, 1951; Tinbergen, 1951), a concept that is generally presumed, with some qualifications, to characterize the communicative vocalizations of nonhuman primate species (Marler, 1975; Marler, Evans, & Hauser, 1992). Fixed vocal signals are sometimes referred to as "calls," and they are presumed to occur in the context of specific social or emotional conditions (see review in Hauser, 1996). Alarm calls are produced in the context of perceived dangers, threat calls in the context of a drive for dominance during conflict, appeasement calls in the context of a drive to avoid conflict, and contact calls in the context of visual separation or reestablishment of contact (greeting). In these examples, the vocalizations in question are *coupled* to the circumstances that inspire their use and the consequent functions they serve. It is in this sense that the signals are "fixed." Both their physical character (the way they sound) and the functions that they serve are relatively constant. Furthermore, there is a presumed one-to-one relation in fixed signals, such that each signal type has one and only one function (although the functions may be broadly defined and applied) and each function corresponds to one and only one signal type. There are empirical qualifications that are worth making about primate fixed signals in this context, and some will be considered below.

With the advent of Contextual Freedom, the coupling of signals and functions is broken. Decoupled vocalizations are not "calls," since they possess (each of them) the *potential* for serving a variety of functions. Examples of Contextual Freedom in mature speech are a bit self-evident, but to contrast the human vocal capability with that of other primates, examples are worth bringing into focus. The examples illustrate the distinction between illocutionary force (roughly, "social function") and semantic content, as formulated by Austin (1962). If an English speaker decides, for example, to say, "There is danger somewhere up in the sky," it can be done to serve a variety of functions (that is, to transmit a variety of illocutionary forces). One such function might be to serve as a *warning* to a listener, who might then be expected to look up for some falling or flying object or to take cover. But there is no requirement in human language that the statement constitute a warning. As stated here, for example (or as could be stated orally in a lecture), the sentence elicits no need for looking for danger from the sky because it is being presented merely as an illustrative example. The sentence's function in the present circumstance is not that of warning, but of *exemplification;* it bears the same semantic content as it does when it serves as a warning, but it has a different illocutionary force. Or the statement might be made to indicate that there is danger for some species other than humans, in which case the sentence again would not be intended as a warning, but would perhaps be intended as an *informational statement* provided for scientific descriptive purposes. Perhaps even more strikingly, a person might decide to produce the sentence for no communicative purpose at all, but rather to *practice* the sounds of the words and the intonations that can be superimposed upon the sentence. Thus, people who know English are capable of producing the sentence "There is danger somewhere up in the sky" (and thus invoking its semantic content) in whatever situation they choose, while at the same time being able to transmit a wide variety of possible illocutionary forces with that same sentence, and they can even produce the sentence in a situation where there is no immediate social function whatever.

The explication of these variable potential uses of the particular example sentence shows that in humans, a particular utterance can have multiple functions, a one-to-many mapping of signal to function. But it should be noted that each of the functions noted could also be served by a wide variety of different utterances. So, if we wished to sincerely issue a *warning* about danger from the sky, we might produce, in addition to the example sentence, other sentences that have the same illocutionary force of warning but include different semantic content: "Yikes, look up" or "Something is careening toward you" or "Look out up in the heavens" or "Hey, a rock's falling toward you" or "There's a plane about to crash on you" or "Mockingbird attack." The fundamental point of these examples is that human language is not limited to having a single utterance or sentence (semantic content) that serves each function. Human language presents the potential of a many-to-one mapping for any function.

Having seen that language offers both one-to-many and many-to-one mappings for individual potential signals and individual potential functions, the necessary conclusion is that humans command a system that is not fixed on either side of the signal-function pairing. Indeed, it is logically necessary to conclude that across the range of possible signals and functions of communication, humans command a many-to-many mapping (because both one-to-many and many-to-one mappings are available), violating the defining characteristics of fixed signaling on both sides. This pattern indicates widely applicable Contextual Freedom.

How Much Vocal Contextual Freedom Occurs in Nonhuman Primates?

A humanlike degree of Contextual Freedom has never been reported for any nonhuman primate vocal system, and we will explicate evidence that even the notable variations that have been reported thus far in the literature do not suggest that any nonhuman primate ever achieves the level of Contextual Freedom found in the first half-year of life in the human, although, of course, future evidence could require revisions to this conclusion. By contrast, with human infants, where vocal Contextual Freedom is in place early, the fixed-signal definition outlined above appears to apply to nonhuman primate vocalizations throughout the life span, with some qualifications, which are of substantial interest but do not unseat the basic point.

Seyfarth and Cheney (1997) provided an overview on this point, citing results from 36 empirical studies of primate vocal development and emphasizing that there are three different perspectives from which to look at the degree of fixity in nonhuman primate vocal systems: (1) the vocal signals themselves, which indicate the "production" capability; (2) the way each signal type functions, which indicates the "usage" capability; and finally (3) the way listeners of the species respond to the signals when they are heard. It turns out that the degree of fixity of the vocal systems of nonhuman primates is markedly different in the three cases.

1. Degree of Vocal Signal Fixity. In the case of the vocal signals themselves, fixity is high, according to Seyfarth and Cheney's evaluation of available studies. Most of the vocalization types that occur in nonhuman primates are easily identifiable auditorily as the same sounds at different ages, even in infancy. Other sounds show "some modification during development," changing from an immature to a more mature form. At the same time, the modification is limited in that primate infant sounds develop into elements of the adult relatively fixed repertoires, not into new kinds of individual sounds. Thus, there is apparently a sharply limited range of sound categories produced at all ages.

What we would expect of an animal with Contextual Freedom would be an ability to produce novel sounds, sounds that are not part of the adult repertoire. These novel sounds would be available for free expression of emotions and states, a pattern that we shall see below does occur in the human infant in the first months of life. In fact, in the human, there are vast differences between the acoustic quality of common identifiable vocalizations in early infancy and in the speech sounds of adulthood (Holmgren, Lindblom, Aurelius, Jalling, & Zetterstrom, 1986; Oller, 1980; Stark, 1981).

There is at least one report of adaptation of sounds by individual macaques cross-fostered with related species (Masataka & Fujita, 1989), but a subsequent study did not confirm the findings (Owren, Dieter, Seyfarth, & Cheney, 1993). A report of "dialect" differences in Japanese macaques living in separate areas (Green, 1975) emphasized minor adjustments in how certain signals were produced in the different groups. So, some shift in the acoustic character of fixed signals may be possible with experience, but that shift appears to be relatively subtle by comparison with the radical variability found in vocalization development of the human infant.

2. Degree of Usage Fixity for Various Signals. On the usage of signals, Seyfarth and Cheney's review suggested that all or virtually all primate sound types are modified with time in accord with experience. The domain of application of each signal type begins by being imperfectly matched with the domain of application found in adults. For example, adults may have contact calls that are different when directed toward subordinates or dominants, but infants may not use these calls precisely, perhaps because they simply do not yet understand the dominance hierarchy. As infants learn where they as individuals fit in the hierarchy, the basis for appropriate use of the sounds is established, and usage is adjusted accordingly.

However, it is worth noting that the apparent errors by infants in domain of application of vocal signals are not radical errors of application that would suggest a general command of Contextual Freedom. Infant primates have not been reported to make the mistake of using contact calls as alarms, for example, or as threats, and more important, they have not been reported to use them in circumstances that lack any immediate social function at all. And as far as the literature indicates, they do not change the emotional valence of sounds—threats, alarm calls, and distress calls are always negative and cannot be adjusted to present positive emotion. The errors of usage that occur appear to be ones of precision, not ones involving general category change with regard to function. Since there are apparently no (or very few) novel sounds available in the infant repertoire, there is no (or very little) basis for creating new signal-function pairings except by reversing the call values of the adult system, which would be perverse and counterproductive from the standpoint of the survival value of the signals within the social systems of nonhuman primates.

There is one notable exception among nonhuman primates that has been reported with regard to the rule that vocal signals have a predetermined (even if somewhat imprecise) function. The pygmy marmoset (*Cebuella pygmaea*) has been found sometimes in the premating period to "babble" in strings of rapidly repeated vocalizations, alternating without a break with other strings of rapidly repeated vocalizations of different categories (Elowson, Snowdon, & Lazaro-Perea, 1998; Snowdon, in press; Snowdon, Elowson, & Rousch, 1997). The great majority of the vocal types in this "babbling" appear to be exemplars of sounds from the adult repertoire, but because the sounds occur so rapidly and change so quickly from category to category, it is hard to see how they could individually have specific fixed functions. Instead, these bouts of vocalization as a whole seem to have a general social function (the bouts occur in social situations), although it is not yet entirely clear what the function might be. Eventually, the great majority of the sound categories that were previously used in babbling bouts come to have the expected mature, species-specific social functions.

This report is extremely important in providing perspective on inter-species differences in primate vocalization capabilities. Yet it is important to focus on both what it shows and what it does not show (without further evidence) about Contextual Freedom. Clearly, it shows that for a time in development, the pygmy marmoset has a vocal repertoire that is not entirely fixed in function. It does not, however, show that the pygmy marmoset can produce any of the *individual* categories of sound that occur in babbling bouts with new functions or even as individual items of vocal play or practice. The babbling seems to occur in bouts where sound types are repeated numerous times within sequences. Generalized Contextual Freedom requires that sounds be producible in any circumstance, not just in mixed repetitive groups; in addition, they must be producible as individual items free of the stimulus conditions that generate them in the adult case. Only then could the sounds be available for free emotional expressivity or pairing through experience with new functions. Even more important, note that the great majority of the sounds produced in the babbling bouts are apparently destined for specific functional fixity: They will, according to the description by

Snowdon and colleagues, eventually serve a particular function such as threat, appeasement, or contact. General Contextual Freedom requires that at least some producible sounds not have any such destiny, but rather that they be free for assignment to new functions in the individual, and the report does not indicate that any infant marmoset sounds acquire free functions.

Of course, further empirical evaluation may uncover additional features of variability in the ability of nonhuman primates to produce sounds. To the present, the reports of Snowdon and colleagues can be interpreted to indicate only a restricted appearance of Contextual Freedom. One possibility is that the pygmy marmoset babbling bouts are manifestations of an innate preparatory exercise for the adult repertoire. Snowdon (in press) has presented evidence that the adult pygmy marmoset repertoire is particularly elaborate among the nonhuman primates. It seems possible, in accord with his reasoning, that the pygmy marmoset has a sort of babbling for the same reason it has an elaborate vocal repertoire, namely, because these are particularly social primates, especially in terms of the importance of cooperative breeding within their societies. Cooperative breeding creates particular opportunities for activities where all parties have joint interests, because the survival and potential reproductive success of their jointly held gene pools are at stake. Such circumstances, Snowdon has argued, may have fostered special growth in vocal communication among caretakers of pygmy marmoset young and may have played an important role in hominid communication evolution as well.

3. Degree of Fixity in Listener Response. While Seyfarth and Cheney's review of the literature suggests notable fixity with regard to both signal production and signal usage in nonhuman primates, they found evidence for extraordinary levels of freedom in how listeners respond to vocalizations or other sounds. One important kind of evidence comes from cross-fostering studies that show that young macaques quickly learn to interpret the sound systems of other species, even though the most recent study has suggested they do not learn to produce those sounds (Owren et al., 1993). Furthermore, various species show an ability to respond to vocalizations of other members of their species in variable ways depending on circumstances (for example, sometimes vocal appeals are ignored, while other times they result in active responses), and they learn to respond to vocal signals even from very different species, such as birds, whose alarm calls sometimes produce flight to safety in groups of monkeys.

All in all, the research reviewed by Seyfarth and Cheney suggests that nonhuman primates show substantial ability to *respond* adaptively to the vocalizations of their species and others species, even when the responses clearly have to be learned. This flexibility of response to sounds stands in stark contrast to the relative fixity of their abilities to *produce* sounds and to pair those used sounds with particular functions. While experience and development do seem to play important roles in the patterns of sound production and usage of nonhuman primates, no amount of experience or development seems to change the basic ground plan where a relatively small number of signal types is destined to have a one-to-one mapping relation with a relatively small number of function types. From the standpoint of the producer, the sounds of nonhuman primates appear to meet the defining requirements of fixed signals.

An Explicated Example: Alarm Calls in Nonhuman Primates

To put the fixed-signal matter in further perspective, it may be useful to consider in more detail the degree of usage flexibility in a particular category of primate communication that has been studied extensively: alarm calls. The most thoroughly investigated nonhuman primate species in this regard is surely the vervet monkey, *Cercopithecus aethiops sabaeus,* which is described to have five types of alarm calls (Cheney & Seyfarth, 1999), three of which pertain to danger from ground-living predators, such as leopards; to danger from snakes; and to danger from flying predators, such as eagles (Struhsaker, 1967). A variety of species of nonhuman primates also have alarm calls of interest to this discussion.

The usage of alarm vocalizations appears to be somewhat flexible for various primate species in that (a) the young tend to become more accurate with time in the usage of these calls in appropriate circumstances; they seem to overgeneralize early, "crying wolf," so to speak, but learn later to use the calls more precisely (Cheney, 1984); (b) there are reported audience effects such that the issuance of an alarm call appears to be more likely if the caller's kin are nearby; and (c) in the context of interactions with humans, instrumental conditioning may sometimes occur with the effect of fundamentally altering certain call functions. Let us consider these three issues of possible flexibility in the usage of alarm calls in turn.

1. Greater Accuracy of Usage of Alarm Calls With Time. Some degree of development (though not apparent teaching) in fixed vocal signals is known to occur in nonhuman primates, with vervets having been particularly well studied. The young have been reported sometimes to produce the "eagle" call, for example, in response to pigeons and other harmless birds (Cheney &

Seyfarth, 1999). Notice that this fact does not, in and of itself, suggest that the calls are issued to serve any function other than alarm by the infant, but merely indicates that infants need to go through learning regarding what to be alarmed about. The fixity of the signal can thus be seen as only marginally challenged by the observation of this sort of development. The scope of the context of danger that inspires the warning call is defined more precisely with time, but the basic nature of the call is not reversed by any aspect of the experience. The function cannot be changed, for example, from a warning to an invitation or a greeting. What *is* unseated by the observation of development in fixed signals is the possible assumption that all fixed signals are present in their final form at birth. Clearly, they are not fixed in final form at birth in many primate species.

2. Audience Effects in the Usage of Alarm Calls. Second, consider the indication that alarm calls may be produced with greater likelihood when kin of the caller are near. This observation suggests that kin selection (Hamilton, 1963) plays a role in fixed-signal usage, allowing gradation of likelihood that a signal will occur. Seyfarth and Cheney's review suggests that a caller is more likely to issue the call with kin in the neighborhood than if more distantly related animals are nearby. Furthermore, solitary animals do not issue alarm calls. The observations suggest that animals have the ability to inhibit alarm calls for self-protection but that this inhibition tends to be released in circumstances where the protection of the caller's kin (and thus the survival of the caller's genes) can be most effectively achieved by the individual's taking the immediate risk of calling. Again, however, it is important to note that this qualification on how the fixed signal is used does not indicate a generalized decoupling of signal from function: The sound remains an alarm call and does not become a greeting or an invitation.

3. The Possibility of Altered Usage in Alarm Calls. The possibility of fundamentally altered or flexible usage of particular calls in the context of instrumental conditioning provides a much more interesting indication that limited vocal Contextual Freedom can occur in nonhuman primates in the context of special living circumstances, such as those that sometimes obtain in interaction with humans. One report that fits this description is from Gibson (1990), who told of Andy, a cebus monkey that lived with her. She reported: "I always come in response to his alarm bark. He frequently uses the alarm bark when there is nothing alarming in the vicinity—he simply wants my attention (p. 211)." The description suggests that the "alarm bark" had been instrumentally conditioned to have a different function from the one it would serve in the wild. In this special circumstance of living with a human, the cebus appeared indeed to have decoupled and recoupled at least one signal and function.

Other reports also indicate that the circumstances of living with or interacting regularly with humans seems to produce some, though generally small, effects on nonhuman primates' abilities to vocalize with Contextual Freedom. Attempts to train chimpanzees to vocalize in ways resembling speech have shown very limited successes indicating some growth of vocal Contextual Freedom (Gardner, Gardner, & Drumm, 1989; Hayes, 1951). And other work with a chimpanzee infant suggests that interaction with humans can foster increases in the amount of vocalization (Kojima, 2001). Furthermore, systematic studies of instrumental conditioning in macaques have suggested that different vocalizations in the macaque repertoire can be trained in an operant task to be produced systematically in contexts that have nothing to do with the normal usage of the sounds, for example, in the context of lights of particular colors (Sutton, 1979). Of course, it is well-known that a variety of nonprimate species (e.g., birds, marine mammals, and canids) can also learn both to produce novel vocalizations and to pair them with new functions in the context of instrumental conditioning. So, perhaps it should not be surprising that primates also are capable, at least in some cases, of learning limited new usages for sounds through operant conditioning.

Tentative Conclusions on Vocal Contextual Freedom in Nonhuman Primates

Research on nonhuman primates is, of course, ongoing, and there will surely be new discoveries of interesting ways that nonhumans can use their vocal systems. Results on operant learning with vocalization in nonhuman primates provide indications that vocal Contextual Freedom can be achieved by these species in many instances given the right circumstances of living. The apparent paucity of vocal Contextual Freedom in the wild may in part be a product of living conditions that discourage it. More direct comparative research is warranted to clarify the relative capabilities of human and nonhuman primates to show vocal Contextual Freedom.

Yet it seems unlikely that the basic pattern reviewed here will change with new evidence. Vocal repertoires of nonhuman primates in intraspecies interaction appear to be well established as fundamental fixed-signal systems, with a limited amount of development of the acoustic character of signals occurring during infancy and more substantial though still limited development and learning occurring for the precise domains of usage of each call type. In the *interpretation* of calls, on the other hand, there appears to be much greater flexibility. Nonhuman primate listeners learn to respond adaptively to vocal signals and other actions of a variety of species. Such flexibility does not appear to occur in *production* and *usage* abilities for vocal signals, where each nonhuman primate call type appears to be largely innately coupled, in one-to-one fashion, signal to function, and substantial environmental change (such as living with humans or being subjected to instrumental conditioning by them) appears to be required in order to produce notable change in the coupling patterns.

Overview of Vocal Contextual Freedom in the Human Infant

Examples above indicate how the adult human can use speech in ways that radically violate the definition of fixed signals. It is clear that speech requires the ability to totally decouple signals from functions, such that any sound sequence can be used in a wide variety of ways to serve a wide variety of potential social functions (Austin, 1962; Searle, 1976). Furthermore, speech sounds and sound sequences can be produced with no immediate social functions at all, merely to practice the sounds themselves.

How soon in human life does full-scale decoupling of signal from function occur? First, it is important to note that the typical human infant does not produce well-formed speech sounds at all during the first half-year of life. They do, however, produce a wide variety of sounds that are identifiable as pertaining to categories familiar to parents and other observers of infants and that appear to be precursors to speech (Koopmans-van Beinum & van der Stelt, 1986; Oller, 1980; Stark, 1980; Zlatin, 1975a). These sound types include squeals, growls, vowel-like sounds, gooing, raspberries, yells, and whispers, among others. Observations made during several longitudinal studies (reviewed in Oller, 2000) of human infant vocal development have produced descriptions that suggest these sounds are used with undeniable Contextual Freedom.

Consider, for example, the quasivowel, the first sound type occurring in the human infant that shows signs of being contextually free. These sounds occur in the first days of life, and during the first month, they tend to be heard in bouts where normal phonation (the kind of phonation that occurs in speech) is produced on the egress of breathing, when the infant appears to be perfectly comfortable. The key here is that these sounds can occur repetitively when the infant is all alone or when there is a caretaker present and there is at first no sign of interactivity in the use of these sounds. We refer to this period as the "Phonation" stage because the infant shows the ability to produce well-formed normal phonation (the kind of voicing that occurs in speech), although without producing the articulatory characteristic of speech.

By the second month of life, the human infant uses quasivowels mixed with longer, normally phonated vocalizations in face-to-face interactions with caretakers. The sounds often have a "gooing" character, in that the supraglottal vocal tract is moved about to produce articulated sounds usually at the back of the throat, occurring in sequence with the quasivowels. We call this period the "Primitive Articulation" stage, because infants show the ability therein to produce some articulation while phonating. Notably, the sounds of the Primitive Articulation stage rarely have the well-formed (or "canonical") character of syllables, in part because they are temporally erratic and extremely variable (sometimes long, sometimes short, sometimes with articulation, sometimes without, and with substantial variation of articulatory movement and fundamental frequency). These 2-month-old sounds cannot be reliably transcribed phonetically, because they are so erratic, but still have some features of speech (normal phonation and articulatory movement) (Oller, 1986; van der Stelt, 1993; Zlatin, 1975b). The variability of the sounds is important to emphasize because that variability is uncharacteristic of the sounds produced by nonhuman primates, where each sound has been naturally selected for a particular function and consequently cannot afford to be too variable. It would clearly be disadvantageous for an animal to mistake an alarm call for a contact call, for instance.

The topography of the interactions of 2-month-old humans with caretakers is also notable. In a typical case, parent and infant are face-to-face, and an exchange of vocalization ensues, with intermittent smiling and turn-taking on both sides (Papoušek, 1994; Papoušek & Papoušek, 1983; Stern, 1974; Trevarthen, 1974). This sort of sustained (sometimes lasting 5 minutes or more) comfortable exchange of vocalization including eye contact may be interpreted as a *bonding* event, and it is important to emphasize that no evidence of interactions with this topography have been reported to our knowledge in any other primate at any age. Fleeting cases of comfortable vocalization with eye contact have been reported (Biben & Bernhards, 1995; Biben, Symmes, & Masataka, 1986), and, of course, vocalization does occur with eye contact in both aggressive displays and play-fighting among nonhuman primates. Still, the structure of the sort of interaction that occurs with human caregivers and 2-month-old infants is very different because of the sustained time frame of the interactions in the humans, the variability of vocalization acoustic characteristics produced by both the human caregiver and the infant, and the wide range of affectively positive or neutral expressions, in contrast with the aggressive or feigned aggressive displays found in vocalization with eye contact among nonhuman primates (Loizos, 1969).

During the period from 3 to 6 months or so (the "Expansion" stage of vocal development), human infants engage in active exploration of the vocal capability. Very early in this period, we see periods of vocalization when the infant is alone and during which many different types of identifiable vocalizations are repeated and systematically alternated as if the infant is engaged in practice (Oller, 1981; Zlatin, 1975a). The sounds (squeals, growls, and vowel-like sounds, for instance) are acoustically variable, but largely distinguishable as three different classes, arranged along a dimension of pitch. Lag sequential analysis of these sound sequences has shown that they do not occur in random sequences, but that the impression of systematic alternation is quantitatively justified (Oller, Buder, & Nathani, 2003). Other sound groups, such as raspberries, yells, and whispers, also occur in systematic alternation in these exploratory bouts of comfortable vocalization (Oller, 1981). The occurrence of these practicelike sequences when the infant is alone and comfortable provides a further indication that the infant commands Contextual Freedom, because *different* sounds occur in the same situation and, importantly, the situation is one in which the only stimulation for vocalization appears to be the infant's internal motivation to explore and practice sounds.

Perhaps equally important, during the Expansion stage, the same sound types that are explored in solitary vocalization are used *expressively in multiple ways*. Each sound category (squeals, vowel-like sounds, and growls, for example) is used with positive, neutral, and negative expressive valences as indicated by facial affect (Oller et al., 2003). For example, an infant may squeal in apparent delight with a smile in one instance but also squeal in frustration with a frown on another occasion. Furthermore, the sounds of the Expansion stage are used both in social interaction, as indicated by eye contact where the infant clearly directs vocalizations toward listeners, and in vocal emotional expressions *without* evidence of directivity to a caregiver who is present, that is, with no eye contact or attempt to obtain it and no indication of attempt to fit the vocalization into a conversational frame.

Summary on Vocal Contextual Freedom in the Human Infant in the First Half-Year

Recalling the definition of the fixed signal and the characteristics of vocalization in nonhuman primates, let us summarize the characteristics of human infant vocalization in the first half-year of life that contrast starkly with vocal characteristics as we understand them in nonhuman primates. One requirement of fixed signals is that the signals themselves must each be mapped just to one function and that function must be itself clear (though it may be broadly defined) and have a clearly social nature. The human infant produces quasivowels in the first month of life, where there is no obvious social function, since the sounds are produced in many instances when the infant is alone. Furthermore, fixed signals require that each be easily identifiable (otherwise, they could not consistently serve their social purposes), and consequently, the sounds must not be too variable in acoustic character. By the Primitive Articulation stage in the second and third months of life, the human infant produces extremely variable sounds during interactions with caregivers and begins to produce similarly variable sounds when alone. By the Expansion stage, human infants produce sounds in identifiable repetitive and systematically alternating sequences when they are alone, indicating a sort of sound-contrast exploratory play and practice. Crucially, these practice sounds are produced when the infant is alone with no obvious emotional expression or social contingency, a pattern that has not been reported in any instance in nonhuman primates—even pygmy marmoset babbling appears to be limited to social situations (Snowdon, in press). Even more important, the human infant sounds are used with multiple expressive valences, and they can be used with or without eye contact or other indications of social directivity.

Consequently, the sounds of the Expansion stage human infant can be said to present an extremely complex many-to-many mapping between signal and function, and the signals themselves are produced with great variability and often with no social function at all. These patterns radically violate the definition of the fixed signal and are not found in nonhuman primates at any age as far as current literature indicates.

The Hominid Break With the Primate Background of Fixed Vocal Signals

What were the selection pressures that drove the hominids in particular to evolve vocal Contextual Freedom, given that other extant species of primates do not show it? We reason that the existence of only one species among the primates with the elaborate communicative system of humans suggests an evolutionary bottleneck, demanding an explanation invoking special living conditions that created a discontinuity between the hominids and other primates. The bottleneck, according to our reasoning, owed to the fact that selection for vocal Contextual Freedom could occur only in somewhat unique circumstances of environment and lifestyle.

To understand the difficulty of selecting for Contextual Freedom in vocalization, it may be instructive to begin by considering the natural selection of fixed signals. The steps that can lead to evolution of a social signal have been discussed by the classical ethologists in terms of a process of "ritualization" (Lorenz, 1951), where actions that are in the repertoire of a species for other reasons come to be interpreted by other members of the species as indicating something about the state of the producer. If these interpretations function to the survival benefit of the progeny of the producer, then the vocalization can be naturally selected to serve a function related to the interpretation. For example, a sound that had occurred sometimes incidentally when an animal experienced sudden fear might have come to be interpreted by other members of the species who heard the sound as an indication that there was danger afoot; that is, the sound might have come to be treated as an alarm signal. As evolution proceeded, members of the species that tended to produce the relevant sound more detectably and more unambiguously might have been able to warn their kin more effectively, thus increasing survival in the lineage. Selection could then have favored successive generations of individuals that produced the sound increasingly detectably and increasingly unambiguously, until the sound had become ritualized as an alarm call. Such a ritualized call would no longer be incidentally related to its interpretation, because the signal-function pairing had been shaped by natural selection. At this point, it could be concluded that the sound had acquired the property of "specialization for communication," a term coined by Hockett (see Hockett & Altmann, 1968).

Fixed signals are, according to this reasoning, selected progressively as communicatively specialized units that serve particular purposes. In the fixed-signal repertoires of nonhuman primates, the purposes can be listed as categories of basic social interaction: threat, alarm, invitation, contact, and distress calling, for example. Note that natural selection for each signal that serves such functions would tend to maximize the clarity of each signal type and its distinctiveness from the others: If the specific functions that the vocalizations serve are themselves the agents of the survival benefit, then we reason that natural selection must operate specifically upon the signals that maximize the transmission of those functions without ambiguity.

But how could contextually free vocalization be selected this way? Contextually free vocalizations (as in the human infant), by definition, can be produced without any clear social function, and such vocalizations are variable in form to such an extent that they can be given any number of possible interpretations. Here, we surmise, is a glimmer of an important aspect of the evolutionary bottleneck. In evolution of fixed signals, natural selection operates upon specific, easily identifiable sounds and molds them to maintain or even increase their acoustic specificity so that they can communicate specific immediate social purposes that have survival benefits for the producer's progeny. In the evolution of contextually free vocalizations, the mechanism of natural selection has to be notably different because the outcome must produce not specificity and fixity of vocalization, but variability of acoustic character, generality of potential function, and the capacity to produce these variable sounds at least some of the time without any immediate social function at all.

How can selection for variability in vocalization then be envisioned? There may exist a number of possibilities, but we are inclined to argue provisionally for the one we outline here. Our goal is to present a scenario that fits a variety of existing kinds of evidence and especially fits with the pattern of progression in vocal development in the human infant.

An Evolutionary Scenario That Could Have Favored Selection of Primates With Greatly Enhanced Vocal Contextual Freedom

We begin with the assumption that because the survival advantages of language depend upon social, communicative, and intellectual skills, the path that led to linguistic skills must have been established in the context of a unique social circumstance, with particular demands upon communication and shared knowledge. Intelligence has widely come to be recognized as a phenomenon that is a product of social complexity (and vice versa) (Byrne & Whiten, 1988), and evolution of communication of the human variety has been widely speculated to have relied upon increases in the sociality of ancient hominids. Dunbar, for example (Dunbar, 1996; Dunbar, in press), following reasoning of Morris (1967), has suggested that as ancient human groups became larger, they reached a critical point where physical grooming could not any longer serve the needs of group cohesion in such a large social group (because there was not enough time in the day for all the necessary grooming) and that vocalization in the ancient humans was then naturally selected as a replacement for grooming. In the context of vocal "grooming," foundations were laid, according to Dunbar's reasoning, for language.

This reasoning about how vocalization in the hominid lineage began to become more elaborate would seem to depend upon other changes in environment that would have created increased human group sizes. The scenario we propose is largely based upon long-standing proposals from the literature on early hominid evolution (see reviews in Leakey, 1994; Morris, 1967). The proposal assumes that group size increased after ancient prehominids began to feed themselves heavily by hunting or fishing or both. An increase in protein in the diet by virtue of this change made it more advantageous (or less disadvantageous) to have a larger brain. Since the brain is disproportionately energy hungry among bodily organs, the carnivorous lifestyle (which affords an especially efficient source of energy) appears to have made the costs of a larger brain manageable for ancient hominids. In turn, the possibility of any increase in brain size may have opened the door to selection for greater skills with regard to hunting and fishing, which would ensure the maintenance or improvement of the food source. It is important to emphasize here that this pattern of growth is seen in our proposal as multifactorial and interactional, with no individual factor fostering change independently of the others. We envision the pattern of change as one of ratcheting, where evolution in one domain (say brain growth) laid the groundwork for further opportunities in others (say communication or hunting skills) and vice versa, back and forth. As time passed, all the factors of growth may have been influencing the potential effects of the other factors.

But brain size increase was not free of other complications. Ancient hominids were bipedal, and their pelvic structure would not have allowed birth of an infant with a large brain (Bogin, 1990, and see review of relevant studies in Locke, 1993). Selection for larger brains appears also to have required selection for a mechanism to change the timing of development so that the human brain would stay relatively small until after birth and would then show particularly significant growth afterward, yielding an extended period of infancy plus an additional period of childhood prior to sexual maturity (Bogin, 1999). During both infancy and childhood, the brain could grow, and because these periods were extended progressively through hominid evolution, not only did the brain have a progressively longer period during which to grow, but there was also a progressively longer period of relative plasticity to exploit the opportunities offered by the larger brain (Bogin, 1990). The change in timing sponsored opportunities for both social and nonsocial learning, and thus for acquisition of information and skills that might be useful later (Bogin & Smith, 1996).

The ancient hominid infant thus appears to have become more altricial than other primates because there was selection pressure for a larger brain (in the adult) in the ancient hominid case, and the means that was naturally selected that could foster brain growth was a felicitous change in timing of development. The prices of these changes were that infants were even more helpless and dependent than in other primate species and had to be cared for longer, and the high-protein food sources had to be continually enhanced to handle growth in brain size. One of the benefits was that introduction of a longer childhood provided the opportunity for much greater social transmission of learnable skills.

Group size of primates could only increase, we presume, with greater success in protein-rich food sources and specifically with a ratcheting increase in the capabilities that allowed success in hunting or fishing or both. The mechanisms that produced the increases in hunting success would have presumably involved a combination of technological advances (better stone tools, for example) and advances in cooperative endeavors throughout the ancient society, including those involved in hunting and/or fishing, such as alliance formation, coordination of group movements, food sharing, and other social advances involved in caregiving and maximizing the value of investments in young.

How might the necessary cooperative endeavors have been advanced? One key would seem to have been increased communication capabilities. We propose that in the context of especially intense social activity and cooperative need within large groups (see Gärdenfors, in press), where the brain could be selected for greater size because the capacity to feed it was in place within the social group, there must have existed a powerful selective pressure in favor of an increase in communication capabilities. The ancient hominids, according to our proposal, were in a position that may have been unique in the paleohistory of primates, where their food sources were sufficient to support a change that would have been too costly in energy requirements for other primates whose food sources were not so protein rich. These unique circumstances may have moved ancient hominids through the first part of the evolutionary bottleneck, after which they were ready for growth in communication.

To this point, our proposal has little that is new, but represents a summary of prior suggestions. Hereafter, however, there is, we believe, substantial novelty to our proposal. The question that may be answerable through this approach is: How did vocal Contextual Freedom come to be selected for, since in all prior cases of primate evolution, it was fixed signaling that had been selected? What was it about the new conditions of larger brain, larger groups, and altriciality that made a selection pressure for *variability* and Contextual Freedom come to the fore to outweigh and overcome the pressures that had previously produced selection only for specific well-defined classes of signals with well-defined functions?

To answer the question, consider two circumstances of social interaction that may have been substantially different for these ancient hominids, now past the first part of the bottleneck because they had increased brain size, protein-rich food sources, greater altriciality of the infant, and a longer childhood. The circumstances that may help explain selection for vocal variability concern both infant-caregiver interaction and adult-adult interaction.

1. Infant-Caregiver Interactions as a Setting for the Growth of Vocal Contextual Freedom. Imagine the ancient hominid infant, during the period after an initial phase of brain size increase in the subspecies, an infant who was more defenseless and helpless than other primate infants and faced a longer period of helplessness and vulnerability than other primate infants. Furthermore, this ancient hominid infant had caregivers with larger brains and presumably more social savvy than prior primates. The caregiving circumstance in this case surely involved an even greater than usual advantage to infants who could deliver messages to their caregivers that would elicit greater investment in their care. These particular infants needed parents and other relatives to bond with them even more fully and for longer periods than other primates. They needed adults to make major commitments to their long-term care and support. They needed a mechanism to elicit that commitment, and we propose that the mechanism that was naturally selected was a new kind of vocal display. In this new vocal system, there was a premium, for the first time in the paleohistory of the primates, on variety and elaborateness, because what the infant needed to do was to exploit the brainpower of the caregiver to recognize the well-being (and perhaps future reproductive capability) of the infant. The elaborate vocal displays that were selected for in that context did have an immediate social function, but that social function was not such as to limit vocal variety with regard to the function, as had occurred in prior primate evolution, but rather to enhance it, because its function was elicitation of care over the long haul. Its goal for each individual infant was *sustained* interaction with the caregiver, designed ultimately to enhance his or her investment in time and effort in the survival of the infant.

On the caregiver side, this interactive experience, presumably often occurring in and around feeding but also extending to other circumstances as the species evolved, may have offered a key opportunity to evaluate the well-being of the infant, the social skills of the infant, and consequently the potential benefits of long-term commitment to this particular infant. In this way, parents had the opportunity to make important decisions (even if tacit ones) about how much energy to invest in each infant (Locke, in press). Of course, parents virtually always feel commitment to their own infants or to those of their blood relatives, but some infants do obtain more investment than others, and in this ancient hominid case, where more subtle evaluation may have been possible (because of increased brain size) and where more subtle information for evaluation could be presented in the form of a new rich vocal display, the selection pressure for variability in vocal display may have been intense, and may have been synergistically enhanced by the interplay of infant and caregiver.

Our proposal regarding this pattern of increase in variability of vocalization in the ancient hominid infant is, of course, inspired in part by the modern observation of human infants and parents interacting in the

Primitive Articulation stage. The interactions appear to foster relationship formation and bonding (Anderson, Vietze, & Dokecki, 1977; Beebe, Alson, Jaffe, Feldstein, & Crown, 1988; Brazelton, Koslowski, & Main, 1974; Trevarthen, 1977; Tronick, Als, & Brazelton, 1977), and they lay the groundwork for more elaborate, interactive relationships in the future. Furthermore, the production of a wide variety of sounds in Primitive Articulation and the presumable production of a wide variety of sounds in ancient interactions of the early hominids of the period we are describing represent a step of Contextual Freedom. While these sounds occur in a circumstance that has a function, that function is not limiting with regard to the kinds of sounds that can occur in it, but instead, the particular function of this kind of interaction fosters a wide range of vocalization, because the goal is sustained turn-taking. Such sustained face-to-face interaction with comfort and vocalization exchange occurs in no other extant primate as far as we know.

The neural substrate that may have made this highly variable vocalization possible was, we propose, built upon in subsequent stages of evolution. Infants who vocalized in the presence of the parent with highly variable sounds were at an advantage, and this may have fostered additional selection pressure on vocalization in other circumstances, where face-to-face interaction did not occur, but where caregivers still might incidentally hear infants producing sounds indicative of the infant's well-being. These vocalizations were, according to this scenario, contextually free from the standpoint of the infant producing them but may still have produced a survival advantage because they increased the probability that their caregivers would support them enthusiastically in growth and development.

In addition, growth of sound-making capabilities in the context of a long childhood and greater learning capability in the subspecies may have led to self-organized development of new ways of exploiting the social opportunities for vocalizing later in development of the individual and/or later in evolution of the species. The Contextual Freedom of the sounds produced by these ancient hominids may have taken on more differentiated communicative forces by creative usage and creative interpretation, with later conventionalization of the pairings that would thus be established between new sounds and new communicative functions.

2. Adult-Adult Interactions as a Basis for Growth in Vocal Contextual Freedom: Effects of Alliances and Sexual Selection. The second circumstance that we wish to consider during the first evolutionary step enhancing vocal Contextual Freedom concerns interactions among more mature members of the ancient hominid group under discussion. These ancient hominids are presumed to have had a more elaborate social structure than at earlier evolutionary stages, with larger groups and thus greater demands on intelligence in order to maintain order in the group and foster coopera- tion in caregiving, defense, and food supply (Dunbar, 1993). The coopera- tive needs of such a group can be assumed to have been greatly enhanced over those of prior primates in the same lineage. Cooperation demands alliance and trust. We propose that contextually free vocalization, also under selection pressure because infant survival in the same population may have depended on caregiving cooperation, provided a new and powerful basis for bonding interactions among adults who could profit from alliance. Vocal capabilities exercised first in infancy became, later in life, a new and potent tool for establishing social connections, evaluating well-being and presumably intelligence, and deciding whom to trust. The members of the groups that most effectively elicited alliances and made the best choices would be in positions of power. Vocal Contextual Freedom would have allowed variable vocalizations to be used as displays (in a way that may be analogized to oratorical advertising, poetry, or music in modern times) (Dessalles, 1998), and as the subspecies continued to evolve, the many pos- sible vocalizations that were developed could come to be attached to new and more subtle social functions of mood manipulation and solicitation of assistance. In this way, vocalization in the ancient hominids could well have taken over roles that had been served in prior times by grooming, but clearly the opportunities for diverse social functions were exploited in vocal interaction to vastly more subtle and powerful ends than grooming could achieve.

Undeniably, sexual selection (Mayr, 1972) could also have fostered growth in the elaborateness of vocal displays among these ancient hominids. Displays of vocalization as entertainment and illustration of social talents may have played a significant role in courtship. That elaborate vocal displays can be important in mate selection is well documented in many bird species (Baptista & Petrinovich, 1986; Nottebohm, 1981; West, King, & Freeberg, 1997). However, in the evolution of birdsong, the sexual selection role for vocal variability is much more limited than in the human line. For songbirds, an elaborate display may be made in courtship, but once courtship has pro- duced its effect, the purpose of the display has been served and no further elaborate vocal display is required for maintenance of the mating relation- ship or rearing of offspring. In the hominid line, mate selection no doubt played a role as well in encouraging elaborate vocal displays, but there were many additional functions served by vocalizations in the hominid line beyond the point of courtship. In our scenario, hominids used elaborate vocalizations not just to secure mates but also to creatively maintain and enhance the activities of cooperative child rearing, cooperative food supply within the family, cooperative protection of the family from competitors within the group, and cooperative defense against outsiders and predators. For the hominids, the extremely complex specific cooperative-breeding functions fostered growth of variable uses of vocalizations to serve particular goals in many different circumstances. Consequently, in the hominid line, mate selection appears to have exerted a supplementary rather than a primary pressure on the evolution of the variable vocal capability, since constant pressure seems to have been exerted beyond the initial point of first vocal Contextual Freedom on the development of sounds that could be brought to the service of a multitude of additional potential social functions.

Getting Through the Bottleneck to Vocal Contextual Freedom

We have proposed that the observation of modern human infancy may provide key clues to how ancient hominids broke free from a pan-primate background where vocal signaling was fixed and where, for many millions of years, there has apparently been an evolutionary bottleneck preventing other primates (and perhaps other animals as well) from profiting from the opportunities that a languagelike communication system offers. We have proposed that the bottleneck consists of a pattern where selection pressures favor fixed signals under the vast majority of living circumstances in social animals. A special circumstance is needed to favor the critical step by which a lineage can break from fixed signals. The circumstance that could have favored evolution through the bottleneck was, we propose, that ancient hominids reached a point where their food supplies were rich enough to support brain growth, where altriciality of infants was required to achieve increased mature brain size, and where the resulting long period of immaturity created an evolutionary premium on investment in the infant and on the infant's ability to elicit that investment. Vocalization and related visual displays were the most powerful available possible tools to evolve toward that social enhancement, we propose, and the young of the species were thus under selection pressure to develop the capability and the motivation to vocalize in an extremely elaborate social manner in order to elicit investment from their caregivers.

Furthermore, we propose the ancient hominid groups that initially made this break with the primate background were able to use the growing vocal system as a display method for a variety of social purposes, such as perhaps increasingly subtle means of appeasement, cajoling, reconciliation, greeting, affection, reprimand, criticism, and maybe even entertainment. With such tools available in the species, both alliance formation and mate selection could have been dramatically enhanced for individuals who were particularly gifted in the manipulation of and by vocalization. Although our reasoning particularly emphasizes analogies with modern child development (as does Locke, in press), the emphasis on cooperation as a key factor in the evolution of communication is in accord with several other current syntheses about the conditions that may have fostered communication growth in the hominid line (Fitch, in press; Gärdenfors, in press; Snowdon, in press).

It is important to note here that nothing we have said about these ancient hominids suggests that they were using the well-formed units of modern natural languages. They presumably were not using words (with, for example, arbitrarily learned references), and, in fact, they did not even have to be using canonical syllables with identifiable consonants and vowels. Their repertoires may well have consisted instead of sounds analogous to those of Expansion stage human infants—squeals, growls, yells, whispers, raspberries, and vowel-like sounds, all produced, as human infants produce them, with enormous variability of pitch contour and volume, of duration and rhythmic character. With such variation available, there could have been substantial opportunities for development of new or more subtle and precise functions for vocalization that may have fostered the survival advantages we have discussed: heightened caregiver investment in the vocally gifted infant, heightened reproductive success due to sexual selection of the most talented vocalizers, and heightened alliance support for vocal friend-makers in the context of a complex society. The vocal gifts of these evolving hominids must have given them an edge over their competitor species and subspecies, presumably because more vocal groups could work together more effectively in the many realms of food acquisition and defense.

The original foundations of language, then, included natural selection for vocal Contextual Freedom in primitive sounds, an ability that is required for the evolution of the capability to produce more elaborate structures, such as well-formed syllables, words, and sentences. Evolution proceeds in steps, and in the case of language, the first step may have been the seemingly unimportant one of gaining the capacity to produce primitive sounds variably and with variable social functions. These primitive sounds, produced in the context of sustained interactions between infants and caregivers, between potential allies, and between potential mates, appear to have opened the door to communicative powers that vastly surpass those of any other species. And it would not have been a trivial added feature of this growth in primitive vocal freedom that ancient hominids, very much like modern human infants, may also have been able to produce vocalizations with no immediate social function at all, just for fun.

References

Anderson, B. J., Vietze, P., & Dokecki, P. R. (1977). Reciprocity in vocal interactions of mothers and infants. *Child Development, 48,* 1676-1681.

Austin, J. L. (1962). *How to do things with words.* London: Oxford University Press.

Baptista, L. F., & Petrinovich, L. (1986). Song development in the white-crowned sparrow: Social factors and sex differences. *Animal Behavior, 34,* 1359-1371.

Beebe, B., Alson, D., Jaffe, J., Feldstein, S., & Crown, C. (1988). Vocal congruence in mother-infant play. *Journal of Psycholinguistic Research, 17,* 245-259.

Biben, M., & Bernhards, D. (1995). Vocal ontogeny of the squirrel monkey, *Saimiri boliviensis peruviensis.* In E. Zimmerman, J. D. Newman, & U. Jürgens (Eds.), *Current topics in primate vocal communication.* New York: Plenum Press.

Biben, M., Symmes, D., & Masataka, N. (1986). Temporal and structural analysis of affiliative vocal exchanges in squirrel monkeys (*Saimiri sciureus*). *Behaviour, 98,* 259-273.

Bogin, B. (1990). The evolution of human childhood. *BioScience, 40.*

Bogin, B. (1999). *Patterns of human growth.* New York: Cambridge University Press.

Bogin, B., & Smith, B. H. (1996). Evolution of the human life cycle. *American Journal of Human Biology, 8,* 703-716.

Brazelton, T. B., Koslowski, B., & Main, M. (1974). The origins of reciprocity: The early mother-infant interaction. In M. Lewis & L. A. Rosenblum (Eds.), *The effect of the infant on its caregiver* (pp. 49-76). New York: John Wiley.

Byrne, R., & Whiten, A. (1988). *Machiavellian intelligence: Social expertise and the evolution of intellect in monkeys.* Oxford, UK: Clarendon Press.

Cheney, D. L. (1984). Category formation in vervet monkeys. In R. Harre & V. Reynolds (Eds.), *The meaning of primate signals.* Cambridge, UK: Cambridge University Press.

Cheney, D. L., & Seyfarth, R. M. (1999). Mechanisms underlying vocalizations of primates. In M. D. Hauser & M. Konishi (Eds.), *The design of animal communication* (pp. 629-644). Cambridge: MIT Press.

Condillac, E. B. d. (1756). *An essay on the origin of human knowledge; being a supplement to Mr. Locke's Essay on the human understanding (Translation of Essai sur l'origine des connaissances humaines).* London: J. Nourse.

Darwin, C. (1859). *The origin of species.* Cambridge, MA: Harvard Press.

Darwin, C. (1871). *The descent of man.* London: Murray.

Dawkins, R. (1996). *Climbing Mount Improbable.* New York: W. W. Norton.

Dessalles, J.-L. (1998). Altruism, status, and the origin of relevance. In J. R. Hurford, M. Studdert-Kennedy, & C. Knight (Eds.), *The evolution of language* (pp. 130-147). Cambridge, UK: Cambridge University Press.

Dunbar, R. (1993). Coevolution of neocortical size, group size, and language in humans. *Behavioral and Brain Sciences, 16*(4), 681-735.

Dunbar, R. (1997). *Grooming, gossip, and the evolution of language.* Cambridge, MA: Harvard University Press.

Dunbar, R. I. M. (in press). Language, music and laughter in evolutionary perspective. In D. K. Oller & U. Griebel (Eds.), *The evolution of communication systems: A comparative approach.* Cambridge: MIT Press.

Elowson, A. M., Snowdon, C. T., & Lazaro-Perea, C. (1998). "Babbling" and social context in infant monkeys: parallels to human infants. *Trends in cognitive sciences, 2*(1), 31-37.

Fitch, W. T. (in press). Evolving honest communication systems: Kin selection and "mother tongues." In D. K. Oller & U. Griebel (Eds.), *The evolution of communication systems: A comparative approach.* Cambridge: MIT Press.

Gärdenfors, P. (in press). Cooperation and the evolution of symbolic communication. In D. K. Oller & U. Griebel (Eds.), *The evolution of communication systems: A comparative approach.* Cambridge: MIT Press.

Gardner, R. A., Gardner, B. T., & Drumm, P. (1989). Voiced and signed responses of cross-fostered chimpanzees. In R. A. Gardner, B. T. Gardner, & T. E. Van Cantfort (Eds.), *Teaching sign language to chimpanzees* (Vol. 165, pp. 664-672). Albany: State University of New York Press.

Gibson, K. R. (1990). Tool use, imitation, and deception in cebus. In S. T. Parker & K. R. Gibson (Eds.), *"Language" and intelligence in monkeys and apes: Comparative developmental perspectives* (pp. 205-218). New York: Cambridge University Press.

Green, S. (1975). Variation of vocal pattern with social situation in the Japanese monkey (*Macaca fuscata*): A field study. In L. Rosenblum (Ed.), *Primate behavior* (Vol. 4, pp. 1-102). New York: Academic Press.

Hamilton, W. D. (1963). The evolution of altruistic behavior. *American Naturalist, 97,* 354-356.

Hauser, M. (1996). *The evolution of communication.* Cambridge: MIT Press.

Hayes, C. (1951). *The ape in our house.* New York: Harper.

Hockett, C. F., & Altmann, S. A. (1968). A note on design features. In T. A. Sebeok (Ed.), *Animal communication: techniques of study and results of research.* Bloomington: Indiana University Press.

Holmgren, K., Lindblom, B., Aurelius, G., Jalling, B., & Zetterstrom, R. (1986). On the phonetics of infant vocalization. In B. Lindblom & R. Zetterstrom (Eds.), *Precursors of early speech* (pp. 51-63). New York: Stockton Press.

Kojima, S. (2001). Early vocal development in a chimpanzee infant. In T. Matsuzawa (Ed.), *Primate origins of human cognition and behavior* (pp. 190-196). New York: Springer-Verlag.

Koopmans-van Beinum, F. J., & van der Stelt, J. M. (1986). Early stages in the development of speech movements. In B. Lindblom & R. Zetterstrom (Eds.), *Precursors of early speech* (pp. 37-50). New York: Stockton Press.

Kroodsma, D. E. (1999). Making ecological sense of song development. In M. D. Hauser & M. Konishi (Eds.), *The design of animal communication* (pp. 319-342). Cambridge: MIT Press.

Leakey, R. (1994). *The origin of humankind.* New York: Basic Books.

Locke, J. (in press). Parental selection of vocal behaviors in the evolution of spoken language. In M. Tallerman (Ed.), *Evolutionary prerequisites for language.* Oxford, UK: Oxford University Press.

Locke, J. L. (1993). *The child's path to spoken language.* Cambridge, MA: Harvard University Press.

Loizos, C. (1969). Play behavior in higher primates: a review. In D. Morris (Ed.), *Primate ethology.* Garden City, NY: Anchor Books, Doubleday.

Lorenz, K. (1951). Ausdrucksbewegungen höherer Tiere. [Expressive displays of higher animals]. *Naturwissenschaften, 38,* 113-116.

Marler, P. (1975). On the origin of speech from animal sounds. In J. F. Kavanagh & J. Cutting (Eds.), *The role of speech in language* (pp. 11-37). Cambridge: MIT Press.

Marler, P., Evans, C. S., & Hauser, M. (1992). Animal signals: Reference, motivation or both? In H. Papoušek, U. Jürgens, & M. Papoušek (Eds.), *Nonverbal vocal communication* (pp. 66-86). New York: Cambridge University Press.

Masataka, N., & Fujita, K. (1989). Vocal learning of Japanese and rhesus monkeys. *Behaviour, 109,* 191-199.

Mayr, E. (1972). Sexual selection and natural selection. In B. Campbell (Ed.), *Sexual selection and the descent of man.* Chicago: Aldine.

Morris, D. (1967). *The naked ape.* New York: Dell.

Nottebohm, F. (1981). A brain for all seasons: Cyclical anatomical changes in song control nuclei of the canary brain. *Science, 214,* 1368-1370.

Oller, D. K. (1980). The emergence of the sounds of speech in infancy. In G. Yeni Komshian, J. Kavanagh, & C. Ferguson (Eds.), *Child phonology: Vol. 1. Production* (pp. 93-112). New York: Academic Press.

Oller, D. K. (1981). Infant vocalizations: Exploration and reflexivity. In R. E. Stark (Ed.), *Language behavior in infancy and early childhood* (pp. 85-104). New York: Elsevier North Holland.

Oller, D. K. (1986). Metaphonology and infant vocalizations. In B. Lindblom & R. Zetterstrom (Eds.), *Precursors of early speech* (pp. 21-35). New York: Stockton Press.

Oller, D. K. (2000). *The emergence of the speech capacity.* Mahwah, NJ: Erlbaum.

Oller, D. K., Buder, E. H., & Nathani, S. (2003, November). *Origins of speech: How infant vocalizations provide a foundation.* Miniseminar for the American Speech-Language Hearing Association convention, Chicago.

Owren, M. J., Dieter, J. A., Seyfarth, R. M., & Cheney, D. L. (1993). Vocalizations of rhesus (*Macaca mulatta*) and Japanese (*M. fuscata*) macaques cross-fostered between species show evidence of only limited modification. *Developmental Psychobiology, 26*(7), 389-406.

Papoušek, H., & Papoušek, M. (1983). Biological basis of social interactions: Implications of research for an understanding of behavioural deviance. *Journal of Child Psychiatry, 24*(1), 117-129.

Papoušek, M. (1994). *Vom ersten Schrei zum ersten Wort: Anfänge der Sprachentwickelung in der vorsprachlichen Kommunikation* [From the first cry to the first word: The onset of speech development in prelinguistic communication]. Bern, Switzerland: Verlag Hans Huber.

Searcy, W. A., & Nowicki, S. (1999). Functions of song variation in song sparrows. In M. D. Hauser & M. Konishi (Eds.), *The design of animal communication* (pp. 575-595). Cambridge: MIT Press.

Searle, J. (1976). A classification of illocutionary acts. *Language in Society, 5*, 1-23.

Seyfarth, R. M., & Cheney, D. L. (1997). Some general features of vocal development in nonhuman primates. In C. T. Snowdon & M. Hausberger (Eds.), *Social influences on vocal development* (pp. 249-273). New York: Cambridge University Press.

Snowdon, C. (in press). Social processes in the evolution of complex cognition and communication. In D. K. Oller & U. Griebel (Eds.), *Evolution of communication systems: A comparative approach*. Cambridge: MIT Press.

Snowdon, C. T., Elowson, A. M., & Rousch, R. S. (1997). Social influences on vocal development in New World primates. In C. T. Snowdon & M. Hausberger (Eds.), *Social influences on vocal development* (pp. 234-248). New York: Cambridge University Press.

Stark, R. (1981). Infant vocalization: A comprehensive view. *Infant Medical Health Journal, 2*(2), 118-128.

Stark, R. E. (1980). Stages of speech development in the first year of life. In G. Yeni-Komshian, J. Kavanagh, & C. Ferguson (Eds.), *Child phonology: Vol. 1. Production* (pp. 73-90). New York: Academic Press.

Stern, D. N. (1974). Mother and infant at play: The dyadic interaction involving facial, vocal, and gaze behaviors. In M. Lewis & L. A. Rosenblum (Eds.), *The effect of the infant on its caregiver* (pp. 187-213). New York: John Wiley.

Struhsaker, T. T. (1967). Auditory communication among vervet monkeys (*Cercopithecus aethiops*). In S. A. Altmann (Ed.), *Social communication among primates* (pp. 281-324). Chicago: Chicago University Press.

Sutton, D. (1979). Mechanisms underlying learned vocal control in primates. In H. D. Steklis & M. J. Raleigh (Eds.), *Neurobiology of social communication in primates: an evolutionary perspective* (pp. 45-67). New York: Academic Press.

Tinbergen, N. (1951). *The study of instinct.* Oxford, UK: Oxford University Press.

Trevarthen, C. (1974). Conversations with a two-month-old. *New Scientist, 2*, 230-235.

Trevarthen, C. (1977). Descriptive analysis of infant communicative behavior. In H. R. Schaffer (Ed.), *Studies in mother-infant interaction*. London: Academic Press.

Tronick, E. Z., Als, H., & Brazelton, T. B. (1977, Spring). Mutuality in mother-infant interaction. *Journal of Communication,* 74-79.

van der Stelt, J. M. (1993). *Finally a word: A sensori-motor approach of the mother-infant system in its development towards speech.* Amsterdam: Uitgave IFOTT.

West, M. J., King, A. P., & Freeberg, T. M. (1997). Building a social agenda for the study of bird song. In C. T. Snowdon & M. Hausberger (Eds.), *Social influences on vocal development* (pp. 41-56). Cambridge, UK: Cambridge University Press.

Zlatin, M. (1975a, November). *Explorative mapping of the vocal tract and primitive syllabification in infancy: The first six months.* Paper presented at the American Speech and Hearing Association Convention, Washington, DC.

Zlatin, M. (1975b). *Preliminary descriptive model of infant vocalization during the first 24 weeks: Primitive syllabification and phonetic exploratory behavior* (Final Report, Project No 3-4014, NE-G-00-3-0077). National Institutes of Health Research Grants, Bethesda, MD.

6

On Why It Takes a Village

Cooperative Breeders, Infant Needs, and the Future

Sarah Blaffer Hrdy

. . . the maternal instinct is the root whence sympathy has sprung and that is the source whence the cohesive quality of the tribe originated.

—Eliza Burt Gamble, 1894

Reconsidering What We Think We Know About Mothers

Anyone who has ever spent time watching chimpanzees will be familiar with the cozy image of a mother tenderly using one arm to hold her newborn baby snug against her body. How natural this seems! The mother-infant

Author's Note: I am indebted to Kristen Hawkes, Jon Seger, and Mary Jane West-Eberhard for discussion and comments. This paper was originally presented as one in the series of Tanner Lectures on Human Values, titled "The Past, Present and Future of the Human Family," delivered at the University of Utah, February 27 and 28, 2001, and published in *The Tanner Lectures on Human Values,* Vol. 23, University of Utah Press.

bond is the first, the most crucial, and in many social creatures, the most enduring social relationship. Who would bother to ask: "Why is that mother carrying her baby?" The answer seems obvious: That's just what primate mothers do. We take it for granted that among our closest primate relations, mothers carry their babies all the time, just as we assume our Paleolithic ancestresses must have.

With few exceptions (and most of these include ruffed lemurs and other prosimians still so "primitive" as to stash their litters in nests), primates bear one baby at a time. The mother then carries her single baby wherever she goes. In ancestral environments, infants left on their own would quickly have succumbed to starvation or predation. This was humankind's "Environment of Evolutionary Adaptedness," according to John Bowlby (1969), who in the 1950s was arguably the world's first evolutionary psychiatrist. No wonder *all* baby primates desperately seek "the set goal" of physical contact with somebody and find it comforting to be close to their mothers, said Bowlby. No wonder a baby monkey becomes emotionally attached to whichever warm and familiar creature reliably responds to its needs. Most often, that individual is the mother.

Today, Bowlby's theory of attachment is basic to our understanding of infant development. But breast-feeding aside, are mothers the only individuals qualified to provide babies with a secure base? This brings us back to the question of *why* chimp mothers carry their babies.

For anyone who has ever had to care for a newborn baby (especially one that can't cling to body hair the way a chimp can), it scarcely comes as news that carrying a baby is awkward, reduces efficiency, and interferes with activities like hunting or even socializing. Adolescent chimps, for example, travel gregariously in groups. Yet after they become mothers, chimps are almost invariably solitary because their slowness puts them at a competitive disadvantage in foraging for ripe fruit (Wrangham, 2000). As gregarious as almost all primates are, chimp mothers carrying babies cannot afford to be. So, why doesn't the mother hand her infant over to a babysitter—say, her adolescent daughter pushily eager to take hold of the baby? The answer is: It's not safe for a chimp mother to do this.

Wild chimps are hunters with a lust for animal flesh. There is a real danger that other chimps in the community might try to wrest her baby away and eat it. A subadult allomother might not be able to prevent that. Unable to take advantage of assistance from other group members, a chimp mother carries her baby everywhere not because this is what the mother instinctively "wants" to do or because it is essential for her infant's healthy development, but because she lacks safe alternatives.

Not long ago, I was visiting a colony of bonobos in Holland and happened to be watching a mother with her baby. A keeper had just given the bonobos some sugarcane. Using one hand to hold the stalk, each bonobo was using the other hand to strip off sweet portions to eat. But this was a daunting challenge for a young, and also subordinate, mother who could not hold her baby and eat at the same time. To do so, she moved away from the other bonobos (who in any event were preoccupied with their own treats) and set her baby down on the straw on the bottom of the cage—something she would never do in the wild. Then she tore into her sugarcane. Clearly, this mother's object was to protect her infant, not necessarily to carry it everywhere. When she had a safe alternative to toting her infant everywhere, she used it. Human apes confront the same trade-off between keeping the infant safe and keeping themselves fed.

Homo Daycarensis?

True, *Homo sapiens* is clever enough to manufacture special devices—woven slings, leather *karosses,* or modern *snuglis*—that make it easier to work with a baby on the mother's body, as well as hammocks and cradles that position infants safely off the ground. We build houses with walls to keep predators out of nurseries. Still, the more incompatible with child care the mother's work is, the more pressure on mothers to delegate care. The more available, willing, and competent caretakers other than the mother or "allomothers" are, the more readily a mother takes advantage of allomaternal assistance. Consider the case of the Efé of Central Africa, the most traditional of pygmy peoples. The Efé still hunt small prey communally with nets, much as archeologists believe humans were doing tens of thousand of years ago (Soffer, Adovasio, & Hyland, 2000).

Among the Efé, infants are passed around among group members on the first day of life. By 3 weeks of age, babies are with allomothers 40% of daytime and with mothers the rest. By 18 weeks, hours with allomothers (60% of the time) exceed time with the baby's own mother. Infants average 14 different caretakers, including fathers, brothers, sisters, aunts, grandmothers, as well as unrelated individuals living in the village; orphans fostered in from other families are especially active caretakers. Similar child care patterns have been reported for some, but by no means all, foraging peoples (e.g., the Aka, Agta, or Andaman Islanders). Yet we take it for granted that the chimplike pattern of *mother exclusively*, which is the pattern made famous for hunter-gatherers like the !Kung, is the normal one. Hence, even the anthropologists studying them still assume that communal care systems like the Efé's are "unique" (Ivey, 2000) or unusual for our species. I'm not so sure.

In just the last quarter century, as anthropologists and sociobiologists have started to compare notes, one of the spectacular surprises has been how much allomaternal care goes on, not just among village and urban as well as foraging people but also, once we started to look, among animals generally. Diverse organisms have converged on cooperative caretaking as a way to rear large litters, offspring that are especially large, or (as in the human case) infants that are both especially large and slow maturing and also (for an ape) closely spaced. In general, cooperative breeders are characterized by unusually flexible and opportunistic breeding systems, as well as by various adaptations that increase the availability of allomothers (group members other than the mother who help her rear her offspring).

Where it occurs, cooperative breeding permits mothers to produce especially costly young or to rear more offspring than otherwise would survive. Among wild jackals, for example, parents raise about two extra pups for every alloparent in the group helping them. Anyone who has ever wondered how social insects, such as bees, wasps, and termites, managed to expand to fully one third of the animal biomass in Amazonian rainforests need look no further than the world's most extensive and reliable communal nurseries. While honeybee queens specialize in doing what they do best, devoting their enormous abdomens to the task of squeezing out 2,000 eggs a day, nonreproductive group members (genetically no different from queens, but never fed the ovary-building special food, or "royal jelly," that transformed their sister into a queen) work away at what they do best: tending the hive and the next generation (Wilson, 1975).

Cooperative breeding allows animals to take advantage of processes and resources (such as honey making or coordinated hunting) as well as allowing them to move into, and even dominate, new habitats that otherwise would not be available. The cooperatively breeding Florida scrub jay, for example, persists where other jays cannot. These avian hunters and gatherers, living on lizards, frogs, and berries, breed in relict patches of scrub oak despite unrelentingly heavy predation pressure on their nests from hawks and snakes. They manage to fledge at least a few young by relying on help from young jays that have not yet started to breed, which serve as lookouts and helpers. Since suitable habitat is scarce, helpers benefit as well by remaining in the group until a breeding position opens up (Woolfenden & Fitzpatrick, 1990). It was cooperative breeding, with its divisions of labor, food sharing, and extra help for mothers, that permitted scrub jays and naked mole rats to occupy novel habitats and social insects and wolves to spread over vast geographic areas. With the emergence of the genus *Homo*, cooperative breeding was to permit a hunting and gathering ape to spread more widely and swiftly than any primate ever had before, moving out of Africa 100,000 years ago, gradually covering and (temporarily at least) dominating the globe.

Flexible Phenotypes

Cooperative breeding is an option only for creatures that already live in groups. For mammals, the story begins with offspring staying near mothers in *philopatric* associations, from the Greek for loving one's natal place, or "home country." Benefits of philopatry include remaining safe in familiar terrain (migrating is dangerous) and continuing to take advantage of remaining near kin, near known resources such as safe sleeping places, fruiting trees, and stored food. On average, these benefits from philopatry must outweigh the advantages from dispersing: leaving competitors behind, finding a new territory, starting to breed in one's own right. Delayed dispersal, along with delayed maturation, means that "prereproductive" group members—teenagers, "spinster" aunts, real and honorary uncles—will be on hand with little better to do (in a Darwinian sense) than stay alive and help kin rear young. But helpers need to be ready to shift to the breeding mode should the opportunity arise. Thus, cooperative breeding requires phenotypic flexibility. The same individual has to be prepared morphologically, physiologically, and behaviorally to assume different roles at different life stages and in response to different opportunities. A female marmoset may be a helper this year, a mother the next. She may have one mate or several.

Phenotypic flexibility lies at the heart of cooperative breeding and has led to fascinating adaptations. Many of these involve delayed or suppressed reproduction, with some fairly bizarre side effects, as in allomothers who, without ever being pregnant or giving birth, start to lactate and suckle babies.

An alpha female wolf, paired for life with one male, will typically be assisted by younger group members, who hunt and devour prey, then return to the den to regurgitate partially digested meat for her pups to eat. Sometimes, the belly of one of these subordinate females will swell up as if she were pregnant. During this pseudopregnancy, she undergoes hormonal transformations similar to real pregnancy and begins to make milk. Vestiges of cooperative breeding frequently crop up in domestic dogs, distant descendants of cooperatively breeding wolves. I once observed a pseudopregnant Jack Russell terrier chase away a mother cat and then adopt and breast-feed her kittens. Suckling young of another species is scarcely adaptive behavior, but in the environment of evolutionary relevance where this female's responsiveness to infant cues evolved, pseudopregnancy followed by lactation increased the milk available to large litters.

So, why doesn't a subordinate female breed herself instead of helping out? In a number of cooperatively breeding species, like wild dogs, wolves, hyenas, dingos, dwarf mongooses, and marmosets, the reason is that if she did, the alpha female would most likely destroy her young. Worse still, sometimes (as has been observed among wild dogs and marmosets) not only are gestational resources from the subordinate female wasted on doomed young, but thereafter, even more somatic resources are diverted to the dominant female's babies, which use the subordinate as a wet nurse (Digby, 2000). The threat of coercion makes postponing (or "suppressing") ovulation the better part of valor, the least bad option, for females that then wait to breed until the coast is clear (Solomon & French, 1997).

Women never evolved the capacity to suppress ovulation or to spontaneously lactate to nurse someone else's baby, although humans sometimes consciously converge upon this pattern by hiring or enslaving wet nurses. But even without suppressed ovulation, human life histories assure the availability of unusually well-qualified allomothers. Delayed maturation means pre-reproductive babysitters are usually on hand, but even better—and uniquely among primates—long life spans after menopause make postreproductive kin available (Hawkes, O'Connell, Blurton-Jones, Alvarez, & Charnov, 1998). Lacking infants of their own, their own reproductive careers behind them, such postreproductive allomothers are likely to be as dedicated and single-minded in caring for immature kin as they are experienced.

The Usefulness of Extra "Fathers"

Unusually flexible mating systems are a hallmark of cooperative breeders. Individuals belonging to the same species can be found living monogamously, polygynously (one male, several females), or in polyandrous groupings (one female, several males) depending on social and ecological circumstances. Such flexibility characterizes our species as well. Looking across traditional societies, mothers can be found in monogamous, polygynous, or polyandrous unions. Since Darwin, however, we have assumed that humans evolved in families where a mother relied on one male to help her rear her young in a nuclear family; yet the diversity of human family arrangements (encompassing as it does the full spectrum of monogamous, polygynous, and polyandrous permutations) is better predicted by assuming that our ancestors evolved as cooperative breeders.

In some traditional matrilineal societies, such as the Moso or the Na peoples of China, mothers remain among their kin without a mate in residence at all. Yet nowhere is it feasible for a mother to rear children on her own. Even in the modern world, where terms such as "single mother" are widely used, survival of mother and young cannot be considered apart from shelter and food provided within a larger social framework. The one absolute constant is that a mother needs assistance, although, as is typical of cooperative breeders, women are flexible and opportunistic concerning just who provides the help they need.

Indeed, human symbol-generating cultural capacities offer interesting bonuses in this regard. Social customs and propaganda are used to increase availability of allomaternal assistance. I like to imagine that it was a cagey white-haired grandmother who, thousands of years ago, first invented the folktale to beat all folktales in terms of its helpfulness to her daughters. According to this folk mythology—which by now has spread over a vast area of South America, encompassing peoples belonging to six different languages groups—each fetus has to be built up from installments of semen contributed by all the men that a woman has had sex with in the 10 months or so prior to birth. Although, in fact, women do not bear litters sired by several fathers, the way wolves, jackals, and some other cooperative breeders do, and there is no such thing as a human baby with more than one genetic father, this biological fiction about partible paternity has proved extremely convenient for mothers who needed to elicit extra assistance rearing their young and getting their children fed.

However it came to pass, from the Aché of Paraguay in the south, to the Mehinaku, Kaingang, Arawete, and Curipaco peoples of central and eastern Brazil, then westward to the Matis of Peru, and northward to the Yanomami and Bari in Venezuela, mothers rely on this convenient biological fiction to line up multiple honorary fathers who will help provision them and their children (Beckerman & Valentine, 2002). Based on data from the Aché when these people still lived as nomadic foragers, anthropologist Kim Hill found that 63% of children were ascribed to more than one father and survived better with two men helping. Among the Bari, a fishing-horticultural people, two dads were similarly optimal. According to Steve Beckerman and his coworkers, 80% of 194 children with one secondary "father" in addition to their primary "father," the man the woman is married to, survived to age 15, compared with a 64% chance of survival for 628 children without a secondary father. This makes sense in societies where provisioning by males is unpredictable, as is often the case with fishing and hunting; and where fathers have a high probability of dying or defecting, relying on several fathers has the same beneficial effects as the presence of many males in marmosets. Not surprisingly, as soon as a woman suspects pregnancy, she attempts to seduce one of the better fishermen or hunters in her group, which may be the flip side of the finding that the best hunters and the best fishermen have the most lovers.

Across cultures, polyandrous arrangements take many forms. Often, polyandrous unions are temporary. For example, among the Shirishana Yanamamo, all marriages begin monogamously; thereafter, if the husband gets his way, an extra wife is added. But if wives are in short supply or there are other problems to be solved, an extra husband is temporarily added to the family unit. The Yanamamo are best known as "the Fierce People," among whom men raid other groups to steal many wives for their harems. But this is only part of their story. Many Yanamamo women spend at least some portion of their married lives in polyandrous unions, a time-honored standby to insure that children get provisioned and tended in a part of the world where children without fathers are at a serious, even lethal, disadvantage.

The South American belief in partible paternity facilitates cooperative provisioning. But even without this myth, an informal style of clan-based polyandry produces the same outcome in parts of central Africa and Asia. Should a husband die, his real and fictional clan brothers will look out for his children.

Ethnocentric Stereotypes

Forget the image of promiscuous women just out to have "fun." At stake is a serious endeavor: mothers making do under difficult circumstances. Mother-centered models force us to rethink long-held assumptions about the nuclear family. Not long ago, a *Wall Street Journal* editorial titled "Feminism Isn't Anti-Sex: It's Only Anti-Family" complained that feminism and especially birth control are responsible for the contemporary breakdown of families in America, with special reference to what is going on in America's inner cities. But given that polyandrous mothers probably predate by thousands of years that most modern of postindustrial luxuries known as "feminism," we would do better to focus instead on demographic and economic realities constraining maternal choices: high rates of male mortality, imprisonment, and defection and job prospects that translate into poor "hunting" prospects, making it impractical for a mother to rely on one man.

Just as surely as romanticized preconceptions about what mothers instinctively want and should do shaped our understanding of what mothers actually did do, ethnocentric stereotypes about mothers evolving in nuclear families shaped the way we viewed the world around us. Even when we observed allomothers caring for young, we assumed the helper must be a coparent and the mother's only mate.

It has been known since the 18th century, for example, that male marmosets are attracted to and carry babies; when zookeepers reported that infants fared better when a male was in the same cage as the mother, primatologists—with the ethnocentrism so characteristic of our species—assumed that Callitrichids must be monogamous, adapted to live in nuclear families. Since the marmoset mother does have better luck rearing young with her mate in the cage with them, the matter might have ended there had primatologists not noticed that mothers, when they could, mated polyandrously with *several* males. Furthermore, these mothers with help from multiple males weaned babies sooner, bred even faster, and had an even higher proportion of their young survive. From the mother marmoset's point of view, reproductively monogamy is fine, but polyandry is even better.

Male care is essential in all the Callitrichids; but for three of the four genera (*Callithrix jacchus, Saquinus mystax, Leontopithecus rosalia*), the more adult males in the group, the higher a mother's reproductive success. Extra males (who may also have mated with the mother) help the parents to carry the infants and provide solid food for the rapidly growing twins so the mother can wean them sooner (Bales, Dietz, Baker, Miller, & Tardif; Snowdon, 1996).

Primability of Caretakers

It would not make a shred of difference, though, how many allomothers were on hand were not other group members inclined to respond to infantile cries or gaping beaks or outstretched hands by picking babies up, delivering food to them, and so forth. Neural and endocrine systems that can be activated, and once activated lead to nurturing, have to be in place. For cooperative caretaking to happen, allomothers have to be susceptible to infant charms and solicitations, amenable to priming.

Fortunately for infants, individuals in many species—including *all* primates—find babies at least interesting and under some circumstances irresistibly attractive. Furthermore, where shared caretaking has paid off and was selected for over time, thresholds for responding have fallen lower, making allomothers more sensitive to the tantalizing signals babies emit.

Typically, it is tougher to elicit nurturing responses from a prereproductive female or from a male than from a recent mother. But it is rarely impossible. Sufficiently primed by the right circumstances, a virgin female or a male eventually responds—even in species where nurturing is not a commonly observed part of the male repertoire. This is one reason why the annals of primatology abound with astonishing adoptions, orphaned chimps adopted by older brothers that never before seemed much interested, or abandoned babies left in the forest and picked up by a female belonging to some other species. As it happens, we know most about priming in rodents.

When male mice encounter a strange pup, they either ignore it or eat it. When sufficiently "primed," however (that is, presented with pup after pup until the males become sensitive to pup signals), males finally quit cannibalizing and caretake: licking pups, gathering them in nests, hovering over them to warm them with their bodies. Primed males do just about everything mothers do, short of lactating. The hormonal basis of such maternal-seeming behavior in males, including humans, is only beginning to be studied.

One reason for the delay had to do with all our preconceived ideas about which individuals "mother." The flip side of the notion that all mothers are nurturing was the idea that "nurturing instincts" are confined to mothers. This was a mistake. When Alan Dixson discovered that male marmosets carrying babies had higher circulating levels of prolactin (the same hormone that is correlated with milk production in mothers) than did males not exposed to babies, the first reaction was skepticism. Even after Dixson's finding was replicated, higher prolactin levels were interpreted as paternal care by a monogamous mammal. Only in the last few years has it become clear that elevated prolactin levels can be found in *any* allomother defending or nurturing immatures, not just in genetic parents. For example, prolactin levels in cooperatively breeding birds, such as scrub jays, go up when nonreproductive helpers are carrying food back to nestlings. Among cooperatively breeding primates, such as marmosets, close contact with infants stimulates release of prolactin in nonreproductives (among *Callithrix jacchus;* Roberts et al., in press) as well as leading to reductions in testosterone (among *Callithrix kuhlii;* Nunes, Fite, & French, 2000). The longer the male carries the infant or the more experienced the male is prior to caretaking, the stronger are these effects.

The biggest surprise, though, was discovering that changes in hormonal levels during a woman's pregnancy might also play a role in priming men living near pregnant women in our species. Prolactin levels in men cohabiting with pregnant women rise over the course of their pregnancies, as do cortisol levels and to some extent estradiol. The most significant effect, though, was a 30% drop in testosterone in men right after birth. Declining testosterone might increase "paternal" behaviors simply by reducing male involvement in other behaviors, such as competing with other males, that might divert them from nurturing. The more responsive to infants men are, the more likely it is that their testosterone will continue to drop (Storey, Walsh, Quinton, & Wynne-Edwards, 2000; Wynne-Edwards & Reburn, 2000).

No one is suggesting that fathers are equivalent to mothers, male caretakers to female ones. Indisputably, hormonal changes during pregnancy and lactation are far more pronounced in mothers than the modest but still detectable changes in men consorting with them. But the point is that *both* sexes are primable in the sense that their thresholds for responding to infants will be lowered by proximity to pregnant mothers and newborn babies. By themselves, proximity and involvement can elicit nurturing. This explains why a fully engaged father, in frequent contact with his infant, can be even more committed to infant well-being than a detached mother. This point tended to be overlooked in early studies because it was taken for granted that mothers evolved to be the sole caretakers of their infants. Attention was riveted by the mother-infant pair, ignoring the social unit around them.

The general primability of both mothers and allomothers helps explain why genetic relatedness by itself can be a surprisingly unreliable predictor of involvement. The fact that humans turn out to be quite primable helps us understand, for example, why adoptive parents, wet nurses, or day care workers can become so emotionally attached to the infants they care for. Based on DNA data, both !Kung San and Aka men have roughly equivalent (95%) chances of being the father of their mates' children, yet the former engage in relatively little infant care, the latter a great deal. The likeliest explanation is the opportunity for priming to matter among Aka men, who remain in close proximity to infants—within arm's reach—roughly 47% of the time (Hewlett, 1988).

In the environments in which humans evolved, immature group members were, more likely than not, relatives. Predispositions to help them evolved according to Hamilton's Rule whereby the cost of helping was less than the benefits calibrated by the probable degree of genetic relatedness to the individual helped. But practically speaking, our ancestors did not think in terms of genes. What mattered were cues from infants processed at an emotional level. This brings us to the source of all these appealing signals: human infants.

The Twofold Tasks of Human Babies

> As soon as we become convinced love is not possible, love becomes impossible.
>
> —Randy Nesse, 2000

Right from birth, newborns are powerfully motivated to stay close, root— even creep—in quest of nipples, which they instinctively suck on. These ancient primate urges to stay close and to get lactation under way are the first instinctive behaviors any of us engage in and are among the most powerful in the human repertoire. But maintaining contact is harder to do for little humans than for other primates. For starters, the newborn's mother has no hair for the baby to catch hold of. The mother herself has to position the baby on her breast and go to some trouble to keep him or her there. The mother must be motivated to pick up her baby hours and days before lactation is under way. There follow myriad decision points where a mother can invest to the fullest extent or take shortcuts.

The mother's commitment to her infant is the single most important determiner of survival prospects. But a long evolutionary history of cooperative breeding has meant that both a mother's commitment to her newborn and the level of support she is able to provide are linked to how much social support she herself has. More than in any other ape, a mother's love is contingent on her circumstances. So, what (in an evolutionary sense) have been the consequences for human infants of their highly precarious dependence?

Within days of birth, human babies are capable of the same kind of contact calls and piteous cries that other primates make, but in addition, they can read and perform all sorts of facial expressions, fully engaging in eye-to-eye contact with people who put their faces within the range that babies can see (around 18 inches). Babies may reward such attentions by imitating the faces peering at them. Orang and chimp babies are also interested in their mothers' faces and take a brief look now and then. But they do not gaze deeply into the mother's eyes like lovers in the early phases of a relationship, what pediatricians call *en face socializing,* the way human babies and their caretakers do. To the extent that psychiatrists and pediatricians thought about this at all, they tended to assume they were witnessing the artifacts of human mental agility and our ability to use language. Interactions between mother and baby, including all the vocal play and intermittent babble, were interpreted (following Colwyn Trevarthen) as "proto-conversations." Yet even babies lacking face-to-face stimulation (say, babies born blind) learn to talk. Furthermore, very few other primates engage in such continuous contact noises or "babbling" (Elowson, Snowdon, & Lazaro-Perea, 1998; Papousek, Papousek, & Suomi, 1991); and although none of these babbling monkey babies learn to talk, all, rather curiously, belong to the cooperatively breeding Callitrichidae, little primates that like human babies may have a more pressing need than most other primates to engage allomaternal attentions. (This is not to say that babbling is not important for learning to talk, only to question which came first: babbling so as to learn to talk or being predisposed to evolve into a talker because that creature was born a babbler!)

But back to my point: Infancy is the most perilous life phase—why linger there? Why not grow big as fast as possible, into a juvenile? Yet instead of using available energy to outgrow their vulnerability, human babies are diverting calories into sophisticated, metabolically costly neurological machinery for eye contact, imitation, emotional expression—into equipment that other primates (who also need to be attached to their mothers) manage perfectly well without. What is all this energetically quite costly infantile face-watching about? One possibility is that the infrastructure for later human cognition is so intricate that babies need to start early. But there is an alternative, not necessarily mutually exclusive, explanation. The baby may also be monitoring his or her mother, learning to read her moods and assaying her level of commitment. If human infants have had to become connoisseurs of maternal responsiveness, this would explain why babies become so upset when experimenters ask their mothers to wear expressionless plastic masks. It could also explain why babies become so unnerved when mothers are depressed.

Ambivalent Mothers and Pathological Outcomes

To the Darwinian-minded John Bowlby, each infant was a composite put together from innumerable past lives forged from what Bowlby (1969) called "the Environment of Evolutionary Adaptedness." Separation from the mother meant death by predation, so that any ape that survived to reproduce must have managed to stay attached. Being attached was normal and led to security; being detached was abnormal. For mid-20th-century attachment theorists, children could be divided into those who were securely attached to their mothers and those who were "maternally deprived," insecurely attached children, at risk for developing into delinquents—the youngsters Bowlby designated in his early writings as "juvenile thieves." These were children who grew up unmotivated to respect "authority"; short on "compliance," empathy, and conscience; less liable to dwell on social consequences and on how others would feel; and liable to take things without asking or paying.

One of the strongest case studies consistent with Bowlby's belief that maternal deprivation put children at risk derives from data compiled in the book *Born Unwanted* (Dytrych, Matejcek, & Schuller, 1988). The centerpiece is a study of 220 children in Prague, Czechoslovakia, born between 1961 and 1963 to married women who had twice sought and twice been denied abortions. On this basis, the mothers' subsequent infants were designated "unwanted." In this study, 110 of the "unwanted" boys and 110 "unwanted" girls were pair-matched with controls of the same age, school class, sex, and birth order who had the same number of siblings and whose mothers were all matched for age and socioeconomic status as determined by the husband's educational level. All were from two-parent homes. (Had young and/or unmarried mothers been included, the results would presumably have been even more dramatic.)

When Professor Zdenek Dytrych, a psychologist at Charles University in Prague, and coworkers relocated 160 of the unwanted pregnancies and 150 of the controls 22 years later, following up on the initial "Prague Cohort," more than twice as many of the "unwanted" children had received criminal sentences (41 versus 19), and more than twice as many (22 versus 9) had been sentenced to prison, all statistically significant differences. Children born "unwanted" were also less likely to describe themselves as happy or satisfied with life, but I focus on the criminal records because the results seem more clear-cut.[1]

This is a remarkable study consistent with the hypothesis that children born unwanted are at greater risk for the behaviors that our society considers deviant. But why? Nothing is known about actual child care.

Much of the research on unwanted children has been done by those advocating particular social agendas. It is not a domain that invites dispassionate analysis. Furthermore, and as always, it is difficult to evaluate causal relationships when many different factors are involved. Was the mother the critical variable? Or was her unwillingness to bear the child merely symptomatic of a nonsupportive social situation when she was pregnant, the same situation that the developing child picks up on after birth? (Note that the Prague study controlled for many variables, but not allomaternal interventions.) And what of all the subjects who did not end up with criminal records? Some mothers may, of course, have grown more committed, or else their "sociopathic" children just did not get caught. But we also want to know: Who else might have been involved in rearing these children? No doubt, Bowlby was right about pathological outcomes for the most extreme cases of maternal and social deprivation. (Neurological and other deficits in the most neglected victims of Nikolae Ceausescu's Romanian orphanages come to mind.) But the idea that insecurely attached youngsters grow up at risk of developing into sociopaths has itself developed in interesting ways since Bowlby.

Why We Need to Consider
Models Based on Cooperative Breeding

So far, most researchers studying development have presumed the antiquity and the normalcy of the nuclear family with a fixed division of labor (mother nurturing, father providing). Variables studied included (a) availability and responsiveness of the mother, (b) presence or absence of the father, and

(c) whether or not the baby was in day care or mother care. Studies with this model in mind reveal that children with less responsive mothers are at greater risk for being noncompliant, becoming aggressive, and doing less well in day care and later in school.

I know of no studies designed to take into account the possibility that humans evolved as cooperative breeders so that infants are cued to the traits most relevant in that context, namely, (a) availability and responsiveness of mother along with (b) availability and responsiveness of allomothers. That is, in terms of developmental outcomes, the most relevant variables might be secure versus insecure, rather than securely or insecurely attached to the mother. Even though we do not know what kind of child care characterized our ancestors in the Pleistocene, it is worth noting that the most comprehensive study we have on the effects of allomaternal care is just as compatible with predictions generated by the hypothesis that humans evolved as cooperative breeders as the same results are with predictions generated by the hypothesis that human babies are adapted to be reared exclusively by mothers.

Alarmed by statistics showing that 62% of U.S. mothers with kids under age 6 are currently working outside the home and that the majority of these mothers are back at work within 3 to 5 months of giving birth, the National Institute of Child Health and Human Development (NICHD) set out to study how the children of these women were faring in different child care arrangements. Beginning in 1991, 1,364 children and their families from diverse ethnic and economic backgrounds were studied in 10 locations around the United States. The main finding of the study was that the maternal and allomaternal sensitivity to infant needs was a better predictor of subsequent developmental outcomes (in terms of traits such as respect for others or "compliance" and self-control) than was actual time spent apart from the mother. In other words, the critical variable was not the presence of the mother per se, but how secure infants presumably felt when cared for by familiar people whom the infants had learned would be sensitive and responsive to their needs.

An Aside on Why We Still Need to Worry About Day Care

Those convinced that babies need full-time care from mothers were no doubt surprised by the results of the massive NICHD study. The study found no ill effects from rampant day care, even day care for infants. No doubt, advocates of day care felt vindicated. The additional information that allomaternal care is not particularly unusual in nature, and may even have been part of our Pleistocene heritage, might tempt some to think that the book is now closed and day care is not something we need to worry about. This would be tragically irresponsible.

Keep in mind what the NICHD study actually showed: Day care was better than mother care when the mother was neglectful or abusive—no one's idea of a good situation. Excluding these "worst" cases, there were no detectable ill effects of day care *provided* that infants had a secure relationship with parents to begin with (which I take to mean that babies felt wanted) and care was of a high quality, meaning plenty of staff, the same caretakers all the time, and caretakers sensitive to infant needs: In short, day care workers who behave like committed kin. These conditions are not easily met.

Where it exists at all, this caliber of infant day care—unless family volunteers happen to be available—is expensive. Down the price range, there can be long waiting lines even for inadequate day care. Such day care as is available may be unlikely to foster secure relationships. *Average* rate of turnover among all workers in day care centers is 30% per year. At least one reason for this is obvious. Day care workers are paid an average hourly wage of $6.12, less than parking attendants ($6.38). Family providers earn even less: $3.37 per hour (from U.S. Bureau of Labor Statistics for 1998, cited in Shonkoff & Phillips, 2000, p. 315). Yet day care places can be so hard to come by that mothers desperate to get back to work may forget to ask "What is the ratio of caretakers to infants?" in their eagerness to inquire "When can we begin?"

So, we return to the crux of the matter: Why should good day care be so developmentally indistinguishable from mother-only care?

Sociobiologists Move Beyond Bowlby

Over the last 20 years, researchers familiar with natural history and a broader array of ethnographic cases have started to move beyond the preconceptions that characterized early attachment theory. New disciplines such as sociobiology have led to a greater awareness of just how variable mothers themselves, their circumstances, and their levels of commitment might be. Along with that awareness came the growing realization that there might be caretakers on the scene *other than the mother* (Hinde, 1982; Hrdy 1999; Lamb, Thompson, Gardner, & Charnov, 1985). So, what about all the conditions intermediate between the two extremes of a totally committed mother and no caretaker at all? And what about the role of allomothers in developmental outcomes?

Since Bowlby, evolutionary-minded developmentalists have speculated that infants are monitoring mothers and other caretakers not just to keep caretakers engaged but also to learn about the kind of world they have been born into, and developing accordingly (Hewlett, Lamb, Leyendecker, & Scholmerich, 2000). A Pleistocene mother responsive enough to make her baby feel secure was likely to be a mother embedded in a network of supportive social relationships. Without such support, few mothers, and even fewer infants, were likely to survive.

This takes us back to the suggestion that babies are up to more than just maintaining the relationship with their mothers: the hypothesis that babies are monitoring mothers to gain information about their social world. Impressed by just how variable rearing conditions could be, evolutionary-minded anthropologists and psychologists, including Pat Draper, Michael Lamb, Jay Belsky, Jim Chisholm, and Mary Main, recognized that over evolutionary time, babies who used their mothers as a cue to determining the kind of world they had been born into, and who developed accordingly, might have a survival advantage. It would be important for a baby to know: Is this world filled with people who are going to help me survive? Can I count on them to share? Can I myself afford to share and to count on others, or should I just take what I need however I can?

The optimal way to behave might differ very much depending, say, on whether the father was around or whether the mother had kin to help. Perhaps one parent was dead and the infant was being reared by someone else. In that case, the baby needs to know: "Will I be better off in this life predisposed to reciprocate and share, or should I be looking out for what I can get and taking it?" Being extremely self-centered or selfish, being oblivious to others or lacking conscience, traits that early attachment theorists assumed to be pathological, might in fact be adaptive, making an individual without much support from kin better able to survive.

As Bowlby was well aware, there would have been pitifully little opportunity among Pleistocene foragers for infants without committed mothers to survive. And if humans evolved as cooperative breeders, few mothers without social support would have been likely to commit. Nevertheless, with increasingly sedentary lifestyles, survival chances for children go up—even those without committed mothers. Over the last tens of thousands of years, as people lingered longer in one place, eliminated nearby predators, built walled houses, stored food—not to mention coming to use rubber nipples and pasteurized milk—infant survival became to some extent decoupled from continuous contact with mothers and other caregivers.

Ragged bands of street urchins or orphans in refugee camps come to mind, surviving all manner of neglect. Even in our own homes, children routinely survive caretaking regimens that an Efé or a !Kung mother would view as appallingly negligent: What kind of mother leaves her baby alone at night? And on this point, our babies would agree. Miraculously, we can leave our infants in cribs and come back hours later to find them still healthy, all 10 fingers and 10 toes intact. Never before in the history of humankind have so many infants deprived of social contact and continuous proximity to caretakers survived so well to reproduce themselves so successfully.

Even If We Persist, Will We Still Be Human?

The truth is that the least-studied phase of human development remains the phase during which a child is acquiring all that makes him most distinctively human. . . .

—John Bowlby, 1969

There are all sorts of humanitarian reasons to worry about this situation. But from my peculiar evolutionary perspective, there is even more at stake here than individual suffering. What I see at stake is loss of the very traits that define us as what we are. When I hear people fretting about the future of humankind in the wake of global warming, emergent diseases and rogue viruses, crashing meteorites, and exploding suns, I find myself wondering: But even if we persist, will our species still be human?

Arguably, the capacity to empathize with others has served humans well. The reason our species managed to survive and proliferate to the tune of this planet's 6 billion current occupants has more to do with how readily we learn to cooperate than with what good conquerors we are. It is no accident that humans are so good at remembering who gave us what or invited us to dinner, predisposed to learn that sharing and reciprocating are rewarding and make us feel good. Reciprocal exchange was part and parcel of our long stint as hunters and gatherers, permitting two families to eat even though providers in one had come home empty-handed (Cashdan, 1985; Wiessner, 1996).

It is because humans are so good at cooperating that we can coordinate complex activities that allow us to exploit resources so effectively. Indeed, it is only because our *Homo ergaster* ancestors could cooperate and share that human mothers could afford to bear such slow-maturing, *Homo-sapiens*-like babies in the first place. But this type of sharing and cooperation breaks down without trust. Emotional habits such as being able to notice what others feel and need, caring about them, and being able to respond to them are learned in the first 3 years of life.

At a rudimentary level, all sorts of creatures are good at reading intentions and movements and anticipating what other animals are going to do. Predators from gopher snakes to lions have to be able to anticipate where their quarry will dart. Other apes can figure out what another individual is likely to know or not know, say, about where an experimenter hid some bananas. But compared with humans, this capacity to entertain the psychological perspective of another individual (what psychologists call "perspective taking") is crude.

The novelist Edmund White has defined *compassion* as "taking an interest in all the details of (other people's) existences and understanding their fears and motives, their longings and griefs and vanities" (White, 2001, p. 14). Cognitive neuroscientists such as Marc Hauser describe compassion as being able cognitively and emotionally to put oneself in someone else's shoes and articulate how that person feels. This is why humans spend time and energy worrying about those they have never even seen, for example, AIDS orphans in Africa. This capacity for articulate empathy is uniquely well developed in humans, so much so that many people (including myself) believe that along with language and symbolic thought, this capacity for compassion is quintessentially human—what along with language defines us as human.

This capacity for articulate compassion is uniquely human. But its expression in any particular human varies with both innate propensities and each person's experiences in the course of development. Heritable capacities and development, nature and nurture, are both involved. First, there is each individual's emotional, empathetic component, which studies show is to some degree heritable. Already by 14 months of age, identical twins (who share all genes in common) were more alike in how they responded when an experimenter pretended to pinch her finger on a clipboard and went "Ooooh" than were fraternal twins (who share only half their genes) (Davis, Luce, & Kraus, 1994; Emde et al., 1992). Second, there is a learned component, having more to do with analytical skills than emotion, as each individual learns to look at the world from someone else's perspective. In most people, learning to adopt someone else's perspective occurs in the context of their earliest relationships with mothers and allomothers, where children are also learning to trust or count on other people.

And this is where someone standing back and taking a long-term view of our species sees a serious problem. There is no reason to think that just because humans have evolved to be smart enough to chronicle our histories and speculate about our origins, evolution has come to a standstill. For gene frequencies in human populations have not ceased to change. Rather, they are in constant flux, which is all evolution ever meant: changes in gene frequencies. (A classic example would be the genes that permit people to continue digesting milk after infancy. They are common in populations with a history of herding and milking cattle, absent among those who never did.) But no matter how useful it might be, natural selection cannot operate on a genetic potential, only on traits that are expressed in the course of development. For example, no one doubts that fish benefit from being able to see. Yet fish reared in darkness, like the small cave-dwelling characin fish of Mexico, never develop their capacity to see. In populations of characins long isolated in caves, youngsters no longer develop eyesight even when reared in the light, because through evolutionary time, traits never expressed are lost.

And this is why the idea of so many children reared without learning to trust in others is so worrisome. Selection works only on developmental outcomes, on phenotypes. But if the human capacity for compassion develops only under certain circumstances and if an increasing proportion of the species is surviving to breeding age without developing these capacities, it won't make any difference how beneficial compassion was among our ancestors. There will be no opportunity for this trait to be selected for. Like sight in cave-dwelling fish, the capacity to empathize will be lost. No matter what the dividends might have been in terms of high levels of interpersonal cooperation, natural selection cannot continue to favor a genetic potential that is not expressed. Worse, as larger proportions of people who never had occasion to develop their capacities for empathy survive, empathetic tendencies themselves become less valuable. Who, after all, will there be worth empathizing with?

No doubt, our descendants thousands of years in the future will be bipedal, symbol-generating apes. They will be adept at using sophisticated technology. But will they still be human in the way we—shaped by a long heritage of cooperative breeding—currently define ourselves?

Note

1. One reason we don't hear more about studies such as the Prague Cohort and others has to do with concerns about stigmatization or what might be seen as "developmental profiling" ("So-and-so is just bound to turn out poorly") as well as with concerns about the pressure such findings put on mothers to love children unconditionally.

References

Note: I have tried to keep the number of references to a minimum. For those wishing more complete documentation, please consult the extensive bibliography in *Mother Nature: A History of Mothers, Infants, and Natural Selection* (New York: Pantheon, 1999).

Bales, K., Dietz, J., Baker, A., Miller, K., & Tardif, S. (2000). Effects of allocare-givers on fitness of infants and parents in Callitrichid primates. *Folia Primatologica, 71,* 27-38.

Beckerman, S., & Valentine, P. (Eds.). (2002). *Cultures of multiple fathers: The theory and practice of partible paternity in lowland South America.* Gainesville: University Press of Florida.

Bowlby, J. (1969). *Attachment.* Middlesex, UK: Penguin Books. (Reissued 1971)

Cashdan, E. (1985). Coping with risk: Reciprocity among the Basarwa of Northern Botswana. *Man, 20,* 454-474.

Davis, M. H., Luce, C., & Kraus, S. J. (1994). The heritability of characteristics associated with dispositional empathy. *Journal of Personality, 62,* 369-371.

Digby, L. (2000). Infanticide by female mammals: Implications for the evolution of social systems. In C. van Schaik & C. Janson (Eds.), *Infanticide by males and its implications* (pp. 423-446). Cambridge, UK: Cambridge University Press.

Dytrych, Z., Matejcek, Z., & Schuller, V. (1988). The Prague Cohort: Adolescence and early adulthood. In H. P. David, Z. Dytrych, Z. Matejcek, & V. Schuller (Eds.), *Born unwanted: Developmental effects of denied abortion* (pp. 87-102). New York: Springer.

Elowson, A. M., Snowdon, C., & Lazaro-Perea, C. (1998). "Babbling" and social context in infant monkeys: Parallels to human infants. *Trends in Cognitive Sciences, 2,* 31-37.

Emde, R. N., Plomin, R., Robinson, J., Corley, R., DeFries, J., Fulker, D. W., Reznick, J. S., Campos, J., Kagan, J., & Zahn-Waxler, C. (1992). Temperament, emotion and cognition at fourteen months: The MacArthur Longitudinal Twin Study. *Child Development, 63,* 1437-1455.

Hawkes, K., O'Connell, J. F., Blurton-Jones, N. G., Alvarez, H., & Charnov, E. (1998). Grandmothering, menopause, and the evolution of human life histories. *Proceedings of the National Academy of Sciences, 95,* 1336-1339.

Hewlett, B. S. (1988). Sexual selection and parental investment among Aka pygmies. In L. Betzig, M. Borgerhoff Mulder, & P. Turke (Eds.), *Human reproductive behaviour: A Darwinian perspective* (pp. 263-276). Cambridge, UK: Cambridge University Press.

Hewlett, B. S., Lamb, M. E., Leyendecker, B., & Scholmerich, A. (2000). Internal working models, trust and sharing among foragers. *Current Anthropology, 41,* 287-297.

Hinde, R. A. (1982). Attachment: Some conceptual and biological issues. In J. Stevenson-Hinde & R. M. Parkes (Eds.), *The place of attachment in human behavior.* New York: Basic Books.

Hrdy, S. B. (1999). *Mother Nature: A history of mothers, infants, and natural selection.* New York: Pantheon.

Ivey, P. K. 2000. Cooperative reproduction in Ituri forest hunter-gatherers: Who cares for Efe infants? *Current Anthropology, 41,* 856-866.

Lamb, M. E., Thompson, R. A., Gardner, W., & Charnov, E. (1985). *Infant-mother attachment: The origins and developmental significance of individual differences in strange situation behavior.* Hillsdale, NJ: Erlbaum.

Nunes, S., Fite, J., & French, J. (2000). Variation in steroid hormones associated with infant care behaviour and experience in male marmosets (*Callithrix kuhlii*). *Animal Behaviour, 60,* 857-865.

Papousek, H., Papousek, M., Suomi, S. J., & Rahn, C. W. (1991). Preverbal communication and attachment: Comparative views. In *Intersections with attachment* (pp. 97-122). Hillsdale, NJ: Erlbaum.

Shonkoff, J., & Phillips, D. A. (2000). *From neurons to neighborhoods: The science of early childhood development.* Washington, DC: National Academy Press.

Snowdon, C. (1996). Infant care in cooperatively breeding species. *Advances in the Study of Behavior, 25,* 643-689.

Soffer, O., Adovasio, J. N., & Hyland, D. C. (2000). The "Venus" figurines: Textiles, basketry, gender and status in the Upper Paleolithic. *Current Anthropology, 41.*

Solomon, N., & French, J. (1997). *Cooperative breeding in mammals.* Cambridge, UK: Cambridge University Press.

Storey, A. E., Walsh, C. J., Quinton, R. L., & Wynne-Edwards, K. E. (2000). Hormonal correlates of paternal responsiveness in new and expectant fathers. *Evolution and Human Behavior, 21,* 79-95.

White, E. (2001, January 7). It all adds up. *New York Times Book Review,* p. 14.

Wiessner, P. (1996). Leveling the hunter: Constraints on the status quest in foraging societies. In P. Wiessner & W. Schiefenhovel (Eds.), *Food and the status quest: An interdisciplinary perspective* (pp. 171-191). Oxford, UK: Berghan Press.

Wilson, E. O. (1975). *Sociobiology: The new synthesis.* Cambridge, MA: Harvard University Press.

Woolfenden, G. E., & Fitzpatrick, J. W. (1990). Florida scrub jays: A synopsis after eighteen years of study. In P. B. Stacey & W. D. Koenig (Eds.), *Cooperative breeding in birds: Long-term studies of ecology and behavior* (pp. 241-266). Cambridge, UK: Cambridge University Press.

Wrangham, R. W. (2000). Why are male chimpanzees more gregarious than mothers? A scramble competition hypothesis. In P. Kappeler (Ed.), *Primate males: Causes and consequences of variation in group composition* (pp. 248-258). Cambridge, UK: Cambridge University Press.

Wynne-Edwards, K., & Reburn, C. J. (2000). Behavioral endocrinology of mammalian fatherhood. *Trends in Ecology and Evolution, 15,* 464-468.

7

Human Emotions as Multipurpose Adaptations

An Evolutionary Perspective on the Development of Fear

Peter LaFreniere

Just as individual or gene-centered views of selection launched the brief, but spectacular, rise of sociobiology a generation ago, the concept of domain-specific adaptations has been the springboard for its replacement, human evolutionary psychology. Because of the enthusiastic assimilation of the first of these theoretical innovations, earlier theoretical advances were prematurely discarded, and it is only recently that there has been growing recognition that human adaptation must be a product of multilevel selection, including group selection (LaFreniere, 2002; MacDonald, 1994, 2002; Sober & Wilson, 1998; Wilson & Sober, 1994). Similarly, I shall argue that evolutionary psychologists must retain a central role for domain-general human adaptations, particularly those adaptations that rely upon cortical processing. In this chapter, I intend to portray human emotions as just such a multipurpose adaptation, embracing both domain-general and domain-specific viewpoints, and showing their interconnections.

Domain-general mechanisms are the hallmark of human adaptation and give our species its unique flexibility to successfully adapt to a wide range of environmental demands. By their very nature, domain-general mechanisms are much better suited than domain-specific mechanisms in environments where individuals face novel and fluctuating problems requiring flexibility and insight (Chiappe & MacDonald, 2004; MacDonald, 1991).

The unique biological evolution of *Homo sapiens* (of course, every species has a unique heritage) requires us to recognize that in our species only, language, symbolism, and culture provide an extraordinary extension of biological adaptations. Emotions are central to that adaptation, representing a vital link with our primate heritage and providing a basis for understanding human universals (Ekman, 1989, 1992). In particular, human nonverbal communication and emotional expression provide a rich domain for research illustrating this interpenetration of biology, language, and culture.

Basic human emotions such as joy, love, anger, fear, and sadness become evident in infancy and are generally recognized across cultures, not just as verbal labels for emotional experience but also as core species-specific motivational systems that organize behavior and development across the life span. In this chapter, I examine one of our most ancient emotion systems, fear, in order to illustrate this adaptive response to environmental challenge. An understanding of human emotions as multipurpose adaptations requires a balanced treatment of both domain-general mechanisms and domain-specific mechanisms in promoting the survival of the organism. We begin by examining the evidence supporting the domain-general viewpoint.

Fear as a Domain-General Adaptation

In everyday life, many fears can be acquired without direct negative experience through observational learning. The primate infant by virtue of its extended period of care and protection can learn to regulate its behavior by observing others, particularly the caregiver. For example, attachment researchers have studied how the presence of the caregiver provides a secure base for the infant's confident exploration of the environment. If something threatening should occur, the infant's attention will be directed to the caregiver's face. Should the caregiver express fear in relation to an event, a fear response can be classically conditioned to that event after a single trial. Evolution is better served by constructing an organism capable of evaluation and observational learning than by constructing hundreds of specific reflexes for the myriad potentially dangerous events facing a primate (LaFreniere, 2000).

This ability of social referencing illustrates the superiority of an open program over a closed program for promoting flexible adaptation to a wide range of environmental stimulation (Mayr, 1982). According to Mayr, a closed program is based on a genotype that does not allow appreciable modifications during the process of development, whereas an open program allows for additional input and modification based on learning and experience throughout the life span. A closed program can be highly adaptive in short-lived species facing relatively constant life challenges, but an open program is more adaptive in long-lived species facing diverse and variable life challenges. The altricial status of primates, including humans, provides an extended period that enables each generation to learn the many variable characteristics of life-relevant stimuli required for successful adaptation.

Without question, the widely successful adaptation of humans to a diversity of environments is due to our ability to solve variable and novel problems. However, not all human challenges involve novelty. In the social environment, important constants in human adaptation are the facial displays and signals of other humans. These may be sufficiently small in number, stereotyped, and important to allow for evolution to construct recognitory programs that are relatively closed. Thus, while emotion expression and regulation may eventually incorporate a high degree of learned behavior, basic emotions, such as fear, also regulate behavior through closed, prewired, genetic programs that control their production and reception. A great deal of evidence now supports the classic Darwinian viewpoint that such processes are innate. As Campos and Barrett (1984) stated, "No social learning appears necessary either for the *reception* of facial and gestural signals (Sackett, 1966), or for the *production* of such (Ekman & Friesen, 1972; Ekman, Sorenson, & Friesen, 1969)" (p. 229).

Most developmental scientists have discarded the notion that the child is born a tabula rasa, or blank slate, upon which the environment acts. Rather, modern developmental perspectives emphasize the child's capacity to actively engage the environment from birth, employing inborn predispositions, preferences, and reflexes that have been shaped by natural selection to provide an adaptive advantage in the environment of evolutionary adaptedness (EEA).

During the infant period, these inborn capacities and preferences of the infant lead to a series of remarkable developments at 3 months. As infants' visual acuity improves and they gain experience with human faces in social interaction, they organize the various elements of the face into a distinct pattern or schema for the human face that may be recognized. At this age, infants can recognize their mother's face in a photograph, and they prefer to look at her rather than a stranger (Barrera & Maurer, 1981b); and soon after, infants can remember and distinguish between faces of different strangers.

Infants also develop the capacity to discriminate between different facial expressions at about 3 months (Haviland & Lelwica, 1987; Nelson, 1987). At this age, infants can discriminate happy and sad faces from surprised faces (Younge-Browne, Rosenfeld, & Horowitz, 1977), smiles from frowns (Barrera & Maurer, 1981a), and smiling faces that vary in intensity (Kuchuk, Vibbert, & Bornstein, 1986). By 4 months, infants are capable of discriminating joyful faces from angry or neutral faces (LaBarbera, Izard, Vietze, & Parisi, 1976), and by 5 months, they are beginning to make discriminations among negative expressions, such as sad, fearful, and angry expressions (Schwartz, Izard, & Ansul, 1985). By the second half of the first year, infants are able to perceive emotional expressions as organized wholes. They can distinguish mild and intense expressions of different emotions (Ludemann & Nelson, 1988), and they respond to happy or surprised expressions differently than sad or fearful faces, even if these emotions are expressed in slightly varying ways by different people (Ludemann, 1991).

Infants also begin to rely upon facial expressions as an important indicator of how to respond emotionally to an uncertain situation or event. This type of social referencing is one of the first clear examples of emotion regulation. Like other examples throughout the first year, it occurs in a dyadic context. As early as 10 weeks, infants begin to respond meaningfully to their mothers' facial expressions (Haviland & Lelwica, 1987), and by 10 months, infants rely on these emotional cues to decide how to respond to a wide variety of events for which they lack experience. For example, maternal facial expressions help regulate the coping behavior of infants to interesting but frightening objects. Klinnert, Campos, Sorce, Emde, and Svejda (1983) exposed 12-to 18-month-olds to three unfamiliar toys, a model of a human head, a dinosaur, and a remote-controlled spider, instructing the mothers to look alternately from the toy to the infant while expressing joy, fear, or a neutral attitude. Infants guided their behavior according to their mothers' expressions, retreating toward her when she showed fear, but approaching the toy when she was happy. In a modification of the "visual cliff" experiment, all 1-year-olds avoided the deeper side when their mothers posed a fearful expression, but 74% of the infants crossed the cliff when their mothers expressed happiness (Sorce, Emde, Campos, & Klinnert, 1985). Because the face carries the most information, by 14 months, infants use it more than any other cue.

Mineka's studies of observational learning in the development of fear of snakes in rhesus monkeys have provided a parallel to studies of infant social referencing and further illustrate the interaction of innate and learned components in the production of adaptive fear responses. In the wild, monkeys show a strong fear of snakes that generalizes to objects that even resemble snakes. Better to err on the side of caution. This fear is so strong and so universal in the wild that early observers, such as Hebb, were inclined to believe that it was innate. Indeed, Hebb (1946) found that a painted wax replica of a coiled snake elicited fear (hair erection and screaming) in 21 out of 30 chimpanzees tested and was second in potency to all stimuli, surpassed only by a skull of a chimpanzee with a movable jaw controlled by a string. Since the chimpanzees that had been born and bred in Hebb's lab were just as likely to show snake fear as the others, Hebb concluded that the fear was a domain-specific adaptation that required no learning.

This question was reopened 40 years later when Mineka and colleagues compared wild-reared and lab-reared rhesus monkeys and found that the lab-reared monkeys did not show fear of snakes (Mineka & Cook, 1993). It is interesting to note that the wild-reared monkeys had been captured and imported from India 24 years prior to the study. Yet they all maintained a strong fear of snakes, despite having had no experience with them for nearly a quarter of a century! This too could have led the investigators to conclude that this was an innate fear. Instead, Mineka and colleagues paired a wild-reared monkey with a lab-reared monkey in order to demonstrate how quickly and permanently fear of snakes could be conditioned. In the test situation, lab-reared monkeys showed no differences in their responses to a live boa constrictor, snakelike objects, or neutral objects that were placed in a Plexiglas box and moved toward them. But when the lab-reared monkeys were exposed to the fearful reactions of the wild-reared monkeys, they quickly learned to fear the snake and snakelike objects. From the standpoint of classical conditioning, it may be that the expression of fear was the unconditioned stimulus and the snake was the conditioned stimulus.

As Mineka's research revealed, the role of learning is interwoven in subtle and complex ways with genetic predispositions to provide for the safety of the primate infant. Clearly, for an organism to adapt to a complex environment of opportunities and dangers, a dynamic balance must be struck between its intrepid exploration of the novel and a measured response to threat, ranging from cautious wariness to terror and rapid flight. Moreover, these responses cannot be acquired over long periods of time through trial and error or gradual shaping. The individual who cannot escape the predator or who falls off a real cliff will be eliminated from the breeding population. One functional solution is to equip the young with the capacity to acquire a fear response to a given stimuli on a single trial, and with no direct experience of it. Clearly, one experience with a poisonous snake or spider, or an aggressive conspecific, will also eliminate the individual. Natural selection would strongly favor individuals capable of using the parent as a source of information from which to quickly learn what to approach and what to avoid. This solution provides for rapid acquisition of the fear response, as well as the capacity for flexible modulation or regulation of the emotion.

Another evolutionary solution to this adaptive problem is to provide the infant offspring with reflexes that quickly mature into adaptive responses and to hardwire certain innate fears into the neural circuitry of the organism. Fear of being alone, heights, and impending collisions would appear to fit this category. In the next section, we turn to evidence from the study of fear supporting the domain-specific viewpoint.

Fear as a Domain-Specific Adaptation

Abundant evidence supports the view that the primate face has been the site of intensive selective pressure for tens of millions of years. This selection pressure has produced an intricate set of facial muscles responsible for controlling the facial expressions of the great apes and humans. In particular, the social ecology of primates, with its challenging flux of coalitions and alliances, has led to finely tuned abilities to produce and conceal subtle expressions and to detect such subtleties in the course of social interaction (de Waal, 1986, 1996). Neurobiological studies reveal that the primate brain has evolved specialized collections of neurons responsible for processing sensory information sensitive to faces, including the recognition of familiar faces and emotional expressions (Hauser, 1997). These evolutionary achievements suggest that the expression and recognition of emotional cues is of central importance for primate adaptation.

Neurological Evidence for an Evolved Fear System

Like his predecessor Paul MacLean, neurobiologist Joseph LeDoux considers evolutionary theory to be essential in understanding the origins of emotion in the brain. However, unlike MacLean, who viewed emotion as a unitary faculty of mind mediated by a single unified system within the brain (MacLean, 1990), LeDoux believes that different emotions may involve different brain systems. Instead of a universal emotion system in the brain, LeDoux believes that different emotions may be mediated by different brain systems and that evolution acted upon each of these basic survival systems somewhat independently. The tendency of cognitive scientists to reduce all processes of the human mind to general cognitive information processing is inconsistent with recent formulations in the neurosciences regarding the relative autonomy of emotional processes. The analogy of the human brain to the information processing of a computer is certainly useful, but to understand human emotions, it may be more useful to remember that it is only an analogy.

Rather than viewing the emotional brain as a general computer, LeDoux (1996), Panksepp (1993, 1998), Plutchik (1980), and others believe that during the long course of its evolution, the brain evolved multiple behavioral-emotional systems, each with its own distinct structural and functional properties. From this perspective, because different emotions are involved in different adaptive tasks, such as seeking protection from the caregiver, defending against danger, securing a mate, and so on, each emotional system may be linked to specific brain systems that evolved for each specific purpose. This idea led LeDoux to propose that scientists investigate one emotion system at a time, without assuming, for example, that the emotion network responsible for activating the organism's response to fear is the same system that activates one's romantic attachments.

The key to understanding this point of view is the idea that natural selection often leads to functional equivalence in evolved systems across diverse species that must successfully solve common problems if they are to survive. As a result, systems have been designed by natural selection for fear, anger, attachment, play, and sexuality that share common ground across diverse species of primates and mammals. This idea is very similar to MacLean's (1990) description of the triune brain, and consistent with MacLean's data that demonstrate functional equivalence across different species regarding the same behavioral display. LeDoux differs from MacLean in assuming that each basic emotional system is somewhat localized anatomically and mediated by separate neural systems. From a research standpoint, one would hypothesize that each system would respond differently to lesions and electrical and chemical stimulation.

Given the arsenal of techniques available to neuroscientists to understand how emotional functions are mediated by specific patterns of neural connections, the only other requirement for progress is selecting a well-defined, reliably measured emotion that is common to a diversity of species.

LeDoux (1996) argued that the emotion of fear is the top candidate for neurological study:

> Fear conditioning is thus an excellent experimental technique for studying the control of fear or defense responses in the brain. It can be applied up and down the phyla. The stimuli involved can be specified and controlled, and the sensory system that processes the conditioned stimulus can be used as the starting point for tracing the pathways through the brain. The learning takes place very quickly and lasts indefinitely. Fear conditioning can be used to study how the brain processes the conditioned fear stimulus and controls defense responses that are coupled to them. It can also be used to examine the mechanisms through which emotional memories are established, stored, and retrieved, and, in humans, the mechanisms underlying conscious fear. (p. 148)

Using a research strategy that combines the classical lesion method with modern neuroanatomical tracing techniques, LeDoux (1996) has developed a process model of the brain that demonstrates how a cognitive appraisal becomes transformed into an emotional response, with all the heart-pounding, bodily sensations that psychologists since James ascribe to fear. The key to this transformation in the brain is the involvement of the amygdala, which LeDoux describes as the hub in the wheel of fear. To illustrate LeDoux's theory of the role of the amygdala in the processing of fearful stimuli, let us consider a hunter walking alone in the Maine woods who is suddenly deafened by the blast of a shotgun fired at close range. Previous models of how the brain responded to such inputs routed the incoming information from the sensory thalamus up to the sensory cortex, where the sound was consciously perceived. The cortex then sent signals to subcortical areas of the limbic system (including the amygdala) responsible for appraisal. After evaluating the emotional significance of the sound as dangerous, the limbic system sent a return message up to the cortex to activate the fear system in the autonomic nervous system, which, in turn, produced the heart-pounding, subjective feeling of fear.

By skillful application of the experimental techniques of lesions and tracing, LeDoux's research revealed that the brain can process the same auditory information via a shorter, more direct route that bypasses the cortex altogether. From an evolutionary vantage point, the direct route evolved first and remains the only pathway available in the lower vertebrates. With the evolution of the cortex, the older, more primitive processing system continued to function alongside the more complex system for millions of years, plenty of time to atrophy if it was not useful. But the direct thalamic pathway to the amygdala is 2 to 3 times faster than the thalamo-cortico-amygdala pathway. However, the increase in speed is offset by reduced cognitive processing, which could be provided only by the cortex. According to LeDoux, this gain in processing time must occasionally provide substantial benefits that more than offset the loss of information, since both pathways remain functional in the human brain, where they converge in the lateral nucleus of the amygdala.

Behavioral Evidence for an Evolved Fear System

The topic of fear has received a great deal of attention not only from neuroscientists like LeDoux but also from ethologists, behaviorists, and cognitive-developmental psychologists. In this section, we discuss stimuli that arouse innate fears in humans and the behavioral systems that are connected to fear. Any description of the ontogeny of fear must be related to advances in cognitive development, since cognitive appraisal is closely connected to the fear response.

In his summary of the early literature on the psychology of fear, Gray (1987, first published 1971) began with J. B. Watson's classic work "Behaviorism" (1924), in which Watson proposed that there were three innate stimuli for fear (pain, sudden loss of support, loud noise) and that all other elicitors of fear were produced by classical conditioning. Watson's view that classical conditioning is a key mechanism that accounts for the diversity of fears acquired by an individual over the course of a lifetime is well-founded, and many experiments have demonstrated that a wide range of behavioral responses associated with fear can be classically conditioned (Gray, 1987).

But classical conditioning alone is insufficient to account for all fear stimuli. According to Gray (1987), at least five general principles are required: intensity, novelty, evolutionary dangers, social stimuli, and conditioned stimuli. Pain and loud noise are examples of intense stimuli, though animals respond in a variety of ways to pain, including anger-aggression as well as fear-avoidance. Novel objects and persons may also give rise to fear, though we shall see below that in humans, temperament, maturation, cognitive development, context, and learning all affect the probability that fear is expressed in response to novel stimulation.

Researchers who observe infant behavior in the first month or two of life are generally in agreement that no specific fear reaction is present at birth. Rather, infants become distressed for a variety of reasons and cry as a response to pain, discomfort, hunger, and other unpleasant experiences. John Bowlby (1969) considered that infant fears are caused by a combination of biology and experience and that infants would more readily respond with fear to events or situations that provided the infant with "natural clues to danger." Bowlby listed only four such cues: pain, being left alone, sudden changes in stimulation, and rapid approach. Gray (1987) has expanded the list of the potential stimuli that might have an evolutionary basis to include fear of strangers; separation anxiety and fear of being alone; fear of open places, heights, falling, or loss of support; fear of the dark; and fear of snakes or spiders. At least four types of infant fears that have been well researched show characteristics consistent with an evolved domain-specific response system: stranger distress, separation anxiety, fear of heights, and fear of impending collision.

Stranger Distress. Stranger distress was originally described by Rene Spitz as an emotion that suddenly appears in all infants at about 8 months. However, we now understand that this emotion is foreshadowed by behaviors that occur at an earlier period of development. At about 4 or 5 months, infants show a distress response to a strange face. At this age, if a stranger stares in silence at an infant, the infant will often return the look and after about 30 seconds begin to cry. Such wariness is interpreted from a Piagetian perspective as a reaction to the failure to assimilate the unfamiliar face to a more familiar schema.

A few months later, infants react negatively and immediately to strangers, especially if approached suddenly or picked up by the stranger. This negative reaction, which can be readily elicited in most infants between 7 and 12 months, is called "stranger distress." Unlike the gradual response arising from failure to assimilate, stranger distress is an immediate reaction to an appraisal of a situation as threatening. This is supported by the observation that infants show even greater distress over the second instance of intrusion by a stranger, a finding that is compatible with the infant's capacity for appraisal and is incompatible with the notion of a failure to assimilate a novel event. If the latter were the instigating cause, the infant should be less frightened by the second approach.

The context and qualitative aspects of the stranger's approach are also critical. If the stranger approaches slowly when the caregiver is accessible, smiling and speaking softly, offering a toy, the infant will often show interest or joy, and distress is unlikely. Finally, the degree of distress shown by an infant to the silent intrusion of the stranger varies greatly from baby to baby, a finding that many believe to be rooted in the genetic temperament of the infant (Kagan, Keasley, & Zelazo, 1978).

While context and cognition play an important role in determining stranger distress, there is nevertheless evidence suggesting a universally precise timetable for its emergence across different cultures, including Uganda (Ainsworth, 1963), Hopi Indian (Dennis, 1940), and the United States (Sroufe, 1979). It would appear that the emergence of this fear response in the second half of the first year is associated with physiological maturation, as well as cognitive development. EEG and heart rate patterns in human infants both show a major developmental shift at this time in response to the presentation of threatening stimuli (Emde, Gaensbauer, & Harmon, 1976).

Comparative physiological and observational data of a variety of other species support a biological basis for the development of this fear response. Observations of the development of stranger distress in human infants resemble the fear of strangers observed in 4-month-old chimpanzee infants by Hebb in his classic 1946 study, "On the Nature of Fear." Hebb argued that this fear emerged at 4 months not as a result of learning, but as a result of perceptual and cognitive maturation. That this fear of strangers is innate is demonstrated by animals reared in the laboratory. That it is dependent on cognitive development is demonstrated by another of Hebb's experiments. Two groups of chimpanzees were reared under two different conditions.

One group was provided with normal visual experiences, including seeing other chimps, while the other group was blindfolded. When exposed to a plaster replica of a chimpanzee head, the first group showed extreme fear, while the blindfolded group showed mild curiosity. Hebb reasoned that the group with normal visual experiences had learned a schema for a chimpanzee that included head, torso, arms, and legs. Confronted by a replica of a head alone, familiar but incomplete, the chimps became extremely upset. Hebb believed that the discrepancy between the familiar and the partially familiar caused the fear response. This violation of expectancies may also be implicated in the maturation of the human response to strangers. Until the schema of the caregiver has developed, no innate fear of strangers is evident in human infants. Other primate data also suggest a biological timetable regulating the onset of social fears. For example, Sackett (1966) found fear responses at about 3 months in isolation-reared rhesus monkeys when they were presented with a picture of an adult with a threatening expression, but not when neutral pictures of infant or adult monkeys were shown.

Separation Anxiety. Like stranger distress, separation anxiety also emerges according to a developmental timetable during the second half-year in human infants. We have noted the changes in the infant's emotional life that reflect advancing physiological and cognitive maturation in the first half-year. By 8 to 10 months, infants become increasingly active in their relationships with their caregivers, as well as increasingly mobile. With this new mobility, the infant expands the capacity for eager exploration of the outer world, returning to the caregiver as a "secure base" (Ainsworth, 1977). At just this time, separation anxiety begins to peak, possibly as a result of the infant's new preoccupation with the presence and location of the caregiver.

Infants from cultures as diverse as Kalahari bushmen, Israeli kibbutzim, and Guatemalan Indians display quite similar patterns in their response to maternal separation, which peaks at the end of the first year and remains elevated for variable lengths of time (Kagan et al., 1978). Cultural practices would also appear to have an impact on separation anxiety. Infants who remain in constant contact with their mothers may show an earlier onset of separation anxiety (Ainsworth, 1977) and possibly more intense and longer periods of reactivity. For example, Japanese infants who are tested in Ainsworth's Strange Situation show more intense reactions to the separation, presumably as a result of cultural norms prescribing constant contact between mother and infant for the first several years of life.

Fear of Heights. Fear of heights in infants has been studied primarily by using a "visual cliff," which consists of a Plexiglas-covered floor with two distinct levels, one shallow and the other several feet deep. The different depths are visually cued by covering the floor with a checkerboard pattern. In a series of experiments, Campos and colleagues (Sorce et al., 1985) have outlined a developmental progression from perception of and heightened attention to the deep side at 5 months to the onset of a fear response at about 9 months. Because of the convergence of the behavioral and physiological data, these studies are particularly convincing regarding the onset of fear. Five-month-olds looked more often at the deep side and showed heart rate (HR) deceleration and no signs of negative affect. HR deceleration has been shown to accompany orienting and attending to new information, and may be assumed to be a sign of interest. In contrast, 9-month-olds showed sharp HR acceleration to the deep side, which many refused to cross, and some began to cry. Other data also show that infants as young as 5 months are capable of perceiving depth (Fox, 1994), but this capacity alone is not sufficient for the onset of fear.

According to Campos, several weeks of crawling experience appears to account for the emergence of fear of heights, since this fear emerges at a relatively constant period after crawling begins, rather than at a fixed chronological age. Most infants learn to crawl at varying ages between 7 and 11 months, and they show fear of the visual cliff at various ages but only after they have been crawling for about 3 weeks (Bertenthal, Campos, & Barrett, 1984). Learning to fear heights is not based on experiences of falling, nor would such trial-and-error learning make sense from an evolutionary perspective. Rather, it appears that this fear, like the fear of strangers and separation from the attachment figure, is programmed into human infants as a consequence of natural selection and requires only normal physiological and cognitive maturation to appear.

Fear of Collision. Another fear that appears to have a biological basis is the fear of an impending collision. Research on "looming" stimuli has been meticulously designed to isolate visual information from other stimuli such as noise or wind, both of which can trigger reflexive responses. In a series of experiments using a shadow-casting apparatus, Yonas, Cleaves, and Pettersen (1978) provided the infant only visual cues of an impending collision, in the form of an exponentially expanding dot that appeared to rush toward them until it covered their entire field of vision. Research on newborns has consistently demonstrated the presence of reflexive blinking, but anticipatory defensive reactions, HR accelerations, and other signs of fear do not appear until 8 to 9 months in normal infants and in the second year for Down syndrome infants (Cicchetti & Beeghly, 1990; Yonas, 1981). Once again, the instinctive defensive response of the infant requires maturation before it appears in the second half-year of life. Again, no evidence has suggested that the timetable for the emergence of this fear is determined by specific learning experiences with colliding objects.

Conclusion

The study of fear illustrates a number of basic issues in the study of emotion. Infancy researchers, like ethologists working with nonhuman primates and other animals, must rely on observable events rather than verbal reports. Researchers who address questions in the ontogeny of fear must, by necessity, confront methodological questions pertaining to its expression. What are the specific criteria that allow one to infer that fear, as opposed to general distress or sadness or anger, is being expressed?

Bowlby (1973) and Charlesworth (1974) have listed a number of observable fear indicators involving expressive and motor behaviors. Bowlby offered the following, not as an exhaustive list, but as a start: "wary watching combined with inhibition of action, a frightened facial expression accompanied perhaps by trembling or crying, cowering, hiding, running away, and also seeking contact with someone and perhaps clinging to him or her" (p. 88). Charlesworth included "momentary arresting or slowing of ongoing behaviors or prolonged freezing, heightened vigilance or awareness, stimulus-distance maintaining or expanding behavior, serious or fearful facial expressions" (p. 263). He went on to note that fear may be followed by withdrawal, flight, wary exploration, or even smiling or laughing. As a consequence of attending to observational methods, facial expressions have become the most reliable and unambiguous indicators of fear in infants and children, and advances have been made in understanding physiological and behavioral precursors to fear and the connections between them.

Comparative analyses have also played a prominent role and have led to an increased understanding of the fear system and its functional significance across many species, including primates. These data indicate that fear reactions emerge precipitously across species according to comparable developmental timetables and that the onset of specific fear responses and fearful mood is accompanied by brain maturational changes involving the integration of corticolimbic systems and developments in the parasympathetic system (Schore, 1994).

The study of fear underscores the critical link between affect and cognition. Discrepancy theories originating in the work of Hebb (1946) and Piaget (1952) provide an account of the steps in the epigenesis of this primary affective system in infancy and demonstrate its dependence on perceptual and cognitive development. Later work has demonstrated the emergence of the psychological emotion of fear based solely on the cognitive appraisal of threat in the environment. The importance of context and meaning have been clearly shown in the work of Sroufe (1996) and others to be the hallmark of the mature fear response, as distinct from the undifferentiated, physiologically based distress of early infancy.

The study of fear allows for an integration with other lines of development in the physical and motor spheres and illustrates the active role of the infant in bringing about the conditions for the experience of separation anxiety and fear of heights, which both become functional very soon after the infant learns to crawl. Such convergent lines of development illustrate the biological unity of development and suggest the functional significance of the timetable itself. Finally, from the perspective of evolutionary psychology, the study of fear illustrates the dual importance of domain-general and domain-specific mechanisms in shaping human adaptation.

References

Ainsworth, M. D. S. (1963). The development of infant-mother attachment among the Ganda. In D. M. Foss (Ed.), *Determinants of infant behavior* (Vol. 2., pp. 67-104). New York: John Wiley.

Ainsworth, M. D. S. (1977). Infant development and mother-infant interaction among Ganda and American families. In P. H. Leiderman, S. R. Tulkin, & A. Rosenfeld (Eds.), *Culture and infancy: Variations in the human experience.* New York: Academic Press.

Barrera, M. E., & Maurer, D. (1981a). The perception of facial expressions by the three-month-old infant. *Child Development, 52,* 203-206.

Barrera, M. E., & Maurer, D. (1981b). Recognition of mother's photographed face by the three-month-old. *Child Development, 52,* 558-563.

Bertenthal, B., Campos, J., & Barrett, K. (1984). Self-produced locomotion: An organizer of emotional, cognitive, and social development in infancy. In R. Emde & R. Harmon (Eds.), *Continuities and discontinuities in development* (pp. 175-210). New York: Plenum.

Bowlby, J. (1969). *Attachment and loss: Vol. I. Attachment.* New York: Basic Books.

Bowlby, J. (1973). *Attachment and loss: Vol. II. Separation, anxiety, and anger.* New York: Basic Books.

Campos, J. J., & Barrett, K. C. (1984). Toward a new understanding of emotions and their development. In C. E. Izard, J. Kagan, & R. B. Zajonc (Eds.), *Emotions, cognition, and behavior* (pp. 229-263). New York: Cambridge University Press.

Charlesworth, W. R. (1974). General issues in the study of fear: Section IV. In M. Lewis & L. A. Rosenblum (Eds.), *The origins of fear* (pp. 254-258). New York: John Wiley.

Chiappe, D., & MacDonald, K. (2004). *The evolution of domain-general mechanisms in intelligence and learning.* Manuscript submitted for publication.

Cicchetti, D., & Beeghly, M. (1990). *Down syndrome: A developmental perspective.* Cambridge, UK: Cambridge University Press.

Dennis, W. (1940). Does culture appreciably affect patterns of infant behavior? *Journal of Social Psychology, 12,* 305-317.

Ekman, P. (1989). The argument and evidence about universals in facial expressions of emotion. In H. Wagner & A. Manstead (Eds.), *Handbook of social psychophysiology* (pp. 143-163). New York: John Wiley.

Ekman, P. (1992). An argument for basic emotions. *Cognition and Emotion, 6,* 169-200.

Emde, R., Gaensbauer, T., & Harmon, R. (1976). Emotional expression in infancy: A biobehavioral study. *Psychological Issues Monograph Series, 10*(No. 37), 1-198.

Fox, N. A. (1994). Dynamic cerebral processes underlying emotion regulation. In N. Fox (Ed.), The development of emotion regulation: Biological and behavioral considerations. *Monographs of the Society for Research in Child Development, 59*(2/3, Serial No. 240), 152-166.

Gray, J. A. (1987). *The psychology of fear and stress.* (2nd ed.). Cambridge, UK: Cambridge University Press. (1st ed. published 1971)

Hauser, M. D. (1997). *The evolution of communication.* Cambridge: MIT Press.

Haviland, J. M., & Lelwica, M. (1987). The induced affect response: 10-week-old infants' responses to three emotional expressions. *Developmental Psychology, 23,* 97-104.

Hebb, D. (1946). On the nature of fear. *Psychological Review, 53,* 259-276.

Kagan, J., Keasley, R. B., & Zelazo, P. R. (1978). *Infancy: Its place in human development.* Cambridge, MA: Harvard University Press.

Klinnert, M. D., Campos, J. J., Sorce, J. F., Emde, R. N., & Svejda, M. (1983) Emotions as behavior regulators: Social referencing in infancy. In R. Plutchik & H. Kellerman (Eds.), *Emotion: Theory, research and experience* (pp. 57-86). New York: Academic Press.

Kuchuk, W., Vibbert, M., & Bornstein, M. H. (1986). The perception of smiling and its experiential correlates in 3-month-old infants. *Child Development, 57,* 1054-1061.

LaBarbera, J. D., Izard, C. E., Vietze, P., & Parisi, S. A. (1976). Four- and six-month-old infants' visual responses to joy, anger, and neutral expressions. *Child Development, 47,* 535-538.

LaFreniere, P. J. (2000). *Emotional development: A biosocial perspective.* Belmont, CA: Wadsworth/ITP.

LaFreniere, P. J. (2002, August). *The role of human emotions in promoting large group cohesion.* In P. LaFreniere & K. MacDonald (Chairs), Evolutionary

Foundations of Human Hypersociality, symposium presented at the International Society for Human Ethology, Montreal, Quebec.

LeDoux, J. E. (1996). *The emotional brain: The mysterious underpinnings of emotional life.* New York: Simon & Schuster.

Ludemann, P. M. (1991). Generalized discrimination of positive facial expressions by seven- and ten-month-old infants. *Child Development, 62,* 55-67.

Ludemann, P. M., & Nelson, C. A. (1988). Categorical representation of facial expressions by 7-month-old infants. *Developmental Psychology, 24,* 492-501.

MacDonald, K. (1991). A perspective on Darwinian psychology: The importance of domain-general mechanisms, plasticity, and individual differences. *Ethology and Sociobiology, 12,* 449-480.

MacDonald, K. (1994). *A people that shall dwell alone: Judaism as a group evolutionary strategy.* Westport, CT: Praeger.

MacDonald, K. (2002, August). *Social and psychological mechanisms of group cohesion.* In P. LaFreniere & K. MacDonald (Chairs), Evolutionary Foundations of Human Hypersociality, symposium presented at the International Society for Human Ethology, Montreal, Quebec.

MacLean, P. D. (1990). *The triune brain in evolution: Role in paleocerebral functions.* New York: Plenum Press.

Mayr, E. (1982). *The growth of biological thought: Diversity, evolution, and inheritance.* Cambridge, MA: Harvard University Press.

Mineka, S., & Cook, M. (1993). Mechanisms involved in the observational conditioning of fear. *Journal of Experimental Psychology: General, 122,* 24-38.

Nelson, C. A. (1987). The recognition of facial expression in the first two years of life: Mechanisms of development. *Child Development, 58,* 889-909.

Panksepp, J. (1993). Neurochemical control of moods and emotions: Amino acids to neuropeptides. In M. Lewis & J. M. Haviland (Eds.), *Handbook of emotions* (pp. 87-107). New York: Guilford.

Panksepp, J. (1998). *Affective neuroscience: The foundations of human and animal emotions.* New York: Oxford University Press.

Piaget, J. (1952). *The origins of intelligence in children.* New York: Routledge.

Plutchik, R. (1980). *Emotion: A psychoevolutionary synthesis.* New York: Harper & Row.

Sackett, G. P. (1966). Monkeys reared in isolation with pictures as visual input: Evidence for an innate releasing mechanism. *Science, 154,* 1468-1470.

Schore, A. N. (1994). *Affect regulation and the origin of self: The neurobiology of emotional development.* Hillsdale, NJ: Erlbaum.

Schwartz, G. M., Izard, C. E., & Ansul, S. E. (1985). The 5-month-old's ability to discriminate facial expression of emotion. *Infant Behavior and Development, 8,* 65-77.

Sober, E., & Wilson, D. S. (1998). Unto others: The evolution and psychology of unselfish behavior. Cambridge, MA: Harvard University Press.

Sorce, J. F., Emde, R. N., Campos, J., & Klinnert, M. D. (1985). Maternal emotional signaling: Its effect on the visual cliff behavior of 1-year-olds. *Developmental Psychiatry, 21,* 195-200.

Sroufe, L. A. (1979). Socioemotional development. In J. D. Osofsky (Ed.), *Handbook of infant development* (pp. 462-516). New York: John Wiley.

Sroufe, L. A. (1996). *Emotional development: The organization of emotional life in the early years*. Cambridge, UK: Cambridge University Press.

de Waal, F. (1986). Deception in the natural communication of chimpanzees. In R. W. Mitchell & N. S. Thompson (Eds.), *Deception: Perspectives on human and nonhuman deceit*. Albany: State University of New York Press.

de Waal, F. (1996). *Good natured: The origins of right and wrong in humans and other animals*. Cambridge/London: Harvard University Press.

Wilson, D. S., & Sober, E. (1994). Reintroducing group selection to the human behavioral sciences. *Behavioral and Brain Sciences, 17*, 585-654.

Yonas, A. (1981). Infants' responses to optical information for collision. In R. Aslin & L. Pettersen (Eds.), *Development of perception: Psychobiological perspectives* (Vol. 2, pp. 313-334). New York: Academic Press.

Yonas, A., Cleaves, W., & Pettersen, L. (1978). Development of sensitivity to pictorial depth. *Science, 200*, 77-79.

Younge-Browne, G., Rosenfeld, H. M., & Horowitz, F. D. (1977). Infant discrimination of facial expressions. *Child Development, 48*, 555-562.

8

Personality, Evolution, and Development

Kevin MacDonald

Research in personality has revealed that five personality dimensions appear regularly in cross-cultural research and among children and adults. The traits of the *five-factor model* (FFM) have been isolated in American English (Goldberg, 1990), Dutch (De Raad, 1992), German (Ostendorf, 1990), Russian (Digman & Shmelyov, 1996), and Chinese (Trull & Geary, 1997), among other languages. In addition to the very large personality literature in adults, the FFM has been supported in children (Graziano & Ward, 1992; John, Caspi, Robins, Moffitt, & Sthouthamer-Loeber, 1994; Kohnstamm, Halverson, Mervielde, & Havill, 1998; Lamb, Chuang, Wessels, Broberg, & Hwang, 2002; McCrae et al., 2002).

An evolutionary approach based on the idea of an evolved system provides a powerful paradigm for personality, a paradigm that would move personality to the very center of thinking about children's development. The basic interest in personality research should be on establishing the set of evolved systems underlying personality differences. Typically, personality research and theory are viewed as fundamentally about individual differences (e.g., Caspi, 1998). Individual differences are certainly an important part of the story, but within a systems perspective, individual differences within the normal range represent variation in evolved systems. Research in neuroscience has revealed that the mammalian brain contains highly specific emotional and motivational systems (e.g., Panksepp, 1998). In the same way, all humans have a respiratory system and a circulatory system that are designed to carry out fundamental biological functions. However, there is important variation among people in these systems, ranging, for example, from relatively high to relatively low lung capacity. These differences have important real-world implications for athletic ability and longevity. Genetic variation is ubiquitous, even for adaptations (e.g., West-Eberhard, 2003). And as discussed below, people are intensely interested in the phenotypic, and by implication, the genetic diversity underlying personality.

The systems perspective focuses on the following questions, none of which would be deemed relevant if individual differences were the only concern (see Figure 8.1):

1. What is the function of the system? Each personality system was designed by natural selection to solve problems of survival and reproduction in ancestral environments. In evolutionary argot, personality systems are therefore adaptations (see Ch. 2, this volume).

2. How does the system change with age, and do age differences conform to evolutionary expectations?

3. Are there sex differences in the system that are understandable in terms of evolutionary theory?

4. Which environmental cues trigger the system? For example, decreased oxygen results in more rapid breathing, and the presence of perceived threat triggers the behavioral inhibition personality system. An important question for personality psychology is whether the cues that trigger particular systems are the result of evolved, domain-specific connections between cues and system responses (e.g., fear of snakes or spiders) or whether they result from general-purpose information-processing mechanisms (e.g., fear resulting from understanding the details of a conspiracy) (see Ch. 2 for a discussion).

5. How does the system interact with other systems? The respiratory system interacts with the circulatory system so that, for example, lowered lung capacity puts pressure on the heart. In the area of personality, there are a great many interactions among systems designed to perform different, often opposing, functions, as between systems designed to obtain rewards, systems designed to inhibit approach to immediate sources of reward in pursuit of long-term goals, and systems designed to avoid sources of threat. A systems theory of personality expects to find conflicts between systems, resulting at times in psychological ambivalence.

6. How do individual differences in the system affect interaction among systems? People who vary in the efficiency of their respiratory systems respond differently to the same environmental stressors, and this affects interactions with other systems. In the same way, fearful people respond

differently to a situation with possible rewards than do people who are less prone to fear. The systems perspective thus sheds light on one of the central problems of personality psychology: how to conceptualize the interactions among situations and personal traits. Because these systems are so intimately interconnected, the genetics underlying personality is extraordinarily complex (see Ch. 2 for a discussion).

7. Along what dimensions does the system vary? Lungs, for example, vary in size, susceptibility to disease, efficiency, and so on. This is perhaps the most difficult and unresearched area of personality psychology, but there is evidence that several types of psychopathology are associated with being extreme on personality systems.

8. What are the systematic group differences in personality systems? Examples include sex differences, age differences, birth order differences, and ethnic differences.

I. Personality Systems as Universal Psychological Mechanisms:
   A. Personality Systems as Universal Design Features of Humans Homologous With Similarly Functioning Systems in Other Vertebrates
   B. System X Context Interactions and Compartmentalization
   C. System X System Interactions
   D. System X Context X Trait Interactions
   E. System-Specific Environmental Influences

II. Approaches to Group Differences in Universal Mechanisms Based on Evolutionary Theory
   A. The Evolutionary Theory of Gender Differences in Personality
   B. Age Differences in Personality Systems
   C. Evolution and Birth Order Differences in Personality
   D. Life History Theory and Personality

III. Evolutionary Perspectives on Individual Differences
   A. Individual Differences Within the Normal Range as Variation in Viable Strategies
   B. Individual Differences at the Extreme Ends of the Normal Range as Maladaptive or High-Risk Strategies
   C. Social Evaluation: Individual Differences in Others' Personalities as a Resource Environment
   D. Self-Evaluation and Self-Presentation of Personality Traits as Mechanisms for Maximizing One's Resource Value in the Social Environment

---

Figure 8.1   Levels of an Evolutionary Perspective on Personality

Personality Systems as Universal Psychological Mechanisms

A basic idea, then, is that there are two worlds of personality psychology, the world of universal psychological mechanisms and the world of individual differences. The mind is conceptualized as a set of mechanisms designed by natural selection to solve adaptive problems. Although the social evaluation of individual differences is indeed an important aspect of an evolutionary approach (see below), at a fundamental level, these mechanisms are conceptualized as adaptive systems that served a variety of social and nonsocial functions in the environment of evolutionary adaptedness (EEA) (see Ch. 2 for a discussion). This perspective expects to find homologous (i.e., inherited from a common ancestor) systems in animals that serve similar adaptive functions, and it expects that these systems will be organized within the brain as discrete neurophysiological systems. It expects that each system will be responsive to particular environmental contexts (resulting in System X Context Interactions) and that different personality systems will be in competition with each other within individuals, leading at times to psychological ambivalence.

An evolved systems perspective does not expect a 1:1 mapping of the factors emerging from factor analysis with evolved mechanisms. There are several reasons for this. Factor rotations are arbitrary in the absence of strong theory. For example, I have argued that an evolutionary perspective is much more compatible with a factor rotation yielding factors of Dominance/Sensation Seeking and Nurturance/Love rather than Extraversion and Agreeableness (MacDonald, 1995, 1999b). (For a contrary view, see Depue & Collins, 1999, who advocate Gregarious/Aloof and Arrogant/Unassuming as fundamental causal dimensions of personality covering the same factor space.) As Trapnell and Wiggins (1990) pointed out, the difference amounts to a rotational difference between two ways of conceptualizing the same interpersonal space. Nevertheless, an evolutionary perspective is better conceptualized with Dominance/Sensation Seeking and Nurturance/Love as the primary axes of interpersonal space, since this conceptualization maximizes theoretically important sex differences and is thus likely to have been the focus of natural selection. Evolutionary theory predicts that in species with sex-differentiated patterns of parental investment, the sex with the lower level of parental investment (typically the males) is expected to pursue a more high-risk strategy compared with females, including being prone to risk taking and reward seeking, and less sensitive to cues of punishment. This follows because the high-investment sex (typically females) is expected to be able to mate relatively easily and is highly limited in the number of offspring (Trivers, 1972). However, mating is expected to be problematic for the low-investment sex, with the result that males must often compete with other males for access to females, while mating for females is much less problematic. Depue and Collins (1999) have claimed that the traits associated with behavioral approach (i.e., sensation seeking, neophilia, exploratory behavior, risk taking, boldness, sensitivity to reward, and impulsivity) are heterogeneous. But within the evolutionary theory of sex, they form a natural unit: They all involve risky behavior that would benefit males more than females. They are thus much more likely to be the focus of natural selection than are Extraversion and Agreeableness.

While there are robust sex differences favoring males in Dominance and Sensation Seeking (Trapnell & Wiggins, 1990; Zuckerman, 1991), sex differences in Extraversion are relatively modest and actually favor females (McCrae et al., 2002; Srivastava, John, Gosling, & Potter, 2003). This is because Extraversion scales include items related to dominance and venturesomeness, which are higher among males, as well as items related to warmth and affiliation, which are higher among females (see discussion in Lucas, Diener, Grob, Suh, & Shao, 2000). From the evolved systems perspective developed here, the concept of a trait consisting of warmth and affiliation does not fit well with a trait consisting of dominance, sensation seeking, and exploratory behavior. And in fact, as discussed below, at the level of brain functioning, these systems are quite separate: There are unique neurochemical and neuroanatomical substrates for love and for behavioral approach, respectively (Bartels & Zeki, 2000; Depue & Morrone-Strupinsky, in press; Panksepp, 1998). Focusing on the highly sex-differentiated traits of Dominance and Sensation Seeking, on one hand, and Nurturance/Love, on the other, is not only much more compatible with a theoretical understanding of how evolution must have worked but is also compatible with what we know of the systems actually found in the brain.

A related reason for focusing on these highly sex-differentiated traits is that they exhibit theoretically expected age changes, while there is little evidence for mean age changes in Extraversion (McCrae & Costa, 1990; McCrae et al., 2002). The "young male syndrome" describes the pattern in which sensation seeking, impulsivity, and aggression—all associated with the behavioral approach systems—peak in young adulthood exactly at the time when young males must compete for mates and establish themselves in the dominance hierarchy.

Furthermore, personality psychology is based on ratings of people by themselves and others, so that the most socially salient features of people are emphasized, and these bear only indirectly on the underlying systems. The factor of Neuroticism refers to a tendency toward negative emotionality, but at the system level, research reveals separate systems of affect intensity (involving a general tendency toward both positive and negative emotionality) and inhibitory systems dominated by the emotions of fear and anxiety. The psychological salience of Neuroticism in everyday evaluations of self and others provides a poor clue to the underlying systems. Similarly, the emergence of Extraversion in factor analysis may well reflect the social salience of these dimensions in everyday life: People who combine positive emotionality, affiliation (close personal bonds, being warm and affectionate), and attention seeking (dominance) are highly valued, while people who are sociopathic, emotionally distant, and withdrawn do not meet other people's interests as friends or companions. But at the systems level, these people differ on two quite separate evolved systems designed for two quite different purposes with two quite different, evolutionarily expected patterns of sex and age differences.

The evolved systems perspective is compatible with a hierarchical analysis in which the superfactors emerging from factor analysis share genetic and phenotypic variance with lower-level mechanisms. For example, Panksepp (1998) has argued that the mammalian brain contains a "foraging/exploration/ investigation/curiosity/interest/expectancy/SEEKING" system (p. 145), what I term "behavioral approach." This system is aimed at obtaining resources, including food and sexual partners, from the environment and overlaps anatomically and neurophysiologically with aggression—not surprising, since aggression is a prepotent way of dealing with the frustration of positive expectancies (Panksepp, 1998, p. 191). To say that this is a system implies some common neurophysiological structure among these different components, but it also is compatible with differences among them, as between aggression and other aspects of behavioral approach or between exploration and interest. There are also species differences in behavioral approach; for example, predatory aggression is a component of behavioral approach in cats, but not in rats (Panksepp, 1998, p. 194). Furthermore, an evolutionist would expect a sex difference in seeking sexual gratification and social dominance but not in seeking food or companionship (sociability). An evolutionary interpretation suggests that these differences accrued over evolutionary time as primitive foraging and mate attraction systems became elaborated and that they effectively resulted in "facets" of personality: mechanisms that share anatomical and neurological structures as well as genetic and phenotypic variance with each other and are therefore nested under one or more of the superfactors of the FFM. However, it is an open question whether each factor of the FFM would have exactly six facets as evolutionarily meaningful mechanisms nested beneath each personality factor, as in the NEO-PI-R (Costa & McCrae, 1992).

These ideas are related to the following thought experiment about how the systems underlying the FFM may have evolved. A functionalist perspective proposes that the systems underlying personality serve very basic needs of the animal. Among even the most primitive mammals, there must be approach systems to obtain resources, prototypically foraging and mate attraction systems. There must also be withdrawal systems to avoid threats, prototypically a fear system (Gray 1987; LeDoux, 1996). There must also be a system of arousal regulation (affect intensity) designed to energize the animal to meet environmental challenges or opportunities; in the absence of such a system, the animal would either be permanently aroused, a highly wasteful posture, or it would be permanently underaroused and less able to meet environmental challenges. For species that develop pair bonds and other types of close relationships involving nurturance and empathy, one expects the evolution of a system designed to make such relationships psychologically rewarding. And for species that must carry out projects requiring attention to detail and inhibiting present pleasures for long-term gains, one expects the evolution of a Conscientiousness system.

Ideally, one would be able to trace the evolution of these systems over time and chart the differentiation of these systems in different lineages, for example, as approach systems become linked with social dominance and aggression and with systems assessing risk (impulsivity, sensation seeking, etc.), self-confidence, and sociability. One would also chart the inhibitory and excitatory connections among these systems. And one would attempt to determine whether natural selection is favoring one extreme of individual differences or the other and what types of psychopathology are linked with being extreme on these dimensions.

Unfortunately, this program of research is still in its infancy. Nevertheless, existing data support several aspects of this model. The functionalist account of the systems underlying the factor space of the FFM is strengthened by findings that individual differences in personality are associated with individual differences in physiological systems common to all humans. There is considerable evidence linking personality systems with specific brain regions and neurochemicals (Eysenck, 1967, 1982; Gray, 1982, 1987; MacDonald, 1988, 1995). Moreover, functionally and neurophysiologically similar systems localized in particular parts of the brain and characterized by particular neurochemical profiles are apparent in animal research; excitatory and inhibitory connections between these systems are well established (e.g., Gray, 1982, 1987; Panksepp, 1998; see below).

There is also evidence for personality traits in wolves (shyness/boldness, social dominance) (MacDonald, 1983) and sunfish (shyness/boldness) (Wilson, 1994) conceptually linked to FFM dimensions, and there is evidence that individual differences in personality among chimpanzees can be understood within the FFM framework (Figueredo & King, 1996; King & Figueredo, 1994). Reviewing the data for 12 quite different species, Gosling and John (1999) found evidence for Extraversion (E), Neuroticism (N), and Agreeableness (A) in most species: E was found in 10 species (but not in rats and hyenas); N was found in 9 species (but not in vervet monkeys, donkeys, and pigs); A was found in 10 species (but not in guppies and octopi). Conscientiousness (C) was found only in humans and chimpanzees. These results surely do not mean that rats and hyenas do not have behavioral approach systems designed to obtain resources or that vervet monkeys do not have fear systems or systems of affect intensity. These findings may indicate that although these animals have these systems, individual differences are not observable. For example, Figueredo and King (1996, 2001) have hypothesized that social species are more likely to show individual differences than nonsocial species. On the other hand, it would not be surprising that guppies and octopi do not have mechanisms of pair bonding and close relationships, since such relationships are not part of these animals' ecologies. Nor would it be surprising that humans and other relatively advanced animals were uniquely involved in long-term projects requiring delay of gratification and close attention to detail (i.e., conscientiousness); less cognitively advanced species, species that respond to environmental challenges mainly via preprogrammed responses, may fail to exhibit differences in focused effort. The point is that the systems perspective expects animal personality psychology to mirror the ecology of the animal.

Personality as a Set of Evolved Systems

I begin with a thumbnail sketch of the systems underlying personality (see MacDonald, 1995).

1. *The Behavioral Approach System.* The behavioral approach system is related to Surgency/Extraversion in the FFM and Dominance in the circumplex model of interpersonal descriptors (Wiggins, 1991; Wiggins & Trapnell, 1996). At the heart of behavioral approach is Dominance/Sensation Seeking, which consists of individual differences in social dominance as well as several other highly sex-differentiated behaviors, including sensation seeking, impulsivity, and sensitivity to reward. Among adults, behavioral

approach is also associated with aggressiveness and higher levels of sexual experiences (Zuckerman, 1991), while impulsivity, "High-Intensity Pleasure," and aggressiveness are components of behavioral approach in young children (Rothbart, Ahadi, Hershey, & Fisher, 2001). The behavioral approach personality systems are designed to motivate approach toward sources of reward (e.g., sexual gratification, social status) that occurred as enduring and recurrent features of the environments in which humans evolved. Approach systems are a human universal, but because of genetic and environmental variation, some of us are more predisposed than others toward social dominance, reward seeking, sensation seeking, and impulsivity.

A theoretically attractive line of research indicates that an important aspect of behavioral approach is dopaminergic reward-seeking mechanisms (Cloninger, 1987; Gray, 1982, 1987; Panksepp, 1982, 1998; Zuckerman, 1991). In rats, the dopaminergic reward-seeking mechanism involves energetic searching, investigating, and sniffing objects in the environment as possible sources of reward, but this seeking behavior is motivationally generalized: It can be directed at any of a variety of specific rewards depending on the context (Panksepp, 1998). The emphasis on reward-seeking mechanisms underlying behavioral approach reflects the typical manner in which evolution shapes the motivation to engage in behavior (Wilson, 1975). Evolution has resulted in affective motivational systems that are triggered by specific types of stimulation (e.g., the taste of sweet foods, the pleasure of sexual intercourse, the joy of the infant in close, intimate contact with its mother), and it is difficult to conceptualize how it could have done otherwise. The evolutionary basis of motivation is the evolution of affective systems underlying particular adaptive behaviors in the environment of evolutionary adaptedness.

Differences in attraction to reward are thus central to behavioral approach. Newman (1987; see also Avila, 2001; Derryberry, 1987) found that compared with its response among introverts, reward has a relatively greater effect on responding among extraverts and especially among disinhibited subjects (psychopaths). The responding of some subjects was actually facilitated by punishment. Gray (1987) proposed close linkages between behavioral approach mechanisms and positive emotions, and Heller (1990) noted that the left hemisphere contains high levels of dopamine reward mechanisms and there are massive projections from the dopamine receptors to the left frontal areas associated with positive affect.

The most sexually differentiated aspects of behavioral approach are maximized during late childhood and early adulthood, while non-sexually-differentiated aspects of behavioral approach appear early in infancy and are strongly associated with positive emotionality. Sensitivity to reward emerges very early in life as a dimension of temperament and is independent of measures of behavioral inhibition, the latter system developing in the second half of the first year (Bates, 1989; Rothbart, 1989b; Rothbart & Bates, 1998). In early infancy, there are individual differences in the extent to which infants approach rewarding stimulation, as indicated by attraction to sweet food, grasping objects, or attending to novel visual patterns. This trait is sometimes labeled "exuberance," defined as an "approach-oriented facet of positive emotionality" (Pfiefer, Goldsmith, Davidson, & Rickman, 2002; see also Fox, Henderson, Rubin, Calkins, & Schmidt, 2001). Children who are high on behavioral approach are prone to positive emotional response, including smiling, joy, and laughter available in rewarding situations and the pleasant social interaction sought by sociable children.

Sensation seeking, including the promiscuous sexual activity loading on the Disinhibition subscale (Zuckerman, 1979), and aggression (Wilson & Daly, 1985) peak in late adolescence and young adulthood, followed by a gradual decline during adulthood. As noted above, this "young male syndrome" is highly compatible with evolutionary thinking: Sex-differentiated systems are expected to be strongest at the time of sexual maturation and maximum divergence of reproductive strategies. Because mating is theorized to involve competition with other males, the male tendencies toward sensation seeking, risk taking, and aggression are expected to be at their peak during young adulthood, when males are attempting to establish themselves in the wider group and accumulate resources necessary for mating. However, boys are higher on behavioral approach even during infancy in cross-cultural samples (see Rothbart, 1989b, for a review); and sex differences in aggression (Eagly & Steffan, 1986), externalizing psychiatric disorders (conduct disorder, oppositional/defiant disorder), risk taking (Klein, 1995), and rough-and-tumble play (which is often associated with aggression) can be seen beginning in early childhood (DiPietro, 1981; Humphreys & Smith, 1987; MacDonald & Parke, 1986; O'Brien & Huston, 1985). Beginning in infancy, boys engage in more large-motor, physically intense activity (Eaton & Enns, 1986; Eaton & Yu, 1989). Increases in activity level are the clearest effect of prenatal exposure of genetic females to androgens (Ehrhardt, 1985; Ehrhardt & Baker, 1974). In factor analytic work, activity level appears to line up in the same area as dominance and sensation seeking (see Larsen & Diener, 1993). The social interactions of boys are also more characterized by dominance interactions and forceful, demanding interpersonal styles (Charlesworth & Dzur, 1987; Cowan & Avants, 1988; LaFreniere & Charlesworth, 1983; Savin-Williams, 1987). On the other hand, females are more prone to depression, which is associated with low levels of behavioral approach (Davidson, 1993; Fox, 1994). Indeed, anhedonia and negative mood are primary symptoms of depression within the *Diagnostic and Statistical Manual of Mental Disorders (DSM-IV;* American Psychiatric Association, 1994) classification.

Taken together, the data on behavioral approach indicate that over development, there is differentiation of behavioral approach from a relatively simple dimension involving differences in activity level and approach to novel objects, visual displays, and sensory stimulation; to sociability and positive emotionality during early infancy; and to aggression, dominance, and rough-and-tumble play during early childhood. This undergoes further differentiation and intensification as children approach reproductive competence and behavioral approach begins to include attraction to sexual gratification.

2. Nurturance/Love. Nurturance/Love, the second factor emerging from the circumplex model, underlies relationships of intimacy and other long-term relationships, especially family relationships involving reciprocity and transfer of resources to others (e.g., investment in children) (Kiesler, 1983; Trapnell & Wiggins, 1990; Wiggins, Trapnell, & Phillips, 1988). This trait is not considered to be a temperament dimension of childhood, but individual differences in warmth and affection observable in early parent-child relationships, including secure attachments, are conceptually linked with this dimension later in life (MacDonald, 1992, 1997, 1999a). Secure attachments and warm, affectionate parent-child relationships have been found to be associated with a high-investment style of parenting characterized by later sexual maturation, stable pair bonding, and warm, reciprocally rewarding, non-exploitative interpersonal relationships (Belsky, Steinberg, & Draper, 1991).

The physiological basis of female pair bonds appears to involve specific brain regions (Bartels & Zeki, 2000) and the hormone oxytocin in humans but not in other mammals (Insel, Winslow, Wang, & Young, 1998; Panksepp, 1998; Turner, Altemus, Enos, Cooper, & McGuinness, 1999). In prairie voles, a monogamous species, oxytocin receptors are found in brain regions associated with reward (Insel et al., 1998), supporting the proposal that pair bonding is a reward-based system that functions to facilitate intimate family relationships and parental investment (Depue & Morrone-Strupinsky, in press; MacDonald, 1992). The stimuli that activate this system act as natural clues (in the sense of Bowlby, 1969) for pleasurable affective response. Intimate relationships and the nurturance of the objects of affection are pleasurable, and such relationships are sought out by those high on this system.

If, indeed, the main evolutionary impetus for the development of the human affectional system is the need for high-investment parenting, females are expected to have a greater elaboration than males of mechanisms related to parental investment. Females, because of their very high investment in pregnancy and lactation, are expected to be highly discriminating maters compared with males and more committed to long-term relationships of nurturance and affection (e.g., Buss & Schmitt, 1993). Females score higher on the IAS-R-B5 LOV scale by a very robust 0.88 standard deviations (Trapnell & Wiggins, 1990). This dimension involves the tendency to provide aid for those needing help, including children and people who are ill (Wiggins & Broughton, 1985), and would therefore be expected to be associated with ideal child-nurturing behaviors. This dimension is strongly associated with measures of femininity and is associated with warm, empathic personal relationships and dependence (Wiggins & Broughton, 1985).

The tendency for females to be more strongly attracted to intimate relationships and pair bonding has empirical support. Girls are more prone than boys to engage in intimate, confiding relationships throughout development (Berndt, 1986; Buhrmester & Furman, 1987; Douvan & Adelson, 1966). Females also tend generally to place greater emphasis on love and personal intimacy in sexual relationships (e.g., Buss & Schmitt, 1993; Douvan & Adelson, 1966). Females are more empathic and desire higher intimacy in relationships (Lang-Takoc & Osterweil, 1992), and both sexes perceive friendships with women as closer, richer, more intimate, more empathic, and more therapeutic (e.g., Wright & Scanlon, 1991). Developmentally, sex differences related to intimacy peak during the reproductive years (Turner, 1981), a finding that is compatible with the present perspective that sex differences in intimacy are related to reproductive behavior.

Being extreme on Nurturance/Love is linked with psychopathology. Dependency disorder is characterized by being unusually prone to needing love and social approval (Widiger, Trull, Clarkin, Sanderson, & Costa, 2002). Several studies have linked dependency disorder to being high on FFM dimensions: Cloninger's (1987) Reward Dependence; Wiggins and Pincus's (1989) IAS-R-B5 LOV; and Widiger et al.'s (2002) Agreeableness. Dependency disorder is overwhelmingly a female disorder (e.g., Kernberg, 1986). Males, on the other hand, are more likely to be at the opposite extreme of sociopathy, characterized by a proneness to cruelty and lack of remorse for harming others (Draper & Harpending, 1988). Being low on Agreeableness is also linked with paranoid personality disorder and antisocial personality disorder (Widiger et al., 2002). Within the IAS scheme, the cold-quarrelsome scale, which is opposite to the warm-agreeable scale, reflects autonomy in interpersonal relationships and "the disposition not to be warm, cooperative, and nurturant when such behaviors would be appropriate" (Wiggins & Broughton, 1985, p. 42).

Finally, Nurturance/Love is separate from security of attachment (MacDonald, 1992, 1999a), with different functions, different emotions, a different distribution among the primates, a different pattern of theoretically expected sex differences, different mechanisms (a neurological reward system versus the internal working model), and different patterns of heritability. Regarding the latter, recently, Bokhorst et al. (2003; see also O'Connor & Croft, 2001) found negligible heritability for attachment security; many studies have shown the heritability of personality dimensions related to Nurturance/Love (e.g., Bouchard, 1996). Nurturance/Love and security of attachment underlie different aspects of close relationships. Reflecting its function as a system designed to protect the infant in times of uncertainty, the attachment system assesses the extent to which others can be trusted to help. The Experiences in Close Relationships Inventory (ECR) (Brennan, Clark, & Shaver, 1998), a measure of adult attachment, contains two factors, labeled Avoidance and Anxiety. The Anxiety factor is a measure of security conceptualized paradigmatically as fear of abandonment, while the Avoidance factor measures the extent to which people are attracted to close relationships for their own sake.

3. *The Behavioral Inhibition System and Conscientiousness.* The behavioral inhibition system (BIS) functions to monitor the environment for dangers and impending punishments (Gray, 1982, 1987; LeDoux, 1996). The BIS responds with the emotions of fear and anxiety to signals of uncertainty or anticipated punishment. Individual differences in behavioral inhibition are observable beginning in the second half of the first year of life with the development of the emotion of fear and expressions of distress and hesitation in the presence of novelty (Rothbart, 1989b; Rothbart & Bates, 1998). Children who are high on behavioral inhibition respond negatively to new people and other types of novel stimulation (Fox et al., 2001; Kagan, Reznick, & Snidman, 1987). Physiological research on behaviorally inhibited children indicates that these children generally have a more responsive sympathetic nervous system. This sympathetic dominance can be seen by the finding that behaviorally inhibited children tend to have a high and stable heart rate in unfamiliar situations, indicating that these children are highly aroused by unfamiliarity. Inhibited children also appear to have a highly sensitive amygdala, a limbic structure implicated in fear reactions (Fox et al., 2001; Kagan & Snidman, 1991). Many behaviorally inhibited children respond intensely to novel situations, and in particular, they tend to be highly prone to tension, anxiety, and fear in these situations.

The Conscientiousness system underlies perseverance in tasks that are not intrinsically rewarding but are important to fulfill long-range goals. The trait of Conscientiousness involves variation in the ability to defer gratification, persevere in unpleasant tasks, pay close attention to detail, and behave in a responsible, dependable manner; not surprisingly, conscientiousness increases with age in children (Lamb et al., 2002). Beginning at about 10 to 12 months of age, temperament research has revealed a trait of effortful control involving focused attention on tasks and the ability to inhibit inappropriate approach tendencies (Rothbart, Ahadi, & Evans, 2000). Rothbart et al. (2001) have shown that this trait is related in adults to Conscientiousness in the FFM.

The psychiatric disorders most associated with Conscientiousness are obsessive-compulsive personality disorder (OCD) and antisocial personality disorder (e.g., irresponsible and delinquent acts, failure to honor obligations or plan ahead) (Widiger & Trull, 1992; Widiger et al., 2002). OCD tends to co-occur with a variety of phobic states and other anxiety disorders (e.g., Marks, 1987; Öhman, 1993). An important aspect of Gray's (1982, 1987) theory is that anxiety is a critical emotion of OCD. Gray views phobias and obsessive-compulsive behavior as linked to the same systems because of the central role for anxiety in these disorders. From this perspective, the adaptive function of the Conscientiousness system is to check for possible threats emanating from the environment, including physical contamination, nonattainment of goals related to self-preservation, and other possible sources of danger and punishment.

The frontal cortex has been implicated in many of the behaviors associated with Conscientiousness. Mesulam (1986; see also Luria, 1980; Tucker & Derryberry, 1992) noted that humans and monkeys with prefrontal cortex damage have difficulty focusing attention, planning orderly sequences of behavior, inhibiting immediate but inappropriate response tendencies, delaying gratification, persevering in tasks that take a great deal of effort, and planning for the future. Furthermore, Tucker and Derryberry (1992) reviewed data indicating that lesions of the frontal cortex were effective for patients with chronic anxiety and sometimes even produced a pathological lack of anxiety, a primary negative emotion of the Conscientiousness system.

There is also evidence for mutual inhibitory influences between the mechanisms underlying Conscientiousness and behavioral approach systems. Mesulam (1986) described reciprocal inhibition between frontal and the parietal lobes, the latter viewed as an approach system characterized by diffuse attention and impulsive responding. There are also reciprocal inhibitory influences between the BIS and the reward-based approach system (Avila, 2002; Fox, 1994; Gray, 1987). In the rat at least, the inhibitory influences from the BIS are more powerful than the reverse. Both systems may be aroused in particular situations, as when a previously rewarded behavior has been punished.

These results have implications for thinking about conflicts between evolved systems as well as for situation specificity. The systems underlying behavioral approach and behavioral inhibition are psychometrically and neurophysiologically independent, implying that individuals can be more or less sensitive to rewards and more or less sensitive to punishment (Avila, 2001; Pickering, Diaz, & Gray, 1995). Nevertheless, each system has inhibitory effects on the other system, so that in a situation with both potential rewards and potential punishments, both systems are activated. Individuals high on behavioral approach evaluate the risks involved and engage in behavioral approach, while introverts, being less attracted to the potential rewards, are more likely to have approach tendencies inhibited. Impending punishments trigger the BIS even for individuals moderately high on behavioral approach; however, a situation characterized overwhelmingly by potential reward with little risk activates the reward/approach systems even for individuals with powerful inhibitory tendencies. The result is what one might term "System X Trait X Situational" variation, where the "System" is understood as a universal mechanism responsive to particular perceived environmental contingencies and the "Trait" represents individual differences in proneness to activating particular systems.

Attentional mechanisms are implicated in Conscientiousness. Indeed, within the FFM, attention deficit hyperactivity disorder (ADHD) is most strongly linked to low Conscientiousness (Nigg et al., 2002). Tucker and Derryberry (1992; see also Tucker & Williamson, 1984) have proposed that left frontal systems mediate attention that is tightly focused on possible environmental threats as well as planning to meet these environmental contingencies. Amphetamine is typically prescribed for individuals with ADHD and helps them engage in effortful, planned behavior and to focus attention on important environmental cues. Large doses of amphetamine result in repetitive, stereotyped (i.e., novelty avoidant), overfocused, hypervigilant, and eventually paranoid behavior. Tucker and Derryberry noted that the compulsions of OCD patients are stereotyped and often tightly focused on imagined threats emanating from the environment (germs, dirt). Unlike the extraverted attention characterized by an habituation bias, the attentional style associated with the attributes of Conscientiousness is narrow, focused, and has a redundancy bias.

The evolutionary theory of sex outlined above suggests that females would tend to adopt a more conservative strategy and thus be higher on measures of Conscientiousness and more prone to anxiety disorders. Nevertheless, males must also be acutely concerned with threats emanating from the environment, particularly the social environment, and be able to defer gratification in the pursuit of long-term benefits. Because the mechanisms underlying behavioral approach are distinct from those underlying Conscientiousness and there are mutually inhibitory relationships between them, the most that could be predicted is that males, because of their high levels of behavioral approach, would have a somewhat greater tendency to be biased toward lower levels of Conscientiousness.

Evolutionary theory predicts that females will be more sensitive than males to physical dangers. Females are more prone to most anxiety disorders, including agoraphobia and panic disorder (e.g., American Psychiatric Association, 1994; Weissman, 1985). Girls report being more fearful and timid than boys in uncertain situations and are more cautious and take fewer risks than boys (Christopherson, 1989; Ginsburg & Miller, 1982). Girls are also more compliant than boys beginning in the toddler period and throughout childhood (Kochanska & Aksan, 1995).

The widespread occurrence of social phobias (Gray, 1987; Marks, 1987) is compatible with evolution of mechanisms finely tuned to evaluation by the group. It is interesting in this regard that the general tendency for females to be higher on phobias and other indicators of fearfulness and caution is not found for social phobia (American Psychiatric Association, 1994; Marks, 1987). Social phobias involve fears of negative evaluations by a group, and one might speculate that there were evolutionary pressures on group-living males for concern for status within the group. Öhman (1993) found that angry faces are among the potentially phobic stimuli (including also snakes and spiders) able to condition autonomic responses that are more resistant to extinction than those conditioned to neutral stimuli—findings that suggest innate feature detectors related to social fears. Feelings of guilt and excessive social responsibility are also common symptoms of OCD, another anxiety disorder that also fails to consistently show a sex difference (American Psychiatric Association, 1994; Weissman, 1985).

4. Affect Intensity. Affect intensity functions to mobilize behavioral resources by moderating arousal in acutely demanding situations in the service of both approach and avoidance behaviors. Affect intensity may be viewed as a general behavioral "engine" that is used in the service of both behavioral approach and behavioral avoidance. It is a behavioral scaling system that allows the organism to scale its responses to current environmental opportunities and threats. This system is well studied at the neurophysiological level, where research implicates catecholamine systems that energize both positive and negative emotion systems (Panksepp, 1998, pp. 109-110, 117). Among temperament researchers, there is general consensus that there are two independent dimensions of reactivity and regulation (see, e.g., Ramsey & Lewis, 2003; Rothbart, 1989a, 1989b; Rothbart & Bates, 1998).

Children who are highly reactive respond intensely to stimulation, reach peak arousal at lower stimulus intensity, and have a relatively low threshold for arousal. These children are often viewed as having a weak nervous system in the sense that they are easily aroused and overstimulated. In the presence of high levels of stimulation, these high-reactive individuals inhibit their responding and tend to withdraw from the source of stimulation. On the other hand, they respond very intensely to even low levels of stimulation. Low-reactive children, on the other hand, may be said to have relatively strong nervous systems in the sense that they have a relatively high threshold of stimulation and do not become aroused by stimulation that would overwhelm a high-reactive individual. Low-reactive individuals are thus more likely to be found in highly stimulating environments, although at extremely high levels of stimulation, even these individuals begin to inhibit their responding and withdraw from stimulation.

Emotionally intense individuals respond relatively strongly to emotional stimulation independent of the emotion involved, including both positive and negative emotions (Larsen & Diener, 1987). People high on affect intensity are prone to fast and frequent mood changes and lead varied and variable emotional lives. Clinically, affect intensity is related to cyclothymia, bipolar affective disorder, neurotic symptoms, and somatic complaints (nervousness, feeling uneasy, shortness of breath). Several developmental studies have found that proneness to both positive and negative emotions under moderate levels of stimulus intensity is associated with reactivity as indicated by measures of vagal tone and event-related potentials (Fox, 1989; Gunnar & Nelson, 1994; Porges, 1991). Recently, Garey et al. (2003) identified a generalized arousal component in the behavior of mice across experiments, investigators, and mouse populations. This factor accounts for about one third of the variance in arousal-related measures.

Affect intensity may be viewed as a generalized motivation-enhancement system that can be directed toward behavioral approach (Dominance/Sensation Seeking) as well as behavioral avoidance and checking for possible threats in the environment (Conscientiousness and Behavioral Inhibition). The catecholamine systems underlying arousal are nonspecific; they induce arousal in a wide variety of systems (Panksepp, 1998). Individuals high on affect intensity are thus highly motivated to intensive interaction with the environment. For example, Fox et al. (2001) found that reactive children who showed continuity of behavioral inhibition were prone to negative emotional responding and had a pattern of right frontal asymmetry in their EEG patterns. On the other hand, highly reactive exuberant children had a pattern of left frontal asymmetry. Reactive children are thus prone to intense emotional response, but they may be biased toward positive or negative emotions.

Of the children classified as unreactive on the basis of EEG data, some were consistently inhibited while others were consistently uninhibited; most were not classifiable as consistently either. Again, these data illustrate the independence of reactivity from behavioral inhibition and behavioral approach systems.

Affect intensity is most closely associated with Neuroticism in the FFM (Larsen & Diener, 1993). Watson and Clark (1992) showed that Neuroticism is associated with all four of their dimensions of negative affect: guilt, hostility, fear, and sadness. However, these negative emotions also tend to be associated with the other systems underlying the FFM: hostility (negatively) with Nurturance/Love, sadness with Introversion, fear with Conscientiousness, and guilt with Nurturance/Love and Conscientiousness. Neuroticism also appears to be related to a wide range of personality disorders that also load on other systems (Costa & McCrae, 1986; Widiger & Trull, 1992). High affect intensity thus energizes negative emotional responding in general. However, affect intensity also provides a powerful engine for positive emotional responses that are central to other physiologically and psychometrically independent systems (Aron & Aron, 1997; Panksepp, 1998, p. 117).

5. Openness to Experience. The Openness to Experience factor taps variation in intelligence and what one might term "optimal Piagetian learning": intrinsically motivated curiosity and interest in intellectual and aesthetic experience combined with imagination and creativity in these areas. Openness increases during adolescence, a time when, with increasing cognitive sophistication, adolescents exhibit greater interest in a wide range of experiences (McCrae et al., 2002). Openness is also related to scores on standardized measures of cognitive ability, including verbal and mathematical achievement tests (John et al., 1994; Lamb et al., 2002). Openness is thus related to domain-general cognitive abilities tapped by such measures and discussed in Chapter 2 as an adaptation to uncertain, rapidly changing environments.

An Evolutionary Perspective on Environmental Influences

The results of behavior genetic research indicate that environmental variation has considerable influence on phenotypic variation in personality, but with the exception of Agreeableness, there is no evidence that environmental variation is shared within families (e.g., Bouchard, 1996). Within an evolutionary systems perspective, environmental influences are conceptualized as involving specific types of stimulation directed at particular evolved systems. Thus, environmental influences affecting the Conscientiousness system would be expected to be events related to inhibiting inappropriate approach behaviors in children (perhaps by parental discipline), while environmental influences related to Nurturance/Love would be expected to involve warmth and affection, which typically occur in close family relationships.

For example, Fox et al. (2001) found that inhibited children placed in day care within the first 2 years were more likely to change to a noninhibited pattern, and they suggested that this may be due to greater experience with nonfamily members. Elsewhere, I have argued that given the status of the human affectional system in promoting close relationships, the primary source of environmental influences would be adult caretakers, typically family members (MacDonald, 1992, 1997). If the relevant environmental stimulation is that which we label warm and affectionate, this type of stimulation is unlikely to come from other sources, at least during infancy and early childhood. It is thus not surprising that Agreeableness shows evidence of shared environmental influence (Bouchard, 1996; Tellegen et al., 1988). Similarly, shared environmental influence has been implicated in security of attachment (Bokhorst et al., 2003). In general, behavior genetics studies have shown more evidence of shared environmental influence in infancy and early childhood (e.g., Plomin, 1994).

Developing emotional ties to children may also be considered an aspect of parental investment. The idea that there was natural selection for high-investment parenting among humans is widely held among evolutionists (e.g., Fisher, 1992; Flinn & Low, 1986; Geary, 1998; Lancaster & Lancaster, 1987; Lovejoy, 1981; MacDonald, 1988, 1992). High-investment parents provide high-quality environments for their children, and these environments contribute to the child's development. Parental investment involves the provision of certain environments, and parents incur a considerable cost in providing these environments: Parental investment includes developing a strong emotional relationship with the child, providing relatively high levels of verbal stimulation and parent-child play, and active parental involvement in monitoring virtually every aspect of the child's life (e.g., children's progress in school, children's peer relationships) (Belsky et al., 1991). From a theoretical perspective, the best evidence that the environments provided by high-investment parents must have benefits is the very clear evidence that they are costly to provide. Theoretically, it is difficult to conceive of a behavior with clear costs remaining in a population without some compensating benefits. For example, if children do not benefit from paternal investment, it is difficult to conceptualize why either males or females would seek such investment. Under these circumstances, males would be better off competing with other males for access to additional females (i.e., increasing their mating effort) than to invest in the offspring of one female (i.e., maintaining high levels of parenting effort). Minimal parenting effort by males is a common pattern in nature, especially among mammals (e.g., Kleiman, 1977, 1981).

While the foregoing argues for the importance of children's environments, it is not inconsistent with evidence that high-investment parenting is itself genetically influenced. There is evidence for reasonably high heritability of all of the behaviors related to parental investment. Thus, measures of parents' and children's perceptions of parental control, and especially parental warmth, are genetically influenced (Rowe, 1994). Parental stimulation and involvement (including measures of parental warmth and control), as measured by the Home Observation for Measurement of the Environment (HOME) and the Family Environment Scale (FES), also have a considerable genetic component (Plomin, 1994). These measures of parental investment covary to a considerable degree with high IQ, which is itself substantially heritable (Plomin 1994; see also below). There is a substantial covariation among the HOME subscales of emotional and verbal responsivity, provision of play materials, maternal involvement, and opportunities for variety of stimulation (Bradley & Caldwell, 1984). Parents who provide verbal stimulation and monitor their children closely also tend to have close emotional relationships with them.

Within an evolutionary paradigm, parental investment is an important aspect of life history theory. Life history theory attempts to understand variation in the reproductive strategies adopted by different life forms. Life history theory implies considerable coherence to individual development because a reproductive strategy involves a coordinated response to the organism's environment resulting from the need to optimally partition mating effort (i.e., the effort expended in attracting mates) and parenting effort (i.e., the effort devoted to nurturing children). The fundamental dimension of reproductive strategies may be construed as a dimension that ranges from a high-parental-investment/low-mating-effort strategy to a low-parental-investment/high-mating-effort strategy.

A reproductive strategy involves a response to a central external ecological contingency that selects for optimum levels of partitioning mating effort and parenting effort. The result is that variables such as mortality rates, longevity, pair bonding, age of first reproduction, period of preadult dependency, and levels of paternal and maternal investment evolve as a coordinated response to the environment. Thus, for example, species adapted to environments where there is a relatively stable, predictable resource base tend to have a suite of traits allowing them to produce highly competitive offspring. Such species would be likely to have traits such as pair bonding between parents, high-investment parenting (including paternal provisioning of the young), low fertility, and delayed maturation of the young.

Theoretically, high-investment parenting is associated with adaptation to ecologically adverse or highly competitive environments where high levels of parental investment are critical to rearing successful offspring (Kleiman, 1977, 1981; Southwood, 1981). This makes intuitive sense because in ecologically adverse or highly competitive situations, male provisioning of food or other resources might tip the balance in favor of offspring compared with the offspring of males who do not provision their young. Indeed, several theorists have proposed that the adverse environment created by the Ice Age had an important role in shaping the intelligence and high-investment reproductive behavior of northern populations (Lynn, 1991; Miller, 1994a, 1994b; Rushton, 1995). Within this framework, natural selection resulted in a uniform tendency toward high-investment parenting as a result of long-term resource scarcity: Males who did not provision their young left few descendants. Long-term selection in resource-scarce environments is therefore expected to lead to high-investment parenting.

The data reviewed by Belsky et al. (1991) illustrate the utility of a life history perspective. They especially noted the large intercorrelations among spousal harmony, parent-child relationship quality, children's interpersonal style, timing of puberty, sexual behavior, and level of parental investment. These qualities would be expected to be most closely related to the Nurturance/ Love system discussed here; Figueredo et al. (in press) found that a single "K-factor" composed of measures of these qualities correlated −0.67 with the closely related factor of psychoticism. The coherence of individual development also appears to involve measures of intelligence (e.g., Rushton, 1995) related to the Openness factor of the FFM. IQ is the single most powerful measure of individual differences psychologists have developed and is related to variation in a very wide range of human activities. Recent studies have suggested that variation in life history strategy is influenced genetically (Comings, Muhlman, Johnson, & MacMurray, 2002; Moffitt, Caspi, Belsky, & Silva, 1992; Rowe, 2000). For example, Comings et al. (2002) reported that father-daughter transmission of a specific X-linked androgen receptor gene is associated with early menarche as well as with parental divorce. Age of menarche is highly heritable, and there is no evidence for shared environmental influence as would be expected in a father absence model (Rowe, 2000).

Evolution and Group Differences in Personality Systems

Several personality systems show systematic, theoretically expected differences between groups, the most important being sex and age differences noted above. Furthermore, because different human groups evolved in somewhat different EEAs, it is not surprising that there is between-group variation on personality systems. For example, children from the Mongoloid gene pool are lower on affect intensity, aggression, and disruptiveness and tend to be more cooperative than Caucasian children (Brazelton, Robey, & Collier, 1969; Freedman & Freedman, 1969; Orlick, Zhou, & Partington, 1990). For adults, Vernon (1982), using a variety of standard personality instruments, found that Mongoloids were more introverted, more anxiety prone, less aggressive, and lower on social dominance than Caucasians, while Rushton (1995) found that Mongoloid samples were less extraverted and more neurotic than Caucasians. Also noting various physical adaptations for extreme cold typical of Mongoloids, including flattened face, narrow eyes, shortened limbs, and the epicanthic fold, Lynn (1991) and Rushton (1995) have theorized that this suite of traits resulted from selection for behavioral restraint during the Ice Age.

Birth order is another source of systematic group differences in personality. Sulloway (1996, 1999; see also Paulhus, Trapnell, & Chen, 1999; Rohde et al., 2003) has provided evidence for modest birth order effects on the five factor dimensions and rebelliousness, and he has provided a compelling evolutionary interpretation of these differences. Firstborns have been found to be lower on Openness, higher on Conscientiousness, lower on Agreeableness, higher on negative emotionality (Neuroticism), higher on social dominance, lower on sociability (a facet of Surgency/Extraversion related also to Agreeableness), and lower on rebelliousness. Birth order—conceptualized as a proxy for differences in age, size, power, status, and privilege—is proposed as the most important systematic unshared environmental influence on personality. Each child attempts to occupy a niche within the family. The oldest child occupies the first available niche, identifies more strongly with parents and with authority, and tends to reject new ideas. Younger children identify less with their parents and are more open to new experience and ideas.

Sulloway's evolutionary perspective draws on parent-offspring conflict theory (Trivers, 1974). Parents tend to favor older offspring because they have a higher reproductive value (i.e., they are closer to reproducing themselves), particularly in situations where resources are limited. This is theorized to increase firstborns' identification with adult values and facilitate the

Conscientiousness system. Because they share only half their genes, siblings also have conflicts with each other over resources, and older siblings are typically able to dominate their younger siblings because of their advantages in size and strength. This strengthens the trait of Social Dominance. Laterborns, on the other hand, resent this domination and develop a suite of strategies that enable them to occupy other niches within the family dynamic, including higher levels of sociability and agreeableness.

Evolutionary Perspectives on Individual Differences in Personality Systems

Despite the claims that individual differences in personality are without adaptive significance (Tooby & Cosmides, 1990), evolutionary perspectives on individual differences is an active area of research and theorizing (Figueredo et al., in press). A basic idea shared by several writers is that personality distributions imply more than one viable adaptive strategy (Belsky et al., 1991; Figueredo & King, 2001; Figueredo et al., in press; Gangestad & Simpson, 1990; MacDonald, 1991; Wilson, 1994; see also discussion in Buss, 1991). Genetic variation in personality and other valued traits serves to facilitate the production of a wide range of variation (within a delimited range), which facilitates the occupation of a wide range of possible niches in the human and nonhuman environment.

One way that this variation could be maintained is via frequency-dependent selection, in which relatively rare phenotypes have an advantage while more common phenotypes have a disadvantage, because they must compete with each other in the same niche (Figueredo & King, 2001; Gangestad & Simpson, 1990; Mealey, 1995). Another possibility is that stabilizing selection (i.e., selection against extremes) occurred (MacDonald, 1995, 1998). Personality systems fundamentally motivate people to approach the world and avoid dangers. Unlike the case with intelligence, it is intuitively plausible that being very high or very low on personality systems is maladaptive. For example, people must be motivated to approach rewards and take some risks in obtaining them, but being foolhardy is dangerous. On the other hand, there is a broad range of genetic variation in the middle of the distribution underlying a range of viable strategies. This approach is consistent with attempts to conceptualize psychopathology in terms of maladaptive extremes on FFM dimensions (e.g., Costa & Widiger, 1994).

Recent evidence suggests the importance of both frequency-dependent selection and stabilizing selection for the 7R allele of the D4 dopamine receptor gene linked with novelty seeking, impulsivity, and ADHD. Harpending and

Cochran (2002) interpreted available data as suggesting natural selection for this allele up to a certain point, followed by stabilizing selection. Despite their extreme behavior, children with this gene did not show common neurological abnormalities related to attention deficits (Swanson et al., 2000), suggesting that this variant of the D4 gene was adaptive during evolutionary history (Harpending & Cochran, 2002; see also Ding et al., 2002). Data for this allele are also relevant to group differences in personality systems: This gene is common among South American Indians, occurs at intermediate levels in Europeans and in most African groups, and is nonexistent among East Asians and the African !Kung (Harpending & Cochran, 2002).

The finding that a gene linked with psychopathology in contemporary environments was adaptive during evolutionary history is consistent with Farley's (1981, 1985) comment that individuals high on sensation seeking are overrepresented in prison populations, but sensation seekers who are well socialized are also overrepresented among highly creative people, including highly successful scientists, artists, political leaders, and entertainers. Similarly, several authors have noted that bipolar affective disorder is linked with creativity in normal or mildly affected relatives of psychiatrically impaired individuals (Andreasen, 1978; Richards, Kinney, Lunde, Henet, & Merzel, 1988), with creativity associated with the manic phase (Isen, Daubman, & Nowicki, 1987). Evolutionists have also theorized that some psychopathology results from the differences between modern environments and the environments in which humans evolved (e.g., Nesse & Williams, 1996). For example, rates of depression may be influenced by contemporary trends toward families removing themselves from close kinship ties as a source of social support. In addition, particular cultural contexts may render certain behavior pathological and maladaptive that would be quite adaptive in a different cultural setting. For example, it has often been informally suggested that although there are exceptions, the behavior of children with ADHD tends to be maladaptive in contemporary societies where children are expected to adjust to educational settings. However, such children might be well adapted to life in societies where the aggressiveness and high energy level of these children would be valued traits.

Personality and Social Evaluation

People are greatly interested in the genetic and phenotypic diversity represented by this range of viable strategies (MacDonald, 1995, 1998). As Buss (1991) noted, personality is an adaptive landscape in which "perceiving, attending to, and acting upon differences in others is crucial for solving problems of survival and reproduction" (p. 471). Hogan's (1996) socio-analytic theory emphasizes social evaluation as central to personality psychology. Individual differences in personality are thus viewed as indicators of whether individuals are suited for particular roles. Each individual is expected to not only appraise the phenotypic traits of others but also to evaluate these traits differently depending on the type of relationship entered into. For example, Lusk, MacDonald, and Newman (1998) found that ideal leaders were expected to be higher than ideal friends in scales intended to tap variation in physical attractiveness, intelligence, conscientiousness, activity, and sociability, but lower in emotionality and disabilities—a trait profile that presumably reflects individuals' criteria for being a good leader. Ideal friends, on the other hand, were expected to be higher than prospective leaders in athletic ability and Intimacy/Warmth, traits that are presumably more important for a successful friendship. Moreover, subjects expected ideal friends to be more similar to themselves than to ideal leaders, and subjects rated themselves as more similar to prospective ideal leaders and ideal friends on categories that they themselves rated highly. Because of the importance of social evaluation of personality, people are motivated to adopt personality profiles that are appealing to other people: the job candidate who attempts to appear conscientious, the suitor who tries to appear loving and nurturing.

Conclusion

The foregoing illustrates how evolutionary theory is able to make an important contribution to personality research. The main contributions are to provide a powerful theory for a great many age and sex differences in personality and to think of personality variation as serving adaptive functions. Another contribution, much stressed here, is to emphasize the central importance of personality systems. In my view, the most neglected area is the failure to think of personality and temperament traits as reflecting variation in evolved systems serving adaptive functions. For historical reasons stemming from the fact that personality research originated long before a solid base in evolution and biological research was possible, we tend to think about variation but not about systems. We therefore miss the complex interactions among systems as being at the heart of personality—interactions that go a long way toward placing personality at the forefront of how people confront their social and nonsocial environments.

References

American Psychiatric Association. (1994). *Diagnostic and statistical manual of mental disorders, 4th edition (DSM-IV)*. Washington, DC: Author.

Andreasen, N. C. (1978). Creativity and psychiatric illness. *Psychiatric Annals, 8,* 113-119.

Aron, E. N., & Aron, A. (1997). Sensory-processing sensitivity and its relation to introversion and emotionality. *Journal of Personality and Social Psychology, 73,* 345-368.

Avila, C. (2001). Distinguishing BIS-mediated and BAS-mediated disinhibition mechanisms: A comparison of disinhibition models of Gray (1981, 1987) and of Patterson and Newman (1993). *Journal of Personality and Social Psychology, 80,* 311-324.

Bartels, A., & Zeki, S. (2000). The neural basis of romantic love. *NeuroReport, 11*(17), 3829-3834.

Bates, J. E. (1989). Concepts and measures of temperament. In G. A. Kohnstamm, J. E. Bates, & M. K. Rothbart (Eds.), *Temperament in childhood* (pp. 3-26). Chichester, UK: Wiley.

Belsky, J., Steinberg, L., & Draper, P. (1991). Childhood experience, interpersonal development, and reproductive strategy: An evolutionary theory of socialization. *Child Development, 62,* 647-670.

Berndt, T. J. (1986). Children's comments about their friendships. In M. Perlmutter (Ed.), *Minnesota Symposia in Child Development: Vol. 18. Cognitive perspectives on children's social and behavioral development* (pp. 189-212). Hillsdale, NJ: Erlbaum.

Bokhorst, C. L., Bakermans-Kranenburg, M. J., Pasco Fearon, R. M., van Ijzendoorn, M. H., Fonagy, P., & Schuengel, C. (2003). The importance of shared environment in mother-infant attachment security: A behavioral genetic study. *Child Development, 74,* 1769-1782.

Bouchard, T. J. Jr. (1996). The genetics of personality. In K. Blum & E. P. Noble (Eds.), *Handbook of psychoneurogenetics* (pp. 267-290). Boca Raton, FL: CRC Press.

Bowlby, J. (1969). *Attachment and loss: Vol. I. Attachment*. London: Hogarth Press and the Institute of Psychoanalysis.

Bradley, R. H., & Caldwell, B. (1984). Children: A study of the relationship between home environment and cognitive development during the first 5 years. In A. W. Gottfried (Ed.), *Home environment and early cognitive development: Longitudinal research*. Orlando, FL: Academic Press.

Brazelton, T. B., Robey, J. S., & Collier, G. A. (1969). Infant development in the Zinacanteco Indians of Southern Mexico. *Pediatrics, 44,* 274-290.

Brennan, K. A., Clark, C. L., & Shaver, P. R. (1998). Self-report measurement of adult attachment. In J. A. Simpson & W. S. Rholes (Eds.), *Attachment theory and close relationships*. New York: Guilford Press.

Buhrmester, D., & Furman, W. (1987). The development of companionship and intimacy. *Child Development, 58,* 1101-1113.

Buss, D. M. (1991). Evolutionary personality psychology. *Annual Review of Psychology, 42,* 459-491.

Buss, D. M., & Schmitt, D. P. (1993). Sexual strategies theory: An evolutionary perspective on human mating. *Psychological Review, 100,* 204-232.

Caspi, A. (1998). Personality development across the lifespan. In N. Eisenberg (Ed.), *Handbook of child psychology* (Vol. 3, pp. 105-176). New York: John Wiley.

Charlesworth, W., & Dzur, C. (1987). Gender comparisons of preschoolers' behavior and resource utilization in group problem solving. *Child Development, 58,* 191-200.

Christopherson, E. R. (1989). Injury control. *American Psychologist, 44,* 237-241.

Cloninger, C. R. (1987). A systematic method for clinical description and classification of personality. *Archives of General Psychiatry, 44,* 573-588.

Comings, D. E., Muhlman, D., Johnson, J. P., & MacMurray, J. P. (2002). Parent-daughter transmission of the androgen receptor gene as an explanation of the effect of father absence on age of menarche. *Child Development, 73,* 1046-1051.

Costa, P. T., & McCrae, R. R. (1986). Personality stability and its implications for clinical psychology. *Clinical Psychology Review, 6,* 407-423.

Costa, P. T., & McCrae, R. R. (1992). *NEO-PI-R professional manual.* Orlando, FL: PAR.

Costa, P. T., & Widiger, T. A. (1994). Summary and unresolved issues. In P. T. Costa & T. A. Widiger (Eds.), *Personality disorders and the five-factor model of personality.* Washington, DC: American Psychological Association.

Cowan, G., & Avants, S. K. (1988). Children's influence strategies: Structure, sex differences, and bilateral mother-child influences. *Child Development, 59,* 1303-1313.

Davidson, R. J. (1993). The neuropsychology of emotion and affective style. In M. Lewis & J. M. Haviland (Eds.), *Handbook of emotions* (pp. 143-154). New York: Guilford Press.

Depue, R. A., & Collins, P. F. (1999). Neurobiology of the structure of personality: Dopamine facilitation of incentive motivation and extraversion. *Brain and Behavioral Sciences, 22,* 491-569.

Depue, R. A., & Morrone-Strupinsky, J. V. (in press). A neurobehavioral model of behavioral bonding: Implications for conceptualizing a human trait of affiliation. *Behavioral and Brain Sciences.*

De Raad, B. (1992). The replicability of the Big Five personality dimensions in three word-classes of the Dutch language. *European Journal of Personality, 6,* 15-29.

Derryberry, D. (1987). Incentive and feedback effects on target detection: A chronometric analysis of Gray's theory of temperament. *Personality and Individual Differences, 8,* 855-865.

Digman, J. M., & Shmelyov, A. G. (1996). The structure of temperament and personality in Russian children. *Journal of Personality and Social Psychology, 71,* 341-351.

Ding, Y. C., Chi, H. C., Grady, D. L., Morishima, A., Kidd, J. R., Kidd, K. K., et al. (2002). Evidence of positive selection acting at the human dopamine receptor D4 gene locus. *Proceedings of the National Academy of Science, 99,* 309-314.

DiPietro, J. A. (1981). Rough and tumble play: A function of gender. *Developmental Psychology, 17,* 50-58.

Douvan, E. A., & Adelson, J. (1966). *The adolescent experience.* New York: John Wiley.

Draper, P., & Harpending, H. (1988). A sociobiological perspective on the development of human reproductive strategies. In K. MacDonald (Ed.), *Sociobiological perspectives on human development* (pp. 340-372). New York: Springer-Verlag.

Eagly, A. H., & Steffan, V. J. (1986). Gender and aggressive behavior: A meta-analytic review of the social psychological literature. *Psychological Bulletin, 100,* 283-308.

Eaton, W. O., & Enns, L. R. (1986). Sex differences in human motor activity level. *Psychological Bulletin, 100,* 19-28.

Eaton, W. O., & Yu, A. P. (1989). Are sex differences in child motor activity level a function of sex differences in maturational status? *Child Development, 60,* 1005-1011.

Ehrhardt, A. A. (1985). The psychobiology of gender. In A. S. Rossi (Ed.), *Gender and the life course.* New York: Aldine.

Ehrhardt, A. A., & Baker, S. W. (1974). Fetal androgens, human central nervous system differentiation, and behavioral sex differences. In R. C. Friedman, R. M. Rickard, & R. L. Van de Wiele (Eds.), *Sex differences in behavior.* New York: John Wiley.

Eysenck, H. J. (1967). *The biological basis of personality.* Springfield, IL: Charles C Thomas.

Eysenck, H. J. (Ed.). (1982). *Personality, genetics, and behavior.* New York: Praeger.

Farley, F. H. (1981). Basic process individual differences: A biologically based theory of individualization for cognitive, affective, and creative outcomes. In F. H. Farley & N. H. Gordon (Eds.), *Psychology and education: The state of the union* (pp. 7-31). Berkeley, CA: McCutchan Publishing.

Farley, F. H. (1985). The Big T in personality. *Psychology Today, 20,* 44-52.

Figueredo, A. J., & King, J. E. (1996). The evolution of individual differences in behavior. *Western Comparative Psychological Association Observer, 2*(2), 1-4.

Figueredo, A. J., & King, J. E. (2001). *The evolution of individual differences.* In S. D. Gosling & A. Weiss (Chairs), Symposium on Evolution and Individual Differences, Annual Meeting of the Human Behavior and Evolution Society, London.

Figueredo, A. J., Sefcek, J., Vasquez, G., Hagenah, B. J., King, J. E., & Jacobs, W. J. (in press). Evolutionary theories of personality. In D. M. Buss (Ed.), *Handbook of evolutionary psychology.* Hoboken, NJ: John Wiley.

Fisher, H. (1992). *The anatomy of love.* New York: W.W. Norton.

Flinn, M. V., & Low, B. S. (1986). Resource distribution, social competition, and mating patterns in human societies. In D. I. Rubenstein & R. W. Wrangham

(Eds.), *Ecological aspects of social evolution: Birds and mammals* (pp. 217-243). Princeton, NJ: Princeton University Press.

Fox, N. A. (1989). Psychophysiological correlates of emotional reactivity during the first year of life. *Developmental Psychology, 25,* 364-372.

Fox, N. A. (1994). Dynamic cerebral processes underlying emotion regulation. In N. Fox (Ed.), The development of emotion regulation: Biological and behavioral considerations. *Monographs for the Society for Research in Child Development, 59*(2/3, Serial No. 240), 152-166.

Fox, N. A., Henderson, H. A., Rubin, K. H., Calkins, S. D., & Schmidt, L. A. (2001). Continuity and discontinuity of behavioral inhibition and exuberance: Psychophysiological and behavioral influences across the first four years of life. *Child Development, 72,* 1-21.

Freedman, D. J., & Freedman, N. C. (1969). Behavioral differences between Chinese-American and European-American newborns. *Nature, 224,* 1227.

Gangestad, S. W., & Simpson, J. A. (1990). Toward an evolutionary history of female sociosexual variation. *Journal of Personality, 58,* 69-96.

Garey, J., Goodwillie, A., Frohlich, J., Morgan, M., Gustafsson, J.-A., Smithies, O., et al. (2003). Genetic contributions to generalized arousal of brain and behavior. *Proceedings of the National Academy of Science, 100,* 11019-11022.

Geary, D. (1998). *Male-female: The evolution of human sex differences.* Washington, DC: American Psychological Association.

Ginsburg, H. J., & Miller, S. M. (1982). Sex differences in children's risk-taking behavior. *Child Development, 53,* 426-428.

Goldberg, L. R. (1990). An alternative "description of personality": The Big Five factor solution. *Journal of Personality and Social Psychology, 59,* 1216-1229.

Gosling, S. D., & John, O. P. (1999). Personality dimensions in nonhuman animals: A cross-species review. *Current Directions in Psychological Science, 8*(3), 69-75.

Gray, J. A. (1982). *The neuropsychology of anxiety.* New York: Oxford University Press.

Gray, J. A. (1987). *The psychology of fear and stress.* Cambridge, UK: Cambridge University Press.

Graziano, W. G., & Ward, D. (1992). Probing the Big Five in adolescence: Personality and adjustment during a developmental transition. *Journal of Personality, 60,* 425-439.

Gunnar, M. R., & Nelson, C. A. (1994). Event-related potentials in year-old infants: Relations with emotionality and cortisol. *Child Development, 65,* 80-94.

Harpending, H., & Cochran, G. (2002). In our genes. *Proceedings of the National Academy of Science, 99*(1), 10-12.

Heller, W. (1990). The neuropsychology of emotion: Developmental patterns and implications for psychopathology. In N. L. Stein, B. Leventhal, & T. Trabasso (Eds.), *Psychological and biological approaches to emotion.* (pp. 167-211). Hillsdale, NJ: Erlbaum.

Hogan, R. (1996). A socioanalytic perspective on the five-factor model. In J. S. Wiggins (Ed.), *The five-factor model of personality: Theoretical perspectives* (pp. 163-179). New York: Guilford Press.

Humphreys, A. P., & Smith, P. K. (1987). Rough and tumble, friendship, and dominance in school children: Evidence for continuity and change with age. *Child Development, 58*, 201-212.

Insel, T. R., Winslow, J. T., Wang, Z., & Young, L. J. (1998). Oxytocin, vasopressin, and the neuroendocrine basis of pair bond formation. *Advances in Experimental Medicine and Biology, 449*, 215-224.

Isen, A. M., Daubman, K. A., & Nowicki, G. P. (1987). Positive affect facilitates creative problem solving. *Journal of Personality and Social Psychology, 52*, 1122-1131.

John, O., Caspi, A., Robins, R. W., Moffitt, T. E., & Sthouthamer-Loeber, M. (1994). The "little five": Exploring the nomological network of the five-factor model of personality in adolescent boys. *Child Development, 65*, 160-178.

Kagan, J., Reznick, J. S., & Snidman, N. (1987). The physiology and psychology of behavioral inhibition. *Child Development, 58*, 1459-1473.

Kagan, J., & Snidman, N. (1991). Infant predictors of inhibited and uninhibited profiles. *Psychological Science, 2*, 40-44.

Kernberg, O. F. (1986). Hysterical and histrionic personality disorders. In R. Michaels (Ed.), *Psychiatry* (Vol. 1, pp. 1-11). Philadelphia: J. B. Lippincott.

Kiesler, D. J. (1983). The 1982 interpersonal circle: A taxonomy for complementarity in human transactions. *Psychological Review, 90*, 185-214.

King, J. F., & Figueredo, A. J. (1994, April). *Human personality factors in zoo chimpanzees?* Paper presented at the Western Psychological Association Convention, Kona, Hawaii.

Kleiman, D. G. (1977). Monogamy in mammals. *Quarterly Review of Biology, 52*, 39-69.

Kleiman, D. G. (1981). Correlations among life history characteristics of mammalian species exhibiting two extreme forms of monogamy. In R. D. Alexander & D. W. Tinkle (Eds.), *Natural selection and social behavior* (pp. 332-344). New York: Chiron Press.

Klein, Z. (1995). Safety-seeking and risk-taking behavioral patterns in *Homo sapiens. Ethology and Sociobiology.*

Kochanska, G., & Aksan, N. (1995). Mother-child mutually positive affect, the quality of child compliance to requests and prohibitions, and maternal control as correlates of early internalization. *Child Development, 66*, 236-254.

Kohnstamm, G. K., Halverson, C. F., Mervielde, I., & Havill, V. L. (1998). *Parental descriptions of child personality: Developmental antecedents of the Big Five.* Mahwah, NJ: Erlbaum.

LaFreniere, P. J., & Charlesworth, W. R. (1983). Dominance, affiliation and attention in a preschool group: A nine-month longitudinal study. *Ethology and Sociobiology, 4*, 55-67.

Lamb, M. E., Chuang, S. S., Wessels, H., Broberg, A. G., & Hwang, C. P. (2002). Emergence and construct validation of the Big Five factors in early childhood: A longitudinal analysis of their ontogeny in Sweden. *Child Development, 73*, 1517-1524.

Lancaster, J. B., & Lancaster, C. S. (1987). The watershed: Change in parental investment and family formation in the course of human evolution. In J. B. Lancaster, J. Altman, A. S. Rossi, & L. R. Sherrod (Eds.), *Parenting across the life span: Biosocial dimensions* (pp. 187-205). New York: Aldine de Gruyter.

Lang-Takoc, E., & Osterweil, Z. (1992). Separateness and connectedness: Differences between the genders. *Sex Roles, 27,* 277-289.

Larsen, R. J., & Diener, E. (1987). Affect intensity as an individual difference characteristic: A review. *Journal of Research in Personality, 21,* 1-39.

Larsen, R. J., & Diener, E. (1993). Promises and problems with the circumplex model of emotion. In M. S. Clark (Ed.), *Review of personality and social psychology: Vol. 13. Emotion* (pp. 25-59). Newbury Park, CA: Sage.

LeDoux, J. (1996). *The emotional brain: The mysterious underpinnings of emotional life.* New York: Simon & Schuster.

Lovejoy, O. (1981). The origin of man. *Science, 211,* 341-350.

Lucas, R. E., Diener, E., Grob, A., Suh, E. M., & Shao, L. (2000). Cross-cultural evidence for the fundamental features of extraversion. *Journal of Personality and Social Psychology, 79,* 452-468.

Luria, A. R. (1980). *The higher cortical functions in man.* New York: Basic Books.

Lusk, J., MacDonald, K., & Newman, J. R. (1998). Resource appraisals among self, friend and leader: Implications for an evolutionary perspective on individual differences and a resource/reciprocity perspective on friendship. *Personality and Individual Differences, 24,* 685-700.

Lynn, R. (1991). The evolution of racial differences in intelligence. *Mankind Quarterly, 32,* 99-173.

MacDonald, K. B. (1983). Stability of individual differences in behavior in a litter of wolf cubs *(Canis lupus). Journal of Comparative Psychology, 2,* 99-106.

MacDonald, K. B. (1988). *Social and personality development: An evolutionary synthesis.* New York: Plenum.

MacDonald, K. B. (1991). A perspective on Darwinian psychology: Domain-general mechanisms, plasticity, and individual differences. *Ethology and Sociobiology, 12,* 449-480.

MacDonald, K. B. (1992). Warmth as a developmental construct: An evolutionary analysis. *Child Development, 63,* 753-773.

MacDonald, K. B. (1995). Evolution, the five-factor model, and levels of personality. *Journal of Personality 63,* 525-567.

MacDonald, K. B. (1997). The coherence of individual development: An evolutionary perspective on children's internalization of cultural values. In J. Grusec & L. Kuczynski (Eds.), *Parenting strategies and children's internalization of values: A handbook of theoretical and research perspectives* (pp. 321-355). New York: John Wiley.

MacDonald, K. B. (1999a). Love and security of attachment as two independent systems underlying intimate relationships. *Journal of Family Psychology, 13*(4), 492-495.

MacDonald, K. B. (1999b). What about sex differences? An adaptationist perspective on "the lines of causal influence" of personality systems. Commentary on "Neurobiology of the Structure of Personality: Dopamine Facilitation of Incentive Motivation and Extraversion," by R. A. Depue & P. F. Collins. *Behavioral and Brain Sciences, 22*(3), 530-531.

MacDonald, K. B., & Parke, R. D. (1986). Parent-child physical play: The effects of sex and age of children and parents. *Sex Roles, 15,* 367-378.

Marks, I. (1987). *Fears, phobias, and rituals: Panic, anxiety, and their disorders.* Oxford, UK: Oxford University Press.

McCrae, R. R., & Costa, P. T. (1990). *Personality in adulthood.* New York: Guilford Press.

McCrae, R. R., Costa, P. T., Terracciano, A., Parker, W. D., Mills, C. J., De Fruyt, F., et al. (2002). Personality trait development from age 12 to age 18: Longitudinal, cross-sectional, and cross-cultural analysis. *Journal of Personality and Social Psychology, 83,* 1456-1468.

Mealey, L. (1995). The sociobiology of sociopathy: An integrated evolutionary model. *Behavioral and Brain Sciences 18,* 523-599.

Mesulam, M. M. (1986). Frontal cortex and behavior. *Annals of Neurology, 19,* 320-325.

Miller, E. M. (1994a). Optimal adjustment of mating effort to environmental conditions: A critique of Chisholm's application of life history theory, with comments on race differences in male paternal investment strategies. *Mankind Quarterly, 34,* 297-316.

Miller, E. M. (1994b). Paternal provisioning versus mate seeking in human populations. *Personality and Individual Differences, 17,* 227-255.

Moffitt, T. E., Caspi, A., Belsky, J., & Silva, P. A. (1992). Childhood experience and the onset of menarche: A test of a sociobiological model. *Child Development, 63,* 47-58.

Nesse, R. M., & Williams, G. C. (1996). *Why we get sick: The new science of Darwinian medicine.* New York: Vintage Books.

Newman, J. P. (1987). Reaction to punishment in extraverts and psychopaths: Implications for the impulsive behavior of disinhibited individuals. *Journal of Personality Research, 21,* 464-480.

Nigg, J. T., Blaskey, L. G., Huang-Pollock, C. L., Hinshaw, S. P., John, O. P., Willcutt, E. G., et al. (2002). Big Five dimensions and ADHD symptoms: Links between personality traits and clinical symptoms. *Journal of Personality and Social Psychology, 83,* 451-469.

O'Brien, M., & Huston, A. C. (1985). Development of sex-typed play in toddlers. *Developmental Psychology, 21,* 866-871.

O'Connor, T. G., & Croft, C. M. (2001). A twin study of attachment in preschool children. *Child Development, 72,* 1501-1511.

Öhman, A. (1993). Fear and anxiety as emotional phenomena: Clinical phenomenology, evolutionary perspectives, and information-processing mechanisms. In M. Lewis & J. M. Haviland (Eds.), *Handbook of emotions* (pp. 511-536). New York: Guilford Press.

Orlick, T., Zhou, Q., & Partington, J. (1990). Co-operation and conflict within Chinese and Canadian kindergarten settings. *Canadian Journal of Behavioural Sciences, 22*, 20-25.

Ostendorf, F. (1990). Sprache und persoenlichkeitsstrucktur: Zur validataet des funf-faktoren-modells der persoenlichkeit [Language and personality structure: On the validity of the five-factor model of personality]. Regensburg, Germany: S. Roderer Verlag.

Panksepp, J. (1982). Toward a general psychobiological theory of emotions. *Behavioral and Brain Sciences, 5*, 407-422.

Panksepp, J. (1998). *Affective neuroscience: The foundations of human and animal emotions.* New York: Oxford University Press.

Paulhus, D. L., Trapnell, P. D., & Chen, D. (1999). Birth order effects on personality and achievement within families. *Psychological Science, 10*, 482-488.

Pfiefer, M., Goldsmith, H. H., Davidson, R. J., & Rickman, M. (2002). Continuity and change in inhibited and uninhibited children. *Child Development, 73*, 1474-1485.

Pickering, A. D., Diaz, A., & Gray, J. A. (1995). Personality and reinforcement: An exploration using a maze learning task. *Personality and Individual Differences, 18*, 541-558.

Plomin, R. (1994). *Genetics and experience: The interplay between nature and nurture.* Thousand Oaks, CA: Sage.

Porges, S. (1991). Vagal tone: A mediator of affect. In J. A. Garber & K. A. Dodge (Eds.), *The development of emotion regulation and dysregulation* (pp. 111-128). New York: Cambridge University Press.

Ramsey, D., & Lewis, M. (2003). Reactivity and regulation in cortisol and behavioral responses to stress. *Child Development, 74*(2), 456-464.

Richards, R., Kinney, D. K., Lunde, I., Henet, M., & Merzel, A. P. C. (1988). Creativity in manic-depressives, cyclothemes, their normal relatives, and control subjects. *Journal of Abnormal Psychology, 97*, 281-288.

Rohde, P., A., Atzwanger, K., Butovskaya, M., Lampert, A., Mysterud, I., Sanchez-Andres, A., et al. (2003). Perceived parental favoritism, closeness to kin, and the rebel of the family: The effects of birth order and sex. *Evolution and Human Behavior, 24*, 261-276.

Rothbart, M. K. (1989a). Biological processes in temperament. In G. A. Kohnstamm, J. Bates, & M. K. Rothbart (Eds.), *Temperament in childhood* (pp. 77-110). Chichester, UK: Wiley.

Rothbart, M. K. (1989b). Temperament in childhood: A framework. In G. A. Kohnstamm, J. Bates, & M. K. Rothbart (Eds.), *Temperament in childhood* (pp. 59-73). Chichester, UK: Wiley.

Rothbart, M. K., Ahadi, S. A., & Evans, D. (2000). Temperament and personality: Origins and outcomes. *Journal of Personality and Social Psychology, 78*, 122-135.

Rothbart, M. K., Ahadi, S. A., Hershey, K. L., & Fisher, P. (2001). Investigations of temperament at three to seven years: The Children's Behavior Questionnaire. *Child Development, 72*, 1394-1408.

Rothbart, M. K., & Bates, J. E. (1998). Temperament. In N. Eisenberg (Ed.), *Handbook of child psychology* (Vol. 3, pp. 105-176). New York: John Wiley.

Rowe, D. C. (1994). *The limits of family influence: Genes, experience, and behavior.* New York: Guilford Press.

Rowe, D. C. (2000). Environmental and genetic influences on pubertal development: Evolutionary life history traits? In J. L. Rodgers, D. C. Rowe, & W. B. Miller (Eds.), *Genetic influences on human fertility and sexuality.* Boston: Kluwer.

Rushton, J. P. (1995). *Race, evolution, and behavior.* New Brunswick, NJ: Transaction.

Savin-Williams, R. (1987). *Adolescence: An ethological perspective.* New York: Springer-Verlag.

Southwood, T. R. E. (1981). Bionomic strategies and population parameters. In R. M. May (Ed.), *Theoretical ecology: Principles and applications* (pp. 30-52). Sunderland, MA: Sinauer Associates.

Srivastava, S., John, O. P., Gosling, S. D., & Potter, J. (2003). Development of personality in early and middle adulthood: Set like plaster or persistent change? *Journal of Personality and Social Psychology, 84,* 1041-1053.

Sulloway, F. J. (1996). *Born to rebel: Birth order, family dynamics, and creative lives.* New York: Pantheon.

Sulloway, F. J. (1999). Birth order. In M. A. Runco & S. R. Pritzker (Eds.), *Encyclopedia of creativity* (Vol. 1, pp. 189-202). San Diego, CA: Academic Press.

Swanson, J., Oosterlaan, J., Murias, M., Schuck, S., Flodman, P., Spence, M. A., et al. (2000). Attention deficit/hyperactivity disorder children with a 7-repeat allele of the dopamine receptor D4 gene have extreme behavior but normal performance on critical neuropsychological tests of attention. *Proceedings of the National Academy of Science, 97*(9), 4754-4759.

Tellegen, A., Lykken, D. T., Bouchard, T. J., Wilcox, K. J., Segal, N., & Rich, S. (1988). Personality similarity in twins reared apart and together. *Journal of Personality and Social Psychology, 54,* 1031-1039.

Tooby, J., & Cosmides, L. (1990). On the universality of human nature and the uniqueness of the individual: The role of genetics and adaptation. *Journal of Personality, 58,* 17-67.

Trapnell, P. D., & Wiggins, J. S. (1990). Extension of the Interpersonal Adjective Scales to include the Big Five dimensions of personality. *Journal of Personality and Social Psychology, 59,* 781-790.

Trivers, R. (1972). Parental investment and sexual selection. In R. Campbell (Ed.), *Sexual selection and the descent of man* (pp. 136-179). Chicago: Aldine-Atherton.

Trivers, R. (1974). Parent-offspring conflict. *American Zoologist, 14,* 249-264.

Trull, T. J., & Geary, D. C. (1997). Comparison of the Big Five factor structure across samples of Chinese and American adults. *Journal of Personality Assessment 69,* 324-341.

Tucker, D. M., & Derryberry, D. (1992). Motivated attention: Anxiety and the frontal executive functions. *Neuropsychiatry, Neuropsychology, and Behavioral Neurology, 5*, 233-252.

Tucker, D. M., & Williamson, P. A. (1984). Asymmetric neural control systems in human self-regulation. *Psychological Review, 91*, 185-215.

Turner, B. (1981). Sex-related differences in aging. In B. B. Wolman & G. Stricker (Eds.), *Handbook of developmental psychology*. Englewood Cliffs, NJ: Prentice Hall.

Turner, R. A., Altemus, M., Enos, T., Cooper, B., & McGuinness, T. (1999). Preliminary research on plasma oxytocin in normal cycling women: investigating emotion and interpersonal distress. *Psychiatry, 62*, 97-113.

Vernon, P. E. (1982). *The abilities and achievements of Orientals in America*. New York: Academic.

Watson, D., & Clark, L. A. (1992). On traits and temperament: General and specific factors of emotional experience and their relation to the five-factor model. *Journal of Personality, 60*, 441-476.

Weissman, M. M. (1985). The epidemiology of anxiety disorders: Rates, risks, and familial patterns. In A. H. Tuma & J. Maser (Eds.), *Anxiety and the anxiety disorders*. Hillsdale, NJ: Erlbaum.

West-Eberhard, M. J. (2003). *Developmental plasticity and evolution*. New York: Oxford University Press.

Widiger, T. A., & Trull, T. J. (1992). Personality and psychopathology: An application of the five-factor model. *Journal of Personality, 60*, 363-393.

Widiger, T. A., Trull, T. J., Clarkin, J. F., Sanderson, C., & Costa, P. T. (2002). In P. T. Costa & T. A. Widiger (Eds.), *Personality disorders and the five-factor model of personality* (pp. 89-99). Washington, DC: American Psychological Association.

Wiggins, J. S. (1991). Agency and communion as conceptual coordinates for the understanding and measurement of interpersonal behavior. In W. M. Grove & D. Cicchetti (Eds.), *Thinking clearly about psychology: Vol. 2. Personality and psychopathology*. Minneapolis: University of Minnesota Press.

Wiggins, J. S., & Broughton, R. (1985). The interpersonal circle: A structural model for the integration of personality research. *Perspectives in Personality, 1*, 1-47.

Wiggins, J. S., & Pincus, A. (1989). Conceptions of personality disorders and dimensions of personality. *Psychological Assessment: A Journal of Consulting and Clinical Psychology, 1*, 305-316.

Wiggins, J. S., & Trapnell, P. D. (1996). A dyadic-interactional perspective on the five-factor model. In J. S. Wiggins (Ed.), *The five-factor model of personality: Theoretical perspectives* (pp. 88-162). New York: Guilford Press.

Wiggins, J. S., Trapnell, P., & Phillips, N. (1988). Psychometric and geometric characteristics of the Revised Interpersonal Adjective Scales (IAS-R). *Multivariate Behavioral Research, 23*, 517-530.

Wilson, D. S. (1994). Adaptive genetic variation and human evolutionary psychology. *Ethology and Sociobiology, 15*, 219-235.

Wilson, E. O. (1975). *Sociobiology: The new synthesis.* Cambridge, MA: Harvard University Press.

Wilson, M. A., & Daly, M. (1985). Competitiveness, risk taking, and violence: The young male syndrome. *Ethology and Sociobiology, 6,* 59-73.

Wright, P. H., & Scanlon, M. B. (1991). Gender role orientation and friendship: Some attenuation, but gender differences abound. *Sex Roles, 24,* 551-566.

Zuckerman, M. (1979). *Sensation seeking: Beyond the optimal level of arousal.* Hillsdale, NJ: Erlbaum.

Zuckerman, M. (1991). *Psychobiology of personality.* Cambridge, UK: Cambridge University Press.

9

An Evolutionary Reconceptualization of Kohlberg's Model of Moral Development

Dennis Krebs

At the end of a program of research my colleagues and I conducted on Kohlberg's (1984) model of moral development, I concluded that it is poorly equipped to account for the kinds of moral judgments and moral behaviors people emit in their everyday lives. My search for a more ecologically valid model of morality led me to what many people would consider an unlikely source, the modern synthetic theory of evolution. In this chapter, I will briefly describe Kohlberg's model of moral development, identify its deficiencies, reconceptualize Kohlbergian structures of moral judgment as evolved decision-making mechanisms, and explain why I believe this reconceptualization gives rise to a more valid model of moral development.

Kohlberg's Model of Moral Development

The two central assumptions of Kohlberg's (1984) model of moral development are that the primary source of morality is moral reasoning and that people become more moral because they acquire increasingly sophisticated structures of moral reasoning. To assess moral reasoning, Kohlberg and his colleagues developed a test containing nine hypothetical moral dilemmas, followed by sets of questions (Colby & Kohlberg, 1987). In the most often cited dilemma, a character named Heinz must decide whether or not to steal an overpriced drug to save his dying wife. Kohlbergians assume that the deontic decisions people make—whether Heinz should or should not steal the drug—stem from structures of moral reasoning. To map these structures, Kohlbergians ask moral decision makers "why" questions designed to induce them to explicate the principles from which they deduced their moral choices.

The main source of support for Kohlberg's model stems from a longitudinal study conducted by Kohlberg and his colleagues. In 1958, Kohlberg gave a cohort of boys an early version of his test, and with the help of colleagues, he retested them every 3 or 4 years for more than two decades (Colby & Kohlberg, 1987). This study produced three main conclusions. First, moral judgments made by individuals are structurally consistent across varying content. That is to say, individuals invoke the same forms of moral reasoning to resolve different kinds of moral dilemmas; moral judgment is organized in "structures of the whole." Second, as children grow older, their structures of moral reasoning normally undergo qualitative changes. According to Colby and Kohlberg (1987), new structures "transform and displace" older structures, giving rise to the six stages of moral development summarized in Table 9.1. Kohlberg and his colleagues found that the participants in his longitudinal study went through these stages in an invariant sequence. Third, because the structures of moral reasoning that define higher stages of moral development are more cognitively sophisticated than those that define lower stages—that is to say, more differentiated, integrated, and logical—and based in more sophisticated perspective-taking abilities, they give rise to more moral decisions (that is to say, moral decisions that are more prescriptive, universal, impartial, and objective).

In 1984, Kohlberg and Candee published a model linking moral reasoning to moral conduct. Kohlberg and Candee (1984) argued that moral judgment is necessary but not sufficient for moral behavior. To behave morally, people must decide what the most moral course of action is, but this does not necessarily compel them to behave morally. To implement moral decisions, people must experience an obligation to carry them out, which entails making follow-up judgments of responsibility. In addition, people must possess sufficient ego strength to do what they think they should.

An Evaluation of Kohlberg's Model of Moral Development

Several years ago, my colleagues and I noted that most of the empirical support for Kohlberg's model stemmed from studies conducted in academic

Table 9.1   Kohlberg's Stages of Moral Development

Stage 1

Morality is defined in terms of avoiding breaking rules that are backed by punishment, obedience for its own sake, and avoiding damage to people and property.

Stage 2

Morality is defined in terms of instrumental exchange, acting to meet one's own interests and needs, and letting others do the same, making deals, engaging in equal exchanges.

Stage 3

Morality is defined in terms of upholding mutual relationships, fulfilling role expectations, being viewed as a good person, showing concern for others, caring for others. Trust, loyalty, respect, and gratitude are important moral values.

Stage 4

Morality is defined in terms of maintaining the social systems from which one benefits.

Stage 5

Morality is defined in terms of fulfilling the social obligations implicit in social contracts that are freely agreed upon, and a rational calculation of the greatest good for the greatest number.

Stage 6

Morality is defined in terms of following self-chosen universal ethical principles of justice, upholding the equality of human rights and respect for the dignity of human beings as individual persons.

contexts in which trained interviewers or experimenters asked university students to make and to justify decisions about how the characters in Kohlberg's dilemmas should resolve hypothetical moral conflicts. We set out to vary parameters of this prototypic situation and determine whether they affected the forms of moral judgment people invoked. To this end, we asked people who differed in a variety of ways to make moral judgments in a variety of nonacademic contexts, to audiences other than experimenters, about moral dilemmas other than those on Kohlberg's test and about people other than the characters in Kohlbergian dilemmas.

The findings from this program of research were reviewed in several publications (see Krebs, Denton, & Wark, 1997; Krebs, Vermeulen, Carpendale, & Denton, 1991; Krebs, Wark, & Krebs, 1995; Wark & Krebs, 1997). To summarize, we found, as Kohlberg would expect, that people tend to make structurally similar—that is to say, same-stage—moral judgments to hypothetical moral dilemmas similar to those on Kohlberg's test. However, we also found that people tend to make lower-stage moral judgments about more real-life-like dilemmas. For example, compared with moral judgments on Kohlberg's test, participants in our studies made relatively low-stage moral judgments to moral dilemmas about prosocial behavior and drinking and driving (Krebs, Denton, Vermeulen, Carpendale, & Bush, 1991), business deals and free trade (Carpendale & Krebs, 1995), prostitution (Bartek, Krebs, & Taylor, 1993), and a variety of real-life dilemmas (Krebs, Denton, Wark, Couch, & Racine, 2002; Wark & Krebs, 1997). Young adults made lower-stage moral judgments about Kohlbergian dilemmas and a dilemma about drinking and driving when they were drinking at bars and parties than they did in academic contexts (Denton & Krebs, 1990). University students made lower-stage moral judgments to a professor of business administration than to a professor of philosophy (Carpendale & Krebs, 1992). Parents and children made relatively low-stage moral judgments about moral dilemmas they experienced in their families (Krebs, Vermeulen, & Denton, 1991). Incarcerated female juvenile delinquents, especially those who scored high on a test of defensiveness, made relatively low-stage moral judgments about moral dilemmas involving prostitution (Bartek et al., 1993). People tended to make different kinds of moral judgments about themselves than they did about others (Krebs et al., 2002; Krebs & Laird, 1998).

Considered as a whole, the findings from our research program did not support Kohlberg's model of moral development. Our data were not consistent with the assumption that moral judgments stem from structures of the whole that have transformed and displaced their predecessors. Instead, our data suggested that people retain old structures of moral judgment after they develop new ones. Moral development is characterized more by an expansion of the range of possibilities than by changes in the overriding structure of the mind. The types of moral judgments people make are not determined solely by the structures of moral reasoning they have acquired; moral judgments are the product of complex interactions between internal qualities of people and the external situational variables they encounter.

Findings from our studies also suggested that the relation between moral judgment and moral behavior is more complex than Kohlberg and Candee (1984) assumed. As postulated by Kohlberg and Candee, in some contexts, people appear to decide what is right, then act on their decisions. However, in other contexts, people appear to act without engaging in moral reasoning, then invoke moral judgments to justify their decisions (Denton & Krebs, 1990; Krebs et al., 2002; Krebs & Laird, 1998).

In the end, I concluded that Kohlberg's model pertains to only one of many functions of moral judgment, namely, to make the most rational moral decision of which one is capable. The methods employed by Kohlbergians are designed to induce people to perform this function. Making moral judgments about Kohlbergian dilemmas in academic contexts is akin to solving problems in logic. As acknowledged by Colby and Kohlberg (1987), Kohlberg's model is a model of "moral competence."

To adequately account for moral development, we must attend to other functions of moral judgment and moral behavior. In real life, people use moral judgments for more social and pragmatic purposes than they do when they make moral judgments on Kohlberg's test. When people tell other people they "should" behave in particular ways, they are rarely trying to explicate their ideal conceptions of morality; rather, they are usually trying to induce the recipients of such judgments to behave in accordance with the moral prescriptions they are pronouncing. They are trying to exert social influence. Recipients of such moral judgments often respond by arguing with those who pronounce them, attempting to persuade them that the prescriptions are unjustified. Negotiations ensue in which parties adduce arguments to support their points of view (Krebs et al., 2002). In real life, people also use moral judgments to approve and disapprove of the behavior of others, to praise, condemn, and blame. In addition, people use moral judgments to guide, justify, and excuse their own behavior; to approve and disapprove of themselves; to enhance their social images; and to foster self-esteem (Denton & Krebs, 1990; Krebs et al., 2002; Krebs & Laird, 1998).

A Functional Reconceptualization of Kohlberg's Elements of Morality

As I have explained, when people make decisions about what the characters in Kohlbergian dilemmas should do, interviewers ask them why, and after interviewees proffer a reason, interviewers ask them why again until interviewees reach the limit of their explanations. For example, an interviewee might say, "Heinz should steal the drug to save his wife's life," and the interviewer might ask, "Why should Heinz save his wife's life?" In response to this probe, the interviewee might answer, "Because he owes it to her." The interviewer might then ask, "Why is it right for Heinz to fulfill his obligations to his wife?" and the person might say, "Because she has done a lot for him" or "Because he made a marriage contract" and so on. Colby and Kohlberg (1987) have classified the reasons people adduce in support of their decisions and labeled them the "elements" of morality (see Table 9.2).

From Kohlberg's perspective, "why" questions induce people to explicate the principles from which they derived their moral decisions. From a more functional perspective, such questions induce people to identify the goals

Table 9.2   Kohlberg's Elements of Morality

Modal Elements

1. Obeying persons or deity

2. Blaming and approving

3. Retribution and exoneration

4. Having a right

5. Having a duty

Value Elements

Egoistic Consequences

6. Maintaining reputation

7. Seeking reward and avoiding punishment

8. Promoting good individual consequences

9. Promoting good group consequences

Ideal or Harmony-Serving Consequences

10. Upholding character

11. Upholding self-respect

12. Serving social ideals or harmony

13. Serving human dignity and autonomy

Fairness

14. Role taking, balancing perspectives

15. Reciprocity or positive desert

16. Maintaining equity

17. Maintaining social contract or freely agreeing

they are advising moral decision makers to pursue, goals such as doing their duty, paying their debts, reciprocating, obtaining approval, avoiding punishment, enhancing their reputations, supporting their groups and so on (see Table 9.2). From a Kohlbergian perspective, the purpose of repeatedly asking "why" questions is to induce people to invoke increasingly abstract principles of morality. From a functional perspective, the purpose of repeatedly asking "why" questions is to get at increasingly ultimate goals and purposes. If you keep asking people functional "why" questions, you will ultimately end up in one of two places, with God or in the theory of evolution. I ended up in the latter.

An Earlier Examination of Relations Between Kohlbergian and Evolutionary Approaches to Moral Development

I was not the first psychologist to adopt a biological approach to morality and view Kohlberg's model from an evolutionary perspective. Kevin MacDonald was. MacDonald (1988) reviewed evidence on moral judgment and moral behavior and concluded that much of it was more consistent with a sociobiological viewpoint than with Kohlberg's cognitive-developmental model. In particular, MacDonald adduced evidence supporting the following eight conclusions. First, children's moral behavior is more self-interested than it appears from the conclusions reached by researchers. Second, people invoke different forms of moral reasoning in different contexts. Third, people perform cost-benefit analyses when they make real-life moral decisions. Fourth, "reasoning about oneself, one's relatives, and significant others is done with a different calculus than is reasoning about hypothetical situations" (p. 148). Fifth, people sometimes fail to behave in accordance with their moral judgments, especially when they conflict with their self-interests. The link between moral reasoning and moral behavior is weak except when the decisions in question involve little cost. Sixth, people use moral judgments to create false impressions and to justify their behavior: "Individuals who are adept at moral reasoning (i.e., perform at the higher stages) are better able to provide reasons which rationalize their self-interested actions in a manner that would justify their behavior to other individuals" (p. 143). Seven, only the first three stages in Kohlberg's sequence are cross-culturally universal. And finally, emotional reactions play an important role in real-life moral decision making.

In the remainder of this paper, I build upon these ideas. I review the basic propositions of evolutionary theory, reconceptualize the structures of moral judgment described by Kohlbergians as evolved mental mechanisms, offer an account of the evolution of moral judgment and moral behavior, and explain why I believe that this account gives rise to a more ecologically valid model of moral development than the one advanced by Kohlberg and his colleagues.

Toward an Evolutionary Model of Morality

Evolutionary theorists assume that the ultimate goal of most (but not all) behavior is to enhance actors' inclusive fitness, defined in terms of the number of replicas of their genes they contribute to future generations. More precisely, evolutionary theorists assume that individuals inherit genes that were selected in ancestral environments because they guided the development of mechanisms that enabled their ancestors to survive, to reproduce, and to pass the genes and mechanisms on to future generations. The function of evolved mechanisms is to help individuals solve adaptive problems pertaining to survival, reproduction, care of offspring, and so on.

There are two basic ways in which genes, or mechanisms, can be selected and increase in frequency, or evolve, over generations. In the first, the vehicles housing the genes or mechanisms—that is to say, individuals—survive until sexual maturity, pass replicas of their genes or mechanisms on to others through asexual or sexual reproduction, then take whatever measures are necessary to ensure that the offspring in whom they have deposited replicas of their genes survive and reproduce. In the second, individuals behave in ways that foster the survival and reproduction of individuals other than their offspring, who possess replicas of their genes—that is to say, individuals who are similar to them genetically. This process is usually referred to as "kin selection." The main difference between the two forms of natural selection is that in the first, individuals create the vehicles that transport replicas of 50% of their genes to future generations, whereas in the second, individuals assist individuals created by others, who may possess varying proportions of their genes.

Evolved Psychological Mechanisms

Evolutionary theorists may attend to different products of evolution. For example, some theorists attend to the frequency of genes in a population, whereas others attend to the number of offspring produced by individuals. Evolutionary psychologists attend to the mental mechanisms that individuals inherit and the behavioral strategies such mechanisms contain. Buss (1999, pp. 48-49) has identified six properties of evolved psychological mechanisms: First, they are shaped by the ways in which they recurrently solved specific adaptive problems over the evolutionary history of the species in which they evolved. Second, they are activated by relatively "narrow slices of information." Third, the information that triggers such mechanisms, the input, pertains to the particular adaptive problems the mechanisms were designed to solve. Fourth, the information processed by such mechanisms is transformed into output by a set of "if-then" decision rules. Fifth, "the output of an evolved psychological mechanism can be physiological activity, information to other psychological mechanisms, or manifest behavior." Finally, "the output . . . is directed toward the solution to a specific adaptive problem." Although it is safe to assume that the strategies implicit in such mechanisms were on average winning strategies in ancestral environments, they need not necessarily produce optimal solutions to the problems that activate them in modern environments.

Kohlberg's Structures of Moral Judgment Reconceptualized as Evolved Psychological Mechanisms

In contrast to learning theorists who posit general-purpose mechanisms, both Kohlbergians and evolutionary psychologists believe the mind is composed of specialized structures or mechanisms designed for particular purposes. Kohlbergians and evolutionary theorists assume that the mental structures that give rise to moral judgments and moral behaviors are activated by particular kinds of problems and that their function is to process information in ways that give rise to particular kinds of decisions. Both types of theorist assume that the form or pattern of the output produced by mental structures reflects the ways in which they are designed and that the primary goal of social scientists is to map the design of the mechanisms by deciphering the operating principles or decision-rules implicit in their output. Kohlbergian and evolutionary psychologists also are attentive to the origin and development of mental structures and mechanisms.

Such similarities notwithstanding, Kohlbergians make different assumptions than do evolutionary theorists about how mental structures originate and the functions for which they were designed. Adopting an ontogenetic perspective, Kohlbergians assume that structures of moral judgment develop through the cognitive processes of assimilation and accommodation and that their function is to enable people to deduce the most moral solution to moral problems. Adopting a phylogenetic perspective, evolutionary theorists assume that evolved mechanisms originate from genetic variations selected in ancestral environments and that their function is to help individuals solve real-life adaptive problems. Kohlbergians focus mainly on the cognitive functions of making moral judgments; evolutionary theorists focus mainly on the adaptive functions of moral behaviors. The central thesis of this paper is that the conception of mental mechanisms derived from evolutionary theory offers a better basis than Kohlberg's conception of structures of moral judgment for explaining the ways in which people make moral decisions and for accounting for moral development. Stated in stronger terms, I believe that most of the moral judgments people make in their everyday lives and most of the moral behaviors they emit are products of the kinds of evolved psychological mechanisms described by evolutionary psychologists, as opposed to the structures of moral reasoning described by Kohlbergians.

The Evolution of Moral Mechanisms

If we assume that people derive moral judgments from evolved mental mechanisms, the first question that arises is, what adaptive functions did such mechanisms serve in ancestral environments; what kinds of adaptive problems did such mechanisms help our hominid ancestors solve? I believe the answer to this question is that the mechanisms that give rise to morality evolved to solve the social problems that occurred when our ancestors banded together to foster their biological interests. Among the many species in the animal kingdom, *Homo sapiens* is among the most social. From the perspective of evolution, mechanisms that dispose animals to aggregate and interact with other members of their species, and for that matter with members of other species, evolve when the mechanisms help animals foster their biological interests. Such mechanisms may help animals enhance their inclusive fitness in several ways. As examples, individuals who band together may be less susceptible to predators than more solitary individuals, and groups may be able to hunt larger game than individuals could kill on their own.

Many of the benefits of sociality stem from cooperative exchanges. Individuals working together can often obtain more for themselves than they could by working alone. Individuals can trade items of relatively little value for items of greater value. Individuals can render valuable assistance to others at little cost to themselves in return for low-cost assistance when they are in need. In such exchanges, both (or all) parties can come out ahead through what economists call "gains in trade."

According to most experts on human evolution, cooperation was instrumental in the evolution of the human species. To quote Leakey and Lewin (1977),

> Throughout our recent evolutionary history, particularly since the rise of a hunting way of life, there must have been extreme selective pressure in favor of our ability to cooperate as a group. . . . The degree of selective pressure toward cooperation . . . was so strong, and the period over which it operated so extended, that it can hardly have failed to have become embedded to some degree in our genetic makeup. (p. 45)

In view of the benefits of cooperation, it might seem that mechanisms disposing individuals to cooperate should evolve without impediment, but unfortunately, this is not the case. In his book *Theory of Justice*, the philosopher John Rawls (1971) explains why:

> Although a society is a cooperative venture for mutual advantage, it is typically marked by a conflict as well as by an identity of interests. There is an identity of interests since social cooperation makes possible a better life for all than any would have if each were to live solely by his own efforts. There is a conflict of interests since persons are not indifferent as to how the greater benefits of their collaboration are distributed, for in order to pursue their ends, each prefers a larger to a lesser share. (p. 4)

Selfish preferences pose a serious problem for the evolution of cooperative mechanisms, because it is in everyone's biological interest to give less than his or her share and to induce others to give more than their share. Inasmuch as the resources in question foster the inclusive fitness of those who possess them, individuals who inherit mechanisms that dispose them to behave selfishly could fare better than those who inherit mechanisms that dispose them to behave cooperatively, mediating the evolution of selfishness and the extinction of cooperation. However, fortunately for the evolution of morality, it is not in individuals' interests to let others treat them selfishly, so we would expect mechanisms to evolve that were designed to counteract selfishness in others.

Most people consider selfish behaviors, defined as fostering one's own interests at the expense of others, immoral; and most people consider cooperative behaviors, defined as fostering one's interests in ways that foster the interests of others, moral. I believe that the biological function of morality is to uphold fitness-enhancing systems of cooperation. Viewing morality in these terms helps us understand its nature. Morality boils down to giving one's share (doing one's duties) and taking one's share (exercising one's rights), cooperating with others by treating them fairly, as one would like to be treated, and resisting the temptation to maximize one's gains at the expense of others. This conception of morality has been espoused in nonbiological terms by many scholars. As one example, Rest (1983) asserted that morality consists in "standards or guidelines that govern human cooperation—in particular how rights, duties, and benefits are [to be] allocated . . . Moralities are proposals for a system of mutual coordination of activities and cooperation among people" (p. 558).

The Social Functions of Morality

In contrast to the purpose of making moral judgments about the hypothetical characters in Kohlbergian dilemmas, people make moral judgments in their everyday lives for two primary purposes: (1) to influence the behavior of others and (2) to guide their own behavior. Let us consider each in turn.

Moral Judgments as Forms of Social Influence

Viewed biologically, moral judgments are a form of communication. Biological analyses of communication assume that animals are evolved to send signals that induce recipients to behave in ways that foster the senders' interests or that manipulate them. Such signals are often deceptive (Dawkins, 1989; Mitchell & Thompson, 1986). Humans' relatively large brains and their capacity for language enable them to employ a significantly larger range of manipulative communication strategies than those available to other species. Senders are able to take the perspective of recipients (referred to as "mind reading" by some psychologists) and plan long into the future. Recipients' reactions to senders' signals are less a function of the physical properties of the signals themselves and more a function of how recipients represent them mentally.

From a biological perspective, when people send second-person moral judgments to others such as "You should help me," "You should keep your promises," and "You are not being fair to me," they are tying to induce recipients to foster their interests by persuading them to behave in accordance with the prescriptions. When people express more abstract judgments such as "Honesty is the best policy" and "People should obey the law," they are attempting to induce recipients to uphold the systems of cooperation from which they benefit. When senders support such judgments with reasons such as "Because you will cultivate a good reputation" and "Everyone will benefit in the end," they are attempting to induce recipients to form cognitive representations of the "if" conditions that activate the behaviors they are prescribing. Such judgments are tools of social influence, tactics of persuasion designed to induce recipients to behave in ways that directly or indirectly benefit those making the judgments.

The Natural Selection of Moral Judgments

Of all the moral judgments people could make, why do they make those observed and classified by Kohlberg and his colleagues? Why do only a few of the many possible moral judgments become normative in all cultures?

Kohlbergian and evolutionary psychologists would agree that people select the moral judgments that are best equipped to solve the moral problems they face, that such problems are social in nature, and that they involve conflicts of interest. However, Kohlbergians would focus on ideal solutions to hypothetical versions of such problems, whereas evolutionary theorists would focus on actual solutions to real problems in which the individuals involved are attempting to foster their biological interests.

Although it might seem that individuals motivated to foster their biological interests would make moral judgments such as "You should sacrifice your interests for my sake," such judgments would not be effective because recipients would not be receptive to them. In effect, recipients of moral judgments are agents of selection, determining what kinds of judgments work. Although those who make moral judgments may well attempt to use them to manipulate and exploit recipients, successful manipulations would have to be subtle, leading recipients to believe that abiding by them would foster their interests. In general, the most effective moral judgments should prescribe behaviors that foster the interests of senders and recipients. Thus, I would expect moral judgments to assume the form "You should foster my interests in ways that foster your interests," which is exactly what most of the moral judgments classified by Kohlbergians do. To summarize, senders do not exhort recipients to behave selfishly, because it is not in senders' interest, and senders do not exhort recipients to behave altruistically, because recipients are unreceptive to such exhortations. Senders exhort recipients to adopt the kinds of cooperative strategies prescribed by Kohlbergian moral judgments, because the mental mechanisms possessed by recipients are designed in ways that make them receptive to such judgments.

The Activation of Stage-Based Moral Judgments

As discussed, we found that in certain contexts, adults invoke moral judgments at all of the stages described by Kohlberg. From an evolutionary perspective, we would expect people to make the kinds of moral judgments that contain the greatest potential to foster their biological interests, which will depend on the "if" conditions implicit in the problems they encounter. So, for example, relatively powerful members of groups should make Stage 1 judgments that exhort weaker members to obey authority in order to avoid punishment. Those who are relatively equal in power should be more inclined to make Stage 2 judgments to each other that uphold mutually beneficial deals. Friends and relatives should make Stage 3 moral judgments that uphold their long-term relationships; and those who have vested interests in maintaining the social order should make Stage 4 judgments. In general, the benefits implicitly promised to those who conform to high-stage moral judgments are more general and delayed than the benefits implicitly promised to those who conform to low-stage moral judgments. Therefore, in general, the "if" conditions invoked to activate higher-stage moral behavior are more tenuous than the "if" conditions invoked to activate lower-stage moral behavior.

Moral Judgments as Forms of Self-Guidance

In Kohlberg's model, which assumes that all the moral judgments people make stem from the same structure of moral judgment, there is no reason to expect any differences between the moral judgments people make to and about themselves and the moral judgments they make to and about others. In contrast, from an evolutionary perspective, we would expect the form of the two types of judgment to differ in significant ways. We would expect the judgments people make about their rights and duties to be more selfish than the judgments they make about the rights and duties of others, for two reasons. First, we would expect people to be motivated to advance their own interests. Second, we would expect the authors of self-serving moral judgments to constitute more receptive audiences than most other recipients. Thus, we would expect people to send messages to themselves such as "You deserve more than your share," "Your contributions are worth more than those of others," and "You should look after your own interests," then graciously receive them with favor.

The magnitude of self-serving biases in moral judgment should, however, vary across a variety of conditions. First, when people express moral judgments about themselves to others, recipients should exert a constraining effect on the selfishness of the judgments in much the same way they exert a constraining effect on the selfishness of second-person moral judgments. We would expect audiences to call people on their selfishness and point out inconsistencies in the standards they are applying to themselves and to others. For this reason, in general, we would expect people to make less selfish moral judgments in public than in private. People also should be selective in the audiences to whom they express their moral judgments, choosing those they anticipate will be most receptive to their points of view (Krebs & Denton, 1997).

Second, the extent to which people apply to themselves the standards they preach to others may depend on the persuasiveness of their communications. When individuals adduce arguments in support of the moral judgments they make to others, they may, in effect, persuade themselves that the arguments are right and buy into them (see Brown, 1986; Taylor, 1989). As suggested by Trivers (2000), believing in the standards one preaches to others may enhance the persuasive power of one's communications. Alternatively, people may compartmentalize moral judgments about themselves and others.

Third, the mechanisms through which people make moral judgments may be designed in ways that contain cognitive representations of others. In effect, internalized images of others may send and receive moral messages. Freud has suggested that introjected images of parents, or more exactly, their superegos, tell people what they ought to do and sit in judgment of them when they fail to live up to their standards. The idea that the psychological mechanism through which people make moral judgments to themselves, often called the "conscience," contains internalized representations of others, especially their parents, has been advanced by scholars from a wide variety of theoretical traditions (e.g., Aronfreed, 1968; Higgins & Eccles-Parson, 1983). However, in the same way that people may direct their moral judgments to audiences who are receptive to their biases, they may invoke internalized audiences who exhort them to advance their own interests and help them justify their self-serving behaviors.

In the end, we must rely on empirical research to map the design of structures that give rise to moral judgments about selves and others. Although a host of studies have reported self-serving biases in social and moral judgments (see Krebs & Denton, 1997; Krebs, Denton, & Higgins, 1988; MacDonald, 1988; Taylor, 1989, for reviews), people differ in the extent to which they harbor such biases, and the biases tend to diminish, disappear, and even reverse themselves when people make judgments about their friends and relatives (Krebs & Laird, 1998).

The Evolution of Moral Behavioral Dispositions

Implicit in the analysis of the evolution of moral judgment I have been advancing is a profoundly important implication, namely, that humans are biologically endowed with the capacity to behave in moral ways. If, as I have argued, people use moral judgments such as those classified by Kohlberg and his colleagues to activate evolved mechanisms that induce recipients to behave in accordance with their prescriptions, recipients must possess such evolved mechanisms. Indeed, I would expect the behavior-producing mechanisms to have evolved before the judgment-producing mechanisms, else the latter would have nothing to activate. But could mechanisms have evolved that dispose individuals to behave morally?

Some very eminent evolutionary theorists think not. Consider for example the following conclusions:

> Nothing resembling the Golden Rule or other widely preached ethical principles seems to be operating in living nature. It could scarcely be otherwise, when evolution is guided by a force that maximizes genetic selfishness. (Williams, 1989, p. 195)

> Be warned that if you wish, as I do, to build a society in which individuals cooperate generously and unselfishly toward a common good, you can expect little help from biological nature. Let us try to teach generosity and altruism, because we are born selfish. (Dawkins, 1989, p. 3)

As much as I admire the work of these theorists, I believe their conclusions about the evolution of morality are incorrect, or at least misleading. When evolutionary biologists talk about selfish behaviors, they mean behaviors that help individuals propagate their genes. Such theorists are, in effect, saying that the mechanisms that give rise to all evolved behaviors (that is to say, behaviors that helped ancestors propagate their genes) are designed in ways that help individuals propagate their genes in modern environments. But this is not necessarily true because, among other reasons, behaviors that were adaptive or genetically selfish in ancestral environments may not be adaptive in current environments. Furthermore, genetically selfish behaviors are not necessarily individually selfish, which is the criterion most people use for morality. As examples, it may be genetically selfish to sacrifice oneself for the sake of one's offspring or other kin, but such behaviors would not be considered individually selfish or immoral. Although cooperative behaviors may foster the genetic interests of cooperators (rendering cooperation genetically selfish), such behaviors may nevertheless qualify as moral.

In my view, there is no necessary inconsistency between behaving morally and fostering one's biological interests. It is not immoral to attempt to survive or to reproduce; indeed, some think people have a moral obligation to preserve their lives and to bear children. The criterion for morality pertains to how we go about fostering our biological interests. In general, we consider it moral to foster our biological interests in ways that foster the interests of others—that is to say, in cooperative ways; and we consider it immoral to foster our interests at the expensive of others—that is to say, in selfish ways. I believe there is little question that mechanisms giving rise to the cooperative strategies prescribed by Kohlbergian Stages 1, 2, and 3 moral judgments have evolved in the human species and in some other species. I also believe that such mechanisms can, under certain conditions, give rise to Stage 4, Stage 5, and Stage 6 moral strategies. I have reviewed evidence supporting this claim in several publications (Krebs, 1998, 2000a, 2000b, 2000c; Krebs & Janicki, 2003). I will briefly summarize here.

The Evolution of Stage 1 Strategies

Stage 1 moral judgments prescribe obeying those who are "older, bigger, or more powerful" than you and the rules they enforce in order to avoid getting "beaten up," "hit," "punished," "put in jail," or "killed." It is easy to see how the strategy implicit in such judgments could pay off better than more selfish attempts to maximize one's gains. Members of groups who are relatively weak face a Hobson's choice: Either defer to those who are more powerful or suffer the consequences. Faced with such choices, it is more adaptive for relatively subordinate members of groups to submit to the authority of the more dominant members in order to make the best of a bad situation and live to fight another day.

There is a spate of evidence that mental mechanisms giving rise to submissive and subordinate behaviors have evolved in many species (see Alcock, 1998; Boehm, 2000; Krebs, 1998, 2000b; Sloman & Gilbert, 2000), including humans (Milgram, 1964; Strayer & Strayer, 1976). In some species, such mechanisms produce dominance hierarchies or pecking orders. Deferential mechanisms are rooted in fear systems, combined perhaps with a touch of awe.

The Evolution of Stage 2 Strategies

Stage 2 moral judgments prescribe helping other people "because you may need them to do something for you one day," keeping promises so the "other person will keep promises to you or give you something in return," and so on. In short, you scratch my back and I'll scratch your back. As pointed out by Trivers (1971) and others, individuals who reciprocate resources may gain more through gains in trade than individuals who do not. In some contexts, individuals are able to bestow huge benefits on others at very little cost to themselves. Trivers (1971) gives the example of someone throwing a drowning person a life preserver.

To evolve, Stage 2 cooperative strategies must contain antidotes to exploitation. One of the strategies prescribed by Stage 2 moral judgments is commonly called "Tit for Tat." Tit for Tat is based in the decision-rule "Make a cooperative overture, then copy the response of your partner in subsequent exchanges." If your partner cooperates, you glean the benefits of the cooperative exchange. If your partner behaves selfishly, you cut your losses (and his or hers!) by behaving selfishly until he or she relents and behaves cooperatively. This aspect of the strategy is prescribed by Stage 2 moral judgments such as "An eye for an eye" and "Don't get mad, get even." Computer simulations of the evolution of social strategies have found that Tit for Tat can defeat more selfish strategies if it enters populations in sufficiently large numbers (Axelrod & Hamilton, 1981). Although Tit for Tat always loses to selfish strategies one-on-one, it ends up winning evolutionary contests by cutting its losses in exchanges with selfish strategies and reaping the benefits of drawing with cooperative strategies, including itself. (When strategies evolve, they become increasingly prevalent in populations; thus, evolved social strategies are usually designed in ways that enable them to do well in exchanges with replicas of themselves.)

Trivers (1971), Dugatkin (1997), and others have adduced evidence demonstrating that mechanisms giving rise to reciprocity have evolved in several species. The exchange of blood in vampire bats is a particularly interesting case in point (Wilkinson, 1990). Gouldner (1960) and others have suggested that reciprocity is a universal moral norm in the human species. As suggested by Trivers (1971), reciprocity is rooted in human psychological systems giving rise to a sense of deserving, a sense of gratitude and indebtedness, and of righteous indignation, retribution, revenge, and vindictiveness, as well as systems instilling a sense of fairness and justice.

The Evolution of Stage 2/3 Strategies

Stage 2/3 strategies prescribe giving those who have transgressed against you a second chance if they have "suffered enough" or if they "feel bad or sorry about cheating you." Such strategies are reflected in aphorisms such as "Forgive and forget" and "Everyone makes mistakes."

Following the publication of Axelrod and Hamilton's (1981) findings, investigators changed parameters in Axelrod and Hamilton's computer simulations and examined the fecundity of other strategies. In general, the closer the environments approximated the actual conditions of evolution, the greater were the benefits from conditionally altruistic strategies. For example, games that allowed for the inevitable errors that occur in social exchanges found that strategies such as "Two Tits for a Tat," "Generous Tit for Tat," "Contrite Tit for Tat," and "Forgiving Tit for Tat" fared better than Tit for Tat because they were equipped to break the self-defeating blood feuds precipitated by one selfish mistake (see Krebs, 2000a, 2000b; Ridley, 1996, for reviews of relevant research). Simulations that enabled players to observe other players and keep track of their strategies (called "image scoring") favored the evolution of altruism through indirect reciprocity (Nowak & Sigmund, 1998).

The Evolution of Stage 3 Strategies

Among the Stage 3 moral judgments classified in Kohlberg's system, there are at least two distinguishable types of strategy. Translated into biological terms, the first one prescribes enhancing one's inclusive fitness by helping members of one's group. The second prescribes conforming to moral norms. The adaptive benefits of the first type of strategy vary in accordance with the relationship between the helper and the recipient of help.

Helping Relatives

Many of the moral judgments contained in Kohlberg's scoring manual prescribe upholding families and helping relatives. It is easy to account for the evolution of mechanisms giving rise to such strategies. It is quite common among mammals for parents to sacrifice their somatic interests for the sake of their offspring. Such self-sacrificial behaviors help the parents propagate their genes. In a classic paper, Hamilton (1964) pointed out that the biological value of parental investment can be extended to relatives other than offspring. The probability of individuals sharing genes varies in proportion to their degree of relatedness. For example, the probability of parents and their offspring sharing genes is .5, and the same for siblings. The probability of grandparents and their grandchildren sharing genes is .25, and so on. Hamilton (1964) explained how a decision-rule could evolve that induced individuals to help others when the coefficient of their relatedness was greater than the cost to the helper of helping, divided by the benefits to the recipient ($r > c/b$). Alcock (1998) and others have reviewed evidence that members of many species behave in accordance with the strategy implicit in Hamilton's equation.

Helping Individuals Who Seem Similar to Relatives

Mechanisms that direct individuals to help their relatives are limited morally because they give rise to nepotistic and discriminatory behaviors, inducing individuals to favor relatives over nonrelatives, close relatives over distant relatives, and more fecund relatives over less fecund relatives. This helps explain the imbalance of helping between parents and children, and grandparents and grandchildren. However, perhaps fortunately, animals may not be able to detect the proportion of genes they share with others directly or exactly (Dawkins, 1989; but see Pfennig & Sherman, 1995; Rushton, 1999). Animals may have to rely on kin recognition cues such as phenotypic similarity, familiarity, and proximity (Porter, 1987). Although such cues may have been highly predictive of genetic relatedness in ancestral environments, they may activate mechanisms that induce individuals to help nonrelatives in modern environments. Inasmuch as the genetic payoffs to individuals from helping nonrelatives are less than those from helping their relatives, helping nonrelatives can be considered more altruistic than helping relatives (see Krebs, 1987).

Helping Friends

Many Kohlbergian moral judgments prescribe helping friends. In part, the evolution of mechanisms that dispose individuals to help their friends can be accounted for in terms of the "misfiring" of kin-selected strategies. Friends usually resemble kin; friends tend to be similar to one another, familiar, and live in relatively close proximity. In addition, such mechanisms probably reaped adaptive benefits through more complex forms of reciprocity than those prescribed by Stage 2 moral judgments.

Tooby and Cosmides (1996) have argued that exchanges between friends do not usually conform to decision-rules such as those that define Tit for Tat strategies. Friends do not pay each other back for every favor they bestow on one another, and they do not typically seek revenge when their partners fail to repay every debt. The give-and-take between friends is more general, averaged over many kinds of resources and over long periods of time. Tooby and Cosmides (1996) discuss the biological significance of a phenomenon they call the "banker's paradox": Banks are least likely to lend people money when they most need it and are least likely to be able to pay it back. In Tooby and Cosmides's view, investing in friends is a strategy aimed at increasing the probability that people will have "bankers" who are willing to lend them "money" when they are in need. Accumulating resources counts for nothing in evolution if they do not enhance individuals' chances of surviving, reproducing, and propagating their genes. Bestowing relatively low-cost favors on friends over long periods of time can be a winning strategy if it induces them to help save your life, help you find a mate, or foster the fitness of your relatives. In this sense, helping friends is akin to investing in insurance.

Helping In-Group Members

Kohlbergian moral judgments also prescribe helping members of one's in-group. Such strategies could stem from mechanisms of social control, which I discuss later, from extensions of kin-selected mechanisms, and from extensions of mechanisms designed to reap benefits from reciprocity. With respect to extensions of kin-selected mechanisms, Sober and Wilson (1998) explained how, under certain (admittedly rare) circumstances, mechanisms disposing individuals to behave in genetically altruistic ways—that is to say, in ways that enhance the fitness of members of their group at the expense of their own inclusive fitness—can evolve when the group as a whole benefits more than do groups containing less altruistic members. The evolutionary process involved is similar to kin selection inasmuch as it is based in propagating genes that dispose individuals to behave altruistically by helping other individuals who possess replicas of such genes. However, it differs from kin selection because the mechanisms that mediate altruism are not calibrated in ways that favor those who are genetically similar to the altruist. In group selection, the costs of helping those who do not possess the genes that give rise to altruism are outweighed by the benefits to the group as a whole, and selfish members are reduced in proportion when groups recombine (see Sober & Wilson, 1998).

Mechanisms that induce individuals to help members of their groups also could have evolved through the benefits of complex systems of reciprocity. Alexander (1987) has argued that the biological function of moral dispositions is to uphold systems of indirect reciprocity. Such systems may assume two forms. In the first, Person A helps Person B, Person B helps Person C, and Person C helps Person A. In the second, all members of a group contribute resources to a central distributor, who redistributes the resources to those who have contributed. Systems of indirect reciprocity have significantly more potential than systems of direct exchange to maximize benefits for all participating members, because they enable each individual to obtain resources of maximum value to them and minimum cost to those who produced them, in exchange for resources of minimum cost to them and maximum benefit to recipients. Such systems encourage individuals to specialize in the cultivation of particular resources, thus reducing the costs of producing them.

The potential gains of systems of indirect reciprocity notwithstanding, mechanisms giving rise to the behaviors necessary to support them could not have evolved without safeguards equipped to protect participating members from being exploited by selfish individuals disposed to give less than their share and to take more than their share. Such safeguards require the detection and punishment of cheaters. Alexander (1987) has outlined three conditions that foster the evolution of systems of indirect reciprocity: (1) Members of groups show a preference for givers over takers as exchange partners; (2) members of groups reward altruists and their relatives by bestowing honors on them; and (3) the success of the groups to which altruistic individuals belong enhances their fitness and the fitness of their relatives. Conversely, cheaters must be punished by rejection, ostracism, losses in prestige, and negative effects on the group that filter back to the cheater and his or her relatives.

As mentioned earlier, the game theorists Nowak and Sigmund (1998) have demonstrated that altruism can evolve through the benefits of indirect reciprocity. In the model they created, they controlled for the benefits of direct reciprocity by minimizing the probability that members of groups would interact with each other more than once. Behaving altruistically enhanced an individual's reputation or "image," and behaving selfishly degraded it. Nowak and Sigmund found that if members of groups showed a preference for those with good reputations, altruism could evolve and become evolutionarily stable. The process that gives rise to the adaptive benefits of indirect reciprocity is similar to the process that gives rise to the adaptive benefits of Tit for Tat: Individuals reap the benefits of cooperating with cooperative members of their groups and avoid the costs of interacting with selfish members of their groups. The difference between the two processes is that in systems of indirect reciprocity, individuals are able to detect selfish members of their groups by observing them and learning about their selfish behavior from others, thus avoiding the costs of being exploited by them directly. The strategy of helping members of one's group publicly in order to cultivate a good reputation is explicitly prescribe by Stage 3 moral judgments such as "Help others 'in order to leave a good impression on the community'" (Colby & Kohlberg, 1987, p. 78).

Conforming to Moral Norms

In addition to moral judgments that encourage people to enhance their inclusive fitness by helping members of their groups, Stage 3 moral judgments encourage people to conform to moral norms. Moral norms are defined as widely practiced types of behavior that members of groups consider right and obligatory. Some moral norms, such as keeping promises and paying debts, appear to be universal (Brown, 1991; Gouldner, 1960; Krebs & Janicki, 2003). Other moral norms, such as those that pertain to food prohibitions, are specific to particular cultures. In my earlier discussion of the evolution of moral judgment, I offered an explanation for the origin of universal moral norms. Here, I make the point that humans are naturally inclined to conform to existing moral norms because conformity pays off. Social learning theorists have demonstrated that people tend to imitate the behavior of those who are successful, powerful, and of high status (Alexander, 1987; Boyd & Richerson, 1985; Burton & Kunce, 1995). Viewed biologically, observing how others behave and copying the behavior of those who fare well would tend to be an adaptive strategy because it would enable individuals to modify their behavior without suffering the potentially adverse consequences of trial and error. The more frequent a type of behavior in a population, the more likely it is to be adaptive. In addition to the benefits of vicarious learning, conforming to moral norms may increase individuals' security by reinforcing their social identities, helping them fit in, and enabling them to avoid the costs of the social sanctions inflicted on those who violate the norms.

The Evolution of Stage 4 Strategies

Stage 4 moral judgments exhort people to obey the law and to conform to moral norms in order to maintain social institutions that promote the common good and provide benefits and protection to all members of society. Stage 4 moral judgments uphold more complex systems of cooperation than do Stage 3 moral judgments. In Stage 4 systems, individuals do not know most other members of their societies, even by reputation. Stage 4 systems are based on complex divisions of labor in which individuals give to and receive from central distributors. A common currency, such as money, enhances the efficiency of such systems.

It is easy to see how Stage 4 systems of cooperation could produce more benefits to all participating individuals than do less complex systems. However, it is equally easy to see that such systems are more susceptible to cheating than the systems upheld by lower-stage moral judgments. Without the antidotes inherent in Stage 2 and Stage 3 systems, Stage 4 systems need policing and legal institutions capable of detecting cheating and punishing cheaters.

If, as most evolutionary theorists believe, our hominid ancestors lived in relatively small groups (Dunbar, 1966), they would not have experienced the adaptive problems or opportunities necessary for the selection of mechanisms specifically designed to uphold Stage 4 systems of cooperation. I believe that the mechanisms that dispose individuals to behave in accordance with Stage 4 moral judgments are extensions of lower-stage mechanisms such as avoiding punishment (Stage 1), making one's best deal (Stage 2), and cultivating a good reputation, conforming, and upholding systems of indirect reciprocity (Stage 3).

Could Structures Mediating
Stage 5/6 Strategies Have Evolved?

Virtually all ultimate moral principles espoused by philosophers of ethics, including those that define Kohlberg's Stages 5 and 6, are based in two prescriptions: (1) Maximize benefits to humankind, and (2) allocate these benefits in a nondiscriminatory way. Indiscriminate cooperation and indiscriminate altruism meet these criteria. Although such strategies could maximize the benefits for everyone if everyone practiced them, I do not believe they have evolved, because they are vulnerable to cheating, nepotism, and discrimination against out-groups.

The vast majority of theorists who have examined the evolution of morality have concluded that mechanisms designed to induce individuals to adopt the strategies prescribed by Stage 5 and Stage 6 moral judgments could not have evolved. Alexander (1987), who concluded that a "modicum" of indiscriminate beneficence could have evolved through indirect reciprocity, seems to be an exception, but the evidence he adduces supports the evolution of only Stage 3 in-group and Stage 4 national systems of indirect reciprocity, with no extension to out-groups or to all of humanity.

Kohlberg's Stages 5 and 6 are different from his first four stages in that they are "colder" and more logical. There is virtually no mention of affect in any of Kohlberg's Stage 5 moral judgments. At least one of Kohlberg's collaborators, John Gibbs (see Gibbs, Basinger, & Fuller, 1992) has concluded that Stages 5 and 6 are "metatheoretical" forms of reasoning, quite different from the forms of reasoning in earlier stages. Researchers have failed to find any evidence of Stage 5 or 6 moral judgments about hypothetical dilemmas in non-Western cultures, and in the many studies my colleagues and I have conducted, we have observed very few participants making Stage 5 and Stage 6 moral judgments about real-life moral conflicts that have consequences for the parties involved.

Implications for Moral Development

Kohlberg's model is a model of moral development, that is to say, how people become increasingly moral over time. What implications does an evolutionary reconceptualization of Kohlberg's model have for ontogenetic moral development? In the animal kingdom, different species develop in different ways. The newborn of some species are essentially the same as adults; they are fully formed and ready to go. In other species, individuals undergo qualitative transformations as they develop. For example, caterpillars change into butterflies. In the human species, females develop breasts at puberty. Viewed from the perspective of evolution, the reason members of some species change as they develop is because they face different kinds of adaptive problems at different phases in their life cycles. As a generalization, the early lives of mammals are dominated by survival problems; when they reach sexual maturity, their lives become dominated by reproductive problems; and in old age, they face problems associated with parental investment.

With respect to morality, we would expect humans to acquire mental mechanisms giving rise to different social strategies in a sequence determined by the types of social problems their hominid ancestors faced at different phases in their lives. In terms of this expectation, the reason young children acquire Stage 1 strategies prescribing obedience to authority is because obeying authority is an adaptive strategy for relatively small, weak, and vulnerable people. The reason older children acquire Stage 2 instrumental exchange strategies is because such strategies reap greater gains in relations with peers.

In Piaget's (1932) pioneering work on the development of moral judgment, he concluded that young children tended to view morality in terms of obedience to adults for two reasons. First, as emphasized by Kohlberg, young children do not possess the cognitive sophistication necessary to understand reciprocity. Second, neglected by Kohlberg but emphasized in evolutionary models, young children's social relations are dominated by adults. According to Piaget, the reason older children acquire a new moral orientation based in cooperation is not only because they develop the capacity to understand cooperation but also because cooperative exchanges are more adaptive than obedience in relations with peers. Contemporary developmental psychologists such as Damon and Hart (1992) and Youniss (1986) have concluded that research evidence supports the more Piagetian interpretation.

During adolescence, children enter new social worlds dominated by relations with the opposite sex and long-term friendships, which activate mechanisms that give rise to Stage 3 moral judgments. During adolescence, social image, reputation, and fear of ostracism become salient (Brown, Lohr, & McClenahan, 1986; Krebs & Van Hesteren, 1994). And as adolescents grow into adults, they enter other social worlds governed by other "moral orders" (Harre, 1984) upheld by Stage 4 moral judgments. As put by Alexander (1987),

> I see Kohlberg's Stage 4 as representing a transition from being primarily a rule-follower to being also concerned with rule-enforcement. This interpretation is consistent with the idea that after having learned and followed the rules one's self, having invested in the system, and having produced and instructed relatives with whose welfare one is ultimately concerned, there is reproductive value in ensuring that one's investment is safe, i.e., that the rules do not change. (p. 134)

Research evidence is consistent with the conclusion that adults who have invested in their social system and who stand to gain from it make Stage 4 judgments but those who do not stand to gain make lower-stage judgments upholding their own interests and the interests of their in-groups (Rest, 1983).

Additive Stage Acquisition

If structures upholding particular systems of cooperation evolved because they were adaptive with respect to particular types of social relations, we would expect people to retain the structures as long as they engaged in the types of social relations the structures evolved to support. Therefore, as discussed, in place of Kohlberg's assumption that new stage structures transform and displace old stage structures, we would expect new stage structures to be added to older stage structures and older stage structures to be retained and activated in the types of contexts in which they were selected in ancestral environments. Krebs and Van Hesteren (1994) have reviewed research supporting this expectation. As examples, adults who make high-stage moral judgments on Kohlberg's test sometimes make Stage 1 judgments in real-life contexts involving relations with powerful authorities (Newitt & Krebs, 1999). Adults behave in the ways prescribed by Stage 1 moral judgments in military contexts, cults, and the contexts created by Milgram (1964) in his classic studies on obedience to authority. Adults invoke Stage 2 strategies in the context of business transactions (Carpendale & Krebs, 1992), Stage 3 strategies when interacting with members of their families and other in-groups (Krebs & Van Hesteren, 1994), and Stage 4 strategies in societal contexts.

On the basis of findings from many studies (see Wark & Krebs, 1997, for a review) we concluded that the moral judgments people make and the moral behaviors they display in their everyday lives are the products of an interaction between the structures of moral judgment they have acquired ontogenetically and the environmental, situational, or contextual factors that govern the activation of these structures. It is misguided to assume that people are "in" stages of moral development, except perhaps young children, who do not have the cognitive sophistication to make high-stage moral judgments. It is more correct to assume that people acquire an increasingly broad range of strategies that enable them to adapt to an increasingly broad range of social contexts. It is misguided to assume that people develop general "structures of the whole" and more correct to assume that they acquire domain-specific structures that evolved in ancestral environments (Buss, 1999).

Inclusiveness

Kohlberg (1984) has argued that new stage structures incorporate or integrate older stage structures within them. Viewed from an evolutionary perspective, this argument is valid inasmuch as more complex systems of cooperation are built upon and include less complex systems of cooperation. For example, it seems quite likely that Stage 4 systems of indirect reciprocity could not have evolved and cannot be maintained without support from Stage 1 obedience strategies, Stage 2 instrumental exchange strategies, and Stage 3 impression management strategies. An evolutionary perspective also offers a clear and simple explanation for why high-stage structures are "better" than low-stage structures: They prescribe strategies that uphold systems of cooperation equipped to produce greater benefits for all contributors.

The Pinnacle of Moral Development

As I have argued, the evidence does not suggest that we are evolved to adopt strategies such as "Give to everyone according to his need," "Do unto others as you would have them do unto you," and "Behave in a way that maximizes the greatest good for the greatest number," though we may well be disposed to preach such strategies to others. This is profoundly tragic, because if we were evolved to uphold the systems of cooperation supported by such strategies, we would be much better off than we are. If we all upheld such systems, social relations would be harmonious; everyone would help and support each other, regardless of race, creed, or color. There would not be any crime or wars. And we could invest the money we saved from the arms race, police, and jails in enhancing the quality of our lives. The problem with systems of cooperation upheld by Stage 5 and Stage 6 moral judgments is that they do not contain any antidotes to selfish and discriminatory strategies and thus are destined to fail. We may well be evolved to uphold systems of indirect reciprocity in relatively small groups of people who know one another by reputation. In such groups, it is possible that low-stage strategies could support some indiscriminate altruism (Alexander, 1987), but the greater the proportion of indiscriminate altruists, the greater the vulnerability of this strategy to selfishness and discrimination.

Summary and Conclusion

In this chapter, I outlined Kohlberg's model of moral development, reviewed research that called it into question, concluded that Kohlberg's model pertains to only one of many functions of making moral judgments, and argued that reconceptualizing Kohlbergian structures of moral judgment as evolved decision-making mechanisms gives rise to a more ecologically valid model. I proposed that the mechanisms that give rise to moral decisions evolved to help our hominid ancestors resolve the inevitable conflicts of interest that arose when they banded together and established systems of cooperation to foster their biological interests. I argued that people use moral judgments to induce others to behave in ways that foster their interests and that recipients of moral judgments are agents of selection. Of the many possible kinds of moral judgments, those that define Kohlberg's stages of moral development were selected because they uphold behavioral strategies that foster the interests of those who send them and those who receive them. In addition to using moral judgments to influence the behavior of others, people use moral judgments to guide their own behavior. Although moral judgments directed toward the self are more self-serving than moral judgments directed toward others, there are several constraints on such self-serving biases.

If people are biologically disposed to behave in accordance with the kinds of moral judgments classified by Kohlberg, then contrary to the conclusions reached by several eminent evolutionary theorists, behaving morally need not be maladaptive and humans may be moral by nature. In the second half of this chapter, I explained how mental mechanisms disposing people to adopt the social strategies prescribed by Stage 1, Stage 2, and Stage 3 moral judgments could have evolved and how the strategies prescribed by Stage 4 moral judgments follow naturally from those that define the earlier stages. I concluded that although it may pay off for people to preach Stage 5 and Stage 6 ethical principles, humans are not biologically disposed to behave in accordance with them.

I ended by considering the implications of the evolutionary model I outlined for moral development. Adopting a life history perspective, I suggested that people acquire structures of moral judgment in the sequence that defines Kohlberg's stages of moral development because such structures helped their hominid ancestors solve adaptive problems that occurred at different phases of their lives. New structures do not transform and displace older structures, as Kohlbergians assume, because people continue to face the adaptive problems the earlier structures were designed to solve. I noted two general implications of my analysis of the evolution of moral dispositions. On one hand, we are moral by nature because we are disposed to behave in accordance with the prescriptions of Stage 1, Stage 2, Stage 3, and Stage 4 moral judgments (for the practical implications of this conclusion, see also Krebs, 2004). On the other hand, we are not completely moral because we are not disposed to behave in accordance with Stage 5 and Stage 6 moral principles. And there is a tragic irony to this, because we all could be better off if we were so disposed.

References

Alcock, J. (1998). *Animal behavior: An evolutionary approach* (6th ed.). Sunderland, MA: Sinauer Associates.

Alexander, R. D. (1987). *The biology of moral systems*. New York: Aldine de Gruyter.

Aronfreed, J. (1968). *Conduct and conscience*. New York: Academic Press.

Axelrod, R., & Hamilton, W. D. (1981). The evolution of cooperation. *Science, 211*, 1390-1396.

Bartek, S., Krebs, D. L., & Taylor, M. (1993). Coping, defending, and the relations between moral judgment and moral behavior in prostitutes and other female juvenile delinquents. *Journal of Abnormal Psychology, 102*, 65-73.

Boehm, C. (2000). Conflict and the evolution of social control. In L. D. Katz (Ed.), *Evolutionary origins of morality* (pp. 79-101). Thorverton, UK: Imprint Academic.

Boyd, R., & Richerson, P. J. (1985). *Culture and the evolutionary process*. Chicago: University of Chicago Press.

Brown, B. B., Lohr, M. J., & McClenahan, E. L. (1986). Early adolescents' perceptions of peer pressure. *Journal of Early Adolescence, 6*, 139-154.

Brown, D. E. (1991). *Human universals*. New York: McGraw-Hill.

Brown, R. (1986). *Social psychology* (2nd ed.). New York: Free Press.

Burton, R. V., & Kunce, L. (1995). Behavioral models of moral development: A brief history and integration. In W. M. Kurtines & J. L. Gewirtz (Eds.), *Moral development: An introduction* (pp. 141-172). Boston: Allyn & Bacon.

Buss, D. (1999). *Evolutionary psychology: The new science of the mind*. Boston: Allyn & Bacon.

Carpendale, J., & Krebs, D. L. (1992). Situational variation in moral judgment: In a stage or on a stage? *Journal of Youth and Adolescence, 21*, 203-224.

Carpendale, J., & Krebs, D. L. (1995). Variations in moral judgment as a function of type of dilemma and moral choice. *Journal of Personality, 63*, 289-313.

Colby, A., & Kohlberg, L. (Eds.). (1987). *The measurement of moral judgment* (Vols. 1-2). Cambridge, UK: Cambridge University Press.

Damon, W., & Hart, D. (1992). Self understanding and its role in social and moral development. In M. H. Bornstein & E. M. Lamb (Eds.), *Developmental psychology: An advanced textbook* (2nd ed., pp. 421-465). Hillsdale, NJ: Erlbaum.

Dawkins, R. (1989). *The selfish gene*. Oxford, UK: Oxford University Press.

Denton, K., & Krebs, D. L. (1990). From the scene to the crime: The effect of alcohol and social context on moral judgment. *Journal of Personality and Social Psychology, 59*, 242-248.

Dugatkin, L. A. (1997). *Cooperation among animals: An evolutionary perspective*. New York: Oxford University Press.

Dunbar, R. (1966). *Grooming, gossip, and the evolution of language*. London: Faber & Faber.

Gibbs, J., Basinger, K. S., & Fuller, D. (1992). *Moral maturity: Measuring the development of sociomoral reasoning*. Hillsdale NJ: Erlbaum.

Gouldner, A. W. (1960). The norm of reciprocity: A preliminary statement. *American Sociological Review, 25,* 161-178.

Hamilton, W. D. (1964). The evolution of social behavior. *Journal of Theoretical Biology, 7,* 1-52.

Harre, R. (1984). *Personal being: A theory for individual psychology.* Cambridge, MA: Harvard University Press.

Higgins, A., & Eccles-Parson, J. E. (1983). Social cognition and the social life of the child: Stages as subcultures. In E. T. Higgins, D. N. Ruble, & W. W. Hartup (Eds.), *Social cognition and social development: A sociocultural perspective* (pp. 137-151). New York: Cambridge University Press.

Kohlberg, L. (1984). *Essays in moral development: Vol. 2. The psychology of moral development.* New York: Harper & Row.

Kohlberg, L., & Candee, D. (1984). The relationship of moral judgment to moral action. In L. Kohlberg (Ed.), *Essays in moral development: Vol. 2. The psychology of moral development.* New York: Harper & Row.

Krebs, D. L. (1987). The challenge of altruism in biology and psychology. In C. Crawford, M. Smith, & D. L. Krebs (Eds.), *Sociobiology and psychology: Ideas, issues, and applications* (pp. 81-118). Hillsdale, NJ: Erlbaum.

Krebs, D. L. (1998). The evolution of moral behavior. In C. Crawford & D. L. Krebs (Eds.), *Handbook of evolutionary psychology: Ideas, issues, and applications* (pp. 337-368). Hillsdale, NJ: Erlbaum.

Krebs, D. L. (2000a). The evolution of moral dispositions in the human species. In D. LeCroy & P. Moller (Eds.), *Evolutionary perspectives on human reproductive behavior. Annals of the New York Academy of Science, 907,* 1-17.

Krebs, D. L. (2000b). Evolutionary games and morality. In L. D. Katz (Ed.), *Evolutionary origins of morality: Cross-disciplinary approaches* (pp. 313-321). Thorverton, UK: Imprint Academic.

Krebs, D. L. (2000c). As moral as we need to be. In L. D. Katz (Ed.), *Evolutionary origins of morality: Cross-disciplinary approaches* (pp. 139-143). Thorverton, UK: Imprint Academic.

Krebs, D. L. (2004). How to make silk purses from sows' ears: Cultivating morality and constructing moral systems. In C. Crawford & C. Salmon (Eds.), *Evolutionary psychology: Public policy and personal decisions* (pp. 319-342). Mahwah, NJ: Erlbaum.

Krebs, D. L., & Denton, K. (1997). Social illusions and self-deception: The evolution of biases in person perception. In J. A. Simpson & D. T. Kenrick (Eds.), *Evolutionary social psychology* (pp. 21-47). Hillsdale, NJ: Erlbaum.

Krebs, D. L., Denton, K., & Higgins, N. (1988). On the evolution of self-knowledge and self-deception. In K. MacDonald (Ed.), *Sociobiological perspectives on human behavior* (pp. 103-139). New York: Springer-Verlag.

Krebs, D. L., Denton, K., Vermeulen, S. C., Carpendale, J. I., & Bush, A. (1991). The structural flexibility of moral judgment. *Journal of Personality and Social Psychology: Personality Processes and Individual Differences, 61,* 1012-1023.

Krebs, D. L., Denton, K., & Wark, G. (1997). The forms and functions of real-life moral decision-making. *Journal of Moral Education, 20,* 131-145.

Krebs, D. L., Denton, K., Wark, G., Couch, R., Racine, T. P., & Krebs, D. (2002). Interpersonal moral conflicts between couples: Effects of type of dilemma, role, and partner's judgments on level of moral reasoning and probability of resolution. *Journal of Adult Development, 9,* 307-316.

Krebs, D. L., & Janicki, M. (2003). The biological foundations of moral norms. In M. Schaller & C. Crandall (Eds.), *Psychological foundations of culture.* Hillsdale, NJ: Erlbaum.

Krebs, D. L., & Laird, P. (1998). Judging yourself as you judge others: Perspective-taking, moral development, and exculpation. *Journal of Adult Development, 5,* 1-12.

Krebs, D. L., & Van Hesteren. (1994). The development of altruism: Toward an integrative model. *Developmental Review, 14,* 1-56.

Krebs, D. L., Vermeulen, S. C., Carpendale, J. I., & Denton, K. (1991). Structural and situational influences on moral judgment: The interaction between stage and dilemma. In W. Kurtines & J. Gewirtz (Eds.), *Handbook of moral behavior and development: Theory, research, and application* (pp. 139-169). Mahwah, NJ: Erlbaum.

Krebs, D. L., Vermeulen, S., & Denton, K. (1991). Competence and performance in moral judgment: From the ideal to the real. *Moral Education Forum, 16,* 7-22

Krebs, D. L., Wark, G., & Krebs, D. (1995). Lessons from life: Toward a functional model of morality. *Moral Education Forum, 20,* 22-29.

Leaky, R. E., & Lewin, R. (1977). *Origins.* New York: Dutton.

MacDonald, K. B. (1988). Sociobiology and the cognitive-developmental tradition on moral development research. In K. B. MacDonald (Ed.), *Sociobiological perspectives on human development* (pp. 140-167). New York: Springer-Verlag.

Milgram, S. (1974). *Obedience to authority.* New York: Harper

Mitchell, R. W., & Thompson, N. S. (Eds.). (1986). *Deception: Perspectives on human and nonhuman deceit.* New York: State University of New York Press.

Newitt, C., & Krebs, D. L. (1999). *Structural and contextual sources of moral judgment.* Unpublished manuscript.

Nowak, M. A., & Sigmund, K. (1998). Evolution of indirect reciprocity by image scoring. *Nature, 393,* 573-577.

Pfennig, D. W., & Sherman, P. W. (1995). Kin recognition. *Scientific American, 272,* 98-103.

Piaget, J. (1932). *The moral judgment of the child.* London: Routledge & Kegan Paul.

Porter, R. H. (1987). Kin recognition: Functions and mediating mechanisms. In C. B. Crawford & D. L. Krebs (Eds.), *Sociobiology and psychology: Ideas, issues, and applications* (pp. 175-205). Hillsdale, NJ: Erlbaum.

Rawls, J. (1971). *A theory of justice.* Cambridge, MA: Harvard University press.

Rest, J. F. (1983). Morality. In J. H. Flavell & E. M. Markman (Eds.), *Handbook of child psychology: Vol. 3. Cognitive development* (4th ed., pp. 556-629). New York: John Wiley.

Ridley, M. (1996). *The origins of virtue: Human instincts and the evolution of cooperation.* New York: Viking.

Rushton, J. P. (1999). Genetic similarity theory and the nature of ethnocentrism. In K. Thienpont & R. Cliquet (Eds.), *In-group/Out-group behavior in modern societies: An evolutionary perspective* (pp. 75-107). Amsterdam: Vlaamse Gemeeschap/CBGC.

Sloman, L., & Gilbert, P. (Eds.). (2000). *Subordination and defeat: An evolutionary approach to mood disorders and their therapy.* Mahwah, NJ: Erlbaum.

Sober, E., & Wilson, D. S. (1998). *Unto others: The evolution and psychology of unselfish behavior.* Cambridge, MA: Harvard University Press.

Strayer, F. F., & Strayer, J. (1976). An ethological analysis of social agonism and dominance relations among preschool children. *Child Development, 47,* 980-989.

Taylor, S. E. (1989). *Positive illusions: Creative self-deception and the healthy mind.* New York: Basic Books.

Tooby, J., & Cosmides, L. (1996). Friendship and the banker's paradox: Other pathways to the evolution of adaptations for altruism. *Proceedings of the British Academy, 88,* 119-143.

Trivers, R. L. (1971). The evolution of reciprocal altruism. *Quarterly Review of Biology, 46,* 35-57.

Trivers, R. (2000). The elements of a scientific theory of self-deception. In D. LeCroy & P. Moller (Eds.), *Evolutionary perspectives on human reproductive behavior. Annals of the New York Academy of Sciences, 907,* 114-131.

Wark, G., & Krebs, D. L. (1997). Sources of variation in real-life moral judgment: Toward a model of real-life morality. *Journal of Adult Development, 4,* 163-178.

Wilkinson, G. S. (1990, February). Food sharing in vampire bats. *Scientific American,* 76-82.

Williams, G. C. (1989). A sociobiological expansion of evolution and ethics. In J. Paradis & G. C. Williams (Eds.), *Evolution and ethics* (pp. 179-214). Princeton, NJ: Princeton University Press.

Youniss, J. (1986). Development in reciprocity through friendship. In C. Zahn-Waxler, M. Cummings, & R. Ianottie (Eds.), *Altruism and aggression: Biological and social origins* (pp. 88-106). Cambridge, UK: Cambridge University Press.

10

Evolutionary Studies of Cooperation, Competition, and Altruism

A Twin-Based Approach

Nancy L. Segal

T he goal of the present chapter is to demonstrate the usefulness and importance of examining human developmental data from the joint perspectives of behavioral genetics and evolutionary psychology. *Behavioral genetics* is concerned with the degree to which genetic and environmental variation underlie individual differences in behavioral traits. It offers a wide range of informative research designs capitalizing on the relative genetic relatedness and rearing circumstances of family members. *Evolutionary psychology* is concerned with across-species uniformities, in particular, the origins and functions of adaptations influencing behavioral patterns and strategies. It also tests the predictive power of broad theories originating in

Author's Note: The writing of this chapter was supported, in part, by an award from the National Institute of Mental Health (NIMH Grant 1 R01 MH63351), an American Fellowship from the American Association for University Women, and a California State University Senior Faculty Research Award.

the field of evolutionary biology, such as Trivers's (1972) evolutionary theory of sexual selection and Hamilton's (1964) kin selection theory. Kin selection theory, which explains cooperation with reference to the relative genetic relatedness of the interactants, is especially relevant to the material to be reviewed.

These perspectives are not intended to replace other theories and approaches; rather, this chapter purports to illustrate, via empirical analyses of twin and adoption data, how a union of behavioral genetics and evolutionary psychology can enrich current theoretical and empirical efforts in the behavioral sciences. It will do so via a review of twins and adoption methods and findings.

Behavioral Genetics and Evolutionary Psychology: Coming Together

The goals and objectives of behavioral genetics and evolutionary psychology differ broadly, as indicated above, yet their common interests have been generally neglected. Mealey (2001) has pointed out that both disciplines are concerned with the concept of kinship. Specifically, identifying traits showing heritable adaptive variation and determining how heritable and nonheritable differences map onto life history strategies would engage the research interests of individuals working within both areas. Evolutionary psychology offers behavioral genetics an additional perspective for interpreting findings, for example, on sex differences in heritability for some traits. Mealey and Segal (1993) found greater genetic influence on reproduction-related behaviors in male than female monozygotic (MZ) twins reared apart. This outcome is consistent with evolutionary expectations that females are more likely than males to be reproductively successful under adverse conditions. Last, behavioral genetics offers evolutionary psychology a rich assortment of research methods for assessing a range of novel hypotheses (Buss, 1984; Scarr, 1995; Segal & MacDonald, 1998; also see Segal, 1993, 2000a, and references therein).

Social Behavior: Genetic and Evolutionary Analyses

This section reviews special subdisciplines of behavioral genetics and evolutionary psychology that bear importantly upon the empirical studies to be reviewed. They include social genetic and kinship genetic theory.

Genetics of Social Behavior

Social genetics is the subdiscipline of behavioral genetics that combines genetic, developmental, and social influences on behavior. It is concerned with the proximal effects of genes on social behavior and organization, with attention to the ecological and evolutionary circumstances of organisms (Hahn, 1990). It has been recognized that almost all behavior expressed by highly social species occurs within social relationships (Scott, 1989, 1997). A key observation is that the genetic backgrounds of social partners may differentially affect individual and joint behaviors (Hahn, 1990).

Most research in this area has used nonhuman samples, given the greater experimental control afforded to investigators. Scott's (1977) classic work with dogs is exemplary. He showed that pairs composed of similar breeds displayed greater cooperation than pairs composed of different breeds and that role differentiation was most likely when partners were chosen from different breeds. In a second experiment, he manipulated dogs' rearing situations so that some animals were raised with animals of the same or different genotype. This procedure revealed that dogs receiving early exposure to different genotypes showed increased cooperation with partners of either the same or different breed during subsequent social encounters.

In contrast with nonhuman studies, human research relies on naturally occurring life situations (e.g., MZ twins reared apart; unrelated children reared together) when conducting analyses of social behavior. Several twin studies have demonstrated this perspective. Von Bracken (1934) studied young MZ and DZ (dizygotic) twins as they completed arithmetic and coding tasks, both in the same room and alone. Key findings were that (a) MZ twins showed greater equality in output when working in close proximity and that (b) DZ twins were more highly motivated to work toward individual goals. Segal (1984) observed more cooperative behaviors between MZ than DZ twin children during puzzle completion and differential productivity tasks, as well as more frequent and meaningful social contacts during school recess.

Social genetics appears to be a natural bridge between behavioral genetics and evolutionary psychology. Few studies have been conducted with this view in mind, but some recent work (reviewed below) has yielded exciting findings.

Kinship

Hamilton's (1964) kin selection theory marked a turning point in evolutionary-based research concerned with the bases of altruism. Prior to his theory, investigators were puzzled by such behaviors. This was because they seemed to reduce Darwinian fitness, as assessed by survival and transmission of one's own genes into future generations, via viable offspring. However, Hamilton argued that natural selection favors behavior that lowers fitness if it improves the fitness of genetic relatives. He further argued that average fitness gains to recipients of altruistic acts must exceed average fitness losses to benefactors multiplied by their coefficient of relatedness. The parent-child relationship is illustrative and is explained in his own words:

> A gene causing its possessor to give parental care will leave more replica genes in the next generation than an allele having the opposite tendency. The selection advantage may be seen to lie through benefits conferred indifferently on a set of relatives each of which has a half chance of carrying the gene in question. (Hamilton, 1946, p. 1)

Hamilton thus recast the concept of classic fitness as *inclusive fitness*, in which fitness is considered a function of one's own survival and reproduction plus that of genetic relatives, weighted by their extent of genetic overlap. This principle would apply not just to parents and children but also to other pairs of relatives who vary in genetic relatedness. Preserving one's genes in future generations is the ultimate cause of such behavior. It is important to recognize, however, that individuals do not consciously calculate genetic overlap prior to performing altruistic acts; rather, they behave as though they do (Dawkins, 1990). The satisfaction individuals gain by assisting close relatives becomes a proximal cause of these behaviors, which most likely works to sustain them.

MZ and DZ twins allow many interesting tests of inclusive fitness because they are exactly the same age and were usually reared together since birth: Kin selection theory predicts that genetic similarity should influence decisions related to cooperation, competition, and altruism. However, it does not specify the proximate psychological mechanism for how people recognize genetic similarity in others. Because being a twin is a relatively infrequent event, it is unlikely that twins have evolved mechanisms designed to influence behavior specifically within twinships. However, it is reasonable to expect that twins, like other humans, would have mechanisms designed to detect and act on genetic similarity in others (Segal, 1997).

What psychological mechanisms may be involved in detecting genetic similarity? How can we know who our relatives are? Physical proximity may be one way to facilitate such knowledge among humans. It is also possible that social bonding is facilitated by neurological mechanisms underlying attraction between individuals who perceive similarities between themselves

(Freedman, 1979). Associations have, in fact, been observed between different forms of recognition and specific emotions, setting off a chain of physiological and psychological events (McGuire, Fawzy, Spar, Weigel, & Troisi, 1994). One proposed mechanism is *phenotypic matching,* the comparison of phenotypes of self with those of others. This allows learning information about one's own characteristics or the characteristics of relatives. The result would be an "image," "template" (Sherman & Holmes, 1985), or "learned standard of appearance" against which the phenotype of an unfamiliar individual could be evaluated. The degree of similarity between the observed phenotype and image offers information about relatedness, albeit approximate. MZ and DZ twins reared apart (MZA and DZA) offer an especially effective test of this concept.

A related topic is that of friends' and spouses' positive assortment for selected physical and behavioral traits. Both unmarried and married partners were found to assort positively for physical traits (e.g., age and bodily attractiveness) and behavioral traits (e.g., humor and imaginativeness), yet married partners showed greater assortment for behavioral traits (Keller, Thiessen, & Young, 1996). Psychological similarity may thus be more meaningful for relationship stability and duration. Other studies have linked attitudinal similarities, personality similarities, and perceptions of similarities with attraction between friends. Rowe, Woulbroun, and Gulley (1994) noted that friends' behavioral similarities are present prior to their relationship formation. Again, MZA and DZA twins offer additional powerful tests of such findings.

Twin Studies: A Brief Overview

Twin Types

Twins can be either identical (monozygotic, or MZ) or fraternal (dizygotic, or DZ). MZ twins result when a single fertilized egg, or zygote, divides during the first 2 weeks after conception. Factors associated with zygotic splitting are not well understood, although the timing of fertilization and implantation have been implicated. MZ twins originate from the same genetic material yet may be subject to multiple sources of difference. For example, fetal anastomoses (shared one-way prenatal circulation) variously affects two thirds of MZ twins. The chronic form can lead to size differences between co-twins in which the smaller donor twin suffers from inadequate nutrition (Bryan, 1992). The acute form occurs during labor and may be associated with birth weight differences and cardiac failure. MZ co-twin differences in chromosomal anomalies (e.g., Turner's Syndrome: 45, XO) may result from chromosomal loss in one twin during embryogenesis (Uchida, DeSa, & Whelan, 1983). Differential X-inactivation (lyonization) is another source of difference between some female MZ co-twins. It involves the random "shutting down" of one X chromosome in every cell nucleus on, or about, the seventh day after fertilization. MZ female twins originating from relatively late zygotic division may show different X-inactivation patterns, making them discordant for conditions such as fragile X syndrome, Duchenne muscular dystrophy, and color blindness (Jørgensen et al., 1992; also see Segal, 2000a; Singh, Murphy, & O'Reilly, 2002).

DZ twins result when two eggs are fertilized by two separate sperm cells. DZ twins share half their genes, on average, by descent. Approximately half of all DZ twin pairs are same sex, and half are opposite sex. There are several intriguing DZ twin variations. *Superfecundated twins* result if two eggs are fertilized on different occasions, either by the same or by different males. In the latter case, the twins would share the same genetic relationship as half siblings because they would have common mothers but different fathers. This event is presumed to be rare, but some cases may go undetected. *Superfetated twins* involve release and fertilization of a second egg several weeks after a first conception has occurred. These twins would show a range of developmental discrepancies at birth (Rhine, Nance, Melin, & Skidmore, 1974). Again, the frequency of such twinning is unknown. *Polar body twins* result from fertilization of a mature egg and a polar body (Bulmer, 1970; also see Segal, 2000a). Depending on subsequent cellular events, these twins may show extremely high or low degrees of genetic relatedness. Last, some twins born to interracial couples can look very different physically, even to the point of appearing unrelated.

Twinning Rates

Research shows that MZ twinning does not run in families, although there has been one recent study to the contrary (Lichtenstein, Olaussen, & Kallen, 1996). Lack of genetic influence on MZ twinning is evidenced by the constant rate at which such twins occur worldwide (the natural twining rate is approximately 1 out of 250 births; see Segal, 2000a). The presence of multiple MZ sets in some families may reflect chance factors, although genetic effects specific to some families cannot be dismissed. In contrast with MZ twinning, DZ twinning does appear to run in families, although the genetic pathways are not well understood. Genetic influences on DZ twinning are also supported by its variable rates across Black populations (16/1,000 births), Caucasian populations (8/1,000 births), and Asian populations (3/1,000 births) (Bomsel-Helmreich & Al Mufti, 1995). DZ twinning has also been linked to frequent intercourse (James, 1992) and periods of sexual abstinence (James, 1986); of course, DZ twins may occur in families lacking some or all of these characteristics.

Twinning rates have escalated substantially in recent years, owing mostly to new assisted-reproductive techniques (ART) but also to advanced maternal age. It is estimated that as of 1999, twins occur in 28.9/1,000 births (Ventura, Martin, Curtin, Menacker, & Hamilton, 2001). One procedure, *in vitro fertilization* (IVF), unites sperm and eggs in a petri dish, then implants multiple embryos in the mother's womb. ART is responsible for a very small percentage of births but has significantly affected the DZ twinning rate. Between 1980 and 1997, twin births increased by 63% among women 40 to 44 years of age and by 1,000% among women 44 to 49 years (Martin & Park, 1999). IVF has also increased the MZ twinning rate but to a lesser extent. Alterations in the membrane surrounding the embryo and/or laboratory manipulation of embryos is thought to induce zygotic splitting, resulting in MZ twins (Hecht, 1995).

Evolutionary reasoning suggests why twins are relatively infrequent in human populations. First, multiple-birth infants pose burdens to families with respect to parental care and resources. Furthermore, twins are often born prematurely and show an excess of congenital anomalies (Mastroiacovo et al., 1999); thus, they may strain parental emotions and finances. Multiple pregnancies are also associated with health hazards for expectant mothers (Krotz, Fajardo, Ghandi, Patel, & Keith, 2002). However, the greater frequency of DZ than MZ twin births is worth exploring. There is evidence that mothers of DZ twins are taller, on average, than mothers of MZ twins and non-twins, a trait that could prove advantageous in some settings (Bulmer, 1970). Mothers of DZ twins also acquire resistance to breast cancer (Murphy, Broeders, Carpenter, Gunnarskog, & Leon, 1997). Another intriguing view is Forbes's (1997) suggestion that the elevated rates of DZ twinning among older mothers may be an adaptive trade-off. That is to say, the risk of having defective children may be offset by the benefits of having two children who may transmit genes to future generations.

Zygosity Diagnosis

Accurate determination of twin type, zygosity diagnosis, is a crucial first step in behavioral genetic research, as will become clear in the section that follows. The best method for determining twin type involves comparing twins' DNA profiles; comparing multiple blood group characteristics is also informative but can be inconvenient and uncomfortable (Richards et al., 1993). Matching DNA patterns or blood groups indicate MZ twins, while differences indicate DZ twins. Physical similarity questionnaires, which show over 90% agreement with blood-typing procedures (e.g., Goldsmith, 1991; Nichols & Bilbro, 1966), are also available and may be substituted when circumstances preclude these other methods.

Twin Research Designs

The logic underlying the classic twin research design, first discussed by Sir Frances Galton in the late 1800s, is simple and elegant: Greater trait similarity between genetically identical twins than between genetically nonidentical twins is consistent with genetic influence on that trait. (The biological bases of twinning had not been worked out in Galton's time, but he correctly reasoned that there were two types of twins, with different degrees of genetic overlap.) Fundamental to twin research is the *equal environments assumption* (EEA), namely that trait-relevant environmental effects are constant for the two types of twins. Considerable studies have supported the EEA for most measured traits (see, for example, Hettema, Neale, & Kendler, 1995).

There are approximately 10 variants of the classic twin research design, summarized in Segal (1990). Only those most relevant to links between behavioral genetics and evolutionary psychology will be reviewed.

Twins as Couples. The "twins as couples" approach focuses on social-interactional outcomes and processes between MZ and DZ twins, with a view toward understanding how genetic relatedness may affect social relations. Units of analysis are thus those that reflect aspects of pair behavior, for example, cooperative events and helping behavior.

Twin-Family Study. When MZ twins marry and have children, the twins become "genetic parents" to their nieces and nephews (the co-twin's children); these nieces and nephews become their "genetic sons" and "genetic daughters." In addition, co-twin's children become "genetic half siblings," in addition to being first cousins, because they have a genetically identical parent. In contrast, DZ twin families preserve traditional family relationships.

Co-Twin Control. Co-twin control uses only MZ twins to assess the relative contributions of maturation and experience to behavioral development. This design involves training one twin and not the other or providing different experiences to each twin. If co-twins show similar behavioral change at testing, this suggests that the intervention did not contribute to the development of that trait and that biological maturation was the more salient factor. However, co-twin differences in development suggest that training did have an effect. This method is infrequently used in psychological research, given concerns over communication between twins and/or incidental learning. It is particularly effective for drug trials or for examining the causes and consequences of co-twin differences in disease susceptibility.

Twin Relationships

A substantial body of data demonstrates closer social relations between MZ than DZ twin pairs (Segal, Hershberger, & Arad, 2003). This difference has been observed consistently among young twins (Segal, 1984, 1997), teenage twins (Mowrer, 1954), and older twins (Neyer, 2002), as well as among twins reared apart and reunited as adults (Segal et al., 2003). Convergence among research findings, despite differences in theory and method, are impressive. There has, however, been less consensus as to the factors underlying observed twin group differences.

Evolutionary Analyses Using a Twin-Based Approach

Evolutionary psychology provides a theoretical framework that can unify multidisciplinary findings (McAndrew, 2002; Mealey, 2001). The next section illustrates the use of twin and other behavioral genetic methods to test evolutionary-based hypotheses, predictions, and questions concerning social relations and relative genetic relatedness. Several ongoing studies will also be reviewed.

"Co-Conspirators" and "Double-Dealers"

Within-Pair Cooperation and Competition. These terms were borrowed from the title of an article, "Co-Conspirators and Double-Dealers: A Twin Film Analysis" (Segal, 2002). This study extends earlier work showing greater cooperation between MZ than between DZ twins on a joint puzzle-solving task (Segal, 1984, 1997). The 47 twin pairs in both analyses were specially selected from a larger sample of 105 twin pairs. Selection criteria were that both co-twins score 100 or higher on the Wechsler IQ Scale for Children-Revised (WISC-R) and that the intrapair difference in IQ score not exceed 6 points (the average MZ twin pair difference). These requirements assured that twins understood the given task and that MZ twins' performance would not be advantaged from having more matched intellectual skills than DZ twins.

Children ranged in age from 6.09 to 11.30 years of age, with a mean age of 7.94 years ($SD = 1.37$). (One pair was eliminated from some analyses due to overexposed film.) Zygosity was assessed via serological analysis or a standard physical resemblance questionnaire completed by mothers. MZ twin pairs were also classified according to concordance (HC) or discordance (HD) for handedness, by observing the hand preferred across 14 unimanual and bimanual activities. Hand discordance suggests that MZ twins originated from relatively late zygotic division, an event associated with a single chorion. Given some evidence of greater personality similarity in one-chorion twins (Sokol et al., 1995), it was of interest to compare twin group behaviors along this dimension.

In the earlier study, filmed sequences were scored for success at task completion, time to completion, positioning of the puzzle, gaze-away rate, facial expressivity, and physical gestures. Nearly all measures supported greater cooperation within MZ twin pairs.

The newer analyses compared subjective impressions of cooperative and competitive behavior provided by three independent judges (Segal, 2002). Perceptions of individuals unfamiliar with the twins bear on the question of whether individuals respond to or create MZ and DZ twins' relative behavioral resemblances and affectional ties. They also afford another approach to common questions surrounding genetic contributions to social relatedness.

Judges viewed the films and rated each along six social-interactional dimensions: Mutuality in goal, sense of "oneness" (0 = *individual effort*; 10 = *joint effort*); nature of interactions (0 = *competitive*; 10 = *cooperative*); accommodation of behavior to needs of the other (0 = *No, very little*; 10 = *Yes, very much*); evidence of role division (0 = *Children are indistinguishable*; 10 = *Children are distinguishable*); involvement in activity (0 = *unequal*; 10 = *equal*); and contribution to finished product (0 = *unequal, not balanced*; 10 = *equal, balanced*). Rank order correlations among the judges across scales ranged from .67 to .80.

Helmert contrasts were used to test hypotheses regarding twin group differences. The groups were ordered with respect to expected magnitude on the six items. The two sets of hypotheses were specified by the order of Items 1, 2, 3, 5, and 6: MZ-HC > MZ > MZ-HD > DZ; MZ-HD > MZ-HC > MZ-HC/DZ > DZ. A reversed ordering was anticipated for Item 4 (role division). In the first set of hypotheses, the overall difference between MZ and DZ twins was significant [F (6,128) = 6.25, $p < .001$]. MZ twins scored significantly higher than DZ twins on mutuality, cooperation, accommodation, involvement, and contribution, and lower on role division, as expected. However, the overall difference between MZ-HC and MZ-HD twin pairs was nonsignificant. In the second set of hypotheses, the overall difference between MZ-HD twins and the combined group of MZ-HC and DZ twins approached significance [F (6,128) = 2.08, $p < .06$]. However, the overall difference between MZ-HC and DZ twins was significant [F (6,128) = 5.30, $p < .001$]. MZ-HC twins scored significantly higher on mutuality, cooperation, accommodation, involvement, and contribution, and lower on role division. These findings, together with the earlier analyses, support the view that individuals respond to, rather than create, MZ and DZ twins' differing interactional styles.

Prisoner's Dilemma: Mutual Versus Individual Gains

The Prisoner's Dilemma (PD) game is a classic in social psychological research and in game theory. This non-zero-sum game, developed in approximately 1950 by Merrill Flood and Melvin Dresher, offers unique opportunities to explore cooperation and trust between two partners. Characteristics of the game come from the situation of two prisoners held separately by police, who wish to determine the perpetrator of a crime. If neither confesses, both will gain similarly; if both betray, then both gain little; but if one confesses while the other remains silent, then the former gains at the expense of the partner. PD has been administered to children, adolescents, and adults, with gender, ethnicity, social status, and familiarity manipulated by investigators. PD is, however, a natural experiment for exploring effects of partners' genetic relatedness on social processes and outcomes. The game is usually repeated over a series of trials. The first genetically informative experiment, using a twin research design, was reported by Segal and Hershberger (1999).

Evolutionary reasoning predicted that MZ twin adolescents and adults would show higher frequency of cooperative choices than DZ twins. Opportunities to explore related issues, such as the relationship of responses over time and possible mechanisms underlying the twins' choices (e.g., intellectual resemblance and social closeness), were also available.

Participants included 59 MZ twin pairs and 37 DZ same-sex twin pairs, ranging in age from 10.92 to 82.67 years. Co-twins were seated back-to-back and given two markers: one blue (indicating cooperation) and one red (indicating competition). When trials were called, each held up a marker and received immediate feedback from the examiner as to choices made and points accumulated. The payoff matrix is displayed in Figure 10.1. Twins were advised to follow an individualistic strategy, such that they should be interested only in their own personal gain.

Multivariate analysis of variance revealed an overall significant effect from zygosity [F (3,90) = 3.27, $p < .05$], with significant univariate effects from cooperative [F (1,92) = 7.11, $p < .01$] and competitive choices [F (1,92) = 4.35, $p < .05$]. The direction of the differences reflected greater

		Twin 1	
		Cooperate (blue)	Compete (red)
Twin 2	Cooperate (blue)	3, 3	0, 5
	Compete (red)	5, 0	1, 1

Figure 10.1   Payoff Matrix in Prisoner's Dilemma Game

cooperation among MZ twin pairs. The effects of sex approached statistical significance, while the Sex X Zygosity interaction was nonsignificant. Consistent with these findings, mutual cooperation increased across trials for MZ twins but decreased across trials for DZ twins. Even though participants completed 100 trials, data degradation was not detected.

Interestingly, despite MZ twins' more frequent cooperation, they still made more competitive than cooperative choices. This outcome suggests a "greater restraint of selfishness" on their part (Axelrod & Hamilton, 1981; Charlesworth, 1996). In other words, perhaps MZ twins cooperate more by competing less. Higher IQ, social closeness, and sharing were all associated with increased mutual cooperation. However, co-twin differences in IQ and in social closeness were unrelated to co-twin differences in cooperative choices. It may be that these two measures are too global, thus lacking specific social dimensions (e.g., trust, loyalty) underlying social cooperation.

Marble-Pull Task: Simultaneous Cooperation and Reciprocal Altruism

An insightful series of experiments was carried out using a 7.6- to 9.7-year-old twin sample from Singapore (Loh & Elliott, 1998). Twins represented Malay, Indian, Chinese, and several other populations. This study tested the hypothesis that cooperation would be greater among MZ than DZ twins but under contrasting conditions. The first condition of simultaneous cooperation (SCO) awarded every player on each successful trial, such that reward distribution was equal. The second condition of reciprocal altruism (RA) offered a reward to the successful twin only, so reward distribution was not necessarily equal. The apparatus used was a marble-pull game, in which a cup of marbles could be pulled toward either twin and delivered into the individually designated cup.

A main effect from zygosity was not detected, but a significant Zygosity X Condition effect was observed. In the SCO condition, MZ twins competed, while DZ twins cooperated. The reverse was true in the RA condition. The authors pointed out that dominance relations can show lack of stability within MZ twinships, as partners often "exchange places"; thus, reward equality offers opportunities to engage in "dominance testing," given the low risk to their relationship (Loh & Elliott, 1998, p. 408). However, when reward equality was uncertain, MZ twins behaved as though equality was a "necessary result" rather than a goal (p. 408). In such circumstances, MZ twins "reverted to their normal mode of cooperative behavior and swiftly divided the results equally between themselves" (p. 408).

In contrast with the MZ twins, DZ twins had little to contest in the SCO condition; thus, most worked in reciprocal fashion, while a few displayed dominance behavior. This was facilitated by the fact that dominance relations show greater stability in DZ twinships. This is probably associated in part with co-twins' differing behavioral styles, partly genetically based, precluding easy exchange of social roles. However, the RA condition with its unequal rewards provided the necessary edge for competition, with which DZ co-twins' behaviors were consistent. Still, despite their competitive tendencies, rewards were generally equal. In this regard, it is worth noting that in Von Bracken's (1934) study, he described two classes of DZ twin behavior: (1) When co-twins perceived ability differences between themselves, competition seemed to dampen as the more skillful twin was confident of his or her superior skill; (2) when co-twins perceived more matched abilities, competition intensified as each co-twin attempted to outdo the other.

The key contribution of Loh and Elliott's (1998) study is the suggestion that MZ and DZ twin relations may be modified by condition and context. The fact that MZ twins sometimes "compete" and DZ twins sometimes "cooperate" does not weaken overall conclusions concerning associations between genetic and social relatedness. This is because the different motivations suggested for MZ and DZ twins' exceptional behaviors make sense with reference to their degree of genetic overlap. Further testing of co-twin cooperation and competition across settings would add informatively to this area.

Fluctuating Asymmetry: Insights Into Reproductive Fitness

Fluctuating asymmetry (FA) is a recent area of interest to evolutionary psychologists. It refers to the body's departure from perfect consistency or symmetry. It has been suggested that greater FA, as reflected by increased right-left differences in wrist circumference, ear length, or facial width, may reflect greater developmental instability associated with stressful biological and environmental events. With respect to behavioral consequences, studies have shown relationships between greater FA and reduced physical attractiveness. There is also evidence that higher-FA individuals have fewer sexual partners than people with lower FA. Both outcomes are associated with reduced reproductive success.

Difficulties with this area of research concern the extent to which genetic fitness may be genetically influenced and the extent to which FA may be just one indicator of fitness. A specific concern has been the inability to separate the effects of FA from other indices of physical attractiveness (e.g., hair color, skin texture). An important step toward resolving this difficulty was undertaken by Mealey, Bridgstock, and Townsend (1999) via a co-twin control design. Standard photographs of 16 male and 18 female MZ twin pairs were used to construct left-left and right-right composite portraits of all individuals. Sixty-three individuals (25 male and 38 female) provided ratings of physical similarity (1 = *not at all similar* to 7 = *extremely similar*) and physical attractiveness (1 = *extremely unattractive* to 7 = *extremely attractive*) scales. Zygosity of the twins was assessed via serological analysis.

It was found that co-twins with lower FA were judged to be more attractive than their higher-FA co-twins. Furthermore, the degree of difference in perceived attractiveness was directly related to the degree of difference in asymmetry. This finding is exciting but is only a first step toward resolving issues of FA and reproductive fitness. Specifically, are higher-FA twins disadvantaged with respect to intelligence and mating prospects relative to their co-twins? Further study along these lines would be informative. A co-twin control design could also illuminate the controversial finding that left-handers show reduced longevity relative to right-handers because of more frequent birth-related difficulties, immune deficiencies, and accidents (Coren & Halpern, 1991). MZ twins share genes linked to disease susceptibility and other medical traits, so earlier death of left-handed (or higher-FA) twins would help clarify factors affecting longevity.

Mealey (2002) extended her line of research to explore the development of parental favoritism. She reasoned that studying MZ twins (who are not truly "identical") might offer a way to map experiential differences onto phenotypic differences and differences in life history strategy (Mealey, 2001). Twenty-five MZ twin pairs (11 male pairs and 14 female pairs) from her original 1999 twin sample completed the Parental Bonding Instrument (PBI), a 25-item, forced-choice (*almost always; frequently; not very often; almost never*) questionnaire (Parker, Tupling, & Brown, 1979). The PBI was used to obtain twins' perceptions of treatment by their mothers and fathers from childhood through age 16 years. Sample items were: "Was affectionate to me," "Tended to baby me," and "Made me feel I wasn't wanted." The primary question was: Did more symmetrical co-twins perceive preferred treatment from their parents?

Significant patterns did not emerge from these data. The only exception concerned Question 16 ("Made me feel I wasn't wanted"); however, the effect was in the reverse direction to what was predicted. In other words, less symmetric twins felt more wanted by their parents than did their more symmetric co-twins. Several explanations were proposed, but it was suggested that parents may not discriminate between twins according to their relative facial symmetry. It is also important to appreciate that childhood FA may differ from later FA, as it may be modified by significant growth periods such as those occurring during adolescence. With regard to Question 16, it was suggested that parental access to adequate resources may allow investing additional care in less healthy twins. Thus, when resources are scarce, it would make better "genetic sense" to invest resources in healthy twins.

Parenting Styles: MZ Within-Pair Differences

Observations of mothers' interacting with each of their extremely low birth weight (ELBW) premature twins tested a series of four interesting hypotheses regarding parenting preferences (Mann, 1992). They were the (1) *Healthy Baby Hypothesis,* maternal preferences are a function of infant health characteristics; (2) *First Home Hypothesis,* maternal preferences are governed by which twin arrives home first since care and attention are directed mostly at this twin; (3) *Fun Baby Hypothesis,* maternal preferences are directed toward healthier twins because they show more positive and less negative behaviors, and (4) *Basic Care Hypothesis,* both twins are likely to receive sufficient maternal care and attention.

Participants included 14 twins, comprising seven sets of ELBW twin pairs and their mothers. Mothers were observed interacting with their twin infants for a 1-hour period within 2 weeks of the twins' 4- and 8-month birthdays. Results supported the Healthy Baby Hypothesis at the 8-month visit: Mothers directed more positive behavior toward healthier twins. (This pattern was also evident at the 4-month period but only with reference to infant crying.) However, mothers who were more involved with healthy twins were also more involved with less healthy twins, and vice versa. Interestingly, mothers showing greater involvement with their twins were from higher-socioeconomic groups yet still responded to infant health status. Mann (1992) suggested that when twins are less premature, mothers might favor less healthy twins, especially when co-twins require less care. Such tendencies would favor the survival of both twins and be reproductively advantageous to the parent. However, a feature of this study compromising interpretation of the results is that the twins' zygosity was not determined. It is possible that mothers' different responses to each twin were a partial function of genetically based differences, as would be likely for DZ pairs.

Twin-Family Study: Twins and Their Preferences for Nieces and Nephews

The twin-family study design has been used to investigate genetic and environmental influences on physical and behavioral characteristics (Segal, 2000a). A particularly elegant application of this method was reported by Gottesman and Bertelsen (1989) using a Danish twin sample. Families composed of MZ and DZ twins discordant for schizophrenia, who were both married with children, were identified from an existing twin study. Children of well and ill MZ co-twins were at similar risk (17.4% and 16.8%), whereas children of well and ill DZ co-twins were at dissimilar risk (2.1% and 17.4%). These findings suggest that MZ twins inherit the same genetically influenced predisposition that can be transmitted to children even by co-twins not expressing the disorder. Furthermore, being raised by a schizophrenic parent is not requisite to children's developing psychopathology. Until now, the twin-family design has been completely ignored by evolutionary psychologists interested in genetic contributions to social relatedness.

An ongoing project at the Twin Studies Center, at California State University, Fullerton, is administering parental preference questionnaires to adult MZ and DZ twins who have nieces and nephews. Recall that MZ twins' nieces and nephews are their "genetic children," so they share closer genetic relations with them than do DZ twins' nieces and nephews. This Internet-based study *(http://psych.fullerton.edu/nsegal/twinparent/)* requests information concerning feelings about caring for the child, being with the child, closeness to the child, and involvement with the child. One prediction is that greater investment in care and concern should be directed to nieces and nephews by MZ twin aunts and uncles than by DZ twin aunts and uncles. Such tests can reveal whether individuals respond to the genetically defined relationship or to the culturally defined relationship. Perhaps both MZ and DZ twin aunts occasionally provide child care for their nieces, with MZ twin aunts doing so more often. One could argue that if MZ twin aunts provide more frequent care for nieces and nephews, then this would explain feelings of increased closeness. However, an evolutionary-based interpretation would consider that the higher proportion of genes shared between MZ twin aunts and their nieces and nephews might underlie the relationship, resulting in more frequent contact.

Twins, Virtual Twins, and Best Friends: Disparate Loyalties?

Virtual twins (VT) are same-age unrelated children raised together since birth. Given that most do not look physically alike, they more closely approach the situation of DZ than MZ twins. They arise when families adopt two near-in-age children at the same time or adopt one child close in time to the delivery of a biological child. Their value in developmental research is that they replay psychological twinship but without the genetic link. Thus, they allow interesting tests of genetic and environmental contributions to behavioral phenotypes.

A study of general intelligence was undertaken based on 90 VT pairs (Segal, 2000b). Participants' mean age at the time of testing was 7.97 years ($SD = 8.50$, $n = 177$) and ranged between 4.01 to 54.84 years. The majority of individuals (70%) were under 7 years of age. An IQ intraclass correlation of .26 was found. Corresponding correlations for reared-together MZ (MZT) and DZ (DZT) twins and MZA twins are .85, .60, and .78, respectively (Plomin, DeFries, McClearn, & McGuffin, 2001). Genetic influence on general cognitive development is thus demonstrated. (Note that the .26 VT correlation is based mostly on children living together, when family effects are most pronounced. In contrast, the .78 MZA correlation is based mostly on adults living apart, when family effects tend to dissipate. Assessing VT pairs as adults would most likely yield a correlation below .26.) Profile analyses of special mental abilities also show genetic influence when compared with findings for twins: MZ: .45; DZ: .24; VT: .08 (Segal, 2000b).

Factors underlying obesity have also been of recent interest, given dramatic increases in overweight children and adults. Joint analyses of MZ and DZ twins and VTs revealed a significant contribution from the shared environment (Segal & Allison, 2002). It was suggested that previous studies may have underestimated this variance component, due to insufficient power or ability to detect it.

VT pairs are a recent addition to behavioral genetic methods. Coupled with twin research designs, they can help address issues of social relatedness. Intuitively, it is reasonable to suppose that VT pairs should show levels of cooperation and competition similar to those of DZ twins, but some preliminary data suggest otherwise. Reproduced below in Table 10.1 are responses to a social relationship survey administered to members of an 18-year-old male DZ twin pair and their near-in-age adopted brother.

Table 10.1   Social Closeness Measures From a DZ Twin Pair and VT Sibling

Respondent	DZ1	DZ2	VT
DZ1	—	Best friends	Casual friends
DZ2	Best friends	—	Casual friends
VT	Best-casual friends	Best friends	—

Both DZ twins characterized their own relationship as that of "best friends" but characterized their relationship to their unrelated brother as that of "casual friends." Note further that the adopted brother views his relationship with each twin as closer than each twin does with him ("casual-best friends" and "best friends," respectively). Thus, there is agreement between the twins and lack of agreement between the two VT pairs. Additional data are being gathered from adult sets in this sample; however, nearly 75% of the sample are children below the age of 6 years.

An ongoing collaborative study, "Twins, Virtual Twins, and Friends: Peers and Adjustment," between researchers at the University of San Francisco (McGuire) and California State University, Fullerton (Segal), is using twins, virtual twins, and best friends to study sibling socialization effects on behavioral similarity and adjustment. Among other things, partners will complete a Prisoner's Dilemma game, coordination tasks, and social relationship questionnaires. Contrasts between twins and VTs will uniquely assess evolutionary-based hypotheses regarding genetic and experiential effects on sibling relations. The VT-best friend comparison will be quite interesting given that VTs do not choose to be together, while best friends do. The twin-friend comparisons will be especially illuminating: Best friends may profess the same or greater loyalty to one another in some contexts (e.g., providing daily assistance) but not in others (e.g., life-and-death situations).

Special Topics in Evolutionary Analysis

Twins Reared Apart: Evolutionary-Based Analyses

Reared-apart twins have been an understandable favorite among behavioral genetic investigators. Studying the rare group of MZA twins provides a direct estimate of genetic influence on measured traits. This is because twins are brought up separately, most often with minimal or no contact until adulthood. Studying DZA twins offers further tests of interactions and offers an important control group. To date, there have been seven major studies of reared-apart twins, conducted in the United States, Great Britain, Denmark,

Japan, Sweden, and Finland (Segal, 2003). A wealth of psychological, physical, and medical science data demonstrate that genetic effects are pervasive across these domains (see Segal, 2000a). At the same time, studies of reared-apart twins also offer keen insights into environmental influences; MZ twin differences are associated with environmental differences (pre-, peri- and/or postnatal), given their genetic identity.

This body of work is not without critics, especially when it comes to studies of general intelligence. Primary objections have concerned age at separation (i.e., twins separated later should be more alike because they spent more time together); reunion in childhood (i.e., twins reunited prior to testing will be more alike than those reunited later); rearing by relatives (i.e., twins reared by relatives will be more similar than twins reared by nonrelatives); and similarity in social environments (i.e., similarity in twins' social environments, including type of school and years of education, will be associated with behavioral similarity) (Taylor, 1980). These arguments have, however, been tested and have been found to be without merit (Bouchard, 1993, 1997; Bouchard, Lykken, McGue, Segal, & Tellegen, 1990).

Twins reared apart are also a natural for assessing many evolutionary-based questions and hypotheses. A seminal paper by Crawford and Anderson (1989) summarized some theoretical and applied aspects of such efforts. This may be the first major paper to have brought a behavioral genetic research strategy to bear upon evolutionary issues.

Life Histories, Strategies, and Tactics

Crawford and Anderson (1989) discussed concepts of genetically organized life histories and environmentally contingent strategies for incorporating them. *Life histories* are genetically organized life courses, including individuals' time, energy, and resource allocation. *Strategies* refer to systematic rules and decisions during different life stages. *Tactics* are behavioral patterns resulting from applying rules and decision-making processes. They encourage attention to behaviors that show low heritability, are related to reproductive function, and whose sensitivity to environmental conditions would have been adaptive during ancestral times.

These authors proposed using MZA twins to assess life histories and their associated features. Specifically, MZA twins would be organized according to hypotheses about genetically based life history traits. This would allow testing of predictions about how environmental conditions and contexts can lead to specific tactics. It is a type of co-twin control design writ large.

A proposed study described in that paper would address the behavioral consequences of father absence and presence in the home on the timing of sexual maturation. Previous research suggests that father absence is associated with precocious pubertal development in females (Belsky, Steinberg, & Draper, 1991; Ellis & Garber, 2000). It is reasoned that girls exposed to early stressful environments, such as that posed by an absent father, would experience depression, weight gain, early sexual development, and unstable relationships. Studying reared-apart twins would allow a closer look at how different environments affect developmental processes in genetically matched individuals. Of course, difficulties in identifying sufficiently large samples of twins reared apart and organizing them by rearing environment makes such efforts unlikely, although not impossible. One difficulty has been lack of an evolutionary perspective by investigators undertaking such analyses in other behavioral domains. In addition, the idea that father absence predicts early sexual maturity has been challenged by behavioral geneticists who find that timing of menarche and pubertal development shows substantial heritability (Rowe, 2000). Other recent work suggests parent-daughter transmission of the androgen receptor genes as an alternative explanation for associations between father absence and sexual maturity (Comings, Muhleman, Johnson, & MacMurray, 2002).

Birth Order

Birth order and its effects on personality have been uniquely addressed in a recent comprehensive theory (Sulloway, 1996). Sulloway reasoned that children in a family, in an effort to secure their share of parental resources, will try to fill specific family niches. Firstborns tend to be traditional, conforming, and upholders of family values, in contrast with laterborns, who are less traditional, less conforming, and avid seekers of rebellious exploits. An informative test of this theory would involve MZA twins who occupied different birth orders within their separate rearing families (Segal & MacDonald, 1998). MZ twins (reared apart and together) show correlations of approximately .50 for most personality traits. It would, therefore, be important to know how twins' different birth positions might modify the Big Five personality trait of Openness to Experience. Again, identifying a sufficient number of pairs to fill essential subject cells is challenging. However, such an analysis is planned using reared-apart twin data from Sweden.

Reproductive Characteristics and Reproductive Success: Twins Reared Apart

To the extent that variation in individuals' reproductive success is related to heritable characteristics, those characteristics will be differentially transmitted into future generations. Mealey and Segal (1993) applied a reared-apart twin approach to assess the extent to which reproduction-related behaviors evidence genetic influence and to identify factors affecting reproduction-related events.

The sample included 82 reared-apart twin pairs, comprised of 21 MZ male pairs, 34 MZ female pairs, 7 DZ male pairs, and 20 DZ female pairs. Mean ages were 38.2 years ($SD = 14.5$) for males and 42.2 years ($SD = 10.7$) for females. All had participated in the Minnesota Study of Twins Reared Apart at the University of Minnesota. Data were drawn from an extensive Life History Interview and the Briggs Life History Questionnaire.

Genetic influence was found for a number of personality and health-related measures, such as activity level, shyness, childhood health, and teenage health. In contrast, genetic effects on number of children were not found, despite genetic influence on age at first date and age at first marriage. Males' reproduction-related behaviors were more highly influenced by both heritable and nonheritable effects than were those of females. Females' responses to items concerned with family dynamics and marital relations were more variously influenced than were those of males. These results support evolutionary models positing sex differences in reproduction-related behaviors. However, reproductive success was related only to childhood health and only in males. It may be that despite genetic influence on relevant proximal mechanisms, these mechanisms are no longer relevant to offspring number.

Social Closeness and Familiarity

A series of social relatedness studies have been undertaken using MZ and DZ twins raised together. However, twins reared apart offer a unique vehicle for exploring the nature of social closeness and familiarity and their underlying mechanisms. This is because the twins have grown up apart in the absence of previous social contact. In the event that twins were reared with near-in-age unrelated siblings, further tests of influences affecting social relatedness become possible. In this case, individuals are frequent interactants but share no common genes. A review of biographical summaries included in previous reared-apart twin studies shows that 40 of the 76 pairs enjoyed close social relations after reunion, while 14 pairs did not (Segal et al., 2003). The remaining 22 pairs were hard to judge, given unclear descriptions and/or because social contact was decided by young twins' adoptive families. However, systematic analyses of social relatedness measures were not completed.

The Minnesota Study of Twins Reared Apart offered a valuable opportunity to compare reunion experiences and subsequent social relations in MZA and DZA twins. Evolutionary reasoning suggested that MZA twins would experience greater social closeness and familiarity than DZA twins. It was also expected that degree of contact prior to assessment would not be associated with social relatedness. Third, it was predicted that twins' perceptions of their degree of physical similarity would correlate positively with the nature of their social relations. Finally, it was anticipated that reunited twins would feel socially closer and more familiar to one another than to the unrelated siblings with whom they were raised. Possible links between social relations and personality traits, interests, values, and education were also assessed.

Participants included 44 MZA twin pairs, 33 DZA twin pairs, and 7 individual twins and triplets. Twins ranged in age from 16 to 70 years, with a mean age of 45.28 years $(SD = 13.68)$. Age at separation ranged from 0 to 54.08 months, with a mean age of 8.03 months $(SD = 12.64)$. Additional descriptive data are available in Segal et al. (2003). Twins completed a comprehensive Twin Relationship Survey, which asked many questions about adoption and reunion. Comparative ratings of four key items (immediate closeness and familiarity, current closeness and familiarity) are presented.

Twins' current perception of physical similarity correlated significantly with current closeness $(r = .28, p < .01, n = 157)$ and with current familiarity $(r = .33, p < .01, n = 157)$. Age and sex were unrelated to perceptions of physical resemblance. A repeated measures analysis of variance compared MZA-DZA twin differences in initial and current closeness and familiarity. The effect of zygosity was statistically significant $[F (1,80) = 6.26, p < .01]$, and, as anticipated, MZA twins indicated greater closeness and familiarity than DZA twins. Significant within-subject effects were observed for Feeling $[F (1,80) = 7.55, p < .01]$ and Time $[F (1,80) = 5.32 p < .05]$. Specifically, twins experienced greater closeness than familiarity toward their co-twins, and current ratings generally exceeded initial ratings. A significant Feeling by Time effect $[F (1,80) = 26.34 p < .001]$ indicated increased familiarity across time but little change in closeness. Interactions involving zygosity were not significant.

Analysis of twins' current closeness and familiarity ratings for their adoptive siblings offered an informative contrast to the reunited twin data. The sample size was reduced, given that some twins had been raised as singletons. Data were analyzed using a repeated measures design that included two within-subject factors: Relative (twin and sibling) and Feeling (closeness and familiarity). All tests of within-subject effects were statistically significant or approached significance: [Relative: $F (1,40) = 26.79, p < .001$; Feeling: $F (1,40) = 3.19, p < .08$; and Relative by Feeling: $F (1,40) = 3.78, p < .06$]. Feelings were stronger for co-twins than for adoptive siblings, and feelings of familiarity were higher than feelings of closeness. Twins rated co-twin closeness and co-twin familiarity equally, but they rated adoptive sibling familiarity higher than adoptive sibling closeness. It is revealing that despite knowing the adoptive sibling for a much longer time than the twin, respondents felt socially closer to their co-twins. This suggests that social rapport was readily established, perhaps via similarities in genetically influenced traits. This issue was also addressed.

Twins' self-reports of personality traits, interests, values, and educational measures were available. However, few statistically significant relationships emerged between these variables and the social closeness measures. Nevertheless, it may be too soon to conclude that social relatedness is unaffected by co-twin resemblance in selected phenotypic traits; perhaps the specific measures used failed to capture features relevant to social relatedness. It may also be that twins' *perceptions* of their similarities in intelligence, personality, and other areas would prove more informative than their self-ratings. Reunited twins' evolving relations may also be a partial function of interpersonal factors not assessed in the present study (e.g., trust and openness), which are highly valued in twin relationships (Foy, Vernon, & Jang, 2001).

Loss of a Twin

Evolutionary hypotheses concerning bereavement parallel those concerning cooperation. If cooperation and closeness are associated with increased genetic relatedness, then response to that loss should also vary as a function of common genes. A twin study tests the prediction that surviving MZ twins grieve more for deceased co-twins than do surviving DZ twins. A comprehensive twin study of bereavement was initiated in 1983 at the University of Minnesota, with the dual objectives of (1) examining differences in grief-related behaviors between MZ and DZ twins and (2) assessing differences in twins' responses to losing a twin and losing other relatives. This study is currently ongoing in the Twin Studies Center at California State University, Fullerton.

Reports from this study vary with respect to sample size, although the current sample exceeds 500. Analyses have demonstrated that surviving MZ twins do, in fact, rate both immediate and current grief intensity higher than surviving DZ twins (Segal, 1997; Segal & Bouchard, 1993; Segal & Ream, 1998). MZ twins also score higher across most bereavement scales of the Grief Intensity Inventory (GEI) than do DZ twins (Segal, Wilson, Bouchard, & Gitlin, 1995; also see Segal & Roy, 2001). Surviving twins (both MZ and DZ) also express more intense grief for the loss of the co-twin than for other relatives. (Fortunately, few twins have lost children, precluding this comparison from the study.)

Recent analyses have continued to apply evolutionary and psychobiological perspectives to questions of grief and mourning. Segal and Blozis (2002) assessed coping and health characteristics immediately following loss (retrospective) and currently. The statistically significant effect of zygosity on current grief implicated correlates of grief in the bereavement process. Consistent with psychobiological theory, the closeness of the twin relationship was associated with grief intensity, which affected physical symptoms and coping efficacy in expected directions. In a related study, Segal, Sussman, Marelich, Mearns, and Blozis (2002) compared retrospective and current GEI scale scores for surviving MZ and DZ twins via discriminant function and profile analysis. The data yielded supportive findings but for the retrospective group only. This was a somewhat surprising finding because earlier analyses showed less change in grief intensity over time for MZ than DZ twins (Segal & Ream, 1998). However, Segal and Ream studied change within individuals, while Segal et al. (2002) studied change across groups.

Summary

The goal of this chapter has been to identify points of commonality between the disciplines of behavioral genetics and evolutionary psychology. This was done chiefly via a series of genetically informed studies whose hypotheses were generated with reference to evolutionary reasoning. Most outcomes were consistent with kinship-genetic expectations, yet evolutionary psychology is not intended to replace other interpretive frameworks. Given that different proximal mechanisms may underlie observed associations between genetic relatedness and altruistic behavior, reference to multiple theoretical perspectives should assist in their identification. For example, Korchmaros and Kenny (2001) found that emotional closeness partly mediates the effect of genetic relatedness on willingness to perform altruistic acts. Leek and Smith (1991) observed that relatives' perceived similarity in personality correlates with various help and conflict measures. It should also be recalled that specific forms of recognition have been linked with specific physiological and psychological events. Finally, qualities such as trust and openness, valued in twin relationships, may affect other relationships, as well (see Foy et al., 2001). Thus, while evolutionary psychology can offer an additional level of analysis, adding richness to our understanding of complex human traits, it can be significantly assisted by other viewpoints and perspectives.

Twin and adoption studies are natural experiments well suited to probing a wide range of hypotheses and questions concerning genetic relatedness and social behavior. While efforts along these lines remain relatively few, new collaborations between behavioral geneticists and evolutionary psychologists are evident. Future work along these lines would be welcome as sophisticated new twin methodologies are being developed. These events, together with data provided by the Human Genome Project, should substantially extend what we know, and can know, from behavioral genetic and evolutionary approaches to human behavioral problems and issues.

References

Axelrod, R., & Hamilton, W. D. (1981). The evolution of cooperation. *Science, 211,* 1390-1396.

Belsky, J., Steinberg, L., & Draper, P. (1991). Childhood experience, interpersonal development, and reproductive strategy: An evolutionary theory of socialization. *Child Development, 62,* 647-670.

Bomsel-Helmreich, O., & Mufti, W. A. (1995). The mechanism of monozygosity and double ovulation. In L. G. Keith, E. Papiernik, D. M. Keith, & B. Luke (Eds.), *Multiple pregnancy: Epidemiology, gestation and perinatal outcome* (pp. 25-40). New York: Parthenon.

Bouchard, T. J. Jr. (1993). Do environmental similarities explain the similarity in intelligence of identical twins reared apart? *Intelligence, 7,* 175-184.

Bouchard, T. J. Jr. (1997). IQ similarity in twins reared apart: Findings and responses to critics. In R. J. Sterberg & E. L. Grigorenko (Eds.), *Intelligence: Heredity and environment* (pp. 126-160). New York: Cambridge University Press.

Bouchard, T. J. Jr., Lykken, D. T., McGue, M., Segal, N. L., & Tellegen, A. (1990). Sources of human psychological differences: The Minnesota Study of Twins Reared Apart. *Science, 250,* 223-228.

Bryan, E. M. (1992). *Twins and multiple births.* New York: Little, Brown.

Bulmer, M. G. (1970). *The biology of twinning in man.* Oxford, UK: Clarendon.

Buss, D. M. (1984). Evolutionary biology and personality psychology: Toward a conception of human nature and individual differences. *American Psychologist, 39,* 1135-1147.

Charlesworth, W. R. (1996). Cooperation and competition: contributions to an evolutionary and developmental model. *International Journal of Behavioral Development, 19,* 25-39.

Comings, D. E., Muhleman, D., Johnson, J. P., & MacMurray, J. P. (2002). Parent-daughter transmission of the androgen receptor gene as an explanation of the effect of father absence on age at menarche. *Child Development, 73,* 1046-1051.

Coren, S., & Halpern, D. F. (1991). Left-handedness: A marker for decreased survival fitness. *Psychological Bulletin, 109,* 90-106.

Crawford, C. B., & Anderson, J. L. (1989). Sociobiology: An environmentalist discipline. *American Psychologist, 44,* 1449-1459.

Dawkins, R. (1990). *The selfish gene* (2nd ed.). Oxford, UK: Oxford University Press.

Ellis, B. J., & Garber, J. (2000). Psychosocial antecedents of variation in girls' pubertal timing: Maternal depression, stepfather presence, and marital and family stress. *Child Development, 71*, 485-501.

Forbes, L. S. (1997). The evolutionary biology of spontaneous abortion in humans. *Trends in Ecology and Evolution, 12*, 446-450.

Foy, A. K., Vernon, P. A., & Jang, K. (2001). Examining the dimensions of intimacy in twin and peer relationships. *Twin Research, 4*, 43-52.

Freedman, D. G. (1979). *Human sociobiology*. New York: Free Press.

Goldsmith, H. H. (1991). A zygosity questionnaire for young twins: A research note. *Behavior Genetics, 21*, 257-269.

Gottesman, I. I., & Bertelsen, A. (1989). Confirming unexpressed genotypes for schizophrenia. *Archives of General Psychiatry, 46*, 867-872.

Hahn, M. E. (1990). Approaches to the study of genetic influence on developing social behavior. In M. E. Hahn, J. K. Hewitt, N. D. Henderson, & R. H. Benno (Eds.), *Developmental behavior genetics: Neurological, biochemical, and evolutionary approaches* (pp. 60-80). New York: Oxford University Press.

Hamilton, W. D. (1964). The genetical evolution of human behaviour. *Journal of Theoretical Biology, 7*, 1-52.

Hecht, B. R. (1995). The impact of assisted reproductive technology on the incidence of multiple gestation. In L. G. Keith, E. Papiernik, D. M. Keith, & B. Luke (Eds.), *Multiple pregnancy: Epidemiology, gestation and perinatal outcome* (pp. 175-190). New York: Parthenon.

Hettema, J. M., Neale, M. C., & Kendler, K. S. (1995). Physical similarity and the equal-environment assumption in twin studies of psychiatric disorders. *Behavior Genetics, 25*, 327-335.

James, W. H. (1986). Dizygotic twinning, cycle day of insemination, and erotic potential of orthodox Jews. *American Journal of Human Genetics, 39*, 542-544.

James, W. H. (1992). Coital frequency and twinning. *Journal of Biosocial Science, 24*, 135-136.

Jørgensen, A. L., Philip, J., Raskind, W. H., Matsushita, M., Christensen, B., Dreyer, V., et al. (1992). Different patterns of X inactivation in MZ twins discordant for red-green color-vision deficiency. *American Journal of Human Genetics, 51*, 291-298.

Keller, M., Thiessen, D., & Young, R. K. (1996). Mate assortment in dating and married couples. *Personality and Individual Differences, 21*, 217-221.

Korchmaros, J. D., & Kenny, D. A. (2001). Emotional closeness as a mediator of the effect of genetic relatedness on altruism. *Psychological Science, 12*, 262-265.

Krotz, S., Fajardo, J., Ghandi, S., Patel, A., & Keith, L. G. (2002). Hypertensive disease in twin pregnancies: A review. *Twin Research, 5*, 8-14.

Leek, M., & Smith, P. K. (1991). Cooperation and conflict in three-generation families. In P. K. Smith (Ed.), *The psychology of grandparenthood: An international perspective* (pp. 177-194). London: Routledge.

Lichtenstein, P., Olaussen, P. O., & Kallen, A. J. (1996). Twin births to mothers who are twins: A registry-based study. *British Medical Journal, 6,* 879-881.

Loh, C. Y., & Elliott, J. M. (1998). Cooperation and competition as a function of zygosity in 7- to 9-year-old twins. *Evolution and Human Behavior, 19,* 397-411.

Mann, J. (1992). Nurturance or negligence: Maternal psychology and behavioral preference among preterm twins. In J. H. Barkow, L. Cosmides, & J. Tooby (Eds.), *The adapted mind: Evolutionary psychology and the evolution of culture* (pp. 367-390). New York: Oxford University Press.

Martin, J. A., & Park, M. M. (1999). Trends in twin and triplet births: 1980-97. *National Vital Statistics Reports, 47,* 1-17.

Mastroiacovo, P., Castilla, E. E., Arpino, C., Cocchi, G., Goujard, J., Marinacci, C., et al. (1999). "Congenital malformations in twins: An international study." *American Journal of Medical Genetics, 83,* 117-124.

McAndrew, F. T. (2002). New evolutionary perspectives on altruism: Multilevel-selection and costly-signaling theories. *Current Directions in Psychological Science, 11,* 79-82.

McGuire, M. T., Fawzy, F. I., Spar, J. E., Weigel, R. M., & Troisi, A. (1994). Altruism and mental disorders. *Ethology and Sociobiology, 15,* 299-321.

Mealey, L. (2001). Kinship: The ties that bind (disciplines). In H. R. Holcomb III (Ed.), *Conceptual challenges in evolutionary psychology: Innovative research strategies* (pp. 19-38). Dordrecht, The Netherlands: Kluwer.

Mealey, L. (2002, June 19-23). *Do parents show favoritism for their symmetric children?* Paper presented at the meeting of the Human Behavior and Evolutionary Society (HBES), New Brunswick, NJ.

Mealey, L., Bridgstock, R., & Townsend, G. C. (1999). Symmetry and perceived facial attractiveness: A monozygotic co-twin comparison. *Journal of Personality and Social Psychology, 76,* 157-165.

Mealey, L., & Segal, N. I. (1993). Heritable and environmental variables affect reproduction-related behaviors, but not ultimate reproductive success. *Personality and Individual Differences, 14,* 783-794.

Mowrer, E. (1954). Some factors in the affectional adjustment of twins. *American Sociological Review, 19,* 468-471.

Murphy, M. F. G., Broeders, M. J. M., Carpenter, L. M., Gunnarskog, J., & Leon, D. A. (1997). Breast cancer risk in mothers of twins. *British Journal of Cancer, 75,* 1066-1068.

Neyer, F. J. (2002). Twin relationships in old age: A developmental perspective. *Personality and Social Relationships, 19,* 155-177.

Nichols, R. C., & Bilbro, W. C. Jr. (1966). The diagnosis of twin zygosity. *Acta Genetica et Statistica Medica, 16,* 265-275.

Parker, G., Tupling, H., & Brown, L. (1979). A parental bonding instrument. *British Journal of Medical Psychology, 52,* 1-10.

Plomin, R., DeFries, J. C., McClearn, G. E., & McGuffin, P. (2001). *Behavioral genetics.* (4th ed.). New York: Worth Publishers.

Rhine, S. A., Nance, W. E., Melin, J. R., & Skidmore, C. E. (1974, October-November). *Familial twinning: A possible example of superfetation in man.* Paper presented at the International Twin Congress, Rome, Italy.

Richards, B., Skoletsky, J., Shuber, A. P., Balfour, R., Stern, R.C., Dorkin, H. L., et al. (1993). Multiplex PCR amplification from the CFTR gene using DNA prepared from buccal brushes/swabs. *Human Molecular Genetics, 2,* 159-163.

Rowe, D. C. (2000). Environmental and genetic influences on pubertal development: evolutionary life history traits? In J. L. Rodgers, D. C. Rowe, & W. B. Miller (Eds.), *Genetic influences on human fertility and sexuality.* Boston: Kluwer.

Rowe, D. C., Woulbroun, E. J., & Gulley, B. L. (1994). Peers and friends as nonshared environmental influences. In E. M. Hetherington, D. Reiss, & R. Plomin (Eds.), *Separate social worlds of siblings: The impact of nonshared environment on development* (pp. 159-173). Hillsdale, NJ: Erlbaum.

Scarr, S. (1995). Psychology will be truly evolutionary when behavior genetics is included. *Psychological Inquiry, 6,* 68-71.

Scott, J. P. (1977). Social genetics. *Behavior Genetics, 7,* 327-346.

Scott, J. P. (1989). *The evolution of social systems.* New York: Gordon & Breach.

Scott, J. P. (1997). Genetic analysis of social behavior. In N. L. Segal, G. E. Weisfeld, & C. C. Weisfeld (Eds.), *Uniting psychology and biology: Integrative perspectives on human development* (pp. 131-144). Washington, DC: APA Press.

Segal, N. L. (1984). Cooperation, competition and altruism within twin sets: A reappraisal. *Ethology and Sociobiology, 5,* 163-177.

Segal, N. L. (1990). The importance of twin studies for individual differences research. *Journal of Counseling and Development, 68,* 612-622.

Segal, N. L. (1993). Twin, sibling and adoption methods: Tests of evolutionary hypotheses. *American Psychologist, 48,* 943-956.

Segal, N. L. (1997). Twin research perspective on human development. In N. L. Segal, G. E. Weisfeld, & C. C. Weisfeld (Eds.), *Uniting psychology and biology: Integrative perspectives on human development* (pp. 145-173). Washington, DC: APA Press.

Segal, N. L. (2000a). *Entwined lives: Twins and what they tell us about human behavior.* New York: Plume.

Segal, N. L. (2000b). Virtual twins: New findings on within-family environmental influences on intelligence. *Journal of Educational Psychology, 92,* 442-448.

Segal, N. L. (2002). Co-conspirators and double-dealers: A twin film analysis. *Personality and Individual Differences, 33,* 621-631.

Segal, N. L. (2003). Spotlights (reared-apart twin researchers); research sampling; literature, politics, photography and athletics. *Twin Research, 6,* 72-81.

Segal, N. L., & Allison, D. B. (2002). Twins and virtual twins: Bases of relative body weight revisited. *International Journal of Obesity, 26,* 437-441.

Segal, N. L., & Blozis, S. A. (2002). Psychobiological and evolutionary perspectives on coping and health characteristics following loss: A twin study. *Twin Research, 5,* 175-187.

Segal, N. L., & Bouchard, T. J. Jr. (1993). Grief intensity following the loss of a twin and other close relatives: Test of kinship-genetic hypotheses. *Human Biology, 65,* 87-105.

Segal, N. L., & Hershberger, S. L. (1999). Cooperation and competition in adolescent twins: Findings from a Prisoner's Dilemma game. *Evolution and Human Behavior, 20,* 29-51.

Segal, N. L., Hershberger, N. L., & Arad, S. (2003). Meeting one's twin: Perceived social closeness and familiarity. *Evolutionary psychology.* Available at *(http://human-nature.com/ep/articles/ep017095.html).*

Segal, N. L., & MacDonald, K. B. (1998). Behavior genetics and evolutionary psychology: A unified perspective. In J. Gilger & S. L. Hershberger (Eds.), *Advances in human behavioral genetics: A synthesis of quantitative and molecular approaches* [Special Issue]. *Human Biology, 70,* 159-184.

Segal, N. L., & Ream, S. L. (1998). Decrease in grief intensity for deceased twin and non-twin relatives: An evolutionary perspective. *Personality and Individual Differences, 25,* 317-325.

Segal, N. L., & Roy, A. (2001). Suicidal attempts and ideation in twins whose co-twins' deaths were non-suicides: Replication and elaboration. *Personality and Individual Differences, 31,* 445-452.

Segal, N. L., Sussman, L. S., Marelich, W. D., Mearns, J., & Blozis, S. A. (2002). Monozygotic and dizygotic twins' retrospective and current bereavement-related behaviors: An evolutionary perspective. *Twin Research, 5,* 188-195.

Segal, N. L., Wilson, S. M., Bouchard, T. J. Jr., & Gitlin, D. G. (1995). Comparative grief experiences of bereaved twins and other bereaved relatives. *Personality and Individual Differences, 18,* 511-524.

Sherman, P. W., and Holmes, W. G. (1985). Kin recognition: Issues and evidence. In B. Hölldobler and M. Lindauer (Eds.), *Experimental behavioral ecology and sociobiology: In memoriam Karl von Frisch 1886-1982* (pp. 437-460). Sunderland, MA: Sinauer.

Singh, S. M., Murphy, B., & O'Reilly, R. (2002). Epigenetic contributors to the discordance of monozygotic twins. *Clinical Genetics, 62,* 97-103.

Sokol, D. K., Moore, C. A., Rose, R. J., Williams, C. J., Reed, T., & Christian, J. C. (1995). Intrapair differences in personality and cognitive ability among young monozygotic twins distinguished by chorion type. *Behavior Genetics, 25,* 457-466.

Sulloway, F. J. (1996). *Born to rebel.* New York: Pantheon.

Taylor, H. F. (1980). *The IQ game: A methodological inquiry into the heredity-environment controversy.* New Brunswick, NJ: Rutgers University Press.

Trivers, R. L. (1972). Parental investment and sexual selection. In B. Campbell (Ed.). *Sexual selection and the descent of man: 1871-1971* (pp. 136-179). Chicago: Aldine.

Trivers, R. L. (1985). *Social evolution.* Menlo Park, CA: Benjamin/Cummings Publishing.

Uchida, I. A., DeSa, D. J., & Whelan, D. T. (1983). 45,X/46XX mosaicism in discordant monozygotic twins. *Pediatrics, 71,* 413-417.

Ventura, S. J., Martin, J. A., Curtin, S. C., Menacker, F., & Hamilton, B. E. (2001). Births: Final data for 1999. *National Vital Statistics Reports, 49,* 1-100.

Von Bracken, H. (1934). Mutual intimacy in twins. *Character and Personality, 2,* 293-309.

11

An Analysis of
Child Maltreatment

From Behavioral Psychology
to Behavioral Ecology

Robert L. Burgess and Alicia A. Drais-Parrillo

I n 1962, Kempe and his colleagues shocked the general public and the
scientific community with their publication of the influential and now
classical paper on "the battered child syndrome" (Kempe, Silverman, Steele,
Droegemueller, & Silver, 1962). Virtually overnight, we were jolted out of
our tendency to view the family, as Christoper Lasch (1977) put it, as a
"haven in a heartless world" and were forced to face the stark realization
that a large number of children were not experiencing the idyllic fictional
childhood portrayed on television. On the contrary, many children were
being grossly abused and neglected. An outraged population, fanned by
media obsessed with this controversial issue, demanded information and
explanations immediately. The scientific community set out to placate and
pacify the public, and there was an explosion of research on the maltreatment of children.

As so often happens in a newly developing area of research, progress was
uneven and made all the more so because researchers from various disciplines and research traditions entered the foray. They arrived with their own

theoretical biases as well as their own customary research methods. For example, the earliest investigators, trained in the various specialties of medicine, emphasized the role of psychopathology (Kempe, 1973; Spinetta & Rigler, 1972). Their research was based on small clinical samples. Psychologists expanded on their efforts and explored the role of certain personality traits, such as depression, aggressiveness, and suspiciousness, as correlates of child abuse and neglect (e.g., Brunquell, Crichton, & Egeland, 1981). In response to this, researchers trained in sociology, social work, and the ecology of individual development argued that our focus should be on the forces in society, such as economic and social impoverishment, that lead adults to abuse or neglect their children (e.g., Garbarino, 1977; Gelles, 1973; Gil, 1970; Straus, Gelles, & Steinmetz, 1981).

All of these early efforts were important and contributed pieces to the puzzle of why parents might behave in ways that were harmful to their own children. Nevertheless, as a researcher trained in the experimental analysis of behavior, the first author was dissatisfied with these early approaches for several reasons. Perhaps the most important was the failure to distinguish between "marker" and "process" variables. Even if poverty conditions or certain personality traits were reliably correlated with maltreatment, it was important to recognize that those connections were not invariant. For example, even if the likelihood of maltreatment was higher under conditions of impoverishment, the fact remained that most poor people did not abuse or neglect their children. What needed to be accomplished was the identification of the actual processes that lead from poverty (or maternal depression) to maltreatment. This led to the formulation of a "social interactional" approach (Burgess, 1979) and a series of investigations termed Project Interact.

A Social Interactional Approach

The social interactional perspective incorporated several features that were unique to the study of child maltreatment at that time. Among those distinctive features were certain assumptions, a few of which we will describe here. The first assumption, based on a behavioral or operant perspective, was that critical process variables were most likely to be found in interpersonal contingencies of reinforcement or punishment operating within families. Following upon the work of Patterson (e.g., 1976), the second assumption was that these contingencies would be evident from the day-to-day social interactions that transpired between parents and their children and that these should be observed and recorded in the natural ecology of the family.

The third assumption was that it would be necessary to observe and record interactions between and among all family members. The basis for this assumption was evidence that maltreatment was sometimes selective within families and that some children may actively contribute to their own maltreatment. These assumptions led Burgess to term this a "social interactional perspective."

There was one other assumption critical to this approach, which we will refer to below. But first, let us return to the distinction between marker and process variables. Given the fact that factors such as parental personality traits (or for that matter, child traits) and ecological conditions such as poverty were only "markers" that identified where important causal processes might be operating, Project Interact identified three types of families to study and compare. Data were collected from families that had either seriously abused or neglected their children. As expected, these families, both single- and two-parent families, were poor and lived below the poverty line. The third type of family had no known history of abuse or neglect matched to the maltreating families in terms of income, education, occupation, family size, and neighborhood.

The primary focus of study was, of course, the patterns of interaction that occurred in each of these three family types. An observational code was carefully designed and was used to record who interacted with whom (verbally and physically), who was the initiator and who was the target, the emotional affect of the behavior, whether the interaction included a command, and, if so, whether the command was followed by compliance or refusal. The intent was to test the assumption/hypothesis that there were patterns of family interaction that distinguished abusive and neglectful families from other families that were similar in most other respects but in which neither abuse nor neglect occurred.

The results from these studies are described in several publications (e.g., Burgess, 1979; Burgess, Anderson, Schellenbach, & Conger, 1981; Burgess & Conger, 1978). When we compared family interactions in abusive and neglectful families with nonmaltreating poverty families, we found that there was a kind of "basic training" for mutually aversive exchanges within the maltreating families. In brief, maltreating parents and their children were observed to reciprocate each other's negative behaviors more than their positive behaviors. This was found to be true for the neglectful families as well as the abusive families. They were found to be more demanding of each other than were the comparison families, but they acceded to each other's demands less often. The largest differences between the maltreating and nonmaltreating families, however, were that the former were less positive to one another and they interacted with each other less often. This was somewhat surprising and was not fully appreciated until later. In any case, other investigators subsequently found a similar pattern. For example, Reid (1984) reported that abusive mothers display approximately twice the rate of punitive behavior as do nonabusive mothers with child management problems and nearly 4 times the rate found in nondistressed, well-functioning families.

So, it seemed that the basic assumptions of the social interactional perspective had merit. In short, the correlates of child maltreatment such as economic deprivation appear to lead to either abuse or neglect if the kinds of coercive interpersonal contingencies described above are activated. Moreover, having identified the importance of the daily patterns of interaction in maltreating families, we had a target for intervention with real promise.

One of the first such efforts was made in Project Interact. The major focus of the intervention program (Burgess et al., 1981) involved teaching abusive and neglectful parents the importance of reinforcement and punishment contingencies, instructing them how to respond to compliance and noncompliance, modeling the behaviors for the parents, and having them role-play and then practice the behaviors. Immediate feedback was given throughout the training phases. In general, the program was promising in the sense that the rate of positive parental behavior could be increased. Nevertheless, gains were hard-earned, small, and difficult to sustain over time despite the fact that the intervention program also addressed the multiple environmental stresses that emerge in these families and that exacerbated conflict and disaffection between the family members. These components of the intervention included (a) relationship establishment between clients and staff, (b) counseling in life management skills, (c) referral to available community agencies for family support services, (d) advocacy by acting as a liaison to community agencies, and (e) offering practical services, such as providing transportation and nutritional and financial management advice. Unfortunately, intervention programs targeting maltreating families continue to have only modest effects today.

In summary, the behaviorally oriented research carried out in Project Interact clearly did add to our understanding of child maltreatment. Nonetheless, a number of questions remained unanswered. For example, why do coercion and rejection seemingly develop so easily among some parents? Why is it so difficult to intervene successfully with maltreating parents? Given that the correlates of child maltreatment are multidimensional, occurring at different levels of analysis, how do we link them together? Is there a general theoretical paradigm that can help us answer questions like these?

In an attempt to answer these questions, the first author returned to the fourth assumption of his social interactional approach, which is based in the branch of evolutionary biology termed *behavioral ecology*, which is concerned with examining the linkages between ecological conditions and adaptive behavior (Burgess, 1979). Thus, in 1988, Burgess, Kurland, and Pensky employed "life history theory" to explain child maltreatment. In the balance of this chapter, we describe a modified version of life history theory to explain how personal, social, and ecological factors and interpersonal contingencies of reinforcement and punishment combine to produce the family dynamics culminating in child maltreatment.

Life History Theory

The central premise of life history theory is the assumption that any evolutionarily successful organism must balance its allocation of time, energy, risk, and other resources to itself—its own growth and maintenance (somatic effort)—with those spent on finding a mate and beginning reproduction (reproductive effort) (Pianka, 1970; Stearns, 1992). Similarly, with respect to reproductive effort, "decisions" are made between strategies that lead to having many offspring, who necessarily receive lower levels of per capita parental investment, as opposed to strategies that involve having fewer offspring, each of whom is capable of being more intensively nurtured.

Evolution-based research has made it clear that reproductive effort is strategic. Evolutionary ecologists have distinguished between r and K reproductive strategies. Organisms that are usually faced with transient and unpredictable environments pursue strategies that permit them to reproduce prolifically. Such organisms are referred to as *r-strategists*. *K-strategists* display evolved traits that are in response to competition with conspecifics under conditions of resource scarcity. Given these circumstances, high levels of parental investment are critical in order to successfully produce offspring that, themselves, will reach reproductive maturity.

For our purposes, the key distinction between r- and K-strategists is the low level of per capita parental investment of the former and the relatively higher level of per capita parental investment of the latter. Even if we accept the common premise that there has been natural selection for high-investment parenting in humans (e.g., Lancaster & Lancaster, 1983), there are undoubtedly individual differences in reproductive strategies (e.g., Draper & Harpending, 1988). Some individuals allocate more energy in the pursuit of finding a mate, sometimes producing offspring from several different mates (a mating or r-strategy), than they do to devoting their energy and other resources to intensively nurturing their offspring (a parenting or K-strategy). Differing levels of parental investment have always reflected a compromise between parental effort, on one hand, and the time, energy, and resources necessary for parental survival and/or successful mating, on the other (Hrdy, 1994). Whether a given parent pursues a low- or high-investment parenting strategy depends on a variety of factors, including the perceived benefits and costs associated with these alternative strategies, an issue to which we will return. Looked at over entire life spans, it is probably the case that most of us pursue a mixed strategy. Nonetheless, there are those who, on a mating-to-parenting-effort continuum, can be found at either extreme.

Whichever strategy a person follows, there are costs and trade-offs that must be made, and these two alternative strategies may be incompatible at the extremes of the reproductive effort continuum. For example, high-investment parenting incurs considerable costs in providing children with the high-quality experiences and environments that eventually contribute to the children's success in ecologically adverse and competitive environments. These costs are not limited to time, money, and energy expenditures. As Trivers (1972) indicated in his classic definition of parental investment, *cost* refers to the parent's compromised ability to invest in other (actual or future) offspring and other mating opportunities.

In summary, we have described the core elements of life history theory and how it has identified two analytically distinct reproductive strategies. These alternative strategies describe different orientations toward the production and care of offspring and are explained by ecological constraints acting on parents. These constraints may be real or imagined. One orientation toward offspring, a K-strategy, is found in predictably adverse and competitive environments where high parental effort enhances offsprings' life chances and subsequent reproductive success. The other, an r-strategy or mating strategy, is found in environments where parents have, or perceive they have, little ability to increase their own life chances or those of their offspring. Under such circumstances, low-investment parenting is likely, which, in turn, can result in child maltreatment. Our task is to identify under what circumstances low parental investment leads to maltreatment.

Social and Ecological Factors

Throughout history, human groups have been exposed to ecological changes that signal improvement or deterioration of their life situations. According to life history theory, ecological instability will affect the behavioral systems associated with mating and parental effort. Specifically, situations in which the availability of necessary resources is variable and social mobility is uncertain contribute to the low level of parental care associated with an r-strategy (MacDonald, 1997).

While it is true that child maltreatment has been found to occur across all social classes, it is also true that maltreatment is disproportionately represented in lower socioeconomic classes (Pelton, 1978). According to Gelles (1992), severe violence toward children is most likely to occur in families where the annual income is below the poverty line. In 1985, The Second National Family Violence Survey found that in families where incomes are below the poverty line, overall violence toward children was 4% higher, severe violence was 46% higher, and very severe violence was 100% higher than in families above the poverty line (Gelles, 1992). Research examining the income-to-needs ratio has revealed that under conditions of chronic and permanent poverty, families meet only 59% and 46% of children's needs, respectively (Ashworth, Hill, & Walker, 1994). Pervasive conditions of poverty can create an environment marked by the unpredictability and uncertainty associated with an r-strategy and result in severe stress, increased irritability, conflict, and punitive behavior (Burgess, 1988). Thus, ecological instability powerfully impacts the costs of parenting and the potential for high parental investment.

Economic hardship, however, does not occur in splendid isolation; it may be buffered or exacerbated by kin, neighborhood, and social supports. It exists, in other words, within a social context. Thus, various ecological circumstances can result in low levels of parental investment. These would include a low potential for paternal investment, especially in environments where such support is essential (Egeland, Jacobvitz, & Sroufe, 1988). Similarly, factors such as social isolation and particular community norms, along with low income (Drake & Pandey, 1996; Wilson, 1987), have been associated with increased levels of child maltreatment. For example, Garbarino and Kostelny (1991) found that certain areas of Chicago tended to have higher rates of child maltreatment than other areas with comparable socioeconomic conditions. Several factors may be operating here. On one hand, there may be a lack of social relationships that can provide parents with the emotional support needed to overcome the stress caused by poverty and provide benefits such as child care resources, parenting information, and social controls sanctioning inappropriate parental actions (Vondra, 1990). In the absence of social exchanges and social visits, there are fewer opportunities for parents to observe family life within other parents' homes. On the other hand, the contacts an abusive parent has with relatives, friends, neighbors, and the larger community or its agencies may serve as mutual reinforcement for socially inappropriate parental behavior. Wahler and Hahn (1984) have shown that rather than interacting with people who form a social support network and who provide assistance, empathy, and problem solving, abusive parents often interact with others who are in similar situations to themselves.

The outcome is that instead of helping each other, they often simply match "war stories," thus exacerbating rather than ameliorating the coercive interactions they have both within and outside of the family. In this way, the abusive parent becomes more and more isolated from helpful social supports and monitoring mechanisms, and maltreatment becomes even more likely.

The association of poverty or resource scarcity with child maltreatment in modern, complex societies is, of course, familiar to everyone. To be sure, there are special stresses and strains experienced by families living in poverty, perhaps especially for those living in communities deficient in appropriate social supports. Nonetheless, poverty or resource scarcity does not inevitably result in low-investment parenting or the maltreatment of children. Poverty as well as stress and deficient social networks are simply marker variables; we need to know more about when and why they are associated with punitive and neglectful parenting. These indicators of ecological instability do seem to intensify conflicts of interest within families, yet they do not inevitably lead to maltreatment. Other factors, at a more microlevel of analysis, allow us to explain individual differences in response to the accumulating stress often associated with resource scarcity.

Individual Factors

Parent Traits

From the perspective of psychology, certain personality traits and a history of abuse have been advanced as determinants of child maltreatment. Evidence for the importance of parental attributes, such as cognitive competence and antisocial behavior, are revealed in several studies. For example, Reid, Kavanaugh, and Baldwin (1987) found that abusive parents tend to rate their children as more deviant than do parents in comparable at-risk families, even though no differences were found in direct observations of the children's behavior. While it was not a study of child maltreatment, the importance of parental personality traits is seen in Elder's longitudinal study of families who experienced the Great Depression (e.g., Elder, Liker, & Cross, 1984), where it was found that economic hardship affected fathers more than mothers, but, more important in the present context, income loss was strongly predictive of arbitrary and explosive parental behavior among only those men who exhibited hostility toward their children before the Depression and who were also experiencing marital problems. For previously friendly and accepting fathers, economic deprivation was not predictive of the nature and degree of paternal involvement.

Concerning cognitive ability or intelligence, Polansky, Chalmers, Buttenweiser, and Williams (1981), in their comprehensive study of child neglect, found the typical neglectful mother to have less than an eighth-grade education and an IQ below 70. In a similar manner, low cognitive competence has been found to be associated with poor prenatal care, low birth weight, low HOME (Home Observation for Measurement of the Environment) scores, difficult child temperament, and problem behaviors such as antisocial behavior and hyperactivity. These findings led Herrnstein and Murray (1994) to conclude that cognitive competence (IQ) has a strong effect on parenting practices.

Additional support for the importance of parental characteristics has been implied in the study of the intergenerational transmission of abuse. Recognition that patterns of personality characteristics and child maltreatment are often found in successive generations has been a mainstay of the child abuse literature. Elder, Caspi, and Downey (1984), in their study of generational relations, reported that an abrasive and irritable interpersonal style is often transmitted from one generation to the next. They found that retrospective ratings of grandmothers' irritability correlated significantly with fathers' and mothers' irritability.

Although no one would assert that intergenerational continuity is a definitive outcome, it does frequently occur (Burgess & Youngblade, 1988; Widom, 1988). Research has yet to conclusively identify how this transmission occurs or what is being transmitted. It is possible, of course, that something more basic than social learning occurs. Given that maltreated children and maltreating parents display similar profiles for heritable personality traits such as aggressiveness and impulsivity (Burgess, 1997), it may be that the capacity for maltreatment is a heritable predisposition. In fact, research has demonstrated that child-rearing styles are traitlike in that they are genetically influenced (Plomin & Bergeman, 1991). Moreover, traits such as intelligence and aggression, which are believed to be associated with child maltreatment, as noted above, have been shown to have strong heritabilities (Rowe, 1994). For example, violent aggressive behavior in males has been linked to heritable testosterone levels (Blum, 1997; Mednick & Volavka, 1980).

It is also possible that fundamental changes occur in an individual's developmental trajectory as a result of early traumatic experiences, such as abuse, neglect, or high levels of stress (Karr-Morse & Wiley, 1997; Widom, 1988). Experiences within the family could induce ontogenetic changes on various levels, from alterations in brain functioning to modeling social behavior. The family itself can function as an important learning environment wherein family members train one another to be increasingly coercive and contentious (Patterson, 1982). This implies that parents who display a pattern of interpersonal irritability use ineffective parenting practices that foster the development of this trait in the next generation via reinforcement contingencies and modeling.

Experiences in the family may have still another role in family members' development. The capacity for child maltreatment may be a stress-induced response to early experience. Exposure to interparental anger may induce emotional stress in children, enmesh children in the parents' problems, or cause anger and aggression that over time will result in the development of dysfunctional behavior. Recent research in the field of brain development has some intriguing implications. Findings have indicated that victims of early traumas in childhood tend to suffer from right-hemisphere impairments; evidence suggests that right-hemisphere deficiencies are correlated with a lack of certain behaviors such as pity, compassion, and attachment (Henry, 1993). Thus, in some cases, the low frequencies of positive interaction and parental care found in abusive families may be due to the fact that the parent has a low capacity to form close bonds with others (Bolton, 1983; Draper & Harpending, 1988). In addition, "Any factors which increase the activity or reactivity of the brainstem (e.g., chronic stress) or decrease the moderating capacity of the limbic or cortical areas (e.g., neglect) will increase an individual's aggressivity, impulsivity, and capacity to display violence" (Perry, 1997, p. 129). The fact that parental aggression toward children is strongly associated with interspousal aggression (Gelles, 1987; Hughes, 1988; Jourlies, Barling, & O'Leary, 1987) is consistent with the idea that the inability to control aggressive impulses and to form close attachment relationships is a generalized response expected from brain impairments experienced early in a child's life.

In sum, intergenerational continuity is not an absolute, and neither low intellectual ability nor a pessimistic disposition correlates perfectly with child maltreatment. Widom's (1988) well-known work on intergenerational transmission and relationships among abuse, neglect, and later antisocial behavior challenged an overly determinististic approach and suggested that child abuse or neglect does not inevitably result in a cycle of maltreatment. There are multiple pathways, and the role of individual traits may interact with ecological conditions during development. In fact, Widom (1988) suggested several factors, including age, intelligence, cognitive appraisal, and temperament, that may influence the effects of child maltreatment on development. Recent research has suggested that individual differences in the long-term consequences of maltreatment may be mediated by individual differences in a particular version of a gene on the X chromosome, monoamine oxidase A, or MAOA (Caspi et al., 2002). Thus, personal characteristics appear to mediate the effects of the environment during childhood as well as mediate the effects of ecological conditions on parental investment.

Child Traits

According to an evolutionary perspective, parents who care for offspring do so altruistically in that they incur considerable costs while benefiting their offspring. Such behavior is considered to be selectively advantageous to the parent only in circumstances that will lead to an increase in parental inclusive fitness (Hamilton, 1964; Trivers, 1972, 1974). If relatedness between parent and offspring is low or uncertain, if the parent's losses are large, or if the benefits to offspring are slight, then parental investment may not necessarily be biologically adaptive. Because of circumstances such as these, parental investment is not invariant over time and is not expected to be indiscriminately distributed among offspring.

If child abuse is a behavioral response influenced by natural selection, then it is more likely to occur when there are reduced inclusive-fitness payoffs due to uncertain or low relatedness. Thus, abuse of stepchildren by stepparents should be more likely than abuse of biological offspring by parents; parents should be more likely to abuse their stepchildren than their biological offspring when both are available ("the Cinderella effect"); and males should be more likely than females to be the abusers. Research has supported such predictions (Daly & Wilson, 1981; Lightcap, Kurland, & Burgess, 1982).

In addition, evolved mechanisms of parental investment should be sensitive to the ability of offspring to convert care into fitness. Therefore, a child's age and health status are critical factors. Research has shown that handicapped children are more likely than nonhandicapped children to be abused (Daly & Wilson, 1981; Lightcap et al., 1982). Younger children are more likely to be abused because of lower reproductive value relative to older siblings; however, escalating parent-offspring conflict as children approach puberty is also crucial. Indeed, it appears that the age-specific rates of child maltreatment form a trimodal distribution with peaks for infants, 2-year-olds, and prepubescent children (Burgess & Richardson, 1984; Lenington, 1981). Consistent with Trivers's (1974) model of parent-offspring conflict, these peaks correspond to periods marked by relatively high parental investment cost-benefit ratios.

Costs and Benefits

We have asserted that parental and child traits in concert with certain ecological factors predict varying levels of observed parental care. However, no one of these markers alone inevitably leads to low-investment parenting.

Thus, a definitive understanding of child maltreatment requires a transition from these various marker variables to the level of actual parental investment to the occurrence of abuse or neglect. The point we address now is how these factors actually effect changes in the level of parental investment.

The general argument advanced here is that natural selection has led to the evolution of psychological mechanisms that enable individuals to adopt specific behavioral alternatives based on cost-benefit decisions, whether in direct or indirect reproductive terms. The rationale for our position is the fact that the 2 million years of the Pleistocene were marked by our ancestors spreading into ecological settings that were incredibly diverse and often changing in fundamental ways due to climatological and geological events (cf. Potts, 1996). Under selection pressures such as these, cognitive mechanisms and facultative responses appropriate to a large variety of social and ecological circumstances should have been favored (Alexander, 1990). Because of this, ancestral humans would have been able to make conditional decisions about the allocation of their energies to somatic, mating, or parental effort. In our estimation, selection forces have led to the tendency to monitor environmental variation and make benefit-cost assessments that typically involve behavioral consequences that historically have been correlated with reproductive success. Examples of such consequences include resource acquisition, status enhancement, and favorable resolutions of interpersonal conflicts of interest. Our view, then, does not assume that inclusive-fitness maximizing necessarily functions as a motive in human affairs. Rather, we are motivated by outcomes that vary in their proximity to the bottom line of reproductive success.

Whether our hypothesis that the tendency to make benefit-cost assessments is a domain-general adaptive psychological mechanism turns out to be correct or not, the fact is, the assumption that individuals attempt for the most part to maximize benefits and minimize costs in their interactions with others has long characterized all of the most useful theories in the behavioral sciences. For example, there is the "matching law" of behavioral psychology, where the relative frequency of a response tends to match its relative frequency of reinforcement (Herrnstein, 1970). Similarly, social exchange theory (Burgess & Nielson, 1974) and microeconomic theory (Becker, 1981) emphasize the importance of cost-benefit analyses. Focusing on proximate outcomes, Becker and Murphy (1988) found that parents' altruistic behavior toward their children depends on the number of children, the benefits expected from each child, and the parents' own perceived needs, because parents typically must reduce their own consumption to increase the time and resources they spend on their children. In the terminology of life history theory and behavioral ecology, individuals are faced with the problem of balancing their allocation of resources to themselves (somatic and mating effort) versus committing those resources to their children and their children's development.

For these reasons, we propose that cost-benefit analysis may be the link between the various marker variables we have described and actual parental effort. The relationship between costs and benefits, as displayed in Figure 11.1, translates into different levels of parental investment. Costs and benefits are not end points on one continuum; if costs increase, benefits do not necessarily decrease. The relationship is more complex, and much remains unknown. However, we propose that parental investment modeled on the ratio of benefits to costs takes the shape of a sine curve (see Figure 11.1). Thus, a general assumption implicit in this model is that there are upper and lower thresholds for high and low parental investment, respectively. The threshold refers to the point where changes in the benefit-to-cost ratio result in minimal changes in parental care. In other words, parental investment attains a plateau, whether it be a high- or low-investment plateau.

The point that distinguishes high and low parental investment has been described in research on altruism and the degree of relatedness. Evolutionary theory implies that altruistic behaviors directed at kin have reproductive value for the altruist if the benefit-to-cost ratio is larger than the inverse of the degree of relatedness (Trivers, 1974). Thus, given that the biological parent-child coefficient of relatedness is one half (Hamilton, 1964), on average, perceived costs must be one half of perceived benefits (i.e., benefits to

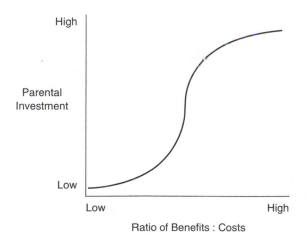

Figure 11.1   Ratio of Benefits to Costs and Parental Investment

costs > 2) to result in acts of high parental investment. Nevertheless, it is important to understand that this curvilinear relationship is individually determined; thus, it may be slightly different between individuals, as well as moderately change through time for an individual.

The threshold for "acceptable" benefit-cost ratios (i.e., those that correspond to higher parental investment) may be influenced by the ecological and individual factors previously described. For example, a parent who has experienced social and economic impoverishment and who has poor problem-solving skills may perceive few benefits contingent on high levels of parental effort. Alternatively, a parent who has suffered a traumatic youth or whose family of origin was abusive may have skewed perceptions of ideal parenting that affect his or her ratio threshold and resultant parental investment. More specifically, and more importantly, these factors influence the perception of costs and of benefits that lead to the second component of our cost-benefit hypothesis.

This second component concerns the relative importance of costs and of benefits in the resulting ratio and associated parental investment. Simply, we suggest that perceived costs are more influential than perceived benefits because costs are more likely to fluctuate and to do so in short spans of time. As shown in Figure 11.2a, when costs are held constant and perceived benefits decrease, parental investment decreases. In contrast, a comparable increase in perceived costs when benefits are held constant results in a greater decrease in parental investment (see Figure 11.2b).

One explanation for the disproportionate role of costs in determining investment may be a general perceptual tendency to track changes in costs more carefully than changes in benefits. The perception of costs and associated increases may be more variable and influenced by more factors than are perceptions of benefits. As Trivers (1974) explained, the costs of a parental act are dependent in part on the condition of the parent, whereas the benefits of a given act are dependent in part on the condition of the offspring. As we have addressed in previous sections, the condition of the parent is multiply determined. Although ecological instability plays a significant role in child maltreatment, ecological factors do not operate in a vacuum. Individual traits work in concert with environmental elements. Indeed, "The same event may be perceived by different individuals as irrelevant, benign, positive, threatening, or harmful" (Widom, 1988, p. 48). For example, the parent with lower cognitive competence and fewer planning skills who endures economic hardship may have an augmented perception of increased costs as compared with a more competent parent who suffers equivalent hardship. The former parent's heightened perception of costs may lead to a greater change in his or her parental investment. However, it is not likely

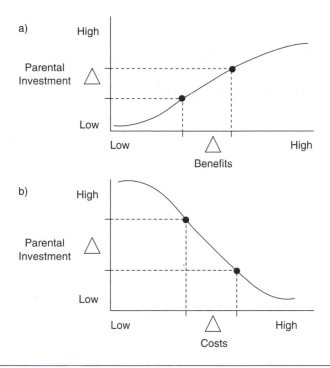

Figure 11.2   Parental Investment as a function of (a) benefits when costs are held constant and (b) costs when benefits are held constant. The conclusion to be drawn from (a) and (b) is that equivalent changes in the predictor (i.e., $\Delta B = \Delta C$) do not result in equivalent changes in the outcome (i.e., $\Delta PI_a \neq \Delta PI_b$). In fact, the change in Parental Investment given a change in benefits is less than the change in Parental Investment given an equivalent change in costs (i.e., $\Delta PI_a < \Delta PI_b$)

that either parent's perception of benefits greatly changed as a result of the economic hardship.

Aversive child behavior may also function to affect perceptions of costs more than those of benefits. Following Trivers (1974), it can be assumed that children have been selected to consume as many parental resources as possible; therefore, parent-offspring conflict must be expected. In this way, child aversive behavior may be functional for the child to extract additional resources in the short term but costly to the child over the long haul, because parental perception of benefits may not dramatically change, but perception of costs would. Thus, parental investment would be likely to decrease as the costs increased over time.

Another possibility for understanding the role of cost centers on the general assumption individuals make about parenting. Although research asserts that benefits do exceed costs in altruistic acts (Trivers, 1974), most parents assume or perceive that they invest more resources in their children than they directly receive in return. This may be another reason why shifts in real or perceived costs play a disproportionate role in the relationship between benefit-cost ratios and degree of parental investment. This is probably also why there has been selection for the "attachment bond" as an evolved domain-specific psychological mechanism. Attachment may function either to encourage parents to pay most of their attention to the positive side of parenting or to simply relax benefit-cost considerations altogether.

Understanding the roles of perceived costs and benefits provides the link between marker variables and parental investment. Ecological factors, parent and child traits, and parental investment are objective variables. Examining benefit-cost ratios and the importance of perceived costs incorporates an additional subjective, personal element to our model.

Parental Investment and Child Maltreatment

Although Trivers (1972) provided a conceptual understanding of parental investment, as well as costs and benefits, operationalizing parental investment remains a difficult task. There is no simple relationship between the costs of high investment to the parents and the benefits to the offspring; that is, excessive costs do not necessarily result in equivalent levels of benefits (Trivers, 1972). Therefore, investment cannot be assessed in terms of costs alone. It may appear rational and easier to assess costs in the present given that benefits of investment must be evaluated over time; however, evaluating costs alone would provide only an estimate of relative parental expenditure or effort (Clutton-Brock, 1991). Benefits to offspring, or rather the effectiveness of parental effort, must also be evaluated to determine the level of parental investment. It should not be surprising that investment has been defined and assessed differently across numerous studies; however, each operational definition describes parental behaviors that are positively associated with benefits to the child. In general, cross-cultural studies have determined levels of parental investment based on behaviors that simply ensure survival to reproductive maturity, whereas research in industrial and postindustrial societies has expanded parental investment to encompass behaviors that benefit offsprings' psychological and physical well-being. For example, Lancaster and Lancaster (1983) implied that continuous body contact and feeding on demand constitute high parental investment among hunter-gatherers. Wilson and Daly (1994) employed a similar definition, including direct and indirect care such as breast-feeding and allocating time to protection. In his investigation of the parenting of Hazda men, Marlowe (1998) measured direct care, such as holding, feeding, talking, listening, and pacifying, and indirect care, such as resource acquisition; however, he concluded that "direct care is probably a more reliable measure of a man's effort than is resource acquisition, which may reflect ability as much as motivation" (p. 403).

Parental investment has become more complex as societies and their demands have grown. Research by developmental psychologists has suggested that a high-investment parenting strategy in modern industrial societies involves a multitude of costly and coordinated activities, including feeling and expressing love toward one's child; possessing a strong emotional attachment to one's child; talking to the child often; reading to the child; playing with the child; actively listening to the child; having empathy for the child; providing emotional support for the child; imparting values such as cooperativeness, honesty, and self-control; monitoring the child's behavior; enforcing rules in a consistent but flexible manner; providing for the child's nourishment and physical health; and attempting to shield the child from harm (Maccoby & Martin, 1983).

As evidenced by the latter complicated set of behaviors constituting high parental investment, simply surviving childhood is not the only goal parents have for their children. Survival does not ensure reproductive success. Physical and psychological fitness (e.g., emotional stability and social and intellectual competence) are important for reproductive success. Thus, parental investment seems more precarious, and distinguishing high from low investment has become more difficult.

Based upon multiagent and multimethod indicators, Patterson and his colleagues have identified four especially critical components of high-investment parenting that contribute to offspring prosocial behavior (e.g., Capaldi & Patterson, 1989). These "family management practices" are (1) contingent positive reinforcement for a child's prosocial behavior, (2) a pattern of discipline that contingently punishes inappropriate behavior in an effective yet humane way, (3) careful monitoring of a child's behavior, including interaction with siblings and the choice of and interaction with peers, and (4) effective problem solving. Based upon more than 25 years of field observation and clinical efforts to intervene in the lives of several hundred problem families, Patterson has documented that breakdowns in these family management practices typically have adverse effects for the child and for general family functioning (Bank, Dishion, Skinner, & Patterson, 1990).

Inept disciplinary tactics, for example, are commonly found in families having problems. In such situations, a parent tends to be extremely negative when interacting with a child, frequently resorting to scolding, threatening, and issuing commands. Moreover, in these situations, the parents usually fail to follow through with consequences for a child's inappropriate behavior. A second breakdown in family management practices found in problem families is the failure of the parent to properly reinforce the child's appropriate and prosocial behavior. This problem can be manifested in two different but often related ways. In one case, the parent may reinforce the child but in an inconsistent and noncontingent way. The other case is found when parents simply display unusually low frequencies of positive reinforcement. Interestingly, the first case may lead to the second (Burgess et al., 1981). The third critical breakdown is in effective monitoring of a child's behavior. Failing to monitor a child's behavior lessens the likelihood that the parent will properly reinforce or punish the child's behavior. The fourth breakdown is in problem-solving procedures, such as identifying a problem; examining potential solutions; and selecting, attempting, and assessing the chosen solution. Difficulties can arise at any or all of these steps toward effective problem solving.

Structural equation analyses by Patterson and Dishion (1988) revealed that these breakdowns in family management practices typically result in aversive child behavior, which, in turn, leads to parental rejection of the child and decreased parental warmth. Moreover, these effects appear to be bidirectional, such that increased rejection results in continued disrupted parenting. In this way, a vicious cycle is set in motion that can lead to a family system out of control and, in extreme cases, to parental disengagement and the maltreatment of the child. The implication here is that microsocial processes operating within a family can short-circuit optimal investment in a child and result in patterns of child abuse and neglect. A comprehensive review of research supportive of this view is found in Cerezo (1997).

Based upon the structural equation analyses of Patterson, Reid, and Dishion (1992), we propose a multiply-mediated model with child maltreatment as the outcome variable. As described above, the most important proximate mechanism explaining problems in parent-child relations is disrupted family management practices. Disrupted parenting is, in turn, controlled by a broad band of contextual and individual variables, such as ecological instability, neighborhood or social network variables, and specific parent and child traits. While these variables all correlate with child maltreatment, their effects are mediated by cost-benefit assessments and whether parental investment is low. This can be seen in Figure 11.3.

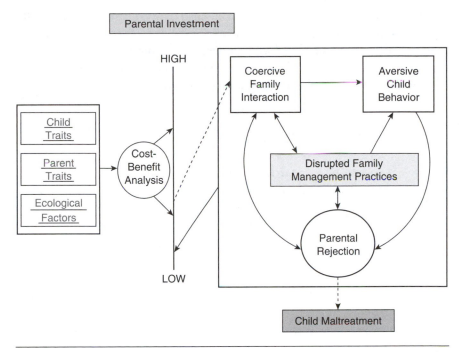

Figure 11.3   A Multiply-Mediated Model. Dotted lines are used to designate the conditional nature of correlations between variables, while solid lines are used to designate causal relationships.

The proximate determinants of child maltreatment, therefore, are to be found in the day-to-day transactions between parents and children. The proximate variable that is most crucial to understanding the link between parental investment and child maltreatment is family management practices. With low parental investment and the breakdown of family management practices, deteriorating ecological conditions ultimately lead to the abuse or neglect of children.

Moreover, there is growing evidence that ecological factors outside the family, as well as individual traits, impact upon child management practices through their effects on the kinds of microsocial and coercive processes operating within families that we found in Project Interact. Because these microsocial processes are dyad-specific and measure the reaction of one family member to the behavior of another, individual parent and child characteristics are invariably involved as well.

As Patterson (1984) has observed, microsocial processes such as these found in maltreating families are often marked by increasingly aversive child behavior and escalating counterattacks. This, in turn, contributes to the parent perceiving the child as deviant and as a costly investment and eventually rejecting the child. All of this makes it increasingly difficult to employ effective child management practices, which then feeds back into the coercive process. The key here is recognition of the bidirectional relation between these coercive microsocial processes and effective family management practices.

Discussion and Conclusions

By now, it should be evident that understanding the causes of child mal-treatment is an interdisciplinary task and requires the synthesis of different levels of analysis, incorporating biological as well as psychological and soci-ological variables. The fact that maltreatment is influenced by biological processes in no way precludes the importance of social and ecological factors operating both within and outside of families for explaining such behavior. Social and ecological conditions do impact a person's reproductive strategy and play important roles in the etiology and persistence of the maltreatment of children. For example, there is substantial empirical support for the assertion that poverty is positively associated with the physical abuse and neglect of children (Drake & Pandey, 1996). Nevertheless, at least in societies where abuse and neglect are nonnormative, resource scarcity does not invariably lead to low-investment parenting or child maltreatment.

Because not all parents with annual incomes below the poverty line resort to low parental investment, individual characteristics must be considered. For example, researchers examining resilience have found that parents of stress-resistant children tend to have more optimistic global opinions about stressful experiences than do parents of stress-affected children; in addition, the researchers suggested that this difference in parents may be attributed to different cognitions of similar, stressful events (Cowen et al., 1997). Thus, psychology offers insights into who tends toward negative perceptions of costs and benefits and low-investment parenting and is thereby most affected by ecological instability. Parental traits such as intelligence and certain per-sonality traits may be markers for situations that lead to disrupted family management practices that culminate in child maltreatment.

The behavioral ecology model we have presented implies that low parental investment results from a combination of factors that impact the perception of benefits to costs, as well as the threshold for acceptable ratios. Because the degree of investment is mediated by cost-benefit analysis, it may be assumed that were perceptions of benefits to costs favorable, observable parental investment would be high, whereas skewed, unfavorable percep-tions would result in low investment.

Low parental investment and child maltreatment are not, however, invariably linked. Proximate antecedents such as coercive family interactions and poor family management practices mediate the relationship between degree of investment and maltreatment. By definition, high-investment parenting is incompatible with a pattern of coercive family interaction and therefore will not culminate in child maltreatment. Thus, persistently coercive family interactions are present only in cases of low parental investment, yet low parental investment is not always accompanied by coercive family interactions and poor family management practices. Nevertheless, a low-investment strategy can result in increasingly coercive family interactions and a breakdown in family management practices that lead to a downward-spiraling, self-perpetuating system of aversive child behavior, increased rejection of the child, escalation of coercive family interactions, poor management practices, and progressively lower parental investment. Child maltreatment is the rock bottom of this downward whirl of interactions. However, abuse and neglect are not the end points of this cycle. Not only might the malignant interactions persist between parent and child, but the pattern may be extended to the next generation via direct and indirect routes, as previously noted.

Although life history theory is able to explain intergenerational continuity as well as new cycles of maltreatment, our central premise has been that an evolutionary explanation that accounts for varying levels of parental investment gains added precision by taking a behavioral ecology perspective that incorporates empirical findings originating from other disciplines and theoretical perspectives. By using the degree of parental investment as a guiding principle in our analysis, we have been able to parsimoniously relate anthropological, psychological, and sociological research to gain a better understanding of child maltreatment and its multiple causes.

References

Alexander, R. D. (1990). Epigenetic rules and Darwinian algorithms: The adaptive study of learning and development. *Etiology and Sociobiology, 11,* 241-303.

Ashworth, K., Hill, M., & Walker, R. (1994). Patterns of childhood poverty: New challenges for policy. *Journal of Policy Analysis and Management, 13,* 658-680.

Bank, L., Dishion, T. J., Skinner, M. L., & Patterson, G. R. (1990). Method variance in structural equation modeling: Living with "glop." In G. R Patterson (Ed.), *Depression and aggression in family interaction* (pp. 247-279). Hillsdale, NJ: Erlbaum.

Becker, G. S. (1981). *A treatise on the family.* Cambridge, MA: Harvard University Press.

Becker, G. S., & Murphy, K. M. (1988). The family and the state. *Journal of Law and Economics, 31,* 1-18.

Blum, D. (1997). *Sex on the brain: The biological differences between men and women.* New York: Viking.

Bolton, F. G. Jr. (1983). *When bonding fails: Clinical assessment of high-risk families.* Beverly Hills, CA: Sage.

Brunquell, D., Crichton, L., & Egeland, B. (1981). Maternal personality and attitude in disturbances of child rearing. *American Journal of Orthopsychiatry, 51,* 680-691.

Burgess, R. L. (1979). Child abuse: A social interactional analysis. In B. B. Lahey & A. E. Kazdin (Eds.), *Advances in clinical child psychology* (Vol. 2, pp. 141-172). New York: Plenum Press.

Burgess, R. L. (1988). Social and ecological issues in violence towards children. In R. T. Ammerman & M. Hersen (Eds.), *Case studies in family violence* (pp. 15-38). New York: Plenum.

Burgess, R. L. (1997). *Behavior genetics and evolutionary psychology: A new look at the transmission of maltreatment across generations.* Presented at Annual Meeting of the Behavior Genetics Association, Toronto, Canada.

Burgess, R. L., Anderson, E. A., Schellenbach, C. J., & Conger, R. (1981). A social interactional approach to the study of abusive families. In J. P. Vincent (Ed.), *Advances in family intervention, assessment, and theory: An annual compilation of research* (pp. 1-46). New York: Columbia University Press.

Burgess, R. L., & Conger, R. D. (1978). Family interaction in abusing, neglectful, and normal families. *Child Development, 49,* 1163-1173.

Burgess, R. L., Kurland, J. A., & Pensky, E. E. (1988). Ultimate and proximate determinants of child maltreatment: Natural selection, ecological instability, and coercive interpersonal contingencies. In K. B. MacDonald (Ed.), *Sociobiological perspectives on human development* (pp. 293-319). New York: Springer-Verlag.

Burgess, R. L., & Nielson, J. M. (1974). An experimental analysis of some structural determinants of equitable and inequitable exchange relations. *American Sociological Review, 39,* 427-443.

Burgess, R. L., & Richardson, R. A. (1984). Child abuse during adolescence. In R. M. Lerner & N. Galambos (Eds.), *Experiencing adolescents: A sourcebook for parents, teachers, and teens* (pp. 119-151). New York: Garland.

Burgess, R. L., & Youngblade, L. M. (1988). Social incompetence and the intergenerational transmission of abusive parental practices. In G. Hotaling, D. Finkelhor, J. T. Kirkpatrick, & M. A. Straus (Eds.), *Family abuse and its consequences: New directions in research* (pp. 38-60). Beverly Hills, CA: Sage.

Capaldi, D. M., & Patterson, G. R. (1989). *Psychometric properties of fourteen latent constructs from the Oregon Youth Study.* New York: Springer-Verlag.

Caspi, A., McClay, J., Moffitt, T., Mill, J., Martin, J., Craig, J. W., et al. (2002). Role of genotype in the cycle of violence in maltreated children. *Science, 297*, 851-854.

Cerezo, M. A. (1997). Abusive family interaction: a review. *Aggression & Violent Behavior, 2*(3), 215-240.

Clutton-Brock, T. H. (1991). *The evolution of parental care.* Princeton, NJ: Princeton University Press.

Cowen, E. L., Wyman, P. A., Work, W. C., Kim, J. Y., Fagen, D. B., & Magnus, K. B. (1997). Follow-up study of young stress-affected and stress-resilient urban children. *Development and Psychopathology, 9*, 565-577.

Daly, M., & Wilson, M. I. (1981). Abuse and neglect of children in evolutionary perspective. In R. D. Alexander & D. W. Tinkle (Eds.), *Natural selection and social behavior.* New York: Chiron Press.

Drake, B., & Pandey, S. M. (1996). Understanding the relationship between neighborhood, poverty, and specific types of child maltreatment. *Child Abuse and Neglect, 20*, 1003-1018.

Draper, P., & Harpending, H. (1988). A sociobiological perspective on the development of human reproductive strategies. In K. B. MacDonald (Ed.), *Sociobiological perspectives on human development.* New York: Springer-Verlag.

Egeland, B., Jacobvitz, D., & Sroufe, L. A. (1988). Breaking the cycle of abuse. *Child Development, 59*, 1080-1088.

Elder, G. H., Caspi, A., & Downey, G. (1983). Problem behavior and family relationships: A multi-generational analysis. In A. Sorenson, F. Weiner, & L. Sherrod (Eds.), *Human development: Interdisciplinary perspectives* (pp. 93-118). Hillsdale, NJ: Erlbaum.

Elder, G. H., Liker, J. K., & Cross, C. E. (1984). Parent-child behavior in the great depression: Life course and intergenerational influences. In P. Baltes & O. G. Brim (Eds.), *Life span development and behavior* (pp. 109-158). New York: Academic Press.

Garbarino, J. (1977). The human ecology of child maltreatment: A conceptual model for research. *Journal of Marriage and the Family, 721* 735.

Garbarino, J., & Kostelny, K. (1991). Child maltreatment as a community problem. *Child Abuse and Neglect, 16*, 455-464.

Gelles, R. J. (1973). Child abuse as psychopathology: A sociological critique and reformulation. *American Journal of Orthopsychiatry, 43*, 611-621.

Gelles, R. J. (1987). *Family violence* (2nd ed.). Newbury Park, CA: Sage.

Gelles, R. J. (1992). Poverty and violence toward children. *American Behavioral Scientist, 35*, 258-274.

Gil, D. (1970). *Violence against children: Physical abuse in the United States.* Cambridge, MA: Harvard University Press.

Hamilton, W. D. (1964). The genetical evolution of social behavior. *Journal of Theoretical Biology, 7*, 1-52.

Henry, J. P. (1993). Psychological and physiological responses to stress: The right hemisphere and the hypothalamo-pituitary-adrenal axis, an inquiry into problems of human bonding. *Integrative Physiological and Behavioral Science, 28*(4), 368-387.

Herrnstein, R. J. (1970). On the law of effect. *Journal of the Experimental Analysis of Behavior, 13,* 243-261.

Herrnstein, R. J., & Murray, C. M. (1994). *The bell curve: Intelligence and class structure in American life.* New York: Free Press.

Hrdy, S. B. (1994). Fitness tradeoffs in the history and evolution of delegated mothering with special reference to wet-nursing, abandonment and infanticide. In S. Parmigiani & F. S. vom Saal (Eds.), *Infanticide and parental care.* London: Harwood Academic Publishers.

Hughes, H. (1988). Psychological and behavioral correlates of family violence in child witnesses and victims. *American Journal of Orthopsychiatry, 58,* 77-90.

Jourlies, E. N., Barling, J., & O'Leary, K. G. (1987). Predicting child behavior problems in maritally violent families. *Journal of Abnormal Child Psychology, 15,* 163-173.

Karr-Morse, R., & Wiley, M. S. (1997). *Ghosts from the nursery: Tracing the roots of violence.* New York: Atlantic Monthly Press.

Kempe, C. H. (1973). A practical approach to the protection of the abused child and rehabilitation of the abusing parent. *Pediatrics, 51,* 804-812.

Kempe, C. H., Silverman, F. N., Steele, B. F., Droegemueller, W., & Silver, H. K. (1962). The battered-child syndrome. *Journal of the American Medication Association, 181,* 17-24.

Lancaster, J., & Lancaster, C. (1983). Parental investment: The hominid adaptation. In D. J. Ortner (Ed.), *How humans adapt: A biocultural odyssey.* Washington, DC: Smithsonian Institution Press.

Lasch, C. (1977). *Haven in a heartless world.* New York: Basic Books.

Lenington, S. (1981). Child abuse: The limits of sociobiology. *Ethology and Sociobiology, 2,* 17-29.

Lightcap, J. L., Kurland, J. A., & Burgess, R. L. (1982). Child abuse: A test of some predictions from evolutionary theory. *Ethology and Sociobiology, 3,* 61-67.

Maccoby, E., & Martin, J. (1983). Parent-child relationships. In P. Mussen (Series Ed.), & E. M. Hetherington (Vol. Ed.), *Handbook of child psychology: Vol. 4. Socialization, personality and social development.* New York: John Wiley.

MacDonald, K. B. (1997). Life history theory and human reproductive behavior: Environmental/contextual influences and heritable variation. *Human Nature, 8*(4), 327-359.

Marlowe, F. (1999, May). Showoffs or providers? The parenting effort of Hazda men. *Evolution and Human Behavior, 20,* 391-404.

Mednick, S. A., & Volavka, J. (1980). Biology and crime. In N. Morris & M. Tonry (Eds.), *Crime and justice: An annual review of research* (Vol. 2). Chicago: University of Chicago Press.

Patterson, G. R. (1976). The aggressive child: Victim and architect of a coercive system. In L. A. Hamerlynck, L. C. Handy, & E. J. Mash (Eds.), *Behavior*

modification and families: Vol. I. Theory and research. New York: Brunner/
Mazel.

Patterson, G. R. (1982). *Coercive family process.* Eugene, OR: Castalia.

Patterson, G. R. (1984). Microsocial processes: A view from the boundary. In
J. Masters & K. Yorkin-Levin (Eds.), *Boundary areas in social psychology*
(pp. 43-67). New York: Academic Press.

Patterson, G. R., & Dishion, T. J. (1988). Multilevel family process models: Traits,
interactions, and relationships. In R. A. Hinde & J. Stenenson-Hinde (Eds.),
Relationships within families: Mutual influences (pp. 283-310). Oxford, UK:
Clarendon.

Patterson, G. R., Reid, J. B., & Dishion, T. J. (1992). *A social interactional
approach: Vol. 4. Anti-social boys.* Eugene, OR: Castalia.

Pelton, L. H. (1978). Child abuse and neglect: The myth of classlessness. *American
Journal of Orthopsychiatry, 48,* 608-617.

Perry, B. (1997). Incubated in terror: Neurodevelopmental factors in the cycle of
violence. In J. D. Osofsky (Ed.), *Children in a violent society* (pp. 124-149).
New York: Guilford Press.

Pianka, E. R. (1970). On r- and K-selection. *American Naturalist, 104,* 592-597.

Plomin, R., & Bergeman, C. S. (1991). The nature of nurture: Genetic influences on
"environmental" measures. *Behavioral and Brain Sciences, 14,* 373-427.

Polansky, N. A., Chalmers, M. A., Buttenweiser, E., & Williams, D. P. (1981).
Damaged parents: An anatomy of child neglect. Chicago: University of Chicago
Press.

Potts, R. (1996). *Humanity's descent: The consequences of ecological instability.*
New York: Avon.

Reid, J. B. (1984). Social-interactional patterns of families of abused and nonabused
children. In C. Zahn-Waxler, M. Cummings, & M. Rake-Yarrow (Eds.), *Social
and biological origins of altruism and aggression.* Cambridge, UK: Cambridge
University Press.

Reid, J. B., Kavanaugh, K. A., & Baldwin, D. V. (1987). Abusive parents' perceptions of child problem behaviors: An example of parental bias. *Journal of
Abnormal Child Psychology, 15,* 457-466.

Rowe, D. C. (1994). *The limits of family influence: Genes, experience, and behavior.* New York: Guilford Press.

Spinetta, J. J., & Rigler, D. (1972). The child-abusing parent: A psychological
review. *Psychological Bulletin, 77,* 296-304.

Stearns, S. (1992). *The evolution of life histories.* New York: Oxford University
Press.

Straus, M. A., Gelles, R. J., & Steinmetz, S. R. (1981). *Behind closed doors:
Violence in the American family.* New York: Anchor/Doubleday.

Trivers, R. L. (1972). Parental investment and sexual selection. In B. Campbell
(Ed.), *Sexual selection and the descent of man.* Chicago: Aldine.

Trivers, R. L. (1974). Parent-offspring conflict. *American Zoologist, 14,*
244-264.

Vondra, J. I. (1990). The community context of child abuse and neglect. *Marriage and Family Review, 15,* 19-39.

Wahler, R. G., & Hahn, D. M. (1984). The communication patterns of troubled mothers: In search of a keystone in the generalization of parenting skills. *Journal of Education and Treatment of Children, 7,* 335-350.

Widom, C. S. (1988). The intergenerational transmission of violence. In N. Weiner & M. E. Wolfgang (Eds.), *Pathways to criminal violence.* Beverly Hills, CA: Sage.

Wilson, M., & Daly, M. (1994). The psychology of parenting in evolutionary perspective and the case of human filicide. In S. Parmigiani & F. S. vom Saal (Eds.), *Infanticide and parental care* (pp. 73-104). London: Harwood Academic Publishers.

Wilson, W. J. (1987). *The truly disadvantaged: The inner-city, the underclass, and public policy.* Chicago: University of Chicago Press.

12

Further Observations
on Adolescence

Glenn E. Weisfeld and Donyell K. Coleman

The study of adolescence in the United States remains highly culture bound. U.S. psychology textbooks focus on contemporary American adolescents to the virtual exclusion of adolescents elsewhere and even adolescents earlier in U.S. history. Social class differences are generally neglected, with most textbook treatments concentrating on middle-class, college-bound adolescents. Although these works pay increasing attention to ethnic differences, this is no substitute for a comprehensive consideration of human adolescence. The exclusion of other cultures from U.S. textbooks is particularly unfortunate, because Americans are notoriously ignorant of other cultures, from which we stand to learn much, particularly concerning adolescent development. American adolescents suffer inordinately from problems such as premarital pregnancy, illicit drug use, violence, low school achievement, and sexually transmitted disease.

This neglect of adolescents in other cultures and times also detracts from our ability to understand the root cause of a given behavior. If we know that the behavior occurs in the United States but remain ignorant of its scope around the world, we cannot determine its origins. Is the behavior characteristic of U.S. adolescents but not of adolescents in other Western industrialized societies? Is it true of U.S. adolescents today but untrue of their parents' generation? Is it a universal finding, in which case we need to seek its explanation in our evolutionary prehistory?

U.S. psychology textbooks consistently report U.S. findings without placing them in context. The reader is led to conclude that these results occur only in the United States and that they are purely cultural phenomena. Alternative historical or evolutionary explanations are tacitly discounted. This tendency is particularly true of reports of sex differences. Many sex differences are cross-cultural, and some are even found generally in mammals or more widely still. Yet one would never suspect this if guided solely by these textbooks. One might attribute this narrowness to a desire to pander to American undergraduates' ethnocentrism and antievolutionism—if one were cynical.

In this chapter, we consider several topics concerning adolescence from a cross-cultural and evolutionary standpoint: dominance competition, romantic relationships, female inhibition in mixed-sex competition, and various forms of delinquent behavior. More comprehensive treatments of adolescence from this perspective include Schlegel and Barry (1991) and Weisfeld (1999).

Dominance Competition

The Dominance Model

The dominance hierarchy model remains an underappreciated tool for making sense of a wide range of social behaviors that are described by mainstream psychology but not analyzed functionally. Behaviors that could be better understood by using this model include striving for social success, allocating resources according to individuals' social success, and the consequences for the individual of habitual success or failure. A surfeit of terms has burgeoned to account for these behaviors. The dominance hierarchy model offers a parsimonious framework for integrating this knowledge and explaining these behaviors functionally.

The basics of this model are as follows: Dominant simians exhibit dominance displays, such as expansive posture, direct gaze, and bodily relaxation, which intimidate rivals. Subordinates exhibit antithetical displays, which convey submission. These displays communicate fighting ability, and individual combatants use this information to reduce the necessity of actual fighting. Dominance carries various prerogatives, notably mating opportunities, but even subordinates exercise the right to be left alone if they duly cede these prerogatives. Animals defend these rights and prerogatives by the threat of force, so that social relations and the allocation of resources are generally stable, regulated, and tranquil. Only when strangers meet is fighting likely to be frequent, until dominance relations are sorted out. Dominant simians show fewer physiological signs of stress and seek out social contact, since this behavior has generally been rewarding. Males tend to be more competitive and dominant than females, with some overlap between the male and female dominance hierarchies. Adaptive adjustments in cortisol, testosterone, and serotonin levels occur as an animal enters into a dominance contest and as the outcome emerges. The amygdala and orbitofrontal cortex are involved in dominance behavior (Weisfeld, 2002).

Analogous findings have been documented in children, adolescents, and adults as well as animals. Yet in lieu of a more parsimonious, comparative explanation, a plethora of concepts has emerged to label these results in humans. These largely superfluous concepts include achievement motivation, self-efficacy, attribution theory, extraversion, social comparison, and social rejection. Many of these findings make sense if considered merely as consequences of success or failure in dominance competition. Successful animals and people receive many social rewards. They develop self-confidence in their abilities, and therefore they seek out social challenges, whereas unsuccessful individuals fear and avoid confrontations. For example, popular adolescents show higher levels of sociability (Newcomb, Bukowski, & Pattee, 1993), and sexually experienced adolescent boys are less likely to be depressed than are virgins (Spencer, Zimet, Aalsma, & Orr, 2002). Successful, self-confident adolescents tend to choose moderately challenging, realistic major subjects (Isaacson, 1964), much as animals challenge those just above them in rank. Students low in self-confidence select very ambitious or very modest career goals, as though avoiding a realistic test of their abilities. Successful individuals expect to succeed, and when they fail, they blame factors other than low ability. Unsuccessful individuals expect to fail, and when they succeed, they cite other factors. Males tend to be more competitive than females. Overrating of self seems to be one means of welcoming challenges; accordingly, males tend to show more overrating of self than females. Since males generally exhibit more competitiveness and self-confidence than females, they more often exhibit a self-confident pattern of attributions.

Why is the concept of dominance avoided? Social scientists who regard humans as fundamentally different from other species are largely responsible. All of us may be reluctant to acknowledge that we are competitive and are guilty of the sin of pride. This reluctance may help explain the fact that while dominance behavior is sometimes acknowledged as occurring in children, it is less often recognized in adolescents and adults. One reason for this distinction may be that children, like animals, fight for dominance, whereas multiple physical and behavioral criteria determine status as development proceeds.

Criteria of Dominance

One reason why even evolutionists sometimes downplay the dominance concept may stem from recognition of the importance of economic competition among males seeking mates. Wealthy men make desirable husbands because they can provide a steady supply of nuptial gifts (Buss, 1994). Nuptial gifts attract females in other species; however, these offerings are species-specific, such as a dead insect, and hence could serve as a releaser to evoke sexual interest. However, given that wealth takes different forms in different human societies, it is unlikely that women possess evolved wealth detectors. Rather, they may be drawn to men who possess some observable proxy for wealth.

A likely candidate for an evolved proxy for male wealth in humans is dominance displays. Wealthy men tend to be socially high ranking, to be deferred to by others, and to exhibit a relaxed self-confidence. Women are attracted to male dominance displays and other indicators of high rank, as are females in many other species (reviewed by Weisfeld & Weisfeld, 2002). Adolescent boys who exhibit nonverbal dominance displays tend to be attractive to girls even though differences in boys' wealth are not yet apparent.

Of course, women (and their parents) can understand the concept of wealth in their particular societies and certainly do consider it in seeking a mate. Cultural criteria, such as clan membership and high-status dress, are also taken into account when choosing a spouse. However, the appeal to women of men's dominant facial, bodily, and vocal features and expressions remains a major factor in explaining female mate choices.

Another possible reason for not using the dominance model to explain human social competition is that the criteria of dominance vary across cultures. Nevertheless, individuals who possess attributes favored in their particular societies exhibit primate dominance displays and gain prerogatives of rank. In China, academic success is highly respected by both sexes, and intelligent adolescents tend to display erect posture, direct gaze, and a relaxed carriage (Dong, Weisfeld, Boardway, & Shen, 1996). By contrast, in the United States, even in relatively elite high schools, academic achievement lends little to a boy's social rank among either boys or girls (Coleman, 1961; Weisfeld, Omark, & Cronin, 1980). Instead, athletic ability and physical attractiveness reign supreme. One recent U.S. study even found that academic success in math and science was negatively related to popularity (Landsheer, Maasen, Bisschop, & Adema, 1998). English and Canadian values seem to be intermediate between these two cases (Brown, 1990; Dong et al., 1996). Thus, culture can dictate the criteria of social competition to some extent, but these values are plugged into the dominance hierarchy behavioral complex.

Young children, like simians, compete for dominance mainly by fighting (Omark, Omark, & Edelman, 1975). Adults compete in culturally variable ways, just as people in different societies satisfy their need for food by eating different things. Dominance competition is not a learned emotion (an oxymoron); rather, we learn some of the criteria by which to compete.

Even though ranks show some long-term stability (see next section), we experience temporary gains and losses in rank and self-esteem. A momentary triumph or failure can alter our dominance displays (Weisfeld & Beresford, 1982). Similarly, we may gain some prestige over someone who generally dominates us by doing him a favor, which elevates our status until the favor is repaid. Wronging another lowers our status vis-à-vis the victim until the misdeed is rectified.

Development of Dominance

Some specifically developmental issues concerning dominance merit attention now. If dominance competition among males is ultimately about gaining mating opportunities, why does it begin early in childhood? There may be two reasons. First, prepubertal children compete for material resources and social opportunities that may contribute greatly to fitness. Children vie for favorite foods and for social opportunities, such as the chance to lead the group at play. Being able to serve as group leader may confer valuable social experience on high-ranking children. A child who is habitually respected and heeded will gain self-confidence and practice social skills that will enhance his or her self-presentation in subsequent social contexts.

The second, related reason for early dominance competition is that childhood ranks tend to carry over into adolescence and beyond (Weisfeld, Muczenski, Weisfeld, & Omark, 1987). Tough boys tended to become dominant, popular leaders who exhibited dominance displays 9 years later ($r = .70$). Presumably, ranks show stability partly because a dominant child develops self-confidence that is instrumental in emboldening him to issue and accept challenges, and in intimidating rivals (Egan & Perry, 1998). The same phenomenon, called "conditioning to success," occurs in animals.

The stability of U.S. boys' ranks suggests that the criteria of dominance remain similar through development. Indeed, physical traits are salient for dominance from childhood through adolescence. Dominant boys are strong, healthy, attractive, physically tough early maturers, who grow up to be strong, athletic, attractive, dominant, early-maturing adolescent leaders (Weisfeld, 1999). Physical attributes are stable, highly correlated, and highly heritable, and so ranks based upon them change little through development (reviewed by Jackson, 1992). In China, on the other hand, we might expect more reversals of dominance ranks over development as the salience of physical traits gives way to respect for intelligence. Similarly, Hopi children compete to be tough, but the pacifistic values of the society eventually discourage fighting and self-aggrandizement (C. C. Weisfeld, Weisfeld, & Callaghan, 1984).

It is often maintained that even in the United States, the criteria for social success change appreciably through development (Pellegrini, 2002). Coercion as a social strategy is said to yield to more prosocial strategies (Hawley, 1999). Aggressive children and adolescents do tend to become unpopular (Cairns, Cairns, Neckerman, Gest, & Gariepy, 1988; Parkhurst & Asher, 1992). But not being aggressive is not the same as exhibiting prosocial behavior. Even if aggression is discouraged, physical attributes such as attractiveness and athletic ability remain salient among peers. Physical traits seem to be compelling criteria of mate choice and leadership everywhere, but especially in the United States. The supposed progression to appreciating prosocial behavior is said to result from children's emerging cognitive capacity for taking another's perspective (Hawley, 1999). If this hypothesis is correct, do U.S. adolescents regress in this capacity, since they mainly value physical attributes, such as attractiveness and (in boys) athletic ability?

Another possible explanation for the developmental decline in dividends from being aggressive is that the type of aggression in question changes through development. Young children seem to tolerate each other's aggression, and an aggressive child is likely to be dominant and popular (Hawley, 1999). But this aggression may constitute play-fighting, which is the norm across cultures in young children, rather than angry aggression or bullying. As ranks are being decided, a tough, dominant boy may fight frequently because he often wins and is reinforced for doing so. Aggression in older children and adolescents detracts from popularity, but perhaps because it is gratuitous—angry aggression or bullying. Popular adolescents seldom fight because they are seldom challenged and are well liked, and they are well liked partly because they seldom attack others.

There may be a streak of wishful thinking permeating the U.S. literature on peer relations in older children and adolescents, with the importance of physical traits being downplayed in favor of prosocial behavior and intelligence. We would like to believe that being smart and nice pays off socially, but the data, especially in the United States, indicate that highly heritable physical traits are paramount. In direct comparisons of the correlation of U.S. adolescent boys' intelligence and athletic ability with dominance, the former pales in comparison (Savin-Williams, 1987). Similarly, being fair was of little advantage to adolescent boys in attracting girls or being popular and influential among boys (Weisfeld et al., 1980; see also Parkhurst & Hopmeyer, 1998). In addition, adolescents are notorious for snubbing subordinates in order not to jeopardize their social standing—not very nice behavior (Eder & Kinney, 1995). Moreover, some studies confuse popularity in the sense of being a good friend with popularity meaning being admired and desired as a friend. Children and adolescents seek friends who are nice to them, but such a friend is not necessarily popular with the group as a whole. We found that Chinese adolescents placed more importance on being a good friend than on popularity, compared with U.S. adolescents (Dong et al., 1996).

Another possible example of wishful thinking is the notion that some boys are low ranking because of a reversible cognitive deficit. Kenneth Dodge (Coie & Dodge, 1983) has argued that rejected, that is, low-ranking, boys get that way by misconstruing the intentions of peers and antagonizing them by reacting with aggression. These boys are said to perceive malice toward them where none exists, and hence they become aggressive in self-defense; this aggressiveness lowers their social standing. The suggested remedy is teaching social skills so that these alleged misperceptions are corrected. (Individual social ranks may be altered by such remedies, but, of course, then other individuals will suffer the slings and arrows of low rank; dominance is a zero-sum proposition.)

The trouble with Dodge's widely accepted explanation is that it fails to explain why these particular boys develop this misperception and why they do not just as often develop the opposite bias and see benevolence where there is malice. Is it not possible that these rejected boys accurately interpret the treatment they receive, that they are in fact rejected and mistreated by their peers? And if so, why are they rejected? Subordinate boys tend to be less attractive and less tough, and are indeed often aggressive (Hodges, Malone, & Perry, 1997), probably because they resent their low status and mistreatment. Dodge (1983) did suggest that rejected boys are less attractive and hence receive less favorable treatment, but he did not follow up this notion. He did, however, discover that boys were more likely to interpret another boy's behavior as hostile if they were the victims than if they observed the same behavior directed toward someone else (Quiggle, Garvber, Panak, & Dodge, 1992). This suggests that this "cognitive deficit" is specific to the treatment that the victim himself receives.

Aggressiveness and Rank

Dodge's finding that rejected boys often withdraw from the group and become aggressive is consistent with the primate dominance model. Subordinate simians tend to withdraw from or be forced from the center of the group, which is a less desirable, more dangerous place to be. If they remain socially withdrawn, they may not get into many fights. However, subordinate animals that remain within the group are sometimes victims of aggression from higher-ranking animals that seek to keep them down and discourage future challenges—exercising their "peck right." Subordinates may also be aggressive in order to rise in the hierarchy; low-ranking vervet monkeys are relatively aggressive (McGuire, Raleigh, & Brammer, 1984). In most studies of children, subordinates are involved in more fights than dominant ones. However, they lose most of these fights. Ethologists define the dominant animal as the one that wins its fights or gains contested resources, not as the one that fights frequently. Studies in which dominance is defined as aggressiveness have yielded confusing results.

The alpha individual is usually less aggressive, but he usually wins when challenged. He has little to gain by challenging others since he cannot advance in rank. Moreover, he can usually intimidate his opponents and so is seldom challenged himself. He enjoys a relative freedom from fighting and can afford to be relaxed and sleeps more soundly. However, in some species, the dominant male is frequently challenged and seldom remains on top for long. This seems to be especially true when the dominant male does all or nearly all of the mating. When the rewards of high rank are great, it will pay for subordinates to challenge their superiors frequently.

Dominance in Females

The dominance model is less successful in explaining female peer relations. As in adolescent boys, dominance, popularity, and leadership in adolescent girls are related closely to physical attractiveness, and high-ranking girls exhibit typical dominance displays (Weisfeld, Bloch, & Ivers, 1984; Zakin, Blyth, & Simmons, 1984). However, females do not generally fight for rank as vigorously as do males (Burbank, 1987), and an aggressive or assertive girl is likely to be unpopular (Dion & Stein, 1978). Instead of using the threat of force, adolescent girls often employ subtler forms of peer competition, such as shunning, gossiping, and criticism (Björkqvist, Lagerspetz, & Kaukiainen, 1992; Crick & Grotpeter, 1995; Eder & McKinney, 1995; Savin-Williams, 1987). But adolescent girls do sometimes fight, just as dominant female simians harass subordinates, potentially reducing the latter's fertility. In a study of British adolescent girls in street gangs, most fights occurred over insults to a girl's sexual reputation (Campbell, 1995).

Campbell (2002) has argued that females avoid fights for adaptive reasons. Females that are pregnant, lactating, or otherwise tending young are especially vulnerable to attack, along with their offspring. Women differ from men in the cascade of hormonal changes that occurs in response to attack and other stressors (Taylor et al., 2000). Men characteristically respond with physical aggression or flight and accordingly undergo pronounced physiological mobilization that is mediated by the sympathetic division and adrenal cortex. In women, fighting and flight are less likely, and mobilization is milder. In response to stressful situations, oxytocin is released at higher levels than in males and promotes affiliation to allies, especially other women, and is soothing and physiologically demobilizing. In many primates, females often support each other, as when one is attacked by the harem master. Similarly, adolescent girls are more likely to turn to same-sex peers for support than are boys (Copeland & Hess, 1995). This sex difference in seeking and offering social support has been reported in an observational study of adolescents (Savin-Williams, 1987) and in subjects of various ages across cultures (Edwards, 1993). The surge in oxytocin under stressful conditions also promotes protection of one's offspring, a response that is usually observed in threatened female mammals (Taylor et al., 2000).

Dominance and Leadership

Another neglected application of the dominance model is its potential for explaining patterns of leadership. Dominant simians tend to attract others' attention because subordinates need to monitor this source of threat. Perhaps partly as a result, dominant primates lead the troop in its movements (Kummer, 1971). A dominant male, because of his prowess, is also often the one to settle disputes among subordinates.

In human society too, high-status individuals tend to be the leaders. Older males lead the group even if they are no longer the strongest males physically. Their experience and wisdom apparently make them desirable leaders, and their success in surviving to middle age may imply some general competence. Among adolescents, a strong, tall, vigorous, competent, attractive peer is desirable as a leader. He or she will have enjoyed many past opportunities to develop leadership skills and will command attention and respect. In an observational study of adolescent boys playing volleyball, the best players praised, criticized, and instructed the poorer players (Weisfeld & Weisfeld, 1984). West Point graduates who possessed dominant, attractive facial features tended to rise in the ranks of officers (Mazur, Mazur, & Keating, 1984). Similarly, younger adolescent girls were observed to pay attention to older, dominant, attractive girls in a dating setting, evidently to learn courtship tactics (Moore, 1995). It presumably pays to seek the assistance of, learn from, and curry the favor of dominant, competent, respected peers. Again, the dominance model offers a starting point for discerning the general outline of peer relations. Dominant, attractive individuals are generally self-confident, outgoing, socially skilled, well-adjusted, respected leaders (reviewed by Jackson, 1992).

Adolescent Romantic Relationships

This topic is gaining increasing attention. Oxytocin has been implicated in formation of pair bonds and in contact comfort (e.g., cuddling in human couples), as well as in other mammalian social bonds (Panksepp, 1998). Oxytocin rises with orgasm in both men and women (Carmichael et al., 1987), and this increase may help to consolidate the bond to the sex partner, especially in women. However, just what developmental events cause the capacity for pair-bonding to develop remain unclear, especially since some children experience "crushes" on a member of the opposite sex before the average age of onset of pubertal hormonal changes (9 years in girls, 10 years in boys). Possibly, adrenal androgens are involved. Adrenarche, the elevation in production of these hormones, occurs quite early, around 7 years of age, and might vary considerably across individuals.

Pair-bonding shows some developmental consistencies, but there is great cross-cultural variability in the extent of premarital sex and the typical age of marriage. The species norm seems to be premarital sexual experimentation (Broude & Greene, 1976; Murdock, 1949), marriage for women around the onset of fertility, and marriage for men when they can afford a wife. Premarital sexual experimentation is thought to allow adolescents to learn their own mate value and those of others, as well as to develop courtship skills. Girls also may receive gifts in exchange for sex. Consistent with a learning explanation, romances last progressively longer as adolescence proceeds (Carver, Joyner, & Udry, 2003; Feiring, 1996), and adolescent marriages are much more prone to divorce than adult ones (Bramlett & Mosher, 2001). Likewise, the fact that promiscuity is relatively high initially (Sorensen, 1973) suggests that learning is being enhanced through contact with a variety of partners. On the other hand, in many societies, marriage occurs at a young age and often with the first sex partner, obviating the opportunity for practice. The romantic bond tends to be strongest with a woman's first sex partner (Kallen & Stephenson, 1982; Peplau, Rubin, & Hill, 1977).

Other proposed functions of sexual experimentation are more dubious from an evolutionary standpoint. Adolescents can learn about sex through premarital practice, but they could gain the necessary practice after marriage. Premarital experimentation might render them more sexually skilled when they enter marriage, but poor sexual skills, unlike refusing sex, do not seem to be a common reason for divorce cross-culturally (Betzig, 1989).

Learning about the opposite sex in more general terms, on the other hand, may be the main benefit of sexual experimentation.

Brown (1999) suggested that adolescent dating allows one to advance in dominance status. Indeed, having a desirable mate can enhance one's status. But this explanation may be culture bound. If it is advantageous to abstain from dating, as in sexually restrictive societies, abstinence enhances a girl's social status and mate value. In addition, Brown has made the compelling observation that as the adolescent dominance hierarchy crystallizes, U.S. adolescents may become less dependent on their peers' opinions of their dates and hence better able to establish romantic relationships based on compatibility. This may contribute to the growing stability of these relationships.

Adolescent romances also seem to play a role in parent-adolescent distancing, a necessary and universal developmental progression. Hazan and Zeifman (1999) reported that before age 8, U.S. children seek emotional support mainly from a parent. From age 8 to age 14, a peer begins to be preferred over a parent. After that, a peer is preferred, typically a romantic partner. A same-sex peer might offer comparable social support in adolescents in more sexually restrictive societies such as China (see above).

Other research has established that secure relationships with parents are linked to stable, intimate romantic relationships (Hazan & Shaver, 1987; Scharf & Mayseless, 2001). Securely attached adolescents are generally comfortable with intimacy and sex. Anxiously attached adolescents have less stable romances. More specifically, anxious/ambivalently attached adolescents tend to fear rejection by romantic partners. They fall in love readily but derive comparatively little enjoyment from sex. Contrariwise, avoidant adolescents exhibit discomfort with intimacy but enjoy sex more (Zeifman & Hazan, 1997).

It makes sense that the internal working model of social relations that develops during childhood would carry over to later relationships. However, another possibility is that a healthy, attractive, pleasant child will inspire closeness in the parents and in romantic partners later on. Attachment status is partly a function of the child's characteristics.

Intense romantic infatuation seldom lasts beyond 2 or 3 years (Fisher, 1992). In the absence of effective contraception, a baby would typically have been born by then, and the parents would need to shift their attention to their helpless newborn. The marriage needs to be maintained indefinitely, however, for the child to continue to benefit from the presence of both parents. The marriage bond seems to be maintained by a less intense affinity based on shared experience and on learning to get along. Mutual satisfaction derived from the baby also probably cements the bond, and neither parent would want to reduce contact with the child through divorce.

Successful reproduction seems by itself to enhance pair bonds in humans and other species (reviewed by Weisfeld & Weisfeld, 2002).

Female Inhibition in Mixed-Sex Competition

Females tend to be less competitive than males in our species and many others. In no culture studied were adolescent girls more competitive than adolescent boys (Schlegel, 1995). Less well-known is the finding that females sometimes reduce their competitiveness when facing male opponents. This phenomenon, referred to as "female inhibition in mixed-sex competition," is most prominent in adolescence and adulthood, that is, during the reproductive years. Any trait with this developmental pattern is likely to relate quite directly to reproduction, so female inhibition probably enhances reproductive success in some way.

Female inhibition has been documented in African American and Hopi adolescents (C. C. Weisfeld et al., 1984), as well as in various Caucasian American populations (Karabenick, Marshall, & Karabenick, 1976). It is not restricted to competitive activities at which males excel, having been demonstrated in spelling bees, at which girls surpass boys (Cronin, 1980). This research and most other studies on this topic have been observational. This is fortunate, because it turned out that the girls studied by C. C. Weisfeld (née Cronin) were mostly unaware that they were holding back when competing against boys and typically denied vehemently that they were doing so. Self-report data alone would not have revealed this female inhibition effect. Observational methods have usually proved to be more sensitive than questionnaire methods in revealing the extent of this phenomenon.

Adult women may or may not (Mausner & Coles, 1978) be aware of exhibiting this behavior. They have been observed to use more tentative speech when addressing a man than a woman (Caspi & Herbener, 1990) and to act more submissively in mixed-sex groups than same-sex ones (Aries, 1982) and toward their husband compared with other men (McCarrick, Manderscheid, & Silbergeld, 1981).

Female inhibition seems to enhance pair bond formation in some way. It occurs vis-à-vis a boyfriend (Peplau, 1976) but seems to be weaker in competition against a brother than against a potential mate (C. C. Weisfeld, 2004). It tends to be exhibited more by women with a rather feminine hormonal profile (reviewed by C. C. Weisfeld, 1986). These high-estrogen, early-maturing women are more interested in marriage and less concerned with attending university and having a career than are less feminine women (Magnusson, 1988; Simmons, Blyth, & McKinney, 1983).

Because competitive success is so important to males, a woman who defeated a man in some competition might discourage him from seeing her again. Female inhibition occurs particularly in cases in which the woman's ability approaches or exceeds that of her male opponent. Cashdan (1993) reported that women who expected to find a husband to support them were less likely to display their own financial resources than those with lower expectations. Furthermore, a woman who felt herself superior to a man might not be romantically interested in him, so she might handicap herself when competing with him in order to maintain a positive view of him. Recall that females of many species, including our own, seek traits reflecting dominance in a male. If a male were subdominant to a female, she might conclude on some mental level that he was beneath her station. Marriages in which the wife dominates the husband are prone to sexual difficulties (Masters & Johnson, 1970) and divorce (reviewed by Weisfeld, 1999). For example, if the wife's income rivals or exceeds the husband's, divorce more often occurs (Booth & Edwards, 1985; Cready, Fossett, & Kiecolt, 1997; D'Amico, 1983).

In sum, the cross-cultural nature of female inhibition, its partially unconscious basis, its relation to hormone levels, its specificity in being directed toward potential mates, and its plausible adaptive value for ancestral hominids argue in favor of an evolved basis and a function in mate formation and maintenance.

Delinquency

Knowledge of ancestral hominid conditions is useful not only for what it tells us about human nature but also because it points out ways in which modern society deviates from the conditions under which humans evolved. For example, if adolescents misbehave, it may be because modern cultural conditions grate against our natural inclinations (Benedict, 1934). What we regard as abnormal behavior may be normal, at least in the statistical sense, when viewed in prehistoric or cross-cultural perspective. If a substantial fraction of adolescents behave in a certain way, a societal rather than individual explanation is usually indicated. Another possibility is that a particular abnormal behavior constitutes a pathological deviation from normality, just as diseases occur because of derangement of normal physiological processes. In other words, the medical model of disease may be extended to behavioral pathology (McGuire & Troisi, 1998). However, pathology, especially with a genetic basis, tends to occur only rarely because it reduces fitness and is selected against. It may be appropriate now to examine adolescent delinquency in the light of these two possibilities—but to bear in mind that many types of juvenile delinquency are status offenses, meaning that these behaviors are acceptable if performed by adults.

Violence

Can adolescent violence be construed as a deviation from normality? Misbehavior by adolescents occurs in numerous preliterate cultures but seldom involves many individuals or extends beyond minor boisterousness (Schlegel & Barry, 1991). Youths may seek to distinguish themselves by committing acts of bravado or by ridiculing or insulting their peers or elders. Humorous repartee is especially common in adolescent boys and men cross-culturally (Apte, 1985). The rise in competitiveness at adolescence probably occurs because sexual competition emerges at this time. Adolescents seek a new, essential object of competition: mating opportunities. Adolescence is the time of maximal reproductive competition, when both sexes are trying to break into the breeding pool. For this reason, bodily prowess and mental aptitude, as indicated by measures of health and fluid intelligence, peak around the end of adolescence (Daly & Wilson, 1983; Schaie & Willis, 1993).

One likely reason for the intensity of sexual competition in male adolescents is that promiscuity abounds during adolescence (Einon, 1994). Research in U.S. high schools has shown that a small number of boys are in great demand; they have many sex partners, whereas most boys have few or none (Forrest & Singh, 1990; Hass, 1979; Sorensen, 1973). This variance in sexual success means that competition is intense among the boys. The great competitiveness of maturing males may help to explain why, in all cultures and historical periods, young males commit the vast majority of assaults and homicides, most of which are related to sexual competition directly or indirectly (Daly & Wilson, 1988).

Can homicides in modern society be interpreted in light of these comparative facts? A landmark Detroit study by Wilson and Daly (1985) indicated that most homicides involved young men who were competing (a) to uphold their reputations (to "save face" even when the material resources at stake were trivial), (b) to secure resources through property crime that would gain them sexual opportunities, or (c) to punish a lover or sexual rival for suspected or threatened violation of their presumed sexual prerogatives. Thus, most "senseless" homicides in this study could be explained in terms of dominance competition, with access to females the ultimate prerogative being contested. Similarly, many fights between street gang members concern disputes over females or competition for gang leadership, which results in greater access to girls (Feldman & Weisfeld, 1973).

Sexual competition is intense for adolescent girls too, since most of them are vying for the same few boys. Furthermore, females are under greater time pressure to acquire husbands, since their mate value declines after adolescence, whereas males' mate value rises as they increase in age and dominance status (Laursen & Jensen-Campbell, 1999). As in males, the assault and homicide rates for females peak in the early reproductive years, when sexual competition is greatest (Daly & Wilson, 1988).

Adolescent aggressiveness and self-display, obsession with one's appearance and social standing, preoccupation with the opposite sex, and deception of potential and current sex partners or rivals (Buss, 1994) may constitute normal expressions of the sexual, romantic, and competitive motives of adolescence. They may reach pathological magnitude in certain individuals or cultures, but such a determination is arbitrary. Other factors to consider include the fact that violence tends to be endemic when police protection is ineffectual, such as when young men are engaged in illegal activities and hence cannot risk summoning the authorities, and when the community lacks political power to secure effective law enforcement. Individuals must then resort to self-help and the collective defense offered by fellow gang members or by kin, in order to protect themselves. Another consideration is Mazur and Booth's (1998) finding that young men in violent neighborhoods tend to have elevated testosterone levels, controlling for various factors. Animals entering into competitive social situations experience a similar rise, presumably to potentiate aggressiveness and competitiveness.

Another plausible interpretation of pathological aggression is that in some cases, it reflects a genetic variant that is maintained in the population by frequency-dependent selection. This variant could remain stable and appreciably common if it conferred an adaptive advantage approximately equal to that of the more common normal variant. Sociopathy might thrive if it did not become too common; people might not suspect that they were being exploited by the sociopath (Mealey, 1995). Sociopathy does appear to have some heritability (Willerman, Loehlin, & Horn, 1992), although almost any trait, whether adaptive or not, exhibits some heritability.

Alternatively, sociopathy may be explained as a purely pathological variant. For example, impulsive homicide is associated with damage to the prefrontal cortex (Raine, 1993). Also, early exposure to lead has been associated with juvenile delinquency, perhaps by impairing cognitive functioning (Dietrich, Ris, Succop, Berger, & Bomschein, 2001). Many criminals are low in intelligence and can be said to enter into illicit pursuits in lieu of competence to compete legitimately.

Sexual Promiscuity

Sexual promiscuity is not pathological if viewed in cross-cultural perspective. In most traditional cultures, especially foragers, adolescent premarital sex is normative, and girls begin their sex lives at puberty, although often with somewhat older boys. Only in economically stratified traditional cultures, in which bride prices are significant, do parents typically restrict their children's sexuality, in order to arrange marriages that benefit the family materially (Friedl, 1975). In these societies, parents try to prevent their children's sexual and romantic liaisons by segregating the sexes, discouraging premarital sex, veiling and draping nubile females, or performing genital mutilation to reduce female libido (van den Berghe, 1979).

Several developmental facts also suggest that premarital sex was normal behavior during hominid evolution. Well before the onset of fertility and the age of marriage in traditional cultures, girls' bodies become prepared for sexual intercourse. The genitals grow, the vaginal rugae develop to stimulate the penis, the vagina thickens, the breasts appear as sexual lures and become sensitive to erotic stimulation, and pubic hair and retropubic fat pad develop to protect the mons veneris during intercourse and to signal sexual maturity (Tanner, 1978). Likewise, boys' genitals and pubic hair develop early in puberty, and orgasm becomes possible about a year before semen is produced. Fertility itself increases only gradually after semenarche. Thus, both sexes are prepared to engage in sex years before fertility begins. Furthermore, puberty seems to prompt a tendency for adolescents to stay up late (Carskadon, Acebo, Richardson, Tate, & Seifer, 1997); this may allow them to engage in sexual relations after meddling adults are asleep.

Unwed Adolescent Motherhood

Because most girls in traditional cultures marry before they reach fertility, early sexual experimentation seldom leads to premarital births. The steady acceleration of menarcheal age between the mid-19th and mid-20th century in the West, as nutrition improved, opened a gap between the onset of fertility and the typical age of marriage. In modern society, fertility begins years before the average age of marriage, leaving a girl vulnerable to premarital pregnancy. Does unwed motherhood in modern society, then, constitute a pathological phenomenon? Certainly, it does in terms of the consequences for the child. Children of single mothers, especially adolescent single mothers, are at risk for a plethora of developmental problems and so are their mothers (Furstenberg, Brooks-Gunn, & Morgan, 1987; Rickel, 1989).

However, many girls who become unwed mothers may be optimizing their reproductive opportunities given their available options (Draper & Harpending, 1988). Many adolescent girls become pregnant not from ignorance about contraception, but because they want to have babies (Lindemann & Scott, 1981; Sorensen, 1973). These girls, often from disadvantaged backgrounds, may get pregnant because they accurately assess their chances of marrying a desirable man to be remote. Given a choice between failure to reproduce and reproduction without a husband, many girls choose the latter.

Wilson (1987) argued that a disproportionate number of African American men are unavailable as husbands due to drug use, incarceration, mental illness, poverty, or premature death. Cross-national and cross-cultural data indicate that men are unmarriageable if they cannot contribute to the family income, so this is not a problem just of Black America (Goode, 1993). As marriageable men become scarcer, they can gain sexual opportunities without offering marriage, and the marriage rate for men (the limiting sex) will decline even further. On the other hand, when women are in short supply, their marriage rate rises (Pederson, 1991). By this analysis, one might conclude that the pathological behavior is societal complacency with endemic poverty. Wilson's recommendation is to increase the number of marriageable men by providing jobs and job training for needy people of any race.

Euphoriant Drug Use

Drug abuse can also be considered from an evolutionary standpoint. Euphoriant drugs act on pleasure centers in the brain, and so, if it is normal to seek pleasure, then self-administering these substances is normal. Wild mammals sometimes ingest euphoriant substances, such as jimsonweed, as do laboratory animals given access to them (Rosenzweig, Leiman, & Breedlove, 1996). Furthermore, it need hardly be pointed out that while many adults indulge in the use of such substances, they condemn the practice in their adolescent children. The hypocrisy of adults in deploring marijuana use (a relatively harmless, nonaddictive drug) while they drink and smoke is well-known. Alcohol and tobacco are addictive and are responsible for virtually all the health and societal damage caused by euphoriant drugs in the United States (Rosenzweig et al., 1996). Furthermore, they are by far the drugs most used by adolescents and are the "gateway" drugs to others (Steinberg, 1996).

Why this animus against these particular drugs but not alcohol and tobacco? Drugs have frequently been stigmatized not because they were especially harmful, but because of their common use by minority groups, such as Blacks, Mexicans, and Chinese, and by the young. If the health risks of a drug were to be invoked as an argument for proscribing it, alcohol and tobacco would head the list of condemned drugs.

Drug use, being so widespread, may be normal. On the other hand, perhaps it is symptomatic of pathology because drugs are used excessively mainly by unhappy people. Drug abuse in adolescence is associated with family and personal problems (Steinberg, 1996). Many victims of societal injustice, depression, and other psychopathies also self-administer euphoriants. Any society with a major drug problem, such as the United States, presumably has a large number of unhappy citizens.

Another factor accounting for the high level of drug use in the United States is, paradoxically, the war on drugs. Cross-national and historical research has demonstrated quite convincingly that the harsh, criminological approach to the drug problem in the United States has created a black market that keeps drug vending profitable and ubiquitous, just as occurred during Prohibition (Miller, 1991). Drugs remain widely available despite extensive programs to interdict supplies and imprison vendors. Temporarily interrupting the supply merely raises the price of drugs and the incentive for selling them. Because of the scope of the war on drugs, many people depend on its perpetuation for their jobs. These include lawyers, judges, police officers, prison guards, private sector employers of prison laborers, construction companies, social workers, counselors, and customs agents. Politicians might also be mentioned, since very few of them have opposed this colossal waste of money. Many impoverished adolescents find selling drugs their only means of employment and the only one offering any realistic chance of economic advancement. However, the associated risks are such that many vendors eventually serve long prison sentences and, upon release, are unable to join society as constructive members.

Other Western countries have adopted a medical approach and have treated their opiates addicts without stigmatizing them (Stimson & Oppenheimer, 1982). Patients are maintained on opiates and generally lead normal, lucid, productive lives. Drugs are administered only to certified addicts under medical supervision, thereby virtually eliminating overdoses, infections, and toxic reactions. Marijuana and cocaine use are tolerated, and only vendors of more dangerous drugs are prosecuted; therefore, selling drugs is not very profitable. Except for tobacco and possibly alcohol, Europeans have lower rates of drug use than Americans (Miller, 1991).

Thus, the extent of a pathological behavior can be affected by governmental policies, and a decriminalization approach may be best. Adopting this approach does not mean that drug use is condoned; rather, it is viewed as symptomatic of basic problems and as a medical problem rather than a moral failure. The resources saved by abandoning a criminological approach could be invested in educating the public about the pharmacological effects of various euphoriant drugs and offering rehabilitation. A harm reduction policy of preventative education, sympathetic rehabilitation with medicinal support, and needle exchange programs would doubtless reduce the consequences of drug use enormously, especially street crime, about half of which is drug related.

General Factors in Delinquency in the United States

Delinquent tendencies in the United States may be aggravated by feelings of neglect and rejection due to the decline of contact with kin. In most traditional cultures, especially foragers, parents are generally more nurturant and attentive toward their children than in ours (Stephens, 1963), particularly where there are multiple caretakers (Werner, 1979). The extended family is the norm for child rearing in our species. Even in intact nuclear families in the United States, contact hours between parents and children are declining and are low compared with the situation in traditional cultures (Louv, 1990). Mothers, even of infants, have increased their working hours dramatically in recent years (Popenoe, 1993), and the U.S. government does not offer paid parental leave. U.S. workers now put in more hours per year than those of any other developed nation. Parents under stress are prone to be curt and hostile toward their children. Parental hostility is correlated with adolescent depression, suicide, and pregnancy (Belsky, 1990).

A related factor is father absence. Drug abuse, running away, criminal offenses, academic and emotional difficulties, financial privation, and premarital pregnancy are more likely in father-absent homes than in other arrangements (Adams & Gullotta, 1989). Also, in such homes, the child or adolescent is at elevated risk of being abused violently or sexually, or even murdered, especially by a stepfather or a boyfriend of the mother (Daly & Wilson, 1988). Furthermore, step-adolescents are especially liable to leave home early or to precipitate their parents' divorces (White & Booth, 1985).

The ubiquitous role of fathers in our species is amply supported by anthropological data, so father absence, even without the presence of another man, is likely to be detrimental. Fathers provide important material resources, defend the family from attack and abuse, and aid children's cognitive, social, and emotional development (Mackey, 1996). In traditional cultures, the father typically assumes a major role in caring for a weanling when the next birth occurs and is the son's main tutor in subsistence skills (Schlegel & Barry, 1991). The direct participation of the father in child care depends on various ecological factors, such as time spent in the settlement and degree of polygyny, and is not as extensive as that of the mother in any society (Friedl, 1975; Stephens, 1963). However, biparentalism—both parents raising their children together—is the norm for our species, notwithstanding the merits of tolerance of other social arrangements.

Another possible example of a lack of fit between contemporary conditions and our evolved behavioral tendencies concerns the performance of useful labor by adolescents. Many contemporary adolescents lack opportunities to gain prestige by helping younger children or performing other useful labor. Many tasks that adolescents perform in preliterate cultures are assigned in modern society to parents or professionals. This reflects the technical difficulty of these tasks and the related necessity for young people to undergo extensive schooling to prepare them for adult labor (Whiting & Whiting, 1973). Also, small family size has reduced older children's opportunities to practice child care. Children and adolescents devote themselves mainly to schoolwork, but this pursuit does not provide the tangible benefits of household and subsistence labor and hence is not very prestigious. Moreover, academic success may garner little respect from peers, compared with the evolved appeal of bodily attractiveness and, perhaps, a lively wit or other social and artistic skills. Deprived of opportunities to gain prestige through societal contributions, some adolescents may resort to other means of attracting attention, such as feats of daring and defiance of adults. Alternatively, they may languish in a state of purposelessness.

Traditional societies provide adolescents with puberty rites: formal training to prepare them for adult roles and societal recognition for entering into adult status (Weisfeld, 1997). Instead of being excluded from the world of adult work and socializing, they are brought along as apprentices from whom much is expected. They are treated as vital and respected contributors, which indeed they are becoming, rather than as outsiders inhabiting a suspicious world of odd dress and musical tastes.

Conclusion

The study of adolescence in the United States would benefit greatly from a cross-cultural, comparative, evolutionary perspective. This perspective can provide a better understanding of normal adolescence and of problem behaviors that result from departures from these ancient functional patterns. In offering this viewpoint, we can provide our still-adolescent university students with a broader outlook on the society that they will eventually lead.

References

Adams, G. R., & Gullotta, T. (1989). *Adolescent life experiences.* Pacific Grove, CA: Brooks/Cole.

Apte, M. L. (1985). *Humor and laughter: An anthropological approach.* Ithaca, NY: Cornell University Press.

Aries, P. (1982). Verbal and nonverbal behavior in single-sex and mixed-sex groups: Are traditional sex roles changing? *Psychological Reports, 51,* 117-134.

Belsky, J. (1990). Parental and nonparental child care and children's socioemotional development: A decade in review. *Journal of Marriage and the Family, 52,* 885-903.

Benedict, R. (1934). *Patterns of culture.* New York: Mentor.

Betzig, L. (1989). Causes of conjugal dissolution: A cross-cultural study. *Current Anthropology, 30,* 654-676.

Björkqvist, K., Lagerspetz, K. M. J., & Kaukiainen, A. (1992). Do girls manipulate and boys fight? Developmental trends in regard to direct and indirect aggression. *Aggressive Behavior, 18,* 117-127.

Booth, A., & Edwards, J. N. (1985). Age at marriage and marital instability. *Journal of Marriage and the Family, 47,* 67-75.

Bramlett, M. D., & Mosher, W. D. (2001). *First marriage dissolution, divorce and remarriage: United States.* Hyattsville, MD: National Center for Health Statistics.

Broude, G. J., & Greene, S. J. (1976). Cross-cultural codes on twenty sexual attitudes and practices. *Ethnology, 15,* 409-429.

Brown, B. (1990). Peer groups and peer cultures. In S. S. Feldman & G. R. Elliott (Eds.), *At the threshold: The developing adolescent* (pp. 171-196). Cambridge, MA: Harvard University Press.

Brown, B. B. (1999). You're going out with who? Peer group influences on adolescent romantic relationships. In W. Furman, B. B. Brown, & C. Feiring (Eds.), *The development of romantic relationships in adolescence* (pp. 291-329). New York: Cambridge University Press.

Burbank, V. (1987). Female aggression in cross-cultural perspective. *Behavioral Science Research, 21,* 70-100.

Buss, D. M. (1994). *The evolution of desire.* New York: Basic.

Cairns, R., Cairns, B., Neckerman, H., Gest, S., & Gariepy, J. (1988). Social networks and aggressive behavior: Peer support or peer rejection? *Developmental Psychology, 24,* 815-823.

Campbell, A. (1995). A few good men: Evolutionary psychology and female adolescent aggression. *Ethology and Sociobiology, 16,* 99-123.

Campbell, A. (2002). *A mind of her own: The evolutionary psychology of women.* Oxford, UK: Oxford University Press.

Carmichael, M. S., Humbert, R., Dixen, J., Palmiana, G., Greenleaf, W., & Davidson, J. M. (1987). Plasma oxytocin increase in the human sexual response. *Journal of Clinical & Endocrinological Metabolism, 64,* 27-31.

Carskadon, M., Acebo, C., Richardson, B., Tate, B., & Seifer, R. (1997). Long nights protocol: Access to circadian parameters in adolescents. *Journal of Biological Rhythms, 12,* 278-289.

Carver, K., Joyner, K., & Udry, J. R. (2003). National estimates of adolescent romantic relationships. In P. Florsheim (Ed.), *Adolescent romantic relations and sexual behavior: Theory, research, and practical implications* (pp. 23-56). Mahwah, NJ: Erlbaum.

Cashdan, E. (1993). Attracting mates: Effects of paternal investment on mate attraction strategies. *Ethology & Sociobiology, 14,* 1-23.

Caspi, A., & Herbener, E. S. (1990). Continuity and change: Assortative marriage and the consistency of personality in adulthood. *Journal of Personality and Social Psychology, 58,* 250-258.

Coie, J. D., & Dodge, K. A. (1983). Continuities and changes in children's social status: A five-year longitudinal study. *Merrill-Palmer Quarterly, 29,* 261-281.

Coleman, J. S. (1961). *The adolescent society.* Glencoe, IL: Free Press.

Copeland, E. P., & Hess, R. S. (1995). Differences in young adolescents' coping strategies based on gender and ethnicity. *Journal of Early Adolescence, 15,* 203-219.

Cready, D. M., Fossett, M. A., & Kiecolt, K. J. (1997). Mate availability and African American family structure in the U.S. nonmetropolitan South, 1960-1990. *Journal of Marriage and the Family, 59,* 192-203.

Crick, N. R., & Grotpeter, J. K. (1995). Relational aggression, gender, and social-psychological adjustment. *Child Development, 66,* 710-722.

Cronin, C. L. (1980). Dominance relations and females. In D. R. Omark, F. F. Strayer, & D. G. Freedman (Eds.), *Dominance relations: An ethological view of human conflict and social interaction* (pp. 299-318). New York: Garland.

Daly, M., & Wilson, M. (1983). *Sex, evolution, and behavior* (2nd ed.). Boston: Willard Grant.

Daly, M., & Wilson, M. (1988). *Homicide.* Hawthorne, NY: Aldine de Gruyter.

D'Amico, R. (1983). Status maintenance or status competition? Wife's relative wages as a determinant of labor supply and marital instability. *Social Forces, 63,* 1186-1205.

Dietrich, K. N., Ris, M. D., Succop, P., Berger, O. G., & Bomschein, R. L. (2001). Early exposure to lead and juvenile delinquency. *Neurotoxicology & Teratology, 23,* 511-518.

Dion, K. K., & Stein, S. (1978). Physical attractiveness and interpersonal influence. *Journal of Experimental Social Psychology, 14,* 97-108.

Dodge, K. A. (1983). Behavioral antecedents of peer social status. *Child Development, 54,* 1386-1399.

Dong, Q., Weisfeld, G., Boardway, R. H., & Shen, J. (1996). Correlates of social status among Chinese adolescents. *Journal of Cross-Cultural Psychology, 27,* 476-493.

Draper, P., & Harpending, H. (1988). A sociobiological perspective on the development of human reproductive strategies. In K. MacDonald (Ed.),

Sociobiological perspective on human development (pp. 340-372). New York: Springer-Verlag.

Eder, D., & McKinney, D. A. (1995). The effect of middle school extracurricular activities on adolescents' popularity and peer status. *Youth & Society, 26,* 298-324.

Edwards, C. P. (1993). Behavioral sex differences in children of diverse cultures: The case of nurturance to infants. In M. E. Pereira & L. A. Fairbanks (Eds.), *Juvenile primates: Life history, development, and behavior* (p. 327-338). New York: Oxford University Press.

Egan, S. K., & Perry, D. G. (1998). Does low self-regard invite victimization? *Developmental Psychology, 34,* 299-309.

Einon, D. (1994). Are men more promiscuous than women? *Ethology and Sociobiology, 15,* 131-143.

Feiring, C. (1996). Concepts of romance in 15-year-old adolescents. *Journal of Research on Adolescence, 6,* 181-200.

Feldman, R., & Weisfeld, G. (1973). An interdisciplinary study of crime. *Crime and Delinquency, 19,* 150-162.

Fisher, H. (1992). *Anatomy of love: The mysteries of mating, marriage, and why we stray.* New York: Fawcett Columbine.

Forrest, J. D., & Singh, S. (1990). Public-sector savings resulting from expenditures for contraceptive services. *Family Planning Perspectives, 22,* 6-15.

Friedl, E. (1975). *Women and men: An anthropologist's view.* New York: Holt, Rinehart & Winston.

Furstenberg, F. F., Brooks-Gunn, J., & Morgan, S. P. (1987). *Adolescent mothers in later life.* New York: Cambridge University Press.

Goode, W. J. (1993). *World changes in divorce patterns.* New Haven, CT: Yale University Press.

Hass, A. (1979). *Teenage sexuality.* New York: Macmillan.

Hawley, P. H. (1999). The ontogenesis of social dominance: A strategy-based evolutionary perspective. *Developmental Review, 19,* 97-132.

Hazan, C., & Shaver, P. (1987). Romantic love conceptualized as an attachment process. *Journal of Personality & Social Psychology, 52,* 511-524.

Hazan, C., & Zeifman, D. (1999). Pair bonds as attachments. In J. Cassidy & P. R. Shaver (Eds.), *Handbook of attachment: Theory, research, and clinical applications* (pp. 336-354). New York: Guilford Press.

Hodges, E. V. E., Malone, M. J., & Perry, D. G. (1997). Individual risk and social risk as interacting determinants of victimization in the peer group. *Developmental Psychology, 35,* 1032-1039.

Isaacson, R. I. (1964). Relations between N-achievement, test anxiety, and curricular choices. *Journal of Abnormal and Social Psychology, 68,* 447-452.

Jackson, L. A. (1992). *Physical appearance and gender: Sociobiological and socio-cultural perspectives.* Albany: State University of New York Press.

Kallen, D., & Stephenson, J. (1982). Talking about sex revisited. *Journal of Youth and Adolescence, 11,* 11-24.

Karabenick, S. A., Marshall, J. M., & Karabenick, J. D. (1976). Effects of fear of success, fear of failure, type of opponent, and feedback on female achievement performance. *Journal of Research on Personality, 10,* 369-385.

Kummer, H. (1971). *Primate societies: Group techniques of ecological adaptation.* Chicago: Aldine.

Landsheer, H., Maasen, G. H., Bisschop, P., & Adema, L. (1998). Can higher grades result in fewer friends: A reexamination of the relation between academic and social competence. *Adolescence, 33,* 185-191.

Laursen, B., & Jensen-Campbell, L. A. (1999). The nature and function of social exchange in adolescent romantic relationships. In W. Furman, B. B. Brown, & C. Feiring (Eds.), *The development of romantic relationships in adolescence* (pp. 50-74). New York: Cambridge University Press.

Lindemann, C., & Scott, W. J. (1981). Wanted and unwanted pregnancy in early adolescence: Evidence from a clinic population. *Journal of Early Adolescence, 1,* 185-193.

Louv, R. (1990). *Childhood's future.* Boston: Houghton Mifflin.

Mackey, W. C. (1996). *The American father: Biocultural and developmental aspects.* New York: Plenum.

Magnusson, D. (1988). *Individual development from an interactional perspective: A longitudinal study.* Hillsdale, NJ: Erlbaum.

Masters, W. H., & Johnson, V. E. (1970). *Human sexual inadequacy.* Boston: Little, Brown.

Mausner, B., & Coles, B. (1978). Avoidance of success among women. *International Journal of Women's Studies, 1,* 30-49.

Mazur, A., & Booth, A. (1998). Testosterone and dominance in men. *Behavioral and Brain Sciences, 21,* 353-397.

Mazur, A., Mazur, J., & Keating, C. (1984). Military rank attainment of a West Point class: Effects of cadets' physical features. *American Journal of Sociology, 90,* 125-150.

McCarrick, A. K., Manderscheid, R. W., & Silbergeld, S. (1981). Gender differences in competition and dominance during married-couples therapy. *Social Psychology Quarterly, 44,* 164-177.

McGuire, M. T., Raleigh, M. J., & Brammer, G. L. (1984). Adaptation, selection, and benefit-cost balances: Implications of behavioral-physiological studies of social dominance in male vervet monkeys. *Ethology & Sociobiology, 5,* 269-277.

McGuire, M. T., & Troisi, A. (1998). *Darwinian psychiatry.* London: Oxford University Press.

Mealey, L. (1995). The sociobiology of sociopathy: An integrated evolutionary model. *Behavioral and Brain Sciences, 18,* 523-599.

Miller, R. L. (1991). *The case for legalizing drugs.* New York: Praeger.

Moore, M. (1995). Courtship signals and adolescents: Girls just wanna have fun? *Journal of Sex Research, 31,* 319-328.

Murdock, G. P. (1949). *Social structure.* New York: Macmillan.

Newcomb, A. F., Bukowski, W. M., & Pattee, L. (1993). Children's peer relations: A meta-analytic review of popular, rejected neglected, controversial and average sociometric status. *Psychological Bulletin, 113,* 99-128.

Omark, D. R., Omark, M., & Edelman, M. S. (1975). Formation of dominance hierarchies in young children: Action and perception. In T. Williams (Ed.), *Psychological anthropology* (pp. 289-315). The Hague, The Netherlands: Mouton.

Panksepp, J. (1998). *Affective neuroscience: The foundations of human and animal emotions.* New York: Oxford University Press.

Parkhurst, J. T., & Asher, S. R. (1992). Peer rejection in middle school: Differences in behavior, loneliness, and interpersonal concerns. *Developmental Psychology, 28,* 231-241.

Parkhurst, J. T., & Hopmeyer, A. (1998). Sociometric popularity and peer-perceived popularity: Two distinct dimensions of peer status. *Journal of Early Adolescence, 18,* 125-144.

Pederson, F. A. (1991). Secular trends in human sex ratios: Their influence on individual and family behavior. *Human Nature, 2,* 271-291.

Pellegrini, A. D. (2002). Affiliative and aggressive dimensions of dominance and possible functions during early adolescents. *Aggressive and Violence Behavior, 7,* 21-31.

Peplau, L., Rubin, Z., & Hill, C. (1977). Sexual intimacy in dating relationships. *Journal of Social Issues, 33,* 86-109.

Peplau, L. A. (1976). Fear of success in dating couples. *Sex Roles, 2,* 249-258.

Popenoe, D. (1993). American family decline, 1960-1990: A review and appraisal. *Journal of Marriage and the Family, 55,* 527-555.

Quiggle, N. L., Garvber, J., Panak, W. F., & Dodge, K. A. (1992). Social information processing in aggressive and depressed boys. *Child Development, 63,* 1305-1320.

Raine, A. (1993). *The psychopathology of crime: Criminal behavior as a clinical disorder.* San Diego: Academic Press.

Rickel, A. U. (1989). *Teen pregnancy and parenting.* New York: Hemisphere.

Rosenzweig, M. R., Leiman, A. L., & Breedlove, S. M. (1996). *Biological psychology.* Sunderland, MA: Sinauer.

Savin-Williams, R. C. (1987). *Adolescence: An ethological perspective.* New York: Springer-Verlag.

Schaie, K. W., & Willis, S. L. (1993). Age difference patterns of psychometric intelligence in adulthood: Generalizability within and across ability domains. *Psychology and Aging, 8,* 44-55.

Scharf, M., & Mayseless, O. (2001). The capacity for romantic intimacy: Exploring the contribution of best friend and marital and parental relationships. *Journal of Adolescence, 24,* 379-399.

Schlegel, A. (1995). A cross-cultural approach to adolescence. *Ethos, 23,* 15-32.

Schlegel, A., & Barry, H. III. (1991). *Adolescence: An anthropological inquiry.* New York: Free Press.

Simmons, R. G., Blyth, D. A., & McKinney, K. L. (1983). The social and psychological effects of puberty on white females. In J. Brooks-Gunn & A. C. Petersen (Eds.), *Girls at puberty: Biological and psychosocial perspectives* (pp. 229-272). New York: Plenum.

Sorensen, R. C. (1973). *Adolescent sexuality in contemporary America.* New York: World Publishing.

Spencer, J. M., Zimet, G. D., Aalsma, M. C., & Orr, D. P. (2002). Self-esteem as a predictor of initiation of coitus in early adolescents. *Pediatrics, 109,* 581-584.

Steinberg, L. A. (1996). *Adolescence* (4th ed.). New York: McGraw-Hill.

Stephens, W. N. (1963). *The family in cross-cultural perspective.* New York: Holt, Rinehart & Winston.

Stimson, G. V., & Oppenheimer, E. (1982). *Heroin addiction: Treatment and control in Britain.* London: Tavistock.

Tanner, J. M. (1978). *Fetus into man: Physical growth from conception to maturity.* Cambridge, MA: Harvard University Press.

Taylor, S. E., Klein, I. C., Lewis, B. P., Gruenewald, T. L., Gurung, R. A. R., & Updegraff, J. A. (2000). Female responses to stress: Tend-and-befriend, not fight-or-flight. *Psychological Review, 107,* 411-429.

van den Berghe, P. L. (1979). *Human family systems: An evolutionary view.* New York: Elsevier.

Weisfeld, C. C. (1986). Female behavior in mixed-sex competition: A review of the literature. *Developmental Psychology, 6,* 278-299.

Weisfeld, C. C. (2004, March). *Female inhibition in mixed-sex competition.* Paper presented at the convention of the Society for Research on Adolescence, Baltimore, MD.

Weisfeld, C. C., Weisfeld, G. E., & Callaghan, J. W. (1984). Female inhibition in mixed-sex competition among young adolescents. *Ethology & Sociobiology, 3,* 29-42.

Weisfeld, G. E. (1997). Puberty rites as clues to the nation of human adolescence. *Cross-Cultural Research, 31,* 27-54.

Weisfeld, G. E. (1999). *Evolutionary principles of human adolescence.* New York: Basic Books.

Weisfeld, G. E. (2002). Neural and functional aspects of pride and shame. In G. A. Cory & R. Gardner Jr. (Eds.), *The neuroethology of Paul MacLean: Convergences and frontiers* (pp. 193-214). Westport, CT: Greenwood Praeger Group.

Weisfeld, G. E., & Beresford, J. M. (1982). Erectness of posture as an indicator of dominance or success in humans. *Motivation & Emotions, 6,* 113-131.

Weisfeld, G. E., Bloch, S. A., & Ivers, J. W. (1984). Possible determinants of social dominance among adolescent girls. *Journal of Genetic Psychology, 144,* 115-129.

Weisfeld, G. E., Muczenski, D. M., Weisfeld, C. C., & Omark, D. R. (1987). Stability of boys' social success among peers over an eleven-year period. In J. A. Meacham (Ed.), *Interpersonal relations: Family, peers, friends* (pp. 58-80). Basel, Switzerland: Karger.

Weisfeld, G. E., Omark, D. R., & Cronin, C. L. (1980). A longitudinal and cross-sectional study of dominance in boys. In D. R. Omark, F. F. Strayer, & D. G. Freedman (Eds.), *Dominance relations: An ethological view of human conflict and social interaction* (pp. 205-216). New York: Garland.

Weisfeld, G. E., & Weisfeld, C. C. (1984). An observational study of social evaluation: An application of the dominance hierarchy model. *Journal of Genetic Psychology, 145,* 89-99.

Weisfeld, G. E., & Weisfeld, C. C. (2002). Marriage: an evolutionary perspective. *Neuroendocrinology Letters, Suppl.* 4(23), 47-54.

Werner, E. E. (1979). *Cross-cultural child development.* Monterey, CA: Brooks/ Cole.

White, L. K., & Booth, A. (1985). The quality and stability of remarriages: The role of stepchildren. *American Sociological Review, 58,* 689-698.

Whiting, J. W. M., & Whiting, B. B. (1973). Altruistic and egoistic behavior in six cultures. *Anthropological Studies, 9,* 56-66.

Willerman, L., Loehlin, J. C., & Horn, J. M. (1992). An adoption and a cross-fostering study of the Minnesota Multiphasic Personality Inventory (MMPI) Psychopathic Deviate scale. *Behavioral Genetics, 22,* 515-529.

Wilson, M., & Daly, M. (1985). Competitiveness, risk taking, and violence: The young male syndrome. *Ethology and Sociobiology, 6,* 59-73.

Wilson, W. J. (1987). *The truly disadvantaged.* Chicago: University of Chicago Press.

Zakin, D. F., Blyth, D. A., & Simmons, R. G. (1984). Physical attractiveness as a mediator of the impact of early pubertal changes for girls. *Journal of Youth & Adolescence, 13,* 439-450.

Zeifman, D., & Hazan, C. (1997). Attachment: The bond in pair-bonds. In J. A. Simpson & D. T. Kendricks (Eds.), *Evolutionary social psychology* (pp. 237-263). Mahwah, NJ: Erlbaum.

13

Amish and Gypsy Children

Socialization Within Cohesive, Strategizing Groups

William R. Charlesworth

In an earlier paper, the present author emphasized that while all behaviors have multiple consequences, one set of behaviors that is indispensable for survival is that of acquiring and retaining resources (Charlesworth, 1988). Without physical, social, and informational resources, no organism can survive and reproduce. Since resources by definition exist outside of the individual, considerable effort must be expended to obtain them. In species with relatively long life spans, the availability of resources usually fluctuates throughout their existence. As a result, acquiring and defending resources is an unremitting task from birth to death.

Being born without mature resource-related skills, human children (in order to survive) are required to obtain the appropriate motivations and behaviors to acquire and use such skills and to do so in culturally acceptable ways. The task of satisfying this requirement is the responsibility of parents or their surrogates. To ensure this requirement is met, parents have to rely on personal knowledge as well as on knowledge of the survival strategies provided by the larger group to which they belong. Without the larger group, the vast majority of families fail to survive (see Hrdy, Ch. 6, this volume).

In the present chapter, the origins and functions of such strategies are viewed in terms of the evolutionary framework proposed by MacDonald (2002). MacDonald posits five evolutionary dimensions to account for how successfully groups employ resource-related strategies: (1) the degree to which the group ensures that its members adapt effective resource strategies, (2) the degree of individual self-interest in the pursuit of resources that may be allowed to supersede group interests, (3) the degree to which the group engages in resource and reproductive competition with other groups, (4) the degree to which a group engages in ecological specialization for its survival, and (5) the degree to which the group allows genetic mixture of group members with members of other groups. MacDonald's dimensions are applied here to help clarify the resource and reproductive strategies funda-mental to the socialization tactics employed by two quite separate cultural groups, Gypsies and Amish. At first glance, Gypsies and Amish appear so bla-tantly different, they could not be reasonably compared (Weyrauch, 2001).

While it is true Gypsies and Amish differ in many, often obvious, respects, it is also the case that they share at least four characteristics in common. For one, both groups have survived culturally over a substantial period of time— at least two millennia in the case of Gypsies and at least three centuries in the case of the Amish—a remarkable feat given the many problems usually accompanying minority status. Second, both groups have been (and still are) reproductively very successful. While they differ significantly in infant/child mortality and general health, substantial numbers of their children never-theless manage to reach adult status and reproduce at a rate greater than the societies surrounding them. This is no mean demographic achievement given that both groups engage in cultural practices frequently at variance with those of the societies around them. Third, the reactions to the cultural prac-tices of both groups are often negative. In the case of the Amish, the reac-tions range from indifference to their "backward" ways to subdued anger at some of their economic practices and unwillingness to serve in the armed ser-vices. Reactions to Gypsies range from indifference and overt discrimination to blatant persecution. And fourth, as will be discussed below in greater detail, Gypsies and Amish share similar strategies in socializing their children and maintaining group cohesion.

Admittedly, these four similarities can be viewed as coincidental given that both groups share very different histories and are so culturally different (Weyrauch & Bell, 2001). However, evolutionary theory allows us to seek what seem to be coincidences for possible biological strategies foundational to all human groups regardless of their cultures and histories (see below). In light of current evolutionary thinking, it is virtually axiomatic that most significant interactions between different biological groups center around resources and the competition required to acquire and defend them. Economics-related behavior is significantly linked to every group's ecology.

Before proceeding further, two general issues must be addressed. First, the use of the term *Gypsy*. The history of the term is complicated. Its first use was based on the misconception that Gypsies were from Egypt. Historical evidence, however, suggests otherwise. Gypsies most likely originated in northern India and became known by outsiders as *Roma,* from the Romani language they spoke. Derived from Sanskrit, Roma connotes "man" or "husband," not a group. The label Roma was imposed on Gypsies in more modern times by outsiders who incorrectly believed they originated in Romania (Lee, 2001). At present, not all Gypsies identify themselves as Romanis, hence the broader term Gypsy is used here, as is customarily used by most current scholars.

The second issue is the general problem of abstracting features from groups (which are not internally homogeneous) and generalizing such features across all members of such groups. Such a problem is impossible to avoid since it is the nature of science to abstract features from heterogeneous phenomena that nevertheless share a sufficient number of features to make generalizations about them. In the case of Gypsies, there are sufficient similarities between individual Gypsies (and Gypsy groups in general) to warrant making tentative categorical statements about them. The same can be said for the Amish. Furthermore, serious scholars and even casual observers can usually identify and label each group as distinctly Gypsy or Amish. While they may make mistakes in generalizing some features, they rarely mistake one group for another. In addition, just as any group with a long history, Gypsies and Amish have come to define themselves as distinct from everyone else.

A rationale for considering Gypsies and Amish as distinct entities has been provided by Ghiselin (1997), who cogently argued that groups (defined as cohesive assemblies of individuals) or species can be usefully conceptualized as unique entities that nevertheless share some basic features. This concept, as he pointed out, is especially applicable to species that have extensive histories. Since history is characterized by a series of nonreplicable contingencies, no abstract typology will satisfactorily generalize across all groups. Therefore (he argued) comparisons between groups can never be perfect. However, similarities between groups can be drawn on the basis of common underlying principles of adaptation that are abstract and hence not subject to empirical contingencies. Evolutionary theory supplies such principles.

Origins: Primate Heritage

Before distinguishing between Gypsies and Amish, it is important to remember that they share a common phylogenetic heritage. Being members of the primate order, all intact members of *Homo sapiens* share more than 98% of their DNA with most other primates, as well as similar physical characteristics, basic behavior patterns, emotions, and cognitive capacities, and many strategies for adapting to their environments (DeVore, 1965; Goodall, 1971; Jolly, 1985). Bearing and caring for immature young, belonging to social groups organized along lines of bond formation and dominance, foraging and hunting for vital resources, maintaining some form of resource-useful territory, toolmaking and building, and responding negatively to strangers are characteristic of most primate species and certainly all humans.

In general, then, humans share a sufficient number of features to support Darwin's hypothesis that they also share a common descent. But that is not the whole story. In addition, all members of *Homo sapiens* also share characteristics that set them off from all other primates: the extraordinary cognitive, language, and learning abilities that make possible social, cultural, scientific, and religious refinements, and technological skills that make *Homo sapiens* the most complex, expansionistic, and adaptively formidable species on earth (Adler, 1967; Dobzhansky, 1962; O'Hear, 1997; Roslansky, 1969). In referring to the singularity of human cognitive abilities, Wilson (1975) noted, "No scale has been invented that can objectively compare man with chimpanzees and other living primates" (p. 548) (see also MacDonald & Hershberger, Ch. 2, this volume). Whether such singularity is qualitative or quantitative may never be clear. What is clear is that despite their primate roots, Gypsies and Amish, like all human groups, share all the distinctive features of *Homo sapiens*.

Ethnicity and Genetic Differences

Not all *Homo sapiens* groups are alike physically and genetically. Races, as major groups that share many similar genes, can still be divided into nine groups on the basis of 72 DNA markers (Senegal Mandenkalu, South African Pgymies, Zaire Pgymies, Europeans, Chinese, Japanese, Melanesians, New Guineans, Australians; see Cavalli-Sforza, 2000). Both Gypsies and Amish are Europeans traditionally subclassified as Caucasian Indo-Europeans. Gypsies appear to be a distinct branch of Caucasians of North Indian origin; the Amish belong to the Germanic branch of Indo-Europeans along with other northern European branches such as Swiss and Dutch.

In terms of physical characteristics, the Amish and Gypsies appear to differ in at least two respects: The Gypsies tend to have darker complexions (Range, 2003), and a higher number of members have black hair. However, as with human populations in general, there is much overlap between the two groups, both at the physical and genetic levels. Furthermore, as is true of many human groups, Gypsies are a mixture of a broad range of genetic strains; this is the case with the Amish as well, but apparently less so.

Recent evidence suggests some differences between the two groups exist in the form of specific hereditary diseases. For example, some Gypsy groups differ from the general population in the frequencies of certain mutations and neutral polymorphisms that are significantly associated with physical and psychiatric disorders associated with inbreeding (Gresham et al., 2001). A number of well-defined hereditary diseases have been found among the Amish, for whom there exist extensive genealogical records. There are two forms of dwarfism (Van Creveld syndrome and cartilage-hair-hypoplasia), pyruvate kinase deficiency anemia, and hemophilia (Hostetler, 1993). The Amish also have a higher frequency of blood type A than surrounding populations (Hostetler, 1993).

Such heredity differences are not surprising, since both populations have historically practiced endogamy, which effectively closed them off genetically from surrounding populations. In addition to cultural constraints on marriage, genetic drift may have also played a role in the relatively high concentration of potentially pathogenic recessives in parts of both populations. In the case of Gypsies, converging evidence from various sources (e.g., linguistic and historical records) indicates that they originally belonged to a single population that separated from a larger Indo-European population several thousand years ago. In contrast, the Amish split off relatively recently from a larger, mostly homogeneous German population in the Rhine River Valley area, for well-known religious reasons.

Cross-Cultural Universals and Differences

As for other common characteristics, the extraordinary adaptive ability of humans compared with other primates appears to be present in both groups. This is also the case for all humans no matter how much they are separated geographically or culturally from each other. Cross-cultural studies by human ethologists and anthropologists reveal many general similarities in basic behavior patterns among groups that are geographically isolated from one another (Eibl-Eibesfeldt, 1989). Furthermore, all cultures share similar (if clearly not identical) strategies to adapt to their physical environments as well as for dealing with kin, friends, and strangers and enemies (especially when resources are at stake); for maintaining group cohesion; and for symbolically representing their concerns for survival, reproduction, and religious fulfillment (Barnouw, 1985; Murdock, 1957).

In many respects, then, the Amish and Gypsies are also very similar. Nevertheless, apart from many daily activities and customs, the two groups differ significantly in population size. Worldwide, there are approximately 12 million Gypsies, approximately 100,000 to 1 million of whom live in the United States. Such figures are very rough estimates because of the absence of any official records (Weyrauch, 2001). The Amish number approximately 100,000 in the United States (Hostetler, 1993; Lee, 2001). As already noted, Gypsies and Amish do share several demographic characteristics of evolutionary significance, namely, their fertility rates. Amish have a mean number of live births of 7 children per married woman. This is considerably more than the national average (between 2 and 3) for the United States, where the vast majority of Amish live. Before 1899, 22.7% of Amish couples had 10 or more children; this figure dropped to 21.8% between 1919 and 1928 (Hostetler, 1993). To be a member of the Old Order Amish is to have many more descendants than the vast majority of larger groups surrounding them.

Estimates of Gypsy live births are much more difficult to estimate. Wide regional differences also exist. In former Czechoslovakia, where approximately 400,000 Gypsies live, Gypsy fertility is 1.5 to 3 times the national average (2.6% annually as opposed to 0.7% for the population as a whole). In Spain, where approximately 500,000 Gypsies live, their population doubles every 13 to 14 years. In Europe as a whole, Gypsies have a birthrate approximately 4 times higher than those surrounding them (Range, 2003).

In short, both the Amish and Gypsies are reproductively much more successful than the societies surrounding them. To achieve such success, both groups, it is assumed here, share similar evolutionary-relevant strategies for maintaining their cultural norms, ensuring group cohesion and identities, and raising children to be reproductively successful adults. The tactics they use, however, to implement such strategies vary greatly from each other as well as from those living around them.

History

As noted above, Gypsies originated in northwestern India, from which they emigrated westward sometime between 950 and 1100 A.D. The reason behind their movement was (it is assumed) to escape from a low-caste status in a quest for a better life as well as to avoid persecution by the Gupta Dynasty and the Afghani occupiers of India at the time. From Persia, Gypsies moved farther westward into Syria, Armenia, and Turkey, and after several centuries into Romania, Hungary, and the former Yugoslavia. By the end of the 15th century, they had settled around the Mediterranean in Egypt, North Africa, and as far west as Spain. Their nomadic lifestyle ultimately brought them into northern Europe by the 16th century, and by the 19th and 20th centuries to North America, Mexico, and Australia. Throughout this whole period, the vast majority of Gypsies were persecuted and often enslaved by those in power around them. Today, the lives of some, however, are improving in several western European countries as well as in the United States (Lee, 2001).

During the 2,000 years of their separate existence, Gypsies have developed their own language, culture, economic strategies, and lifestyle, which obviously aided them to survive but also set them apart as a minority in the societies around them. During virtually all of their history, no single authority (apart from those who enslaved them) has ever managed to govern them for any period of time. They have survived by doing odd jobs and jobs no one else wanted (hanging criminals, dogcatching, slave trafficking, bear training), by manufacturing everyday objects out of metal and wood, entertaining others in various ways (at circuses, fairs, street shows), by trading and generally scratching together a desperate existence that often included stealing, begging, and engaging in scams.

As for resources (see Charlesworth, 1988, for an in-depth account of resources), most Gypsies have never owned land. As a result, their major physical resources have consisted of whatever local materials they can acquire (via purchasing, stealing, or borrowing) to satisfy their economic and cultural needs. Their social resources have usually consisted of people around them with certain unsatisfied needs, such as getting dirty jobs done, having their fortunes read, and so on. Their informational resources consist of the tribal memories of elders passed on to them orally and of what can be learned from the daily activities and behaviors of the peoples around them.

As outsiders who manage to keep much of their life secret, Gypsies have often been perceived as dangerous, parasitical, and unworthy of assimilation. The result of this has been, as already noted, discrimination and sometimes horrific persecution, the most recent being the murder of approximately 500,000 of them in Nazi concentration camps. Today, the great majority of Gypsies scattered throughout central and western Europe and the small number of them living in the United States and Canada are relatively free from harsh discrimination (Lee, 2001).

The Amish, in contrast, have a shorter, much less cataclysmic history than the Gypsies. Originally Mennonites (one of several late 16th-century Anabaptist groups originating in Switzerland), the Amish became followers of Jacob Amman, a 17th-century elder whose piety and religious beliefs led him and his followers to separate from the main body of Mennonites in Europe at the time. Viewed as heretics and persecuted by various religious groups in mostly urban western Europe, the Amish moved into rural areas and became farmers. By living frugally and engaging in hard work, they survived in a relatively simple agrarian economy outside the mainstream of their surrounding societies. Their semi-isolation was achieved partly by maintaining strict group discipline and speaking their own language (a German dialect), along with the local language, wearing distinctive clothes, and avoiding contact as much as possible with surrounding societies.

In the early 1700s, many Amish immigrated to North America and settled in large numbers in Pennsylvania, Ohio, Indiana, and Iowa and later in Canada and other midwestern states. While harsh persecution ceased, different opinions about education, military conscription, government regulations concerning vaccination, milk, and vehicle inspection, and farm purchasing and selling made the Amish somewhat unpopular with surrounding societies. Nevertheless, their excellent farming strategies and skill and work ethic as carpenters, barn builders, and manual laborers helped win the respect of the non-Amish. Such skills also made them very successful resource competitors. Their frugal living allowed them to buy up much farmland as well as underbid on labor on community-wide projects. Today, despite their idiosyncratic lifestyle and pressures from the outside to modernize their habits, the Amish are flourishing.

So, we have two groups of humans with very different histories, cultures, and geographical locations. Currently, both are living for the most part as social or quasi-social isolates in scattered populations. Both are sufficiently different from their surrounding communities to be of some concern to the latter, the Gypsies eliciting much more concern from local populations than the Amish. Nevertheless, as already noted, both groups are enjoying higher fertility rates than their surrounding societies and are still managing to preserve their identities. Even though both groups face defection of some of their young, they still remain distinct cultural groups that show no immediate signs of shrinking in size nor of being assimilated into modern society. Of course, this could change as a result of exposure to the mainstream media or because of population pressure.

As for success in resource competition with surrounding groups, the Amish have been comparatively more successful. Their prosperity is modest and for most, if not all members, apparently quite satisfactory. The benefits of their efforts are more equally distributed across their families. In contrast, Gypsies vary greatly in economic status. The more disadvantaged have to scrape hard for a living, while others (much fewer in number) live fairly well by holding more or less steady jobs and living in their own homes. This number is apparently growing (Lee, 2001).

Cultures

The term *culture* covers such a wide range of phenomena, it is impossible to treat it comprehensively or in any detail. As a substitute, the present author lists here predominant features characterizing Gypsies and Amish. These features can be found in a wide range of scholarly and scientific literature, journalistic accounts, and travelogues; they are considered here as modal for both groups. Ethnocentric or cultural biases (both negative and positive) may have helped spread the use of such features. Nevertheless, without referring to such features, there is no way to make shorthand distinctions between Gypsies and Amish. Hopefully, those listed below are sufficiently representative of the both groups. Features Gypsies and Amish appear to share are listed in Table 13.1; features that differentiate them are listed in Table 13.2. Discussion of some of these features follows the tables to help

Table 13.1   Modal Similarities Between Gypsies and Amish

Are scattered geographically (Gypsies much more so)
Maintain minority status
Adhere to explicit and implicit traditions
Are culturally isolated from many host practices
Resist assimilation
Have a history of persecution (Gypsies more so)
Are bi- or multilingual
Are not always cooperative with all of host's laws
Reject military service of host country
Are socially distinguishable in dress (Amish more so)
Live relatively simply (Gypsies often by necessity, Amish by choice)
Practice endogamy
Have high fertility compared with surrounding groups
Adhere to strict internal codes of group behavior
Emphasize strong cooperation between kin
Highly cohesive as social groups
Possess own judicial system
Use banishment for serious group offenses
Exploit local (rather than remote) resources
Control or exclude reading material for children
Exercise somewhat similar socialization practices

Table 13.2   Modal Differences Between Gypsies and Amish

Gypsies	Amish
Nomadic, migratory	Sedentary
Occupy wide-ranging niche patches	Occupy narrow-range niche patches
Opportunistic workers, scavengers	Specialist farmers
Seekers of new resources	Creators, defenders of resources
Major resources: local materials	Major resource: arable land
Daily tasks: foraging, fortune-reading, cheating outsiders, entertaining	Daily tasks: farming, odd or seasonal jobs, making furniture, quilts, household items, constructing/painting buildings
Permit opportunistic begging	Proscribe begging
Somewhat large between-family difference in income	Relatively small between-family difference in income
Moderate within-group conflict	Low within-group conflict
Generally impoverished	Generally comfortable
High friction with neighbors	Low friction with neighbors
Frequently harshly discriminated against	Occasionally discriminated against
Frequently law-free or lawless	Mostly law abiding
Relatively high incarceration rates	Virtually no incarceration rates
Maximal contact with strangers	Minimal contact with strangers
High-risk lifestyle	Low-risk lifestyle
Non- or opportunistically nationalistic	Partially nationalistic
Relatively short life span	Relatively long life span
Relatively high incidence of physical/mental problems	Relatively low incidence of physical/mental problems
Emotionally unrestrained	Emotionally restrained
Irreligious, opportunistically religious	Christian religious

account for and interpret how the Gypsy and Amish socialization practices reflect the role of their belief systems, economics, and life situations.

Beliefs

Beliefs are viewed here as core cognitive and emotional dispositions that motivate and guide behavior as well as make sense of one's life (religiously or philosophically) and govern relationships with one's group and the outside environment. Shared beliefs motivate members of groups to maintain their identities, cooperate with one another, and sustain themselves in a world quite different from theirs.

Gypsies do not have written documents explicitly stating their religious or secular beliefs. Their traditions are passed on orally and expressed daily in interactions with each other and during rituals such as marriages and trials. Some Gypsy populations, however, adopt some of the rituals of traditional religious peoples with whom they coexist (Fraser, 1995). Thus, there are Catholic Gypsies, various groups of Protestant and Orthodox Gypsies, and Muslim Gypsies. Some Gypsy groups in Europe go on pilgrimages and celebrate major church holidays with Christians. It is difficult, if not impossible, to determine whether their affiliations with these majority religions are based on conventional piety or are opportunistic efforts to ensure security and economic support from wealthy churchgoers, as well as to enjoy religious holidays and celebrations with the latter.

Gypsies have two powerful taboos, one having to do with fear of the dead and the other with physical or social contamination or pollution. For Gypsies universally, the dead become spirits, *mulo*, who remain close by to watch over the activities of the family to ensure that no family members defile Romani values (Williams, 2003). Fear of the mulo is very strong. The taboo of contamination or pollution, *marime*, applies to two spheres of Gypsy life, physical and social. The former involves personal cleanliness, which applies mostly to women and the lower parts of their bodies, especially during puberty, menstruation, pregnancy, and immediately after childbirth. A possible adaptive function of the physical taboo has to do with hygiene. Gypsies make great efforts to have clean bodies and inside living quarters. The appearance of their dwellings from the outside is frequently unpromising.

The social aspect of the contamination taboo has to do with having physical contact with non-Gypsies, *gadzo*, who are considered to be polluted, as well as lacking in the proper sense of shame, ignorant of Gypsy life and rules, and potentially dangerous. To be accused of pollution through contact with non-Gypsies is to experience great shame and possible exclusion from the tribe. Marriage with gadzo is prohibited, but if consummated can lead to serious consequences, such as permanent banishment.

One obvious adaptive function of this social taboo is that it establishes a cultural barrier between Gypsies and outsiders. Such a taboo has economic consequences as well, since it prevents workers from getting permanent employment with non-Gypsies. At the genetic level, the taboo greatly restricts any gene mixing between Gypsies and outsiders.

In contrast to Gypsy beliefs, Amish beliefs are based on the Bible, which is viewed and interpreted primarily from a Protestant viewpoint, with emphasis on Old Order Mennonite interpretation and practice. In this respect, the Amish are conservative post-Reformation Christians trusting in the word of God as provided by the Old and New Testaments, interpreted by each individual (or local community) independently of traditional Christian institutions. Such interpretations foster adhering to the daily practices of the early church, believing in adult (rather than infant) baptism, and refusing to bear arms or to take oaths to secular institutions.

Amish religious beliefs advocate Jesus's love of each other and neighbor, and proscribe all evil acts, including abortion, birth control, sodomy, and homosexuality. They strongly abjure any form of violence and support conscientious objection to war. Economically, they maintain that loving and caring relationships with all persons are far more important than acquiring wealth, social status, and power. Many of these moral desiderata are also a traditional part of the Quaker vision, in which biblical injunctions concerning love and mutual aid are daily preached.

The Amish have no church buildings (they worship in homes or barns). Their settlements are divided into autonomous church districts composed of all baptized members. Each district has a bishop and several preachers and elders. Church attendance is weekly, and Bible reading or quoting from the Bible is a more daily occurrence. While the Amish eschew accumulating material wealth, their religion nevertheless supports sound economic practices, ensuring them of reliable and relatively risk-free economic viability. Since modern machinery is usually not used, good farmland and very efficient labor-intensive agricultural practices allow them to meet not only physical demands but social ones as well.

Living on farms in thinly populated areas allows the Amish to maintain their distance from the outside world so they can practice their religion in private and educate their children with minimal outside intrusion. *Ordnung* (discipline or order) is a rule of conduct that plays an important part in their religious as well as social life. This rule of conduct, which some Amish contest, has no apparently direct biblical origin and is the principle of holding the line that keeps all Amish socially together and adhering to their faith. As Beiler (1989) noted, Ordnung "creates a desire for togetherness and friendship . . . binds marriages, generates peace, love, contentment, equality, and unity" (p. 84). In short, Ordnung requires obedience, not self-opinion. A minor violation of Ordnung means public confession and some form of repentance and reformation. A more serious violation could lead to shunning or excommunication from the community as a whole.

In several respects, then, the Amish religious belief system (despite its otherworldly principles) has adaptive social value as well as economic utility. By requiring modesty, frugality, great patience, hard work, and the renunciation of many amenities of modern living (such as electricity), their religion aids them greatly in acquiring resources for survival, avoiding intrusions from the outside, and flourishing in a world pretty much of their own choice. Their psychic isolation reinforces their separation in a very effective way. In this respect, they are a society that has achieved a degree of utopian living (somewhat restricted but satisfying) not enjoyed by the vast majority of the world populations.

Marriage and the Family

Both groups encourage large families, both explicitly or implicitly mandate and expect conjugal fidelity and high fertility, and forbid contraception and abortion (although this is currently being questioned by both groups) and infanticide. Both groups also expect that parents (especially mothers) invest as much in their young as circumstances permit.

Among the Gypsies, the father usually is in charge of finding a bridegroom for his daughter, who usually is no older than 14 years of age. His choice is based on his assessment of the groom's family for reciprocation and harmony once connected to the family. According to tradition, the groom's family must pay a bride price after extensive negotiation with the bride's family. After the wedding, the bride then moves in with the groom's family.

Marriage is expected of all eligible young persons because such unions strengthen alliances with other Gypsies (distant relatives if possible) and create mutual obligations between families. Given the diversity among various Gypsy groups, such customs may vary. However, in general, their marriage customs contribute greatly to group integrity and cohesion as well as keep any economic surplus within the Gypsy community.

Among the Amish, the family (and by extension, the whole Amish community) plays a significant role in guiding marriages. Amish youth start dating in their midteens and marry in their early 20s. Their partners are invariably Amish from other settlements, occasionally with distant cousins (although first cousins are taboo). Eventually and ideally, the newly married couple moves into their own house, having been amply supplied with household items and furniture by family, relatives, and others in their community. As with the Gypsies, Amish marriage practices contribute greatly to group integrity and cohesion as well as to economic stability.

Child Rearing and Socialization

As already intimated, socialization of the young is absolutely essential for any group to survive physically and to maintain its identity across time.

It is difficult to make generalizations about Gypsy child rearing because of the lack of firsthand systematic accounts of it. While anecdotal accounts of it are available, they are not comprehensive enough to apply to all Gypsy groups, since the groups involved are often culturally diverse and their daily lifestyles dependent on local social and economic conditions. Hence, what follows must be taken with reservation (Fonseca, 1995).

Since the family and the wider kinship group (clan) are the core of Gypsy life, children, beginning at birth, are nourished and cared for by their mothers (as well as by older girls, sibs, or relatives). Being bathed, swaddled, bundled up, and continuously fussed over, newborns enjoy a safe and comfortable existence. However, once they become toddlers and begin to walk, older sibs and neighbors are usually put in care of them. The young child's life at this point becomes more representative of what is to come. Since they are no longer babies, they may be treated roughly, shooed away when too curious, yelled at, or smacked, but usually with no cruelty or gratuitous brutality. Surrounding adults are always present to treat the child with love and discipline. Although they gradually become independent and physically and psychically tough, their family and clan are always there to offer assurance and care whenever needed.

As for household chores, young children learn them as soon as they are able, and over time, they become aware of what is necessary to earn a living outside the home. Their learning takes place primarily by imitation, trial and error, and ad hoc instruction depending on the task. In addition to learning basic adaptive skills, Gypsy children are also strenuously socialized to respect all elders, attend group activities and rituals, and to associate only with members of their group. In more modern terms, they are generally home-schooled in the sense that their education takes place in the home and hence is usually in the form of spontaneous, sporadic on-the-job training. Historically, Gypsies have never gone to public schools (unless forced): Their wandering lifestyle did not permit it, nor did their fear of being polluted by the values and activities of outsiders.

As with the majority of preliterate human groups, Gypsies have done the most adaptive thing they could do for their children without the assistance of written formulas or catechetical instruction. They have succeeded in keeping their children exclusively within their group, socializing them into group loyalty, and ensuring that they are able to work for a living and have children themselves. This strategy appears to have contributed greatly to their survival as a group. That their wisdom is not shared by many current groups can be seen, in contrast, in the enormous amount of current written literature written by experts informing anxious parents how to raise and educate children.

As with the Gypsies, the Amish view childhood socialization as crucial for them to survive culturally and economically. However, in contrast to the Gypsies, the Amish view worldly material success and involvement as an anathema. This is especially true in the domain of accumulating and displaying wealth, engaging in modern business and legal practices, and being instructed or informed by the media and public education in general. Learning to avoid contact with the outside world and to acquire blameless conduct are seen as necessary for the Amish child to acquire eternal salvation. Their religious beliefs require no less.

Beginning at a very young age, the Amish child is required to do chores around the home and work with parents and community members whenever required. In the home, the child is taught major gender-appropriate skills to satisfy the basic economic family and community needs. Obeying and respecting elders are viewed as absolutely necessary to achieve this. The education of Amish children, whether formal as in elementary school or informal at home, is directed almost exclusively at achieving practical, life-related goals. The strategy behind this is to achieve sufficient economic success to be independent of the outside society as well as to strengthen social cohesion by learning to cooperate with and respect other Amish.

Abstract learning as found in standard academic disciplines such as science, literature, and social studies is viewed as unnecessary and distracting. Outside books and periodicals are carefully screened for any material that may be subversive or ungodly.

Like Gypsy children, Amish children spend nearly all of their lives in the presence of their families and with other Amish. Without television, telephones, and unscreened reading material and with only occasional contact with strangers, Amish children are immersed in a single, homogeneous culture that peacefully but relentlessly dictates their values and beliefs, and structures their work skills around the daily tasks of making a living and caring for family. Because radio and television are nonexistent in Amish homes, Amish children are presented daily with models only of good conduct, hard work, and skilled artisans. Imitating such models is comparatively easy, since there is no competition. Being of few words, most adults have no need or inclination to articulate what is expected of the child. Just doing what adults do is all that is necessary. The average Amish child, then, grows up in the family as a worker for the good of the community, isolated from outside influences and consistently reminded by daily prayer, religious services, and admonitions to become a pious and humble servant of the Lord. In other words, the child is viewed and treated as a blank slate upon which Amish values and economic skills are imprinted exclusively and relentlessly, with little opportunity for pollution by the outside world.

In this respect, the Amish approach to child raising and education is totalitarian, no different in many respects from many other groups who want to ensure that they will protect their identities and survive and flourish in the future. The socialization of Gypsies and Amish have strategies in common: Parents begin socialization very early by surrounding their children day-in and day-out with family and group members who constantly look after them, require them early to do household chores, and teach them how to make a living. Given their unique position amongst outside groups, parents feel compelled to teach their children to avoid outsiders and when in contact with outsiders, to be cautious. The positive affective relationships between children and other family members provide the former with a strong sense of group identity and the need for group cohesion (MacDonald, 1984). Without such relationships, the demands for altruism toward the group would be difficult, if not impossible, to enforce.

Resources and Strategies to Exploit Them

As in all human groups, Gypsies and Amish have to identify resource potentialities in their environments and develop ways to exploit them within the contexts of their own particular needs, capabilities, and cultural standards, as well as current relationships with their neighbors. Since, historically, their neighbors have been indifferent to their existence or even hostile, both groups have the additional task of avoiding negative repercussions of their behavior in acquiring resources. The nature of the majority of resources available to both groups is quite different.

For Gypsies, resources are frequently scattered materials requiring opportunistic scavenging of local materials, followed frequently by reprocessing them and selling or trading them. Collecting and reworking scrap metal into kitchen utensils is an example. Material resources already possessed by the neighbors can be acquired by offering services for them or by begging, stealing, and cheating. Services range from fortune-telling to washing cars, cleaning cesspools, and doing jobs avoided by others.

Historically, most Gypsy resources are usually quickly exhausted. Scavenging can deplete material resources, and host societies can lose interest in requiring their services or, feeling cheated by Gypsy dealings, avoid them or drive them out. As a consequence, Gypsy material and service resources are usually not predictably available. Their economic activities often require sporadic, unregimented labor and frequently involve a higher-than-average risk, especially when socially proscribed or illegal activities are engaged in. As a consequence, to be economically successful, Gypsies have to be quick learners, clever, highly flexible, and able to withstand the tensions that result from contacts with potentially threatening outsiders. Since engaging with outsiders runs the risk of pollution, Gypsies also have to be knowledgeable about the behavior of strangers to avoid being entrapped by them into revealing their nature and strategies. Their language and their nimble use of its many nuances aid them in this respect.

Gypsy children, when old enough, accompany their elders in the latter's economic activities and learn firsthand what is required to make a living. Frequently, some tasks, such as begging, are left primarily to young children because they are less liable to prosecution if caught. Other tasks, such as caring for younger sibs and doing housework in general, in the case of girls is furthered because of the safety their homes provide them.

The main physical resources for the Amish are farmland and the products taken from it. Both are relatively predictable. Producing food, firewood, and other farm products for their own use and for sale to others requires a great deal of discipline, perseverance, industriousness, and group stability. While farming is dependent on weather and other factors, it is much less risky than the economic activities required of Gypsies. As for satisfying the needs of others, contact with outsiders is usually limited to providing services such as home building and painting, helping with harvests, and marketing their own products, such as quilts and furniture.

Compared with the Gypsies, the Amish are more specialists operating within a comparatively narrow economic niche. A major difficulty associated with Amish economic activities is their lack of machine-powered farm equipment, automobiles, and electric power, which puts them at a competitive disadvantage with neighbors. Their strict honesty and frequent willingness to work for less financial gain than their neighbors often offsets such disadvantages. Perhaps the biggest disadvantage of interacting with their non-Amish neighbors is the risk (as with Gypsies) of being influenced by ideas and values contrary to their beliefs.

As a consequence of their resource strategy, Amish have to be industrious, clever, and conscientious workers to extract the maximum from their land without diminishing it. Generally, they do very well in conserving their land and improving the quality of whatever they extract from it. In dealing with outsiders, they have to maintain a reputation of being honest and trustworthy—even if they appear as somewhat odd (in their dress, language, and social habits). If any dissonance between them and the non-Amish world arises, it frequently has to do with the fact that they regularly buy up farms for children and relatives. Their large families require them to be continually expanding their tillable acreage. Another source of dissonance has to do with occasional instances of noncompliance with local, state, and federal laws. Resistance to sending their adolescent children to public schools and their young men to military conscription has also caused them some problems.

Conclusion

Gypsies and Amish are minority cultures of relatively great durability despite the fact that their customs, behaviors, and beliefs often run counter to the larger society around then. What appears to be responsible for such durability is a variety of complex interlocking biological, cultural, ecological, and developmental causes. Taking MacDonald's (2002) aforementioned view of evolutionary strategies for adaptation, both groups can be seen as engaging in quite different forms of ecological specialization to meet their resource needs. Gypsies scavenge, work for others opportunistically, shift their efforts as a direct function of changes in the availability of local material and social resources, and respond rapidly to variations in social acceptability of their behavior. In doing so, they pay a greater social and economic cost for their form of specialization, especially when their economic behavior elicits hostility. The consequences of the latter may be responsible for their widespread poverty.

In contrast, the Amish are more sedentary, shape local agricultural conditions to meet their needs, and avoid dependency on their neighbors, as well as avoid making their neighbors angry. Not having to periodically shift their efforts according to outside response, the Amish greatly benefit economically from steadfast, systematic, and labor-intensive work habits. In this respect, then, they differ greatly from Gypsies.

Both specializations, nevertheless, are clearly not maladaptive, suggesting that human groups can exploit resources in a wide variety of ways and still survive and flourish. What is clearly evident is that both groups make great efforts to prevent genetic and culture mixture with other groups. Group fealty is stressed in the socialization of children and in the control of adult behavior. For both groups, individual self-interest is stressed as absolutely secondary to group interests. The necessity of group cohesiveness for survival through within-group cooperation is a cultural axiom that plays an integral part of daily interactions. And both groups, while not culturally dominant and in the case of the Gypsies hardly economically advantaged, nevertheless reproductively outcompete the larger societies surrounding them. In this respect, both groups meet the minimum subsistence requirement for reproductive success.

The question their achievements pose is why Gypsies and the Amish are successful given the many reasons why they should not be. They amass no amount of material wealth, nor do they have any political strength; they make little or no effort to keep up with the outside modern world (unless it is worth their while to meet minimum material needs); and they always run the risk, especially in the case of the Gypsies, of being persecuted or pressured to emigrate.

The Gypsy and Amish strategies for adapting to the larger world have been very successful: They maintain strong group cohesion both to preserve their traditions and to compete against others for economic survival, and they have the savvy to deal with outsiders to ensure their economic survival. Their distinctive languages, clothes, and daily behavior aid in determining who belongs to the group and who does not. And they adhere to strict rules for ensuring group fidelity and for identifying and punishing dissenters or freeloaders.

An additional factor in their favor may well be genetic. Gypsies and the Amish resemble each other because they draw directly on obligate (evolutionarily and hence genetically hardwired) strategies for group survival. Such strategies may be based on individual personality traits such as perseverance, indoctrinability, loyalty to kin, and absolutist thinking about in-group and out-group relations.

At present, we have no hard evidence that such traits are genetically based, but it is conceivable that individuals possessing such traits collected in common gene pools through natural selection or genetic drift. As Maynard Smith (1989) pointed out, large, random-mating populations may break up into trait groups, that is, into groups of individuals sharing similar genotypes. Because of the relative small size of the groups, over a relatively short period of time, the genetic composition of the group becomes more homogeneous. It is conceivable, then, that individual differences in resistance to outside interference have a genetic basis. If this is the case, it could be argued that Gypsies did not exist as a group until persistent persecution of like-temperament individuals (who looked and acted differently from the majority) led them to unite and eventually to emigrate to safer regions. Similarly, the Amish as a group conceivably would not have survived if the counter-Protestant reformation persecution of stubborn, freedom-loving people had not driven like-minded resisters into forming coalitions. In short, selection for certain individual personality traits related to ethnocentrism could have served as a magnet for individuals possessing a degree of genetic homogeneity to join together into groups (MacDonald, 2004). At this point, natural selection or genetic drift took over.

As far as early socialization is concerned, individual similarities must also be taken into consideration along with individual differences. The fact that most children in both groups accept the socialization practices imposed on them suggests some genetic homogeneity toward compliance with parental and group impositions put upon them by their elders. There have always been defectors from both groups, and some resistance to group pressure is to be expected. If defectors are prereproductive when they defect, within-group homogeneity would increase both genetically and culturally. Those who defect would not be available to mislead the group's young. Furthermore, being a marginal society with often unpopular customs may play an equally strong role along with genetic similarities in motivating group members to hold together (MacDonald, 2004). Instilling minority status in children helps them share more with each other and work harder in case the future turns bad for them as a result of outside threats and competition. Without a modicum of threat and persecution, group fealty and cohesion can be greatly weakened.

Economic abundance can have similar effects. Affluence allows for greater individual expression, since it usually allows more free individual time to be exposed to and enjoy nongroup influences and tends to be associated with less danger. It would be interesting to see how cohesive Gypsies and Amish were if they became more prosperous. It can be argued that group coherence would decline and dissent increase with increased economic opportunity. Since the ability to become prosperous is distributed unevenly across individuals in any group, it would not be surprising if the rate of defections from the group increased. The tactical differences between both groups in manifesting their strategies in everyday behavior can be viewed as facultative; that is, everyday behaviors are subject to adaptive modification depending on local ecological and social conditions as well as historically established cultural rules. Such facultative flexibility would account for the many differences in behavior between both groups that nevertheless serve similar functions.

Ideally, more empirical evidence will be obtained to ensure that present accounts are indeed accurate of how both groups came into existence and continue to survive in a world of ever-increasing social influence. For certain, bringing the knowledge and insights of the biological and cultural sciences together will always be necessary to interpret such evidence.

References

Adler, M. (1967). *The difference of man and the difference it makes.* New York: Holt, Rinehart & Winston.

Barnouw, V. (1985). *Culture and personality* (4th ed.). Belmont, CA: Wadsworth Publishing.

Beiler, J. F. (1989). On the meaning of Ordnung. In J. A. Hostetler (Ed.), *Amish roots* (pp. 84-85). Baltimore, MD: Johns Hopkins University Press.

Cavalli-Sforza, L. L. (2000). *Genes, people, and languages.* Berkeley: University of California Press.

Charlesworth, W. R. (1988). Resources and resource acquisition during ontogeny. In K. B. MacDonald (Ed.), *Sociobiological perspectives on human development* (pp. 24-77) New York: Springer-Verlag.

DeVore, I. (Ed.). (1965). *Primate behavior: Field studies of monkeys and man.* New York: Holt, Rinehart & Winston.

Dobzhansky, T. (1962). *Mankind evolving: The evolution of the human species.* New Haven, CT: Yale University Press.

Eibl-Eibesfeldt, I. (1989). *Human ethology.* New York: Aldine de Gruyter.

Fonseca, I. (1995). *Bury me standing.* New York: Vintage Books.

Fraser, A. (1995). *The Gypsies* (2nd ed.). Oxford, UK: Blackwell.

Ghiselin, M. T. (1997). *Metaphysics and the origin of species.* Albany: State University of New York Press.

Goodall, J. (1971). *In the shadow of man.* Boston: Houghton Mifflin.

Gresham, D. (et al. 16 other authors). (2001). Origins and divergence of the Roma Gypsies. *American Journal of Human Genetics, 69,* 1314-1331.

Hostetler, J. A. (Ed.). (1989) *Amish roots.* Baltimore, MD: Johns Hopkins University Press.

Hostetler, J. A. (1993). *Amish society* (4th ed.). Baltimore, MD: Johns Hopkins University Press.

Jolly, A. (1985). *The evolution of primate behavior* (2nd ed.). New York: Macmillan.

Lee, R. (2001). The Rom-Vlach Gypsies and the Kris-Romani. In W. O. Weyrauch (Ed.), *Gypsy law: Romani legal traditions and culture* (pp. 188-230). Berkeley: University of California Press.

MacDonald, K. (1984). An ethological-social learning theory of the development of altruism: Implications for human sociobiology. *Ethology and Sociobiology, 5,* 97-109.

MacDonald, K. (2002). *A people that shall dwell alone: Judaism as a group evolutionary strategy, with diaspora peoples.* Bloomington, IN: 1stbooks Library. (Originally published 1994, by Praeger, Westport, CT)

MacDonald K. (2004). *Separation and its discontents: Toward an evolutionary theory of anti-Semitism.* Bloomington, IN: 1stbooks Library; (Originally published 1998, by Praeger, Westport, CT)

Maynard Smith, J. (1989). *Evolutionary genetics.* Oxford, UK: Oxford University Press.

Murdock, J. (1957). World ethnographic sample. *American Anthropologist, 59,* 664-687.

O'Hear, A. (1997). *Beyond evolution: Human nature and the limits of evolutionary explanation.* Oxford, UK: Clarendon Press.

Range, P. R. (2003). *A phantom nation seeks justice.* New York: Ford Foundation Reports. Available at *(http://www.fordfound.org/publications/ff_report/view_ff_report_detail.cfm?report_index=272).*

Roslansky, J. D. (Ed.). (1969). *The uniqueness of man.* Amsterdam: North Holland Publishing.

Weyrauch, W. O. (Ed.). (2001). *Gypsy law: Romani legal traditions and culture.* Berkeley: University of California Press.

Weyrauch, W. O., & Bell, M. A. (2001). Autonomous lawmaking: The case of Gypsies. In W. O. Weyrauch (Ed.), *Gypsy law: Romani legal traditions and culture* (pp. 11-87). Berkeley: University of California Press.

Williams, P. (2003). *Gypsy world: The silence of the living and the voices of the dead.* Chicago: University of Chicago Press.

Wilson, E. O. (1975). *Sociobiology: The new synthesis.* Cambridge, MA: Harvard University Press.

14

Evolutionary Psychopathology and Abnormal Development

Linda Mealey

Typically, in its everyday usage, the term *abnormal* connotes undesirability—with an implied corollary desire to change or improve the undesirable condition. When applied to a person's psychology, it may amount to rejection of that individual's core identity. Use of the term *abnormal* thus has profound social implications.

Scientists and clinical practitioners are often considered guilty of indifference or lack of empathy when they go about their business of studying, diagnosing, and treating physical and psychological disorders. This apparent effect is, however, partially a result of the fact that scientists and practitioners are often using a different definition of abnormal than what is most typically implied. Unfortunately, they are sometimes not even using the same definition of a particular disorder, with one result being a lack of unified, programmatic effort into understanding the etiology and development of psychopathology. To begin this discussion, it is then perhaps best to begin with an introduction to the various uses of "normal" and "abnormal." What may be considered abnormal from an everyday, a scientific, or a clinical perspective may not be considered abnormal from an evolutionary perspective.

Five Traditional Approaches
to Defining Normality and Abnormality

There are at least five common ways of defining normality: *statistical normality,* the *medical model, psychological normalcy, socially prescribed norms,* and *legal norms.* Each of these has its value within a particular framework, but each also has drawbacks that prevent it from becoming the only, or even the "best" definition.

Statistical Normality

The easiest way to define normality has to do with statistical variation: anything that is *common* is normal, and anything that is *uncommon* is abnormal. Scientists usually apply a 5% cutoff, defining anything in the top or bottom 2.5% of a distribution as unusual, as well as any process, event, or outcome that happens in fewer than 5% of cases. This may be the most objective way to define normality and abnormality, but there are several problems with it. First, why use a 5% cutoff? Why not a 1% cutoff, or a 10% cutoff? If you are familiar with the recent debate over the incidence of homosexuality in the United States, you can see that part of the reason this debate has become so passionate is that some people want to define homosexuality as an abnormality and some people want to define it as a normal sexual variation. For those who use a statistical definition of normality, actual percentages are critical: An incidence of 4.9% may mean that homosexuality is abnormal, while an incidence of 5.1% may mean that it is normal. The statistical definition is a problematic definition for the same reason that it is objective: The 5% cutoff is, in itself, quite arbitrary.

Another problem with the statistical definition is that what is considered normal or abnormal changes as the incidence of various behaviors changes. If the incidence of homosexuality in the United States were to fluctuate up and down around the 5% level, then using this definition, the normality or abnormality of homosexuality would flip-flop from year to year; this is hardly a helpful attribute. In a related vein, according to a statistical definition, a behavior may be normal in one culture but at the same time be abnormal in another culture, just because its frequency differs. Should we consider homosexuality to be normal in San Francisco but abnormal in Santa Fe? Perhaps. Societal values are certainly relevant to our everyday concept of normality. But by using this "objective" statistical definition, a person could change from normal to abnormal and back just by changing residence! A final problem with the statistical definition of normality is that behaviors or events that are equally rare must be classified in the same way, even if one seems to be a desirable event and the other undesirable. Using the statistical definition, a great artist is just as abnormal as someone with schizophrenia, simply by virtue of being equally uncommon.

The Medical Model

The medical model of normality is based on the idea that everything has a function: If something works the way it is supposed to, it is normal; if it doesn't work, it is nonfunctional and therefore abnormal. One problem with the medical approach is that it is predicated on assumed knowledge that we simply do not have. As deftly pointed out by Nesse and Williams (1991, 1994), we do not always know the function of a physiological process, and what might appear to be abnormal might actually be functionally appropriate to the circumstances (e.g. fever, anemia). Furthermore, many processes may have more than one function, some of which are as of yet unknown (e.g., sleeping, crying). To label something as abnormal when in fact we do not understand its genesis or function is to act out of ignorance.

Another problem with the medical model of abnormality is that it does not necessarily reflect the concerns or perspective of the labeled individual. A person with functional but visually ambiguous genitalia would be considered normal using this definition, but might feel abnormal and seek treatment. On the other hand, a person who desires to be childless might be quite pleased to discover that he or she has an abnormal inability to procreate; since the "condition" renders the problems of contraception irrelevant, the person may consider it to be liberating and have no desire to be "fixed." (No pun intended here, but the use of "fixed" to refer to the sexual neutering of a pet animal constitutes an interesting linguistic reversal of the assumptions of the medical model and simultaneously provides interesting insight to human concerns.)

Psychological Normalcy

The psychological approach to normality and abnormality is the one that focuses on the value of a behavior or condition from the perspective of the labeled individual. This is the definition that clinicians often use when treating a client: The goal is to relieve distress and increase individual happiness, satisfaction, and self-esteem.

One problem with this definition is that some people, despite being both statistically and medically normal, might still be uncomfortable with their situations and want to change. A big issue in clinical medicine is whether to treat people for concerns that to them may seem very real but which to an outside observer or practitioner may seem petty, exaggerated, or even fabricated (e.g. baldness, shyness, short stature).

The reverse problem also occurs with this definition: There are many conditions that individuals feel comfortable with and don't want to change but which society finds undesirable; drug "abuse" often falls into this category, as does antisocial personality. For some "expert" or authority to determine what is "best" for someone else can be seen as a dangerous precedent to individual freedom. Besides, how do we really know what is best for someone else? And even when we think we do know, what do we do when what is best for one person is not what is best for another?

Social Norms

The fourth definition of normality is based on social prescriptions and proscriptions: What society promotes as expected and proper is considered normal, and what it shuns or frowns upon is considered abnormal. This may be the most commonly used definition of normal and abnormal and is therefore a very important definition in terms of human social interaction, expectations, and psychology.

Social norms can through peer pressure channel people into lifestyle choices that may not be the most desirable for them as individuals, even if somehow this restriction of individuality might be good for the society. Furthermore, this definition shares some of the same problems as the statistical definition: It can be arbitrary; it can change rapidly over time; and it can vary substantially across times, cultures, age groups, and even neighborhoods.

Legal Norms

Legal normality is defined as what is allowable and unpunishable by law; abnormality is whatever is restricted and/or punished. In many cases, legal norms are set to try to prevent harm; in these circumstances, they are closely tied to the perceived social value of a behavior. In other cases, legal norms attempt to preserve individual freedom of choice in the face of pressures from the social majority. Different cultures set different weightings in their decisions to promote "the good of the one" versus "the good of the many."

An Evolutionary Perspective on Normality and Abnormality

When we have to make decisions about whether to try to promote, prevent, or intervene in the development of various psychological traits or behavioral outcomes, our lack of a singular definition of normality proves to be a major stumbling block. While an evolutionary approach cannot provide an algorithm for decision making, it can provide novel, often helpful, insight. After presenting an evolutionary approach to the concepts of normality and abnormality (adapted from Mealey, 1997), five "abnormal" psychological conditions will be discussed using an evolutionary perspective.

Normality as Adaptiveness

Using the evolutionary perspective, we might start by considering normality to be anything adaptive and abnormality to be anything mal- adaptive. In this sense, "adaptive" would mean evolutionarily adaptive; that is, *the trait confers an advantage to its bearer in terms of contributing to successful survival and reproduction.* This definition is perhaps most similar to that of the medical model in that both rely on the concept of func- tion. Evolutionary adaptiveness/maladaptiveness does not, however, map directly onto medical functionality/dysfunctionality; the difference is that from the evolutionary perspective, functionality of a trait is defined purely in terms of the reproductive advantage it ultimately confers, rather than in terms of the smooth operation of a specific physiological or mechanical process.

As with the other definitions, there are problems involved with the evolutionary approach. First, just because a behavior, trait, or mechanism may owe its existence to the fact that it once had adaptive value does not necessarily mean that it is still adaptive in our modern, technological envi- ronment (Crawford, 1998). Second, even a trait that is still evolutionarily adaptive may not be obviously correlated with successful reproduction: It may be that the trait is only one of several variations present at equilibrium frequencies, with each having a similar net effect on survival and reproduc- tion; or it may be that the trait is part of a contingency strategy that is adap- tive only in the sense of "making the best of a bad job" (Dawkins, 1980; discussion below). Third, a trait that evolved because it is adaptive for its bearer may have maladaptive consequences for someone other than the bearer (Mealey, 1997). For these reasons, a trait that is normal in an evolu- tionary sense is not necessarily normal using any of the other definitions.

Furthermore, as a colleague who read a draft of this chapter reminded me, most zygotes (fertilized eggs) do not reach maturity and do not repro- duce. Evolution happens because of the mathematical fact that in all species (humans included), only a few individuals actually make it through all stages of development and become successful parents, grandparents, and great- grandparents. This fact is the basis of natural selection. It is fanciful and incorrect for us to think of evolution as a process that leads to perfection:

Death is normal, illness is normal, stress is normal, and for some individuals to do better than others is also normal.

Often, evolutionary psychologists are criticized for committing what is called "the naturalistic fallacy"; that is, they assume that whatever is natural is, by definition, good. To expect that happiness and contentment are the normal state of the human psyche, we commit the inverse of the naturalistic fallacy: We assume that whatever we perceive as good must be what is natural! But this too is a fanciful and incorrect assumption. Although we each might strive for happiness as a personal goal, we are not "designed" for happiness; happiness is probably a luxury of modern living that most of our ancestors (indeed, most of our contemporaries) never dreamed of. My colleague's comment brought to mind the wisdom of Thomas Jefferson, who, when drafting the U.S. Declaration of Independence, changed his original wording so that among the inalienable rights of all men (sic) was not "happiness," but only "the pursuit of happiness." This insight, whether derived from evolutionary theory, philosophy, or political history, can sometimes be useful.

True Pathologies

In an evolutionary scheme, "true pathologies" are traits or attributes that are clearly maladaptive *from the perspective of the single, individual human who is directly affected*. This category would include disruptions of physical or psychological development resulting from external (nonhuman) assaults, such as from toxins (e.g., alcohol), infectious disease (e.g., HIV), or injury (e.g., brain trauma). Abnormalities in this category are likely to reduce the affected individual's prospects for survival and reproduction. They can be recognized by the fact that the assault elicits an automatic combative (healing) response from the individual. Toxins, infectious disease, and injury, for example, all elicit complex physiological defenses and attempts at tissue repair; these responses are proof of selection pressures in the past, demonstrating that the insult has a history of causing harm.

Modern Pathologies

Like true pathologies, "modern pathologies" are traits or attributes that are maladaptive *from the perspective of the individual who is affected* and are likely to lead to a reduction in fitness. They can be discriminated from true pathologies, however, in that there is no identifiable, coordinated, counterresponse from the affected individual; indeed, the source of the problem may actually seem to be *internal* (e.g., obesity, compulsions; Nesse, 1991a;

Nesse & Williams, 1994). Modern pathologies are likely to represent adaptations gone awry. Although they have a complicated genesis that consists of a variety of coordinated changes in physiological and/or psychological states, the changes reduce, rather than enhance, adaptive functioning, suggesting that an evolved response has been triggered but that its deployment is not appropriate in the current environment, with its different sets of contingencies.

Ethical Pathologies

"Ethical pathologies" are traits or attributes that may be functional and adaptive for one party but have maladaptive consequences for one or more others (e.g., antisocial personality, Mealey, 1995c; sexual coercion, Mealey, 1999b). In most societies, social and legal norms require that in such situations, it is the actor (or shall we use a more emotionally laden term such as *aggressor*, or *manipulator?*) who is labeled as abnormal, even though from an adaptive perspective, we might think the reverse. (This is a touchy issue for many reasons; see below.) Ethical pathologies can be identified by finding *complex, corresponding, coevolved, complementary response sets among the different parties involved.* Deception, for example, will be countered by strategies for deception detection (e.g., Alexander, 1987; Cosmides, 1989; Mealey, Daood, & Krage, 1996); rape and incest will be countered by strategies for rape and incest avoidance (Shepher, 1983; Thornhill, 1996); theft will be countered by protective measures (Cohen & Machalek, 1988; Ellis, 1990; Vila, 1997), and so on.

Evolutionary Compromises

Based on my colleague's comment discussed above, I have added a new, fourth category. There are a variety of medical and psychiatric conditions that we think of as abnormalities because they are undesirable but which are, in fact, the result of "evolutionary compromise." One type of compromise is based on the phenomenon of *genetic pleiotropy*: the fact that any particular gene has multiple effects and it is the gene's net effect that determines whether it remains in a population. Maladaptive disease states or psychological predispositions may represent the negative side of some trait that has a less noticeable positive side. For example, a genetic benefit may be accrued by some individuals at a genetic cost to their relatives: Sickle cell anemia is the classic medical example; homosexual orientation may be a psychological example (Turner, 1995a, 1995b). Alternatively, the multiple effects of a gene may appear in the same individual, conferring an advantage at some stages in life but with a cost during another later stage (e.g., bipolar or manic-depressive disorder; Goodwin & Jamison, 1990, as cited in McGuire, Troisi, & Raleigh, 1997). There is also the possibility that a gene may have different effects under different conditions; and it may confer either positive or negative effects depending on the presence or absence of other genes and features of the environment (e.g., schizophrenia; Allen & Sarich, 1988).

A compromise may also result when an individual's options are seriously restricted, again, "making the best of a bad job." The "victims" of ethical pathologies, for example, may have nonoptimal choices forced upon them (e.g., battered women, veterans of war), and they may manifest "abnormal" behavior (e.g., posttraumatic stress disorder) that is actually normal for people in their situations. The fact that such interpersonal conflicts have occurred for a long part of our evolutionary history means that the responses of victims will be complex, coordinated, and adaptive given the circumstances. Paradoxically, partly because of society's insistence on labeling the perpetrator of these bad situations as abnormal and partly to avoid "blaming the victim," there has been a reluctance to label the victims as abnormal, and only recently have victim syndromes been recognized by the psychiatric profession. Given the many, somewhat arbitrary ways of defining abnormality, it is unfortunate that to some extent, this reluctance prevented many people from obtaining help. Thus, most insurance companies, as well as government hospitals and programs, will not pay for medical or psychological treatment unless an agreed-upon "diagnosis" can be made. As mentioned in the introductory paragraph to this chapter, which of the many definitions of normal is used in a particular context can have profound social implications.

Evolutionary Psychopathology

This section describes evolutionary ideas on several prominent types of psychiatric disorders. (See also MacDonald, Ch. 8, this volume, for discussion of several important psychiatric disorders as extremes on personality systems.)

Depressions

Depression manifests varying levels of severity, from everyday sadness to psychosis and sometimes suicide. Evolutionary models have been proposed to explain each form. Everyday sadness and *exogenous* depression, that is, depression that is clearly triggered by an external event (such as a death, loss of job, foundered love affair), can be explained by Nesse's (1991b) evolutionary model of mood. Nesse has suggested that the psychological system we call "mood state" is similar to the various systems we call "emotions" in that both evolved to selectively motivate situation-appropriate behaviors in response to changing temporal conditions. (Indeed, the word *emotion* has the same root as the words *motive, motivation,* and *motion;* emotions instigate action.) According to Nesse, mood is a mid- to long-term response to prevailing conditions, whereas emotion is a short-term, immediate response to a specific stimulus. (See also Griffiths, 1990, and Plutchik, 1980, on the evolution of emotion.)

Nesse has argued that positive mood is a reflection of past success and anticipation of future success. Sad affect, on the other hand, reflects feelings of loss, failure, or pessimism. Positive (or "high") moods motivate the individual to take advantage of the opportunities and resources available in favorable conditions; sadness (or "low" mood) motivates the individual to avoid potentially dangerous situations, to seek and obtain help, to conserve resources, and to contemplate a variety of alternative strategies. Through its depressive effects on the body and mind, sadness inhibits the kind of risk taking that optimism might inspire, which is, of course, appropriate to situations in which a person has recently experienced loss.

In support of Nesse's model, Leith and Baumeister (1996) found that individuals experiencing low moods, such as sadness, are less likely than others to engage in risk-taking behaviors. Individuals experiencing low moods also experience lower levels of curiosity compared with individuals in high or neutral mood states (Rodrigue, Olson, & Markley, 1987). When sadness reaches an intensity we might call depression, we see the appearance of nonconscious cognitive biases and selective attention to negative information that prolong the motivational state (Mineka & Sutton, 1992; Nesse, 1991b; Sloman, 1992).

Low levels of depression (sadness) thus seem to be normal, adaptive, functional states (McGuire et al., 1997; Neese, 1998; Nesse & Williams, 1997; Price, Sloman, Gardner, Gilbert, & Rohde, 1994). Severe and prolonged depression, however, is classified as a psychiatric mood disorder and is seen as dysfunctional by medical practitioners as well as by those who experience it. Severe depression is associated with reduced survival and reproduction (McGuire et al., 1997). From an evolutionary perspective, severe depression may be an example of a modern pathology, in which a normal, adaptive response has gone awry under the conditions of modern society: We see a complex, coordinated set of changes in the affected individual's physiology and psychology, but rather then being adaptive (as they are in mild cases), they are maladaptive.

That severe depression might be a modern pathology is supported by the fact that it is more common in modern, Western cultures with dense, but loosely structured populations. Indeed, in Western societies, we see large, recent increases in depression significant enough to use the metaphor of an *epidemic*. The metaphor is apt, for although depression is not a "communicable" disease, it seems that our sadness mechanism is triggered by exposure to certain environmental circumstances that are much more common in some habitats and social situations than others. Relevant features of the modern environment that perhaps serve to trigger and maintain this coordinated symptomatology include the change from living in extended families to nuclear families; increasing numbers of "broken" and "blended" families; larger, more hierarchical employment situations where individual competence may not be recognized and each worker is replaceable by an anonymous other; and increased access to information about the opportunities, wealth, and status available to others but not to oneself (see, e.g., de Catanzaro, 1995; Gilbert, 1992; McGuire et al., 1997; Price et al., 1994).

Looking at this list, it is easy to imagine that some depressions might also fall into the category of evolutionary compromises, being the best one can do in a bad situation with limited options. Furthermore, to the extent that some of these "bad" situations are the outcome of competition with other people who are benefiting from the interactions, some depressions might be categorized as ethical pathologies. It is likely that depressions are heterogeneous in form and etiology (McGuire et al., 1997) and that modern conditions can trigger more than one form.

The most extreme (clearly maladaptive) consequence of depression is suicide. As de Catanzaro (1995) pointed out, some suicides are explicable in terms of the above model: When individuals see no hope at all for the future, they anticipate no changes in their prospects and therefore no changes in their mood states. This form of suicide is typical among the elderly, who may be quite accurate in their assessment, and also among younger individuals who have suffered what they consider (at the time) to be an irreplaceable loss.

There is another, increasingly common "motive" for suicide among younger people, however, that may or may not be classified as depression and in some ways seems the antithesis of the model just presented: That is, some suicides can be seen as extreme forms of risk taking, seen most often in young men (Gardner, 1993; Stein & Stanley, 1994). Of course, the causes of some deaths are not possible to classify as suicide versus accident, even knowing the antecedent conditions and circumstances surrounding them (Irwin, 1993; Wilson & Daly, 1985).

Whereas depression and its consequent withdrawal are associated with losses and failures in the past and lack of prospects for the future, anger and its consequent risk taking are often seen in situations where both the past and the future are unpredictable and risk taking might actually improve one's prospects (Hill, Ross, & Low, 1997; Wilson & Daly, 1985, 1993). This strategy seems, like the depression/withdrawal strategy, to involve a complex, coordinated set of physiological and psychological responses, perhaps too representing an adaptation gone awry.

A very wise person (my mother) once said that depression is anger without the enthusiasm. If depression and anger are, indeed, related, as not just my mother, but many clinicians and psychometricians believe (see e.g., Gilbert, 1992), it may be that the key feature distinguishing the two is an element of hope. The clinical implications arising from this possibility include that we might sometimes consider anger to be a "positive," "assertive" mood rather than a "negative," "dysphoric" mood (Mealey & Theis, 1995) and that channeling anger into appropriate action might be a first step in the treatment of depression (Price et al., 1994).

Anxiety and Phobias

Like depression, anxiety can range from mild, normal, and adaptive to severe, abnormal, and maladaptive. Mild anxiety, like sadness, is evoked in situations when it might serve a function. Under conditions of minor threat or unpredictability, for example, anxiety can increase alertness and sensitivity to environmental cues (Hansen & Hansen, 1994; Marks & Nesse, 1994; Mathews & MacLeod, 1985). Thus, both depression and anxiety lead to cognitive distortions that make sense from an evolutionary perspective (Gilbert, 1998; Mineka & Sutton, 1992).

Common phobias also seem to have at their root an innate predisposition to avoid potentially dangerous stimuli and conditions: Fear of heights, fear of drowning, and fear of lightning, for example, make sense in terms of their function of ensuring safety (Leckman & Mayes, 1998; Marks & Nesse, 1994). In fact, certain phobias are easier to acquire than others, suggesting that the human nervous system is biologically "prepared" to learn certain important associations (Seligman, 1970): People can more easily acquire phobias of snakes and spiders, for example, than flowers or trees, the former being potentially dangerous and the latter generally innocuous or even useful.

Debilitating phobias and panic attacks seem to be learned, exaggerated responses to stimuli and situations that are perceived as threatening even if they are, in actuality, harmless. Our brains are bestowed with several mechanisms that automatically heighten our vigilance toward, and awareness of, potential threats (Davey, 1992; Hamm, Vaitl, & Lang, 1989; Hugdahl & Johnsen, 1989; Mealey, 1995a; Merckelbach, van den Hout, Jansen, & van der Molen, 1988; Ohman, 1992; Stein & Bouwer, 1997); this situation makes a "false alarm" likely. The redundancy of so many mechanisms, however, pays off in terms of the relative rarity of severe accidents consequent to inappropriate fearlessness (Nesse, 1997).

Obsessive-compulsive disorder and posttraumatic stress disorder (PTSD) also appear to be learned exaggerations of psychiatrically normal and adaptive responses to threat (Rapoport & Fiske, 1998; Silove, 1998). Obsessions and compulsions, like phobias, are typically related to a perceived (if not actual) threat. Hand-washing and other germ-phobic compulsions are obvious examples, as are compulsions of checking and rechecking whether stoves are turned off and doors are locked; hoarding of food or objects is a hypothetical foil against potential starvation or disaster. PTSD includes obsessive and intrusive thoughts about a real, previously experienced threat (e.g., Shipherd & Beck, 1999). Those who suffer from PTSD often mentally rehearse the event, and many experience obsessive feelings of personal guilt, even if unfounded. Both the cognitive rehearsal and the feelings of guilt would be adaptive if the threat were likely to recur and the intrusive thoughts led to enhanced alertness and novel avoidance strategies (Silove, 1998).

Anorexia

Like other female mammals, women seem to have evolved a variety of physiological mechanisms for "deciding" not to reproduce; these include suppression of ovulation, embryo resorption, and fetal miscarriage (Baker & Bellis, 1995; Wasser & Barash, 1983). The first of these "decisions" is based on level of body fat (Frisch, 1984; McFarland, 1997; Pond, 1997). Specifically, if a potential mother does not have sufficient body fat, she will not have enough caloric resources to maintain a pregnancy and subsequent lactation. In this circumstance, the hypothalamus reduces its hormonal output, precluding ovulation and possible pregnancy under conditions when the body may need to reserve its energy for nonreproductive purposes. Like adaptive depression, suppression of ovulation is an evolved strategy to "make the best of a bad job" until the situation improves.

In addition to body fat, ovarian function also tracks nutrition, energy balance, and aerobic activity (Bailey et al., 1992; Ellison, 1990). This explains why in contemporary technological societies where food is abundant, female athletes involved in strenuous sports and, especially, endurance sports, are sometimes anovulatory (do not ovulate) and/or amenorrheic (do not menstruate). Physicians generally treat this condition as if it were a medical abnormality, but from an evolutionary perspective, it is an adaptive mechanism at work.

Wasser and Barash (1983) speculated that the adaptive responsiveness of reproductive physiology to various aspects of physical condition might be extended in social species (like humans) to include responsiveness to aspects of social conditions. According to their reproductive suppression model (RSM), social and psychological stressors should trigger the same physiological reaction as physical stressors, because individuals under social and psychological stress are just as unsuited to pregnancy and raising offspring as individuals under physical stress (Wasser, 1990).

Based on this reasoning, Surbey (1987), Voland and Voland (1989), and Anderson and Crawford (1992) applied the RSM to humans to try to explain anorexia in contemporary industrialized societies. Basically, they suggested that anorexia may be a modern pathology in response to a "social emergency": Body fat is minimized in situations when it would be disadvantageous for a girl to become pregnant or even to show signs of sexual maturity that would attract sexual attention. This model explains several otherwise inexplicable features of the anorexia "epidemic": (a) that it develops almost exclusively in girls and younger women, rather than in boys and men (for whom sperm production requires very little energy and no fat reserves) or older women (for whom further delay of reproduction probably means no reproduction at all); (b) that it is frequently associated with a first (often early and often undesirable) sexual experience; (c) that it is increasing rapidly only now, at this point in history, and only in the richest, most developed countries (where malnutrition is now a less common stressor than unwanted sexual attention); and (d) that it afflicts mostly middle- and upper-class girls and women (for whom single motherhood has a social stigma that isn't shared among the lower classes).

Does this mean that anorexia is adaptive? Perhaps. The overwhelming majority of cases of anorexia do not reach life-threatening levels. Surbey (1987) reported that "In general, developing anorexia nervosa appears to alter a girl's developmental trajectory from that of an early maturer to that of a late maturer without decided ill effects" (p. 568). On the other hand, anorexia is obviously maladaptive for the 10% (of those diagnosed) who reach a level that endangers life. Anorexia is similar to depression in this way, too: At low levels it may be adaptive, whereas at more intense levels, which appear to be more common now than in the past, it seems to be an adaptation that has gone awry (Abed, 1999; Crawford, 1998).

The recent increase of anorexia (and bulimia) in modern Western societies may, in fact, parallel the increase of depression because they share one or more increasingly common environmental precipitants. Changes in social structure have led to increased sexual abuse and to increased female competition, either of which could precipitate these disorders. While competition is typically regarded as a feature of male, rather than female, interactions (Daly & Wilson, 1988; Wilson & Daly, 1985, 1993), this is actually true only in terms of physical aggression. Both sexes engage in what Schmitt and Buss (1996) have called "competitor derogation," and women and girls are more likely than men and boys to use subtle forms of aggression, such as starting and perpetuating rumors, talking "behind someone's back," or otherwise trying to manipulate the social "Who's Who" (Buss, 1988; Cashdan, 1996, 1998; Hood, 1996). Nonphysical but otherwise intense competition between women is probably a cross-cultural universal (Burbank, 1987; Campbell, 1999).

One way women might compete is by inhibiting the attractiveness and reproductive capacity of other women. Wasser and Barash (1983) cited studies of reproduction among !Kung women showing that during a 10-year period, fewer than 50% of reproductive-age women had two or more children, while more than 40% had none at all; they interpreted this "inequality" as the reproductive manipulation of subordinate women by dominants. In contemporary Western society, anorexia may be the manifestation of a similar, socially induced reproductive suppression (Mealey, 1999a, 2000).

If so, who is suppressing whom? Although "the media" are generally blamed for promoting thinness as a cultural ideal, when it comes to advertising, consumers "call the shots," and it is women, not men, who claim that the ideal female figure is one of below-average weight. (Men actually prefer plumper female figures than do women; Anderson, Crawford, Nadeau, & Lindberg, 1992; Cohn et al., 1987; Fallon & Rozin, 1985; Furnham & Radley, 1989). When it comes to assessments of physical attractiveness, women are more influenced by the opinions of other women than by the opinions of men (Graziano, Jensen-Campbell, Shebilske, & Lundgren, 1993). Perhaps dominant women use this fact to manipulate others.

Antisocial Personality

According to the *Diagnostic and Statistical Manual of the American Psychiatric Association (DSM),* antisocial personality is a psychiatric disorder. Few psychiatrists, however, could use the medical model to identify something "wrong" with individuals so diagnosed, and certainly there is no medical treatment for it. Indeed, the diagnosis of antisocial personality does not really derive from the medical model, but, as the more common term *sociopath* reveals, reflects the social and legal meanings of normality. I have argued (Mealey, 1995b, 1995c, 1997) that from an evolutionary perspective, antisocial personality is both normal and adaptive: As a trait that confers value on its bearer by imposing costs on others, it falls under the category of an ethical pathology.

Ethical pathologies, by definition, involve two or more "competing" parties in that one party can benefit only if the other loses. Situations such as this are referred to in mathematical terms as *zero-sum games* and can be modeled using the principles of mathematical game theory. Game theorists can predict the final outcome of a social "game" if they know the various "strategies" used by the "players": Different combinations of strategies can be "played out" on computers over many trials to see which strategies work best under which conditions (the different conditions being the "stakes" of the game, the "payoffs," and what strategies other players are playing). Game theory can be used to model the potential value of various strategies for real games (such as poker or tic-tac-toe), as well as for "war games," "business wars," or interpersonal "battles." It has also been used to model the interactions between two or more parties in coevolutionary relationships such as those of predator and prey, male and female, and host and pathogen (Pool, 1995).

In game theory, an *evolutionarily stable strategy* (ESS) is a strategy that, although it may be "beaten" occasionally in particular situations, cannot be beaten by any other strategy when played in repeated contests over the long term. Translated into real evolutionary terms, a trait is an ESS if it allowed its bearers to have equal or greater reproduction than individuals without the trait. Maynard Smith (1974, 1978; Maynard Smith & Price, 1973) showed that sometimes there is no single best strategy, and a variety of strategies can persist in a stable mix. This feature of evolutionary games is what allows for the long-term maintenance of genetic diversity and behavioral flexibility within a species, and it is the basis of my evolutionary model of sociopathy (Mealey, 1995b, 1995c, 1997).

DSM diagnoses are based on outward signs (symptoms) rather than on etiology (Lilienfeld, 1994), and just as people can become depressed following a variety of paths, I argue that people can also become antisocial following a variety of paths. Game theory tells us that behavioral diversity can be maintained in at least five ways (Mealey, 1995c), providing us with at least five paths to similar outcomes. Specifically, behavioral variability can appear in a population as

1. genetically based (stable) individual differences in strategy;

2. specieswide, but random, use of mixed strategies;

3. environmentally contingent (opportunistic) use of mixed strategies;

4. stable, developmentally canalized individual differences; and

5. stable individual differences in strategy as a result of differential canalization of different genotypes.

Translating these into less technical terms, they are equivalent to (1) the psychological concept that people have inborn, genetically determined personalities; (2) the military concept that sometimes the safest strategy in battle is to be unpredictable, and so everyone is born with the ability to play "different strategies" somewhat randomly; (3) the social psychology concepts of states and scripts—that we all have the ability to play different strategies (show different aspects of ourselves), but rather than play them (or "act") randomly, we play them depending on what is best in the particular circumstances; (4) the behavioral psychology idea that each person is born as a *tabula rasa*, or "blank slate" and that personality is molded by features of the environment and specific experiences; and (5) the behavior genetics concept of a gene-environment interaction, in which people respond differently to their environments depending on their inborn personalities—something of a realistic compromise between the extreme positions of (1) and (4).

Applying these to antisocial personality, we come up with the possibilities that (1) some people are born antisocial; (2) we are all sometimes antisocial; (3) we can all be antisocial under certain circumstances; (4) some of us become antisocial because of our early environments and experiences; and (5) some people become antisocial because that is how their particular inborn personalities respond to their particular early environments. There is evidence for all of these ideas, and I believe they are not mutually incompatible (Mealey, 1995b).

1. Some people do seem to be born with an ability to feel the *primary emotions* (anger, happiness, sadness, disgust, fear, surprise) but not the *social emotions* (love, shame, guilt, trust, sympathy, remorse). These people are classic psychopaths; their inability to empathize makes them inherently *asocial*, so it is very easy for them to engage repeatedly in antisocial behavior.

2. Most of us, at some time, have seemed to lash out for no reason at all. This behavior has the effect of keeping others "on their toes" and not taking us for granted. Occasionally, people admit to using it as a conscious strategy: One teenage girl living in a dangerous neighborhood said that the best way to be sure that no one "messed" with her was to act a little crazy, a little violent, a little unpredictable.

3. Most antisocial behavior is exhibited by young males in competitive situations (Daly & Wilson, 1988; Wilson & Daly, 1985), and when the situation changes, they cease their antisocial behavior. Financial success, social success, finding a new friend or new job, getting married or having a child, all of these can result in the abrupt cessation of antisocial behavior by people whose motives are situational rather than related to personality.

4. Some people seem to acquire antisocial personalities as a result of critical or ongoing traumatic life events (such as abuse from an alcoholic parent

or continuous social rejection). The result is a stable antisocial personality that is difficult to change.

5. Sociological models of crime suggest a diathesis-stress model, in that people with certain psychological predispositions (impulsivity, high activity levels, low intelligence) will become antisocial when exposed to difficult situations that people with more sedate personalities or more advanced skills would be able to cope with. Thus, children from single-parent homes who grow up in disadvantaged neighborhoods with few role models, who have few opportunities, and who are perhaps also more often exposed to disease and environmental toxins are most at risk for developing antisocial behavior.

Schizophrenia

Of all the mental disorders, schizophrenia is probably the most debilitating and the least understood. Of those it afflicts, only one third experience spontaneous remission; of the rest, half can be helped with modern antipsychotic drugs but will be forever in and out of hospitals, and half will never again experience life as most of us know it. The aspects of mental life that are most distorted by schizophrenia are the ones we consider to be so particularly human: language, reason, planning, self-identity, empathic interpersonal relationships, and sense of humor.

Schizophrenia is not a specifically modern disease. In its various forms, it affects 1% of people worldwide, and it seems to have always existed at the same general rate (Allen & Sarich, 1988; Crow, 1997). Schizophrenia has a significant genetic basis (see Gottesman, 1991), yet unlike the other disorders discussed herein, it provides no apparent benefit—actual or potential—to its sufferers. Because the prevalence rate of schizophrenia is far above what could result from spontaneous mutation, several investigators have sought a genetic/evolutionary explanation.

Crow (1991, 1993, 1995, 1997) has suggested that schizophrenia is a side effect of the intense and rapid selection for the very phenomena that it destroys. Specifically, he argued that schizophrenia results from the brain asymmetries that developed as we evolved language, the ability to plan, and the ability to empathize with the perspective of others. According to this model, normal human functioning requires a delicate and complex interaction of processes that only recently in human evolution became lateralized in the brain. Partly because lateralization is such a recent phenomenon and partly because it means a loss of functional redundancy, the fine-tuning of this precarious balance is easy to disrupt. Presumably, according to this model, humans are still undergoing directional selection for brain lateralization, and until we reach a point where the costs outweigh the benefits, the genetic and developmental mechanisms underlying lateralization will not stabilize sufficiently to prevent errors such as schizophrenia.

Not everyone is satisfied with this explanation. Allen and Sarich (1988) believe that we are already at a point where selection has stabilized but that of those individuals with a genetic predisposition for schizophrenia, only some individuals in some cultures experience dysfunction. This model reflects the idea of an adaptation gone awry due to environmental mismatch, and Allen and others (Kleinman & Cohen, 1997) have claimed that schizophrenia rates are not, after all, similar across cultures.

Some researchers even dispute the assumption that schizophrenia is highly genetic. Although schizophrenia runs in families and is more likely to be found in both members of an identical-twin pair than in a fraternal-twin pair, this familial transmission could be explained by shared, nongenetic factors. Davis (Davis & Bracha, 1996; Davis, Phelps, & Bracha, 1995) has suggested that schizophenia is much more likely to be shared by twin pairs who shared the same fetal membranes and the same placenta than twins who did not, regardless of the fact that the twins are genetically identical. This finding supports a long-standing argument that schizophrenia is actually a viral or retroviral disease, like influenza or AIDS, and that transmission occurs in the womb (e.g., Murray, Jones, O'Callaghan, Takei, & Sham, 1992; Wright & Murray, 1993).

Conclusions

Evolutionary approaches are often stereotyped as simplistic and ignoring the rich tapestry of mechanisms that actually exist. The approach sketched here is clearly not monolithic; that is, it provides several different evolutionary scenarios for psychiatric diagnoses: true pathologies, maladaptive responses to evolutionarily novel environments, evolutionary compromises, and strategies that may be adaptive for the individual but that oppose the interests of others.

These categories also apply to the psychiatric disorders of children. Several of the diagnoses discussed above apply to children (e.g., anorexia, depression, anxiety, and phobias). Conduct disorder in children, like antisocial personality, often involves violating the rights of others and is thus not necessarily maladaptive for the individual. Present evidence has indicated that mental retardation and autism have biological origins (e.g., Drew, Hardman, & Logan, 1996), presumably examples of true pathologies.

Several authors have suggested that attention deficit/hyperactivity disorder (ADHD) involves a maladaptive response to the modern world, where children are expected to sit still and pay attention to a teacher in a classroom setting. Despite academic problems resulting from inattention, overactivity, aggressiveness, and impulsivity, ADHD children achieve occupational success and satisfaction equal to that of their peers, quite possibly because they find jobs that reward their strengths (Campbell, 2000). Cantwell (1990, 1992) has reported that some adults identified as having exhibited the symptoms of ADHD as children went on to achieve high levels of success as entrepreneurs and salesmen and that some had achieved success in the entertainment industry. These individuals exhibited a great deal of drive and an extraordinary amount of energy in pursuit of their goals. Such examples also suggest the relevance of the idea of evolutionary compromises: ADHD children represent a high-risk compromise between a high-energy, reward-driven, extraverted attentional style and the demands of the environment for caution and successful inhibition of behavior for long-term goals.

While still in its infancy, there is little doubt that evolutionary thinking is making a major contribution to the conceptualization of psychiatric diagnoses. It is hoped that this contribution will inspire future efforts to understand the evolutionary origins and functions of psychiatric diagnoses.

References

Abed, R. (1998). The sexual competition hypothesis for eating disorders. *British Journal of Medical Psychology, 71*, 525-547.

Alexander, R. D. (1987). *The biology of moral systems.* New York: Aldine de Gruyter.

Allen, J. S., & Sarich, V. M. (1988). Schizophrenia in evolutionary perspective. *Perspectives in Biology and Medicine, 32*, 132-151.

Anderson, J. L., & Crawford, C. B. (1992). Modeling costs and benefits of adolescent weight control as a mechanism for reproductive suppression. *Human Nature, 3*, 299-334.

Anderson, J. L., Crawford, C. B., Nadeau, J., & Lindberg, T. (1992). Was the Duchess of Windsor right? A cross-cultural review of the socioecology of ideals of female body shape. *Ethology and Sociobiology, 13*, 197-227.

Bailey, R. C., Jenike, M. R., Ellison, P. T., Bentley, G. R., Harrigan, A. M., & Peacock, N. R. (1992). The ecology of birth seasonality among agriculturalists in Central Africa. *Journal of Biosocial Science, 24*, 393-412.

Baker, R. R., & Bellis, M. A. (1995). *Human sperm competition.* London: Chapman & Hall.

Burbank, V. K. (1987). Female aggression in cross-cultural perspective. *Behavioral Science Research, 21*, 70-100.

Buss, D. M. (1988). The evolution of human intrasexual competition: Tactics of mate attraction. *Journal of Personality and Social Psychology, 54*, 616-628.

Campbell, A. (1999). Staying alive: Evolution, culture, and women's intrasexual aggression. *Behavioral and Brain Sciences, 22,* 203-252.

Campbell, S. B. (2000). Developmental perspectives on attention deficit disorder. In A. Sameroff, M. Lewis, & S. Miller (Eds.), *Handbook of child psychopathology* (2nd ed., pp. 383-401). New York: Plenum.

Cantwell, D. (1990, March). Paper presented at the Department of Pediatrics, University of Minnesota.

Cantwell, D. (1992, May). Paper presented at the Department of Pediatrics, University of California-Irvine.

Cashdan, E. (1996). Women's mating strategies. *Evolutionary Anthropology, 5,* 134-143.

Cashdan, E. (1998). Are men more competitive than women? *British Journal of Social Psychology, 37,* 213-239.

de Catanzaro, D. (1995). Reproductive status, family interactions, and suicidal ideation: Surveys of the general public and high-risk group. *Ethology and Sociobiology, 16,* 385-394.

Cohen, L. E., & Machalek, R. (1988). A general theory of expropriative crime: An evolutionary ecological approach. *American Journal of Sociology, 94*(3), 465-501.

Cohn, L. D., Adler, N. E., Irwin, C. W. Jr., Millstein, S. G., Kegeles, S. M., & Stone, G. (1987). Body-figure preferences in male and female adolescents. *Journal of Abnormal Psychology, 96,* 276-279.

Cosmides, L. (1989). The logic of social exchange: Has natural selection shaped how humans reason? Studies with the Wason selection task. *Cognition, 31,* 187-276.

Crawford, C. (1998). Environments and adaptations: Then and now. In C. Crawford & D. Krebs (Eds.), *Handbook of evolutionary psychology: Ideas, issues, and applications.* Mahwah, NJ: Erlbaum.

Crow, T. J. (1991). The origins of psychosis and "The Descent of Man." *British Journal of Psychiatry, 159,* 76-82.

Crow, T. J. (1993). Sexual selection, Machiavellian intelligence, and the origins of psychosis. *The Lancet, 342,* 594-598.

Crow, T. J. (1995). A Darwinian approach to the origins of psychosis. *British Journal of Psychiatry, 167,* 12-25.

Crow, T. J. (1997). Schizophrenia as failure of hemispheric dominance for language. *Trends in Neuroscience, 20,* 339-343.

Daly, M., & Wilson, M. (1988). *Homicide.* New York: Aldine de Gruyter.

Davey, G. C. L. (1992). An expectancy model of laboratory preparedness effects. *Journal of Experimental Psychology: General, 121,* 24-40.

Davis, J. O., & Bracha, H. S. (1996). Prenatal growth markers in schizophrenia: A monozygotic co-twin control study. *American Journal of Psychiatry, 153,* 1166-1172.

Davis, J. O., Phelps, J. A., & Bracha, H. S. (1995). Prenatal development of monozygotic twins and concordance for schizophrenia. *Schizophrenia Bulletin, 21,* 357-366.

Dawkins, R. (1980). Good strategy or evolutionarily stable strategy? In G. W. Barlow & J. Silverberg (Eds.), *Sociobiology: Beyond the nature/nurture debate.* Boulder, CO: Westview.

Drew, C. J., Hardman, M. L., & Logan, D. R. (1996). *Mental retardation: A life cycle approach* (6th ed.). New York: Macmillan.

Ellis, L. (1990). The evolution of collective counterstrategies to crime: From the primate control rule to the criminal justice system. In L. Ellis & H. Hoffman (Eds.), *Crime in biological, social, and moral contexts.* New York: Praeger.

Ellison, P. T. (1990). Human ovarian function and reproductive ecology: New hypotheses. *American Anthropologist, 92,* 933-952.

Fallon, A. E., & Rozin, P. (1985). Sex differences in perceptions of desirable body shape. *Journal of Abnormal Psychology, 94,* 102-105.

Frisch, R. E. (1984). Body fat, puberty and fertility. *Biological Reviews, 59,* 161-188.

Furnham, A., & Radley, S. (1989). Sex differences in the perception of male and female body shapes. *Personality and Individual Differences, 10,* 653-662.

Gardner, W. (1993). A life-span rational-choice theory of risk taking. In N. Bell & R. Bell (Eds.), *Adolescent risk-taking.* Newbury Park, CA: Sage.

Gilbert, P. (1992). *Depression: The evolution of powerlessness.* New York: Guilford Press.

Gilbert, P. (1998). The evolved basis and adaptive functions of cognitive distortions. *British Journal of Medical Psychology, 71,* 447-463.

Gottesman, I. I. (1991). *Schizophrenia genesis: The origins of madness.* New York: W. H. Freeman.

Graziano, W. G., Jensen-Campbell, L. A., Shebilske, L. J., & Lundgren, S. R. (1993). Social influence, sex differences, and judgments of beauty: Putting the interpersonal back in interpersonal attraction. *Journal of Personality and Social Psychology, 65,* 522-531.

Griffiths, P. E. (1990). Modularity, and the psychoevolutionary theory of emotion. *Biology and Philosophy, 5,* 175-196.

Hamm, A. O., Vaitl, D., & Lang, P. J. (1989). Fear conditioning, meaning, and belongingness: A selective association analysis. *Journal of Abnormal Psychology, 98,* 395-406.

Hansen, C., & Hansen, R. (1994). Automatic emotion: Attention and facial efference. In P. M. Niedenthal & S. Kitayama (Eds.), *The heart's eye: Emotional influences in perception and attention.* New York: Academic.

Hill, E. M., Ross, L. T., & Low, B. S. (1997). The role of future unpredictability in human risk-taking. *Human Nature, 8,* 287-325.

Hood, K. E. (1996). Intractable tangles of sex and gender in women's aggressive development: An optimistic view. In D. M. Stoff & R. B. Cairns (Eds.), *Aggression and violence: Genetic, neurobiological and social perspectives.* Mahwah, NJ: Erlbaum.

Hugdahl, K., & Johnsen, B. H. (1989). Preparedness and electrodermal fear-conditioning: Ontogenetic vs. phylogenetic explanations. *Behavioral Research and Therapy, 27,* 345-353.

Irwin, C. E. Jr. (1993). Adolescence and risk taking: How are they related? In N. Bell & R. Bell (Eds.), *Adolescent risk-taking*. Newbury Park, CA: Sage.

Kleinman, A., & Cohen, A. (1997). Psychiatry's global challenge. *Scientific American, 276,* 74-77.

Leckman, J. F., & Mayes, L. C. (1998). Understanding developmental psychopathology: How useful are evolutionary accounts? *Journal of the American Academy of Child and Adolescent Psychiatry, 37,* 1011-1021.

Leith, K. P., & Baumeister, R. (1996). Why do moods increase self-defeating behavior? Emotion, risk-taking and self-regulation. *Journal of Personality and Social Psychology, 71,* 1250-1267.

Lilienfeld, S. O. (1994). Conceptual problems in the assessment of psychopathy. *Clinical Psychology Review, 12,* 641-662.

Marks, I. M., & Nesse, R. M. (1994). Fear and fitness: An evolutionary analysis of anxiety disorders. *Ethology & Sociobiology, 15,* 147-161. (Reprinted in S. Baron-Cohen (Ed.), *The maladapted mind: Classic readings in evolutionary psychopathology.* London: Erlbaum/Taylor & Francis, 1997)

Mathews, A., & MacLeod, C. (1985). Selective processing of threat cues in anxiety states. *Behaviour Research and Therapy, 23,* 563-569.

Maynard Smith, J. (1974). The theory of games and the evolution of animal conflict. *Journal of Theoretical Biology, 47,* 209-221.

Maynard Smith, J. (1978). The evolution of behavior. *Scientific American, 239,* 176-192.

Maynard Smith, J., & Price, G. R. (1973). The logic of animal conflict. *Nature, 246,* 15-18.

McFarland, R. (1997). Female primates: Fat or fit? In M. E. Morbeck, A. Galloway, & A. L. Zihlman (Eds.), *The evolving female: A life-history perspective.* Princeton, NJ: Princeton University.

McGuire, M. T., Troisi, A., & Raleigh, M. M. (1997). Depression in evolutionary context. In S. Baron-Cohen (Ed.), *The maladapted mind: Classic readings in evolutionary psychopathology.* London: Erlbaum/Taylor & Francis.

Mealey, L. (1995a). Enhanced processing of threatening stimuli: The case of face recognition. *Behavioral and Brain Sciences, 18,* 304-305.

Mealey, L. (1995b). Primary sociopathy psychopathy is a type, secondary is not. *Behavioral and Brain Sciences, 18,* 579-599.

Mealey, L. (1995c). The sociobiology of sociopathy. *Behavioral and Brain Sciences, 18,* 523-541.

Mealey, L. (1997). Heritability, theory of mind and the nature of normality. *Behavioral & Brain Sciences, 20,* 527-532.

Mealey, L. (1999a). Evolutionary models of female intrasexual competition. *Behavioral and Brain Sciences, 22,* 254.

Mealey, L. (1999b). The multiplicity of rape: From life history strategies to prevention strategies. *Jurimetrics, 39,* 217-226.

Mealey, L. (2000). Anorexia: A "losing" strategy? *Human Nature, 11,* 105-116.

Mealey, L., Daood, C., & Krage, M. (1996). Enhanced memory for faces of cheaters. *Ethology and Sociobiology, 17,* 119-128.

Mealey, L., & Theis, P. (1995). The relationship of mood and preferences among natural landscapes: An evolutionary perspective. *Ethology and Sociobiology, 16,* 247-256.

Merckelbach, H., van den Hout, M. A., Jansen, A., & van der Molen, G. M. (1988). Many stimuli are frightening, but some are more frightening than others: The contributions of preparedness, dangerousness, and unpredictability to making a stimulus fearful. *Journal of Psychopathology and Behavioral Assessment, 10,* 355-366.

Mineka, S., & Sutton, S. K. (1992). Cognitive biases and emotional disorders. *Psychological Science, 3,* 65-69.

Murray, R. M., Jones, P. B., O'Callaghan, E., Takei, N., & Sham, P. C. (1992). Genes, viruses and neurodevelopmental schizophrenia. *Journal of Psychiatric Research, 26,* 225-235.

Nesse, R. M. (1991a). Psychiatry. In M. Maxwell (Ed.), *The sociobiological imagination.* Albany: SUNY Press.

Nesse, R. M. (1991b). What is mood for? *Psycoloquy* (an electronic journal) 2.9.2.1.

Nesse, R. M. (1997). An evolutionary perspective on panic disorder and agoraphobia. In S. Baron-Cohen (Ed.), *The maladapted mind: Classic readings in evolutionary psychopathology.* London: Erlbaum/Taylor & Francis.

Nesse, R. M. (1998). Emotional disorders in evolutionary perspective. *British Journal of Medical Psychology, 71,* 397-415.

Nesse, R. M., & Williams, G. C. (1991). The dawn of Darwinian medicine. *Quarterly Review of Biology, 66,* 1-22.

Nesse, R. M., & Williams, G. C. (1994). *Why we get sick: The new science of Darwinian medicine.* New York: Random House.

Nesse, R. M., & Williams, G. C. (1997). Are mental disorders diseases? In S. Baron-Cohen (Ed.), *The maladapted mind: Classic readings in evolutionary psychopathology.* London: Erlbaum/Taylor & Francis.

Ohman, A. (1992). Orienting and attention: Preferred preattentive processing of potentially phobic stimuli. In H. Hayne & R. Richardson (Eds.), *Attention and information processing in infants and adults: Perspectives from human and animal research.* Mahwah, NJ: Erlbaum.

Plutchik, R. (1980). *Emotion: A psychoevolutionary synthesis.* New York: Harper & Row.

Pond, C. M. (1997). The biological origins of adipose tissue in humans. In M. E. Morbeck, A. Galloway, & A. L. Zihlman (Eds.), *The evolving female: A life-history perspective.* Princeton, NJ: Princeton University.

Pool, R. (1995). Putting game theory to the test. *Science, 267,* 1591-1593.

Price, J., Sloman, L., Gardner, R. Jr., Gilbert, P., & Rohde, P. (1994). The social competition hypothesis of depression. *British Journal of Psychiatry, 164,* 309-315.

Rapoport, J. L., & Fiske, A. (1998). The new biology of obsessive-compulsive disorder: Implications for evolutionary psychology. *Perspectives in Biology and Medicine, 41,* 159-175.

Rodrigue, J. R., Olson, K. R., & Markley, R. P. (1987). Induced mood and curiosity. *Cognitive Therapy and Research, 11,* 101-106.

Schmitt, D. P., & Buss, D. M. (1996). Strategic self-promotion and competitor derogation: Sex and context effects on the perceived effectiveness of mate attraction tactics. *Journal of Personality and Social Psychology, 70,* 1185-1204.

Seligman, M. E. P. (1970). On the generality of the laws of learning. *Psychological Review, 77,* 407-418.

Shepher, J. (1983). *Incest: A biosocial view.* New York: Academic.

Shipherd, J. C., & Beck, J. G. (1999). The effects of suppressing trauma-related thoughts on women with rape-related posttraumatic stress disorder. *Behaviour Research and Therapy, 37,* 99-112.

Silove, D. (1998). Is posttraumatic stress disorder an overlearned survival response? An evolutionary-learning hypothesis. *Psychiatry: Interpersonal and Biological Processes, 61,* 181-190.

Sloman, L. (1992). How mood variation regulates aggression. *Psycoloquy* (an electronic journal) 3.1.1.3.

Stein, D. J., & Bouwer, C. (1997). A neuro-evolutionary approach to the anxiety disorders. *Journal of Anxiety Disorders 11,* 409-429.

Stein, D. J., & Stanley, M. (1994). Serotonin and suicide. In R. D. Masters & M. T. McGuire (Eds.), *The neurotransmitter revolution: Serotonin, social behavior and the law.* Carbondale, IL: Southern Illinois University.

Surbey, M. K. (1987). Anorexia nervosa, amenorrhea, and adaptation. *Ethology and Sociobiology, 8,* 47S-61S.

Thornhill, N. W. (1996). Psychological adaptation to sexual coercion in victims and offenders. In D. Buss & N. Malamuth (Eds.), *Sex, power, conflict: Evolutionary and feminist perspectives.* New York: Oxford University Press.

Turner, W. J. (1995a, May 25-27). *Asexuality, homosexuality and transsexuality.* Paper presented at The International Behavioral Development Symposium on the Biological Basis of Sexual Orientation and Sex-Typical Behavior, Minot, ND.

Turner, W. J. (1995b). Homosexuality, Type 1: An Xq28 phenomenon. *Archives of Sexual Behavior, 24,* 109-134.

Vila, B. (1997). Human nature and crime control: Improving the feasibility of nurturant strategies. *Politics and the Life Sciences, 16,* 3-21.

Voland, E., & Voland, R. (1989). Evolutionary biology and psychiatry: The case of anorexia nervosa. *Ethology and Sociobiology, 10,* 223-240.

Wasser, S. K. (1990). Infertility, abortion, and biotechnology: When it's not nice to fool Mother Nature. *Human Nature, 1,* 3-24.

Wasser, S. K., & Barash, D. P. (1983). Reproductive suppression among female mammals: Implications for biomedicine and sexual selection theory. *Quarterly Review of Biology, 58,* 513-538.

Wilson, M., & Daly, M. (1985). Competitiveness, risk-taking, and violence: The young male syndrome. *Ethology and Sociobiology, 6,* 59-73.

Wilson, M., & Daly, M. (1993). Lethal confrontational violence among young men. In N. Bell & R. Bell (Eds.), *Adolescent risk-taking.* Newbury Park, CA: Sage.

Wright, P., & Murray, R. M. (1993). Schizophrenia: Prenatal influenza and autoimmunity. *Annals of Medicine, 25,* 497-502.

Author Index

Subject Index

About the Editors

Robert L. Burgess is Professor of Human Development at Penn State University. He has degrees in anthropology, psychology, and sociology, including his PhD from Washington University, St. Louis. He has published numerous articles in journals and chapters in books dealing with topics such as theory construction, the development of criminal behavior and illicit drug use, cooperation and competition in children's groups, the development and consequences of power differences in dyads involved in exchange relationships, and the role of imitation in retarded children. He is also coauthor (with Don Bushell Jr.) of *Behavioral Sociology: The Experimental Analysis of Social Process,* and (with Ted L. Huston) of *Social Exchange in Developing Relationships.* Drawing upon research methods developed by primatologists, he conducted one of the first observational studies of abusive and neglectful families in their own homes. Recently, he has published articles examining the convergence of evolutionary biology and behavior genetics for understanding human development.

Kevin MacDonald is Professor of Psychology at California State University-Long Beach. His research has focused on developing evolutionary perspectives in developmental psychology, certain historical phenomena (e.g., the origins of monogamous marriage), and ethnic relations. After receiving a master's degree in evolutionary biology, he received a PhD in biobehavioral sciences, both at the University of Connecticut. His dissertation focused on behavioral development in wolves. He continued developmental research during a postdoctoral fellowship at the University of Illinois, performing research on human parent-child play, particularly rough-and-tumble play characteristic of fathers. In the area of developmental psychology, he is the author of *Social and Personality Development: An Evolutionary Synthesis* (Plenum, 1988). He is also the editor of two books: *Sociobiological Perspectives on Human Development* (Springer-Verlag, 1988) and *Parent-Child Play: Descriptions and Implications* (State University of New York Press, 1993).

About the Contributors

William R. Charlesworth received his PhD at Cornell University. He is Professor Emeritus at the Institute of Child Development at the University of Minnesota. His scholarly interests include human ethology, as well as cultural, ontogenetic, and evolutionary adaptations. Most recently, he has investigated terrorist behavior.

Alicia A. Drais-Parrillo is a Research Associate at Child Welfare League of America, Washington, DC. Her main areas of interest are parent-child interaction and the social development of children, specifically the development of antisocial and aggressive behavior. She received her PhD in human development and family studies from Penn State University.

Donyell K. Coleman is a graduate student in developmental psychopathology at Wayne State University. She is a research assistant funded through the National Institute of General Medical Science's Initiative for Minority Student Development. She received her MA from Wayne State University and is currently pursuing her PhD. Her major research interests center on the relationship between parental influences and adolescent psychopathology. Her research has focused on the association between maternal depression and children's behavior problems. Coleman is currently working on a project looking at parental perceptions of adolescent risk behaviors.

Mark Flinn is Associate Professor in the Departments of Anthropology and Psychological Sciences at the University of Missouri-Columbia. He received his PhD from Northwestern University and was a Postdoctoral Fellow and Assistant Professor in the Department of Anthropology, the Division of Biological Sciences, and the Society of Fellows at the University of Michigan. He has conducted a longitudinal study of childhood stress, family environment, and health in a rural community in Dominica for the past 16 years. His current research investigates how naturalistic events in children's everyday lives are associated with neuro-endocrine stress response, immune function, morbidity, and psychological development. He is more broadly concerned with relations among biology, psychology, and culture from an evolutionary perspective.

David C. Geary is Department Chair and Professor of Psychological Sciences at the University of Missouri-Columbia, and from 2000 to 2003, he was the University of Missouri's Middlebush Professor of Psychological Sciences. He has published more than 110 articles and chapters across a wide range of topics, including cognitive and developmental psychology, education, evolutionary biology, and medicine. His first two books, *Children's Mathematical Development* (1994) and *Male, Female: The Evolution of Human Sex Differences* (1998), were published by the American Psychological Association, as will his next book, *The Origin of Mind: Evolution of Brain, Cognition, and General Intelligence* (2004).

Ulrike Griebel, Visiting Assistant Professor, Department of Biology, The University of Memphis, completed her PhD from the University of Vienna, Austria (1992), in marine biology. She has held a postdoctoral fellowship at the Konrad Lorenz Institute for Evolution and Cognition Research, Altenberg, Austria, where she remains a member. Her research has focused on psychophysical studies of vision and evolution of vision in marine mammals and on cephalopod learning and communication systems. She is author of numerous articles and is coeditor with D. K. Oller of *The Evolution of Communication Systems: a Comparative Approach* (in press, MIT Press).

Scott L. Hershberger is Professor of Psychology at the California State University, Long Beach. He holds a doctorate in psychometrics from Fordham University and has published extensively in the areas of multivariate statistics, measurement, latent variable models, behavior genetics, and analysis of clinical trials.

Sarah Blaffer Hrdy is Professor Emeritus of Anthropology at the University of California, Davis. She received her PhD from Harvard University. Her work in primate sociobiology has led to a number of publications, including *The Woman that Never Evolved* (1981), a *New York Times* Notable Book; and *Infanticide: Comparative and Evolutionary Perspectives* (1984, coedited with Glen Hausfater), a *Choice* Outstanding Academic Book. Her most recent book, *Mother Nature: A History of Mothers, Infants, and Natural Selection* (1999), was chosen by both *Publishers Weekly* and *Library Journal* as a Best Book of 1999, was a finalist for the PEN USA (West) 2000 Literary Award for Research Non-Fiction, and won the Howells Prize of the American Anthropological Association.

Dennis Krebs is currently a Professor of Psychology at Simon Fraser University. He received his PhD from Harvard University and is a Fellow of the Center for Advanced Study in the Behavioral Sciences. He has published many articles and books on altruism, morality, and self-deception, and will soon publish a book on the evolution of morality.

Peter J. LaFreniere is Professor of Developmental Psychology and Director of the Child Study Center at the University of Maine. He received his PhD from the Institute of Child Development, University of Minnesota in 1982. His research has investigated processes of social and emotional development and adaptation from an evolutionary perspective, particularly as they relate to early childhood. He is currently the editor of the *Human Ethology Bulletin* and the author of *Emotional Development: A Biosocial Perspective* (2000).

Linda Mealey, until her untimely death in 2002, was Professor of Psychology at the College of St. Benedict, St. Joseph, Minnesota. (See a tribute to Linda by Nancy L. Segal in the Foreword.) She was a prolific author in the area of evolutionary psychology and behavior genetics. Her 2000 textbook, *Sex Differences: Development and Evolutionary Strategies,* was well received and widely reviewed.

D. Kimbrough Oller, Professor and Plough Chair of Excellence, The University of Memphis, School of Audiology and Speech-Language Pathology, completed his PhD from the University of Texas in psycholinguistics (1971). He has held faculty positions at the University of Washington, the University of Miami, and the University of Maine. He is a member of the Konrad Lorenz Institute for Evolution and Cognition Research, Altenberg, Austria. His work includes many publications on the development and evolution of vocalization and speech in humans, and a book, *The Emergence of the Speech Capacity* (Lawrence Erlbaum, 2000).

Dr. Nancy L. Segal received a PhD degree from the University of Chicago in 1982. She is currently Professor of Psychology and Director of the Twin Studies Center at California State University, Fullerton. Dr. Segal is the author of *Entwined Lives: Twins and What They Tell Us About Human Behavior* (Dutton, 1999; Plume 2000). She is also senior editor of *Uniting Psychology and Biology: Integrative Perspectives on Human Development* (APA Press, 1997). Dr. Segal received a 2003-2004 American Fellowship from the American Association of University Women for writing a second book on twins, to be published by Harvard University Press. She is coprincipal investigator of an NIMH supported study "Twins, Virtual Twins and Friends: Peers and Adjustment."

Glenn Weisfeld is a professor of psychology at Wayne State University. He received his doctorate at the University of Chicago. He has conducted research, much of it cross-cultural, on dominance hierarchies in adolescents, marital satisfaction, street gangs, and kin recognition through olfaction. With Nancy L. Segal and Carol C. Weisfeld, he coedited *Uniting Psychology and Biology: Integrative Perspectives on Human Development* (American Psychological Association, 1997). Dr. Weisfeld's *Evolutionary Principles of Human Adolescence* (Basic Books, 1999) received a faculty recognition award at Wayne State. He is vice president of the International Society for Human Ethology, and formerly edited its *Human Ethology Bulletin.*